INCONTINENCE OF THE VOID

SHORT CIRCUITS
Mladen Dolar, Alenka Zupančič, and Slavoj Žižek, editors

The Puppet and the Dwarf: The Perverse Core of Christianity, by Slavoj Žižek

The Shortest Shadow: Nietzsche's Philosophy of the Two, by Alenka Zupančič

Is Oedipus Online? Siting Freud after Freud, by Jerry Aline Flieger

Interrogation Machine: Laibach and NSK, by Alexei Monroe

The Parallax View, by Slavoj Žižek

A Voice and Nothing More, by Mladen Dolar

Subjectivity and Otherness: A Philosophical Reading of Lacan, by Lorenzo Chiesa

The Odd One In: On Comedy, by Alenka Zupančič

The Monstrosity of Christ: Paradox or Dialectic?, by Slavoj Žižek and John Milbank, edited by Creston Davis

Interface Fantasy: A Lacanian Cyborg Ontology, by André Nusselder

Lacan at the Scene, by Henry Bond

Laughter: Notes on a Passion, by Anca Parvulescu

All for Nothing: Hamlet's Negativity, by Andrew Cutrofello

The Trouble with Pleasure: Deleuze and Psychoanalysis, by Aaron Schuster

The Not-Two: Logic and God in Lacan, by Lorenzo Chiesa

What Is Sex?, by Alenka Zupančič

Liquidation World: On the Art of Living Absently, by Alexi Kukuljevic

Incontinence of the Void: Economico-Philosophical Spandrels, by Slavoj Žižek

INCONTINENCE OF THE VOID

ECONOMICO-PHILOSOPHICAL SPANDRELS

Slavoj Žižek

THE MIT PRESS   CAMBRIDGE, MASSACHUSETTS   LONDON, ENGLAND

This book was set in Copperplate Gothic Std and Joanna MT Pro by Toppan Best-set Premedia Limited. Printed and bound in the United States of America.

Library of Congress Cataloging-in-Publication Data is available.

ISBN: 978-0-262-03681-8

10   9   8   7   6   5   4   3   2   1

CONTENTS

A short circuit occurs when there is a faulty connection in the network—faulty, of course, from the standpoint of the network's smooth functioning. Is not the shock of short-circuiting, therefore, one of the best metaphors for a critical reading? Is not one of the most effective critical procedures to cross wires that do not usually touch: to take a major classic (text, author, notion), and read it in a short-circuiting way, through the lens of a "minor" author, text, or conceptual apparatus ("minor" should be understood here in Deleuze's sense: not "of lesser quality," but marginalized, disavowed by the hegemonic ideology, or dealing with a "lower," less dignified topic)? If the minor reference is well chosen, such a procedure can lead to insights which completely shatter and undermine our common perceptions. This is what Marx, among others, did with philosophy and religion (short-circuiting philosophical speculation through the lens of political economy, that is to say, economic speculation); this is what Freud and Nietzsche did with morality (short-circuiting the highest ethical notions through the lens of the unconscious libid.inal economy). What such a reading achieves is not a simple "desublimation," a reduction of the higher intellectual content to its lower economic or libid.inal cause; the aim of such an approach is, rather, the inherent decentering of the interpreted text, which brings to light its "unthought," its disavowed presuppositions and consequences.

And this is what "Short Circuits" wants to do, again and again. The underlying premise of the series is that Lacanian psychoanalysis is a privileged instrument of such an approach, whose purpose is to illuminate a standard text or ideological formation, making it readable in a totally new way—the long history of Lacanian interventions in philosophy, religion, the arts (from the visual arts to the cinema, music, and literature), ideology, and politics justifies this premise. This, then, is not a new series of books on psychoanalysis, but a series of "connections in the Freudian field"—of short Lacanian interventions in art, philosophy, theology, and ideology.

"Short Circuits" intends to revive a practice of reading which confronts a classic text, author, or notion with its own hidden presuppositions, and thus reveals its disavowed truth. The basic criterion for the texts that will be published is that they effectuate such a theoretical short circuit. After reading a book in this series, the reader should not simply have learned something new: the point is, rather, to make him or her aware of another—disturbing—side of something he or she knew all the time.

Slavoj Žižek

THE USE OF USELESS SPANDRELS

Incontinent the void. The zenith. Evening again. When not night it will be evening. Death again of deathless day. On one hand embers. On the other ashes. Day without end won and lost. Unseen.

Samuel Beckett, *Ill Seen Ill Said*

The term "spandrels" originated in architecture (where it designated the space between a curved figure and a rectangular rectilinear surround) and was then appropriated by evolutionary biology, where it stands for features of an organism arising as byproducts, rather than adaptations, that have no clear benefit for the organism's fitness and survival; however, precisely as such, they can be "ex-apted" and acquire a new unexpected role crucial to the organism's functioning. For Gould and Lewontin, many functions of the human brain, especially language, emerged as spandrels.[1] Reflections in this book operate in the same way: they fill in the empty spaces that emerge in the interstices between philosophy, psychoanalysis, and the critique of political economy. It seems that today the most interesting theoretical interventions emerge in such interstices, without clearly and fully belonging to any particular field.

This "spandrelization" of the content in no way implies a confused, nonsystematic structure. The book's three parts follow the triad of UPS: the universal dimension of philosophy, the particular dimension of sexual difference, the singular dimension of the critique of political economy. The passage from one dimension to another is strictly immanent: the ontological Void of the barred One is accessible only through the impasses of sexuation, and the ongoing prospect of the abolition of sexuality, i.e., of the change in "human nature" itself, opened up by the technoscientific progress of global capitalism, compels us to shift the focus to the critique of political economy. Each of the two parts of the book deals with these passages: Part I ("SOS: Sexuality,

Ontology, Subjectivity") with the passage from ontology to sexuation; Part II ("The Belated Actuality of Marx's Critique of Political Economy") with the passage from sexuation to the critique of political economy.

In the dimension of *philosophy*, (1) the limit of ontology is first approached through the notion of an excessive element, an element structurally out of place that gives body to radical negativity; (2) this negativity inscribes itself into the order of being as the antagonism of sexual difference, which is why the human subject is constitutively sexualized; (3) a "unified theory" of the four discourses and the formulas of sexuation is outlined; (4) the explosive combination of biogenetics and digitization clearly discernible in today's global capitalism opens up the prospect of a nonsexual reproduction of life, and thus poses a threat to the very existence of subjectivity.

In the dimension of the *critique of political economy*, (1) the excess detrimental to every ontology assumes the form of surplus-value, the key Marxian notion that is elaborated in its homology with three other notions of excess: Lacan's surplus-enjoyment, scientific surplus-knowledge, and political surplus-power; (2) this brings us to a Lacanian reading of the "labor theory of value" and of the self-propelling circulation of capital, and (3) to the question of how the capitalist discourse (social link) fits into Lacan's matrix of four discourses (Master, University, Hysteria, Analyst). (4) Although, in the Lacanian perspective, alienation is irreducible, constitutive of human subjectivity, this does not mean that alienation is the ultimate horizon of political activity: Lacan posits separation as a move that supplements and overturns alienation, so the question raised is that of a politics of separation.

The second part concludes with an appendix which, rejecting the utopian notion of Communist society as one in which tensions such as resentment disappear, deals with the obscure topic of the libidinal paradoxes that would persist in an imagined future Communist society. Although this last topic may appear irrelevant in view of the state of today's Left, it casts its shadow on today's struggles.

*

This book is a weird one. It repeats the paradox of Spinoza's *Ethics*: while it focuses on "eternal" topics (the basic structure of being, etc.), it gets caught up in many very specific debates on contemporary issues. It contains some passages from my earlier books, which are all included in new contexts, and thus given a new spin.[2] Especially in the first part, it is largely a dialogue with the recent work of Alenka Zupančič, for which I have the highest appreciation. So it brings something old, something new, something borrowed, something ... *red*, not blue!

PART I

SOS: SEXUALITY, ONTOLOGY, SUBJECTIVITY

There are two main meanings of "UPS" in our everyday language: United Parcel Service and uninterruptible power supply (a power supply that includes a battery to maintain power in the event of an outage—for example, a UPS keeps a computer running for several minutes after an outage, enabling the user to save data). However, the target of this book is another UPS: the good old philosophical triad of Universal, Particular, and Singular, and in a very precise sense. Universal stands for ontology, Particular for sexuality, and Singular for subjectivity—a triad of SOS.[1] Why? Is there more than an irrelevant pun at work in this SOS? A careful reader must have noted that SOS inverts the order of the terms with regard to UPS: in SOS we get PUS, (particular) sexuality, (universal) ontology, (singular) subjectivity. Why this precedence of sexuality over ontology, and why does it trigger an SOS, a distress signal? A simple answer: because it signals the ultimate failure and limitation of every ontology. From the Lacanian standpoint, "there is no sexual relationship" is not merely the axiom that underlies human sexuality, determining it as fundamentally antagonistic, it is an axiom with radical ontological implications, an axiom that posits the antagonistic (incomplete, "flawed") character of reality itself, the impossibility of grasping it as a Whole; and subjectivity can arise only in a reality that is ontologically incomplete, traversed by an impossibility.

This also means that the subject is immanently, constitutively, sexed: it is not enough to say that the subject emerges when the substance is non-all, antagonistic, inconsistent; the mediating term here is sexuality, that is to say, in order to have a subject, the antagonism (impossibility) that cuts across reality has to acquire a form of sexuality, of the impossibility of the sexual relationship. And vice versa, of course: if we just combine ontology and sexuality (sexual difference) without subjectivity, we get the traditional cosmological vision of reality characterized by the eternal struggle of the two "principles," masculine and feminine (yin and yang, light and darkness, form and matter, etc.). Plus the third variation: if we combine just sexual difference and subjectivity, and leave out the ontological implications, we get not subjectivity proper but mere sexualized human agents who fit neatly into a realist ontology as its special sphere, i.e., we regress from the Kantian rupture back into traditional ontology. It was Kant who, in deploying the antinomies of pure reason, took the first step toward the triangle of failed ontology, subjectivity, and the ontological implications of sexual difference: once we take into account the Lacanian conceptualization of sexual difference, the strict formal homology between Kant's duality of mathematical and dynamic antinomies and Lacan's formulas of sexuation is evident. Furthermore, Kant interprets antinomies of pure reason as an a priori limitation on any attempt to construct a consistent ontology.

Why, then, our emphasis on the impossibility of ontology? The current age is one in which deconstructionist discourse analysis is losing ground to the proliferation of new ontologies: from the hypercritical transcendental questioning of every ontological claim (What are its conditions of possibility? On what hidden presuppositions must it rely? etc.) we are passing over to a multiplicity of new ontologies which replace the critical stance with (sometimes feigned) realist naivety (new materialism, speculative realism, object-oriented ontology …). The project of SOS is to formulate a third way: to break out of the critico-transcendental approach without regressing into precritical realist ontology. Many of the critical remarks aimed at my work are due to the critics' misunderstanding of this central point. In his perspicacious review of the volume *Repeating Žižek*, Jamil Khader notes how some contributors interrogate

> Žižek's credentials as a philosopher, especially in relation to Badiou's critique of Lacan's anti-philosophical position. Hamza points out, in fact, that philosophers who are Žižekian are always reminded that compared to Žižek, "it is not a difficult task to be a follower of Badiou, or a Badiousian in philosophy, due to his very well-structured system." To this extent, Noys cautiously reiterates Badiou's claim that Žižek is "not exactly in the field of philosophy," only to proposes that Žižek is a "reader of philosophy," someone who offers not a philosophy but a method.
>
> Bruno Bosteels makes this case against a Žižekian philosophy more forcefully. He claims that after his international career took off, Žižek has been struggling very hard to disassociate himself from the field of cultural studies, in which his work was initially received and "misrecognized," and to reclaim his name as a philosopher. Bosteels writes: "Thus, whereas Badiou after the completion of *Being and Event* speaks from within the bastion of a classically or neoclassically styled philosophy, waving the banner of Platonism with sufficient self-confidence to accept the challenge of an

anti-philosopher such as Lacan, Žižek is still at pains to downplay the late Lacan's anti-philosophical provocations for the sake of gaining respectability as a philosopher." For Bosteels, this seems to offer a seamless explanation of Žižek's "proverbial nervousness." His tics simply betray an anxiety about being excluded from prestigious institutional apparatuses and departments of philosophy, whether in Slovenia, Britain or France. As such, he performs the role of the hysteric to the "master's discourse of a stoically unfazed Badiou."[2]

I find these critiques of my work problematic on more than one count, even if I discount the—to put it mildly—very problematic "grounding" of my bodily tics (incidentally, the result of an organic disease for which I am taking medication!) in my anxiety about being excluded from academic apparatuses and not recognized as a "serious" philosopher. (Can one even imagine the politically correct outcry if another thinker—one who was, say, a lesbian feminist—were to be "analyzed" on such a level?) First, I *do* propose a kind of "ontology": my work is not just a deconstructive reflection on the inconsistencies of other philosophies, it *does* outline a certain "structure of reality." Or, to put it in brutally simplified Kantian terms: the last horizon of my work is not the multiple narrative of cognitive failures against the background of the inaccessible Real. The move "beyond the transcendental" is outlined in the first part of my *Absolute Recoil*, where I deploy in detail the basic dialectical move, that of the reversal of epistemological obstacle into ontological impossibility that characterizes the Thing itself: the very failure of my effort to grasp the Thing has to be (re)conceived as a feature of the Thing, as an impossibility inscribed into the very heart of the Real. (Another move in this direction is my elaboration of the quasi-ontology of "less than nothing" in my reading of the ontological implications of quantum physics.)

But the heart of the problem lies elsewhere: in the application to philosophy of the opposition between the Master and the Hysteric. To cut a long story short: if we identify true philosophy with a stoically unfazed Master's discourse, then philosophers such as Kant and Hegel are no longer philosophers. After Kant, "classically or neoclassically styled philosophy," i.e., philosophy as a "world-view," as a great rendering of the basic structure of the whole of reality, is simply no longer possible. With Kant's critical turn, thinking is "not exactly in the field of philosophy," it offers "not a philosophy but a method": philosophy turns self-reflexive, a discourse examining its own conditions of possibility—or, more precisely, of its own impossibility. In short, Kant is typically engaged in prolegomena to metaphysics proper, a preparatory dance endlessly postponing the jump into the cold water of the thing itself. Metaphysics (the description of the hierarchical rational structure of the universe) gets necessarily caught in antinomies, illusions are unavoidably needed to fill in the gaps in the structure—in short, with Kant, philosophy is no longer a Master's discourse, its entire edifice gets traversed by a bar of immanent impossibility, failure, and inconsistency. With Hegel, things go even further: far from returning to precritical rational metaphysics (as Kantians accuse it of doing), the whole of Hegelian dialectics is a kind of hysterical undermining of the Master (the reason Lacan called Hegel "the most sublime of all hysterics"), the immanent self-destruction and self-overcoming of every metaphysical claim. In short, Hegel's "system" is nothing but a systematic tour through the failures of philosophical projects. In this sense, all of German Idealism is an exercise in "anti-philosophy": Kant's critical thought is not directly philosophy but a prolegomenon to future philosophy, a questioning of the conditions of (im)possibility of philosophy; Fichte no longer calls his thinking philosophy but *Wissenschaftslehre* ("teaching on scientific knowledge"); and Hegel claims that his thought is no longer a mere philo-sophy (love of wisdom) but true wisdom (knowledge) itself. This is why Hegel is "the most sublime of all hysterics": one should bear in mind that for Lacan, only hysteria produces new knowledge (in contrast to University discourse, which simply reproduces it).

Insofar as philosophy (traditional ontology) is a case of Master's discourse, psychoanalysis acts as the agent of its immanent hystericization. The topic "Lacan and philosophy" can be adequately approached only when we avoid the trap of the clear line of demarcation between the two: psychoanalysis as a specific clinical practice on the one side, philosophical reflection on the other. When Lacan emphatically asserts *je m'insurge contre la philosophie*, he, of course, identifies philosophy with a "world-view," a view of the universe as a Whole encompassing all divisions and inconsistencies. When a philosopher dismisses the philosophical relevance of psychoanalysis, he, of course, reduces it to a specific clinical practice dealing with a particular ontic phenomenon (of psychological pathologies). They are both wrong: what they both miss is (not some higher synthetic unity of the two but) their intersection: their relationship is that of the two sides of a Möbius strip, so that if we progress to the very heart of each of the two, we find ourselves in its opposite. Throughout the entire span of his teaching, Lacan was engaged in an intense debate with philosophy and philosophers, from ancient Greek materialists to Plato, from Stoics to Thomas Aquinas, from Descartes to Spinoza, from Kant to Hegel, from Marx to Kierkegaard, from Heidegger to Kripke. It is through reference to philosophers that Lacan explains his fundamental concepts: transference through Plato, the Freudian subject through Descartes's *cogito*, *objet a* as surplus-enjoyment through Marx's surplus-value, anxiety and repetition through Kierkegaard, the ethics of psychoanalysis through Kant, and so on. Through this continuous engagement, Lacan is of course distantiating himself from philosophy (just recall his—rather unfortunate—continuous mocking of the Hegelian *Aufhebung*, or his self-consciousness as opposed to the Freudian divided/barred subject); however, all this desperate effort to draw the line of separation again and again reasserts his commitment to philosophy—as if the only way for him to delineate the basic concepts of psychoanalysis is through a philosophical detour. Although psychoanalysis is not philosophy, all its subversive dimension comes from the fact that it is not simply a particular science or practice but has radical consequences for philosophy: psychoanalysis is a "no" to philosophy that is internal to it, i.e., psychoanalytic theory refers to a gap/antagonism that philosophy blurs, but that simultaneously grounds philosophy (Heidegger called this gap ontological difference). Without this link to philosophy—more precisely, to the blind spot of philosophy, to what is "primordially repressed" in philosophy—psychoanalysis loses its subversive dimension and becomes just another ontic practice. The Real with which psychoanalysis is dealing is not just the reality of the subject's psychological suffering but, much more radically, the (anti-)philosophical implications of Freud's reading of this suffering.

Only such a philosophy-traversed-by-psychoanalysis can survive the challenge of modern science. That is to say, what is philosophy today? The predominant answer of contemporary scientists is: its time is over. Even the most basic philosophical problems are increasingly becoming scientific ones: the ultimate ontological questions concerning reality (Does our universe have a limit in space and time? Is it caught in determinism, or is there a place for genuine contingency in it?) are today questions addressed by quantum cosmology; the ultimate anthropological questions (Are we free, i.e., do we have free will? etc.) are addressed by evolutionary brain science; even theology is allotted its place within brain science (which aims at translating spiritual and mystical experiences into neuronal processes). At most, what remains of philosophy are epistemological reflections on the process of scientific discoveries.

In today's antideconstructionist turn, there are, however, many attempts to return to a realist ontology, with all the usual caveats (it's not really a return, because it's a new ontology of radical contingency, etc.). Perhaps the main precursor of this return to ontology is Louis Althusser's "aleatoric materialism." In his two great manuscripts published posthumously, *Initiation à la philosophie pour les non-philosophes* (1976) and *Être marxiste en philosophie* (1978), Althusser (among other things) outlines a specific theory of philosophy which overlaps neither with his early "theoreticist" concept of philosophy as "theory of theoretical practice" nor with his later notion of philosophy as "class struggle in theory"; while closer to the second notion, it serves as a kind of mediator between the two. Althusser's starting point is the omnipresence of ideology, of ideological abstractions which always structure our approach to everyday life and reality; this ideology has two levels, the "spontaneous" everyday texture of implicit meanings, and the organized religion or mythology which initiated a systematic system of these meanings. Then, in ancient Greece, something new and unexpected happened: the rise of science in the guise of mathematics. Mathematics deals with pure, abstract numbers deprived of all mythic reference, it is a game of axioms and rule in which no cosmic meaning resonates, there are no sacred, lucky or damned numbers. Precisely as such, mathematics is subversive; it threatens the universe of cosmic meaning, its homogeneity and stability. A weird incident that happened on a departing American Airlines flight from Philadelphia to Syracuse on May 7, 2016, shows that this fear of mathematics persists even today. An economics professor was solving a differential equation on a piece of paper, and a lady passenger seated at his side thought he might be a terrorist because of what he was writing, so she passed a note to a flight attendant, claiming that she was too ill to take the flight. The plane returned to the gate, the lady was taken from the plane and voiced her suspicion to ground staff; security members then removed the economics professor from the plane and questioned him. ...[3]

The true break happens here, not between mythic ideology and philosophy but between the mythical universe and science—and the function of philosophy is precisely to contain this break. Formally, philosophy also breaks with the mythical universe and obeys the rules of science (rational argumentation, thinking in abstract conceptual terms, etc.), but its function is to reinscribe scientific procedure into the religious universe of cosmic meaning. To put it in mock-Hegelian terms: if science is a negation of religion, philosophy is a negation of negation, i.e., it endeavors to reassert religious meaning within the space (and with the means) of rational argumentation:

> All of Plato—the theory of ideas, the opposition of knowledge and opinion, and so on—is based on the break that the first science represents. In a sense, this is because all of Plato is an attempt to control and in a way to "sublate" this break, in a profoundly inventive but also profoundly reactive dialectic. Philosophy, in its idealist Platonist matrix, is thus a *reactive invention*: the displacement of (the ideological functions of) religion onto the plane of pure (abstract) rationality. It draws from these sciences its "form, the abstraction of its categories, and the demonstrativeness of its reasoning," as a pure reasoning directly carried out on "abstract" objects, but its *function* is an ideological one, a mandate and a service delegated, explicitly or otherwise, by the dominant class.[4]

Here is the link with Althusser's second definition of philosophy as class struggle in theory: this pressure to contain the scientific threat, to reassert the all-encompassing religious world-view, is not grounded in some kind of disembodied tendency toward meaningful totalization of our experience, but is pressure exerted as part of the class struggle in order to guarantee the hegemony of the ruling-class ideology. All great philosophers after Plato repeat this gesture of containment, from Descartes (who limits the domain of science to the material world) and Kant (who limits the domain of science to the phenomenal world in order to open up the space for religion and ethics) to today's neo-Kantian theorists of communication who exempt communication from scientific rationality. Against this predominant idealist form of philosophy (Plato, Aristotle, Aquinas, Descartes, Kant, Hegel ...), Althusser asserts the subterranean tradition of materialist counterphilosophy, from the early Greek materialists and Epicureans (who assert the material world of contingent encounters) through Spinoza and even Heidegger. Is not one of the great episodes in this struggle Cantor's profoundly materialist reconceptualization of the infinite? His basic premise is the multiplicity of infinities which cannot be totalized into an all-encompassing One. Cantor's great materialist breakthrough concerns the status of infinite numbers (and it is precisely because this breakthrough was materialist that it caused so many psychological traumas to Cantor, a devout Catholic): prior to Cantor, the Infinite was linked to the One, the conceptual form of God in religion and metaphysics, while with Cantor, the Infinite enters the domain of the Multiple—it implies the actual existence of infinite multiplicities, as well as the infinite number of different infinities.

But is Platonism really a reaction to the subversive abstraction of mathematical science? Is it not also (or mainly) a reaction to other tendencies like sophist philosophy or pre-Platonic materialism? Moreover, did the ideological recuperation of mathematics not begin prior to Plato, with the Pythagoreans who imbued numbers with cosmic meaning? It is worth mentioning here the continuing dialogue between Alain Badiou and Barbara Cassin, which is best characterized as the new version of the ancient dialogue between Plato and the sophists: the Platonist Badiou against Cassin's insistence on the irreducibility of the sophists' rupture. From the strict Hegelian standpoint, Cassin is right to insist, against Badiou, on the irreducible character of the sophist's position: the self-referential play of the symbolic process has no external support which would allow us to draw a line, within the language games, between truth and falsity. Sophists are the irreducible "vanishing mediators" between *mythos* and *logos*, between the traditional mythical universe and philosophical rationality, and, as such, a permanent threat to philosophy. Why? They broke the mythical unity of words and things, playfully asserting the gap that separates words from things; and philosophy proper can be understood only as a reaction to the sophists, as an attempt to close the gap opened up by the sophists, to provide a foundation of truth for words, to return to *mythos* in the new conditions of rationality. This is where one should locate Plato: he first tried to provide this foundation by his teaching on Ideas, and when, in *Parmenides*, he was forced to admit the fragility of this foundation, he engaged in a long struggle to reassert a clear line of separation between sophistry and truth. (The opposition between the sophists and Plato is also echoed in the opposition between democracy and corporate organic order: sophists are clearly democratic, teaching the art of seducing and convincing the crowd; while Plato outlines a hierarchical, corporate order in which every individual is in his/her proper place, allowing for no position of singular universality.) The irony of the history of philosophy is that the line of philosophers who struggle against the sophists' temptation finishes with Hegel, the "last philosopher" who, in a way, is also the ultimate sophist, asserting self-referential play with no external support of its truth: for Hegel, there is truth, but it is immanent to the symbolic process—the truth is measured not by an external standard, but by the "pragmatic contradiction," the inner (in)consistency of the discursive process, by the gap between the enunciated content and its position of enunciation.

Is not the way Althusser relates to philosophy one of the clearest cases of the gap that separates the position of enunciation from the enunciated (content)? At the level of the enunciated content, he is all modesty: he strongly opposes the idealist philosophical pretension to grasp the structure of the entire universe, to "know it all," to reveal the absolute truth (or the truth of the Absolute). Against this idealist pretension, he praises accepting limits, openness to contingent encounters, etc., which characterize the materialist undercurrent from Epicurus through Spinoza up to Heidegger (although one might add here that it is difficult to imagine a more "arrogant" philosopher than Spinoza, whose *Ethics* claims to reveal the inner working of God-Nature—if nothing else, it can be shown that here Spinoza is much more "arrogant" than Hegel ...).

> Idealist philosophers speak for everyone and in everyone's stead. They think, in fact, that they are in possession of the Truth about everything. Materialist philosophers are much less talkative: they know how to shut up and listen to people. They do not think that they are privy to the Truth about everything. They know that they can become philosophers only gradually, modestly, and that their philosophy will come to them *from outside*. So they shut up and listen.[5]

However, in what Althusser actually does when talking about philosophy, his "process of enunciation," his approach to philosophy, we can easily discern the exact opposite of what he characterizes as a materialist approach: brutally simplified universal statements which pretend to define the universal key features of philosophy, with no modest provisos. Philosophy as such is class struggle in theory, the eternal battle of two lines, "idealist" and "materialist"; it functions as an empty repetition of the line of demarcation idealism/materialism which produces nothing new; etc., etc. In short, Althusser acts as a supreme Judge imposing his Measure on the wealth of philosophies. No wonder, then, that Althusser is so adamantly anti-Hegelian: Althusser's opposite here is Hegel, whose enunciated (content) may appear "arrogant" ("absolute Knowing," etc.), but whose actual approach is much more radically "modest," "deconstructing" every pretense to directly reach the Absolute, demonstrating how each such claim fails owing to its inherent inconsistencies. The extreme case of this "arrogance" of Althusser's is his treatment of the digitization/computerization of our lives, which he brutally reduces to technocratic idealism: when the bourgeoisie loses its ability to generate idealist philosophical systems that guarantee the hegemony of its ideology, it begins to rely on the apparently non-ideological "automatism of computers and technocrats," the "neutral" expert knowledge to which our lives should be entrusted:

> In a time in which the bourgeoisie has even given up on producing its eternal philosophical systems, on the prospects and guarantees that ideas can provide it with, and in which it has entrusted its destiny to the automatism of computers and technocrats; in a time in which it is incapable of proposing a viable, conceivable future to the world, the proletariat can rise to the challenge; it can breathe new life into philosophy and, in order to liberate men and women from class domination, make it "an arm for the revolution."[6]

Sounds nice, albeit a bit naive: today, when science seems to be fully incorporated into capitalism, the standard situation in which the task of philosophy is to contain the subversive potential of the sciences seems almost inverted, so that philosophy itself becomes a tool against technocratic domination. ... However, the very conjunction "computers and technocrats" should immediately arouse our suspicions: as if the two are synonymous, as if there is no potential tension between the two, as if (as should be abundantly clear from today's ferocious struggles for the control of cyberspace) cyberspace is not one of the privileged terrains of class struggle today, when state apparatuses and corporations desperately try to contain the monster they themselves helped to unleash: "Althusser misunderstands the nature and transformative potential—the proletarization, perhaps—of computation and computer science. In so doing he appears ignorant of the strength of the scientific tools for rethinking and resisting technocratic rule."[7] In ignoring all these ambiguities and tensions, in brutally imposing a simple universal scheme, it is Althusser who acts like the worst idealist philosopher; consequently, it is Althusser who should have followed his materialist formula: "shut up and listen."

The more basic problem with Althusser here is that he is unable to think the shift in the very basic functioning of ideology that characterizes late capitalism: the shift from the prohibitive authority of the (patriarchal) Law to the permissive-hedonist superego ideology. To formulate his limitation in the terms of individual names, what Althusser was not able to think was a capitalist universe "structured like the Spinozan absolute," i.e., the reemergence of Spinoza as the paradigmatic thinker of late capitalism.

1.1 THE REAL AND ITS VICISSITUDES

The Three-Body Problem, Liu Cixin's sci-fi masterpiece,[1] the first part of the trilogy Remembrance of Earth's Past, begins in Mao's China during the Cultural Revolution: Ye Wenjie, a young woman, has just seen her father killed for continuing to teach (and proclaim his belief in) Einstein's theory of relativity. Disgusted by humanity, she hijacks a government program intended to make contact with aliens, and attempts to encourage extraterrestrials to invade Earth. The story then moves to the near future, where the old Wenjie is contacted by Wang Miao, a researcher developing a new nanotechnology who starts having strange experiences. Scientists he knows are killing themselves because they say the laws of physics are no longer working as expected. When he takes photos with his fancy new camera, there is a countdown on the negatives when they are developed. When he tries to explore possible linkages between these phenomena, he finds himself drawn into "Three Body," a virtual-reality game in which players find themselves on an alien planet, Trisolaris, whose three suns rise and set at strange and unpredictable intervals: sometimes far too far away and horribly cold, sometimes far too close and destructively hot, and sometimes not seen for long periods of time. The players can somehow dehydrate themselves and the rest of the population to weather the worst seasons, but life is a constant struggle against apparently unpredictable elements. Despite that, players slowly find ways to build civilizations and attempt to predict the strange cycles of heat and cold. After contact is established between the two civilizations, our Earth appears to the desperate Trisolarians as an ideal world of order, and they decide to invade it to ensure that their race will survive. The outcome of this encounter will probably be that each civilization will have to de-idealize the other, realizing that the other also has its faults—something akin to what Lacan called "separation." There is another Lacanian theme in the novel: the virtual game which turns out to simulate real life on Trisolaris reminds us of Lacan's motto that truth has the structure of a fiction.

However, the most interesting feature of the novel is how the opposition between Earth and Trisolaris echoes the opposition between the traditional Confucian view of Heaven as the principle of cosmic order and Mao's praise for Heaven in disorder: is not the chaotic life on Trisolaris, where the very rhythm of seasons is perturbed, a naturalized version of the chaos of the Cultural Revolution? Is not the terrifying insight that "there is no physics," no stable natural laws, the insight that pushes many scientists to suicide, the insight into how, as Lacan put it, there is no big Other? Nature itself today is in disorder, not because it overwhelms our cognitive capacities but primarily because we are not able to master the effects of our own interventions into its course—who knows what the ultimate consequences of our biogenetic engineering or of climate change will be? The surprise comes from ourselves, it concerns the opacity of how we ourselves fit into the picture: the impenetrable stain in the picture is not some cosmic mystery, like a mysterious explosion of a supernova, the stain is we ourselves, our collective activity. It is against this background that one should understand Jacques-Alain Miller's thesis: *Il y a un grand désordre dans le réel.*[2] "There is a great disorder in the real." That is how Miller characterizes the way reality appears to us in our time, in which we experience the full impact of two fundamental agents, modern science and capitalism. Nature as the Real in which everything, from stars to the sun, always returns to its proper place, as the realm of long reliable cycles and of stable laws regulating them, is being replaced by a thoroughly contingent Real, a Real outside the Law, a Real that is permanently revolutionizing its own rules, a Real that resists any inclusion into a totalized World (universe of meaning), which is why Badiou characterized capitalism as the first worldless civilization.

How should we react to this constellation? Should we adopt a defensive approach and search for a new limit, a return to (or, rather, the invention of) some new balance? This is what bioethics endeavors to do with regard to biotechnology, this is why the two form a couple: biotechnology pursues new possibilities of scientific interventions (genetic manipulations, cloning …), while bioethics endeavors to impose moral limitations on what biotechnology enables us to do. As such, bioethics is not immanent to scientific practice: it intervenes in this practice from outside, imposing external morality onto it. But is not bioethics precisely the betrayal of the ethics immanent to scientific endeavor, the ethics of "do not compromise your scientific desire, follow its path inexorably"? A new limit is also what the slogan of the Porto Allegro protesters, "A new world is possible," basically amounts to, and even ecology offers itself at this point as the provider of a new limit ("we cannot go further in our exploitation of nature, nature will not tolerate it, it will collapse …").

Or should we follow the opposite path mentioned above (of Deleuze and Negri, among others) and posit that capitalist disorder is still too much order, obeying the capitalist law of surplus-value appropriation, so that the task is not to limit it but to push it beyond its limitations? In other words, should we risk here also a paraphrase of Mao's well-known motto: there is disorder in the Real, so the situation is excellent? Perhaps this is the path to follow, albeit not in the sense advocated by Deleuze and Negri in their celebration of deterritorialization? Miller claims that the pure lawless Real resists symbolic grasp, so that we should always be aware that our attempts to conceptualize it are mere semblances, defensive elucubrations; but what if there is still an underlying *order* that generates this disorder, a matrix that provides its coordinates? This is what also accounts for the repetitive sameness of the capitalist dynamic: the more things change, the more everything remains the same. In short, what Miller ignores is that the obverse of the capitalist dynamic is a clearly recognizable order of hierarchic domination. Here is a long passage from his programmatic text:

> This is something indicated by Lacan's examples to illustrate the return of the real in the same place. His examples are the annual return of the seasons, the spectacle of the skies and the heavenly bodies. You could say ... based on examples from all antiquity: Chinese rituals of course used mathematical calculations of the position of the heavenly bodies, etc. You could say that in this epoch the real as nature had the function of the Other of the Other, that is, that the real was itself the guarantee of the symbolic order. The agitation, the rhetorical agitation of the signifier in human speech was framed by a weft of signifiers fixed like the heavenly bodies. Nature—this is its very definition—is defined by being ordered, that is, by the conduct of the symbolic and the real, to such an extent that according to the most ancient traditions all human order should imitate natural order.
>
> The real invented by Lacan is not the real of science, it is a contingent real, random, in as much as the natural law of the relation between the sexes is lacking. It is a hole in the knowledge included in the real. Lacan made use of the language of mathematics—the best support for science. In the formulas of sexuation, for example, he tried to grasp the dead-ends of sexuality in a weft of mathematical logic. This was like a heroic attempt to make psychoanalysis into a science of the real in the way that logic is. But that can't be done without imprisoning jouissance in the phallic function, in a symbol; it implies a symbolization of the real, it implies referring to the binary man-woman as if living beings could be partitioned so neatly, when we already see in the real of the 21st Century a growing disorder of sexuation. This is already a secondary construction that intervenes after the initial impact of the body and *lalangue*, which constitutes a real without law, without logical rule. Logic is only introduced afterwards, with the elucubration, the fantasy, the subject supposed to know, and with psychoanalysis.

Until now, under the inspiration of the 20th Century, our clinical cases as we recount them have been logical-clinical constructions under transference. But the cause–effect relation is a scientific prejudice supported by the subject supposed to know. The cause–effect relation is not valid at the level of the real without law, it is not valid except with a rupture between cause and effect. Lacan said it as a joke: if one understands how an interpretation works, it is not an analytic interpretation. In psychoanalysis as Lacan invites us to practice it, we experience the rupture of the cause–effect link, the opacity of the link, and this is why we speak of the unconscious. I am going to say it in another way: psychoanalysis takes place at the level of the repressed and of the interpretation of the repressed thanks to the subject supposed to know.

But in the 21st Century it is a question of psychoanalysis exploring another dimension, that of the defence against the real without law and without meaning. Lacan indicates this direction with his notion of the real, as Freud does with his mythological concept of the drive. The Lacanian unconscious, that of the latest Lacan, is at the level of the real, let us say for convenience, below the Freudian unconscious. Therefore, in order to enter into the 21st Century, our clinic will have to be centred on dismantling the defence, disordering the defence against the real. The transferential unconscious in analysis is already a defence against the real. And in the transferential unconscious there is still an intention, a *wanting to say*, a *wanting you to tell me*. When in fact the real unconscious is not intentional: it is encountered under the modality of "that's it," which you could say is like our "amen."

Various questions will be opened up for us at the next Congress: the redefinition of the desire of the analyst, which is not a pure desire, as Lacan says, not a pure infinity of metonymy but—this is how it appears to us— the desire to reach the real, to reduce the other to its real, and to liberate it of meaning. I would add that Lacan invented a way of representing the real with the Borromean knot. We will ask ourselves how valid this representation is, of what use it is to us now. Lacan made use of the knot to arrive at this irremediable zone of existence where one can go no further with two. The passion for the Borromean knot led Lacan to the same zone as Oedipus at Colonus, where one finds the absolute absence of charity, of fraternity, of any human sentiment: this is where the search for the real stripped of meaning leads us.[3]

Many things in these quoted paragraphs are problematic. The problems begin with the notion of the Real as Nature in its regularity, as that which always returns to its place; as Lacan noted, for the ancient Aztecs and other civilizations of sacrifice, the natural Real was not simply a regularity that nothing can perturb. The ancient Aztecs organized human sacrifices to guarantee—what? Not a special favor from the gods but the very regularity of Nature at its most elementary: human lives have to be sacrificed so that

Nature will rotate in its regular way, so that the sun will rise in the morning, etc. In short, the Real of the natural order where "everything returns to its own place" needs a symbolic intervention, it has to be guaranteed by rituals. There is a key passage from this Real sustained by symbolic sacrifice to the Real of modern science, the Newtonian Real of natural laws, of the network of causes and effects—it is only this Real that functions in itself, without the help of any symbolic intervention:

> With the infinite universe of mathematical physics nature disappears; it becomes solely a moral instance. With the philosophers of the 18th Century, with the infinite universe nature disappears and the real begins to be unveiled.
>
> Fine, but I have been asking myself about the formula *there is a knowledge in the real*. It would be a temptation to say that the unconscious is at this level. On the contrary, the supposition of a knowledge in the real appears to me to be an ultimate veil that needs to be lifted. If there is a knowledge in the real there is a regularity, and scientific knowledge allows prediction, it is so proud of prediction, in so far as this demonstrates the existence of laws. And it does not require a divine utterance of these laws for them to remain valid. It is by way of this idea of laws that the old idea of nature has been preserved in the very expression *the laws of nature*.[4]

Miller goes much too fast here: the break between traditional Nature and the Nature of modern science is more radical. In contrast to traditional Nature, whose regular rhythm is supposed to point toward a deeper cosmic sexualized meaning (day and night as the regular exchange of masculine and feminine principles, etc.), scientific laws of nature are themselves contingent, there is no deeper meaningful necessity sustaining them, they are, to quote Miller, discovered precisely "under the modality of 'that's it,' which you could say is like our 'amen.'"

Furthermore, Miller's search for the "pure" Real outside the Symbolic, a Real not yet stained by it, that he attributes to Lacan has to be abandoned as a Deleuzian blind alley: in a very Deleuzian way (repeating literally a formula from *Anti-Oedipus*), Miller speaks of the "true" pre-Oedipal Unconscious "beneath" the Freudian one, as if we first have the "pure" pre-Oedipal movement of drives, the direct interpenetration of signifying material and *jouissance* baptized by Lacan *lalangue*, and it is only in a (logical, if not temporary) afterward that this flux is "ordained" by symbolic elucubrations, forced into the symbolic straitjacket of binary logic, of paternal Law and castration that sustain sexual difference as the normative structure of two sexual identities, masculine and feminine. According to Miller, even Lacan's "formulas of sexuation" fall into this category of symbolic elucubrations that obfuscate the "pure" Real outside the Law. Today, however, things are changing; we "see in the real of the 21st Century a growing disorder of sexuation," new forms of sexuality are emerging which undermine "the binary man-woman as if living beings could be partitioned so neatly."

From a strict Lacanian standpoint, something is terribly wrong with this line of reasoning: Miller passes directly from the Real as Nature (which follows its regular rhythm or its laws) to the pure lawless Real—what goes missing here is the Lacanian Real itself, the Real which is *nothing but* a deadlock of symbolization or formalization ("Le réel est une impasse de formalization," as Lacan put it in *Seminar XX*), the Real which is an immanent impossibility of the symbolic, a purely formal obstacle that thwarts/distorts the symbolic from within, the Real of an antagonism inscribed into the heart of the symbolic, the self-limitation of the symbolic. This impasse is not caused by an external real, as Miller implies when he qualifies Lacan's formulas of sexuation as elucubration on the Real: symbolic interpretations of sexual difference are such elucubrations, but not the Real of the difference itself. Sexual difference is not binary/differential, it is an antagonism that binary symbolic difference tries to "normalize" by translating it into symbolic oppositions. (And, in a strictly homologous way, class antagonism is not a symbolic elucubration on the lawless Real of social life but the name of the antagonism obfuscated by ideologico-political formations.) In equating capitalism with the Real outside the Law (outside castration), Miller takes capitalism at its own ideology, ignoring Lacan, who saw clearly the antagonism masked by capitalist perversion. The vision of today's society as a capitalist Real outside symbolic law is a disavowal of antagonism, not a primary fact, in exactly the same way that the notion of the sexual Real outside the Law is a disavowal of sexual antagonism.

What Real, then, are we talking about? In "Was geschah im 20. Jahrhundert?" (What happened in the twentieth century?), a chapter in the book of the same title,[5] Peter Sloterdijk endorses Badiou's thesis, from his *Le siècle*, that the defining feature of the twentieth century was "the passion for the real," the gravitational pull toward the real basis of our lives (economic base, libido, will, etc.). What we witness is the reversal of the traditional relation between public theology and occult materialism preached in elite circles— today, materialism is public while gnostic theology grows in the underground. ... Passion for the Real is not just a realist-cynical stance of reducing ideological chimeras to their "actual base" ("it's all really about the economy, power, sex"), it is also sustained by a messianic logic of extermination: the cobweb of (religious, moral, etc.) illusions has to be ruthlessly erased, and it has to be done now. The twentieth century was a time of extremism, of *passage à l'acte*, not of hope for some future. Sloterdijk, of course, for this very reason sees the twentieth century as the age of extremism and ethical catastrophes, from Nazism to Stalinism. The twenty-first century should oppose to this gravitational stance of reducing all phenomena to their actual base the stance of floating in the air, the antigravitational elevation—even our earth is a spaceship Earth floating in the air.

So, again, what notion of the Real are we talking about? Sloterdijk adheres to the traditional "realist" notion of the Real, ignoring the Lacanian Real as the minimal difference, the purely formal gap accessible through the act of (what Badiou calls) subtraction, not violent reduction. (Badiou himself, well aware of the trap of violent reduction to which Stalinism and Maoism succumbed, sees the new century as providing an opening into a different passion for the Real.) The stakes here are the highest imaginable; they concern the ultimate philosophical question, which is, or so we are told:

1.2 WHY IS THERE NOTHING RATHER THAN SOMETHING?

For critics of science, this is *the* question, the question even the most advanced science will never be able to answer, since science always and by definition has to presuppose that there is something (its object). Quantum cosmologists retort that this, precisely—the rise of something out of nothing—is something they *can* account for: the entire universe, from the fireball of the Big Bang to the star-studded cosmos we now inhabit, popped into existence from nothing at all, and this had to happen because "nothing" (the quantum void) is inherently unstable.

Perhaps, however, we should turn the big question around: why is there (also) nothing and not (just) something? More precisely: how could nothing arise out of something? Insofar as "something" stands for the brute Real, and "nothing" for negativity at the core of subject, the negativity proper to the symbolic order (as Lacan repeats again and again, negativity is introduced into the Real only through the rise of the symbolic order), the question is thus, in Hegelese: how can subject arise out of substance? Here we encounter the first paradox: while subject arises through the symbolization of the Real (subject is by definition subject of the signifier), it is strictly correlative to the failure of symbolization: subject's objectal counterpart is a remainder of the Real that resists symbolization. In other words, complete symbolization would have realized a structure without subject, a structure that would no longer be symbolic. The key to this paradox is that symbolization is as such, in its very notion, incomplete, non-all, failed; it is a structure of its own failure. And here things get really interesting.

One of the most pervasive anti-idealist themes not only of "deconstruction" but of the entire post-Hegelian critique of absolute idealism is the one of an "indivisible remainder"—Schelling, the first great critic of Hegel, coined the term: *der nie aufgehende Rest*. The idea is that every process of conceptualization, of rational apprehension, of symbolization, every attempt by *logos* to seize reality, produces a remainder; the Real resists full symbolization.

We thus have a process in three steps: first, there is the raw presymbolic Real; then, there is the process of its symbolization, of getting caught up in the symbolic network; but the symbolization cannot be completed, and Lacan's name for what remains is *objet petit a*. Lacan's formula of the discourse of the Master provides the matrix of this process: a subject is represented in a signifier for other signifiers, and this operation produces a remainder, *a*. The relationship between the presymbolic Real and *a* can thus be formulated as the relationship of before and after (similar to the stupid advertisements for effective diets where we get a person with a big stomach "before" and a flat stomach "after"): the Real precedes symbolization, while *a* is what remains of the Real after it goes through the symbolic, a monument to the ultimate failure of symbolization. Insofar as the process of symbolization vaguely coincides with what Hegel called *Aufhebung* (sublation: transposition of the raw contingent Real into the order of symbolic necessity, its idealization), the topic of the indivisible remainder readily offers itself as an indicator of the limit of *Aufhebung*: this remainder is the raw piece of the Real that cannot be sublated into a moment of the ideal symbolic texture, so it can also be called *der nie aufhebbare Rest*. (Incidentally, for a Hegelian, it would be easy to counter that the indivisible remainder is an immanent part of the dialectical process, its concluding moment—recall Hegel's concept of monarchy, where the person of the king whose only legitimization is his birth, i.e., the "irrational" natural contingency of his parents, not what he has made of himself, his subjective self-sublation, has to be added to the rational network of social relations in order to constitute it as the actual totality of a State.)

There is, however, a problem with this simple triadic structure: it ignores the radically ambiguous status of *objet a* which, in Lacan, stands for the coincidence of opposites at its purest—it is simultaneously the "irrational" (alogical, contingent, material) remainder of the process of symbolization, something that resists getting caught up in the symbolic form, *and* a purely formal moment, a hypothetic X that is never encountered but ex-sists as a virtual point of reference. In his commentary on Lacan's *Seminar XVI*, Miller elaborated the crucial change in the status of *objet petit a*, the object-cause of desire: the passage from corporeal specimen (partial object: breast, feces ...) to a pure logical function; in this seminar,

> Lacan does not really describe *objets a* as corporeal specimens, he constructs them as a logical consistency, logic being there in the place of biology. The logical consistency is like a function that the body must satisfy through different bodily deductions.[6]

This passage is the passage from the foreign intruder, the pieces of sand heterogeneous to the signifying machine, preventing its smooth functioning, to the total homogeneity of this machine. When Lacan is describing the loops and twists of the symbolic space on account of which its interiority overlaps with its exteriority ("ex-timacy"), he does not merely describe the structural place of *objet a* (surplus-enjoyment): surplus-enjoyment is *nothing but this structure itself*, this "inward loop" of the symbolic space. Let us clarify this with a reference to the gap that separates drive from instinct: while drive and instinct have the same "object," the same goal, what differentiates them is that drive finds satisfaction not in reaching its goal but in circulating around it, repeating the failure to reach it. One can say, of course, that what prevents the drive from reaching its goal is the *objet a* which is decentered with regard to it, so that, even if we reach the goal, the object eludes us and we are condemned to repeat the procedure; however, this *objet a* is purely formal, it is the curvature of the space of drive on account of which the "shortest way" to reach the object is not to aim directly at it but to encircle it, to tour around it repeatedly.

Repetition is not only repetition of something that cannot be repeated and, in this sense, repetition of the impossibility of repeating, but repetition of something that does not exist in itself, that emerges only retroactively through its repetition. This emergence can be discerned apropos of the two versions of Doctorow's *Billy Bathgate*, the original book and the cinema version. The movie is basically a failure, but an interesting one: a failure which nonetheless evokes in the viewer the specter of a much better novel. However, when one then goes on to read the novel on which the film is based, one is disappointed—this is *not* the novel the film evoked as the standard with regard to which it failed. The repetition (of a failed novel in the failed film) thus gives rise to a third, purely virtual, element: the better novel. This is an exemplary case of what Deleuze describes in a crucial passage from *Difference and Repetition*:

> while it may seem that the two presents are successive, at a variable distance apart in the series of reals, in fact they form, rather, *two real series which coexist in relation to a virtual object of another kind*, one which constantly circulates and is displaced in them. ... Repetition is constituted not from one present to another, but between the two coexistent series that these presents form in function of the virtual object (object = x).[7]

With regard to *Billy Bathgate*, the film does not "repeat" the novel on which it is based; rather, they both "repeat" the unrepeatable virtual X, the "true" novel whose specter is engendered in the passage from the actual novel to the film. This virtual point of reference, although "unreal," is in a way more real than reality: it is the *absolute* point of reference of the failed real attempts. This is how, from the perspective of materialist theology, the divine emerges from the repetition of terrestrial material elements, as their "cause" retroactively posited by them. Deleuze is right to refer to Lacan here: this "better book" is what Lacan calls the *objet petit a*, the object-cause of desire that "one cannot recapture in the present, except by capturing it in its consequences," in the two really existing works, the book and the film. The nonexistent "better book" is what both existing works repeat (and fail in their endeavor to repeat), it is what maintains a distance between the two, the interruption between the two.

Does not this irreducible ambiguity of *objet a* compel us to turn around the usual RSI of the presupposed Real, its symbolization, and the imaginary-real remainder of this process? What if we risk the inverted triad which begins with the real excess or remainder, goes on with the attempt to deal with this excess through its symbolization, and ends up with the fantasy of some imaginary presymbolic Real, a fantasy engendered retroactively by the process of symbolization itself? The ontological premise here is that excess (surplus) is not excess with regard to some stable standard—excess is original; if we subtract excess, then not even *nothing* remains, because nothing "is" only with regard to excesses. (In capitalism, this paradox is openly staged, which is why capitalism is the truth of prehistory: in the cycle of its self-reproduction, capital circulates around its void.)

The question that arises here is: how has this nothing to be structured so that excess can emerge out of it? The answer is indicated by quantum physics: this void is not the Void of inner peace, of withdrawal into the neutral medium of earthly conflicts, it is inherently unstable, the utter contradiction of an X which "is" its own impossibility—in short, zero is in itself a barred One. However, we should be more specific here: the void of the impossible/barred One is not the same as the void of the vacuum state, which is not truly empty but contains fleeting electromagnetic waves and particles that pop in and out of existence; the Void of the barred One is not the void pregnant with virtualities but the void of the pure self-contradiction, of the utter tension crushing a One which persists only as its own impossibility. Traditional notions of the Void always confront the problem of how and why the Void is disturbed so that particular entities emerge out of it (and their answer is mostly the evocation of some inexplicable loss of balance, similar to Fichte's *Anstos*, which sets in motion the differentiation of the I and the non-I). What we should do is to fully identify the two: there is no peaceful and balanced Void beyond *disturbances*, the Void *is* the radical disturbance/impossibility/tension out of which entities emerge, entities which bear the trace of their origin and are by definition thwarted, antagonistic.

This, then, is the original correlation: the pure Real as a purely formal bar, the Void of its own impossibility, and the excess which is an excess with regard to nothing—or, in Lacan's mathemes, $barred{S}$ and a. Note how one should here think $barred{S}$–a as prior to the signifying representation, not as its outcome.

(We will leave aside for the time being the key question: how is the $\$$ of the Void related to the $\$$ of subjectivity?)

But is not the claim that being is grounded in its own impossibility already contained in Hegel's old dictum that "contradiction" is the *movens* out of which all particular entities emerge? Lacan said: "Discourse begins from the fact that here there is a gap. ... But, after all, nothing prevents us from saying that it is because discourse begins that the gap is produced."[8] Did he also not assert here the full coincidence of discourse (signifier) with its own impossibility? A discourse is thwarted by a gap which is consubstantial with discourse, so that it is simultaneously its condition of impossibility and its condition of possibility. It is this ultimate coincidence of opposites which is lacking in Badiou's ontology, where

> pure being is inconsistent, but it is all fully there, so to speak. Being as
> such is not ridden with any impossibility. The latter only pertains to, or
> originates in, its (re)presentation, and leads to the theory of the Event
> and its ontological impossibility or prohibition. What follows from Lacan's
> conceptualizations, on the other hand, is that the two are related: an Event is
> possible (can happen) because of the impossibility inherent to being. ... It
> is precisely because of this impossibility which it keeps repeating that being
> is a domain where things *can* happen; it has the potential for Events. And
> this, of course, is an important difference with regard to Badiou, for whom
> the interruption of being by an Event comes from an absolute "elsewhere."[9]

The ontological gap between the order of Being and the interruption/cut that an Event introduces into this order is thereby transposed back into the order of Being which is traversed by an immanent antagonism/impossibility. (The Freudian name for this gap is "death drive," and it is no wonder that Badiou reacts in a quite allergic way to any mention of the death drive.) One should thus reject positions (which, of course, are far from being identical) such as the Buddhist notion of reality as a flow of inconsistent insubstantial phenomena against the background of Nothing, or Badiou's pure multiplicity as the ultimate ontological category. In this view, reality is the inconsistent multiplicity of multiplicities which cannot be generated by or constituted from (or reduced to) some form of Ones as its elementary ("atomic") constituents. Multiplicities are not multiplications of One, they are irreducible multiplicities, which is why their opposite is not One but zero, the ontological Void: no matter how far we progress in our analysis of multiplicities, we never reach the zero level of simple constituents, the only "background" of multiplicities is zero itself, the Void.[10]

So the primordial opposition is not that of One and Zero, but that of Zero and multiplicities, and the One emerges later. To put it even more radically: since only Ones fully "really exist," multiplicities and Zero are the same thing (not *one and* the same thing): Zero "is" multiplicities without Ones which would guarantee their ontological consistency. This ontological openness of the oneless multiplicity allows us to approach in a new way Kant's second antinomy of pure reason, whose thesis is: "Every composite substance in the world consists of simple parts; and there exists nothing that is not either itself simple, or composed of simple parts."[11] Here is Kant's proof:

> For, grant that composite substances do not consist of simple parts; in this case, if all combination or composition were annihilated in thought, no composite part, and (as, by the supposition, there do not exist simple parts) no simple part would exist. Consequently, no substance; consequently, nothing would exist. Either, then, it is impossible to annihilate composition in thought; or, after such annihilation, there must remain something that subsists without composition, that is, something that is simple. But in the former case the composite could not itself consist of substances, because with substances composition is merely a contingent relation, apart from which they must still exist as self-subsistent beings. Now, as this case contradicts the supposition, the second must contain the truth—that the substantial composite in the world consists of simple parts.
>
> It follows, as an immediate inference, that the things in the world are all, without exception, simple beings—that composition is merely an external condition pertaining to them—and that, although we never can separate and isolate the elementary substances from the state of composition, reason must cogitate these as the primary subjects of all composition, and consequently, as prior thereto—and as simple substances.[12]

What, however, if we accept the conclusion that, ultimately, "nothing exists"? (A conclusion which, incidentally, is exactly the same as the conclusion of Plato's *Parmenides*: "Then may we not sum up the argument in a word and say truly: If one is not, then nothing is?") Such a move, although rejected by Kant as obvious nonsense, is not as un-Kantian as it may appear: it is here that one should apply yet again the Kantian distinction between negative and infinite judgment. The statement "material reality is all there is" can be negated in two ways: in the forms "material reality *isn't all there is*" and "material reality *is non-all*." The first negation (of a predicate) leads to the standard metaphysics: material reality isn't everything, there is another, higher, spiritual reality. ... As such, this negation is, in accordance with Lacan's formulas of sexuation, inherent to the positive statement "material reality is all there is": as its constitutive exception, it grounds its universality. If, however, we assert a nonpredicate and say "material reality *is non-all*," this merely asserts the non-All of reality without implying any exception; paradoxically, one should thus claim that the axiom of true materialism is not "material reality is all there is," but a double one: (1) there is nothing which is not material reality, (2) material reality is non-All.[13] However, again, such an ontological vision of an inconsistent plurality against the background of the Void is not enough. As we have already seen, the first thing to do is to specify the nature of this void: it is not the void of a neutral ground of all phenomena but the Void of the impossible One, the Void of an extreme antagonism, tension, self-contradiction, the Void of the impossibility of the One's becoming itself.

In other words, while the order of Being is, for Badiou, an inconsistent multiplicity of multiplicities, there is no impossibility/antagonism that thwarts it. This brings us back to our basic theme of void and surplus: "the 'wandering excess' is not the implication of the multiple (multiplicity), but of the One-less, of the minus-one" (AZ, 131). And, surprising as it may sound, this notion of surplus as a supplement to the ontological Void/impossibility has profound political implications. Recall all the vivid descriptions (in Deleuze, Rancière, and Badiou) of the "part of no-part," of "supernumerary" elements which are part of society without having a proper place within it, i.e., cannot be counted and accounted for as its immanent parts. The properly political tension here is the tension between the hegemonic Totality and the supernumerary parts which resist being included in it, so that emancipatory struggle appears as the struggle for the redefinition of Universality, for a new All which will encompass supernumerary elements. For example, in a society in which patriarchal heterosexuality is imposed as a norm, homosexuals and other non-heterosexual orientations function as "parts of no-part": even if they are tolerated, they are perceived as marginal deviations, so the task is to redefine the entire field of sexuality in order to abolish the subordinate role of homosexuals. ... What is missing here? From the Lacanian-Marxist standpoint, the tension between (the hegemonic figure of the) social All and its "parts of no-part" is strictly secondary with regard to the basic social antagonism/"impossibility" that cuts across the social body—or, to put it in Freudian terms, "supernumerary" elements are symptoms of this antagonism ("class struggle"). Let us take another example, that of sans-papiers, the undocumented illegal immigrants who are de facto part of our societies and even play a considerable economic role in it (as a cheap unprotected labor force), but without being properly included in it with full rights. These sans-papiers are a

contemporary political instance of the wandering excess. For Badiou this is an example of being which obviously exists, yet has no symbolic status, which is why it can be treated, at the level of the state and its mode of representation, as if it did not exist. It is an unrepresented (uncountable) excess of the state-multiple beyond itself. The difference with Lacan in this respect is of course not that for Lacan something like the sans-papiers would not count as a critical problem; it resides in the formulation of what exactly is the problem here (where it lies), and hinges on the distinction between the symptom and the Real. Briefly put: a symptom is a formation of being, whereas the Real is its deadlock (non-being) which this formation keeps repeating. ... They are the symptom as material embodiment of a fundamental deadlock (of a given whole). (AZ, 131)

In short, the tension between the hegemonic order and its symptoms (parts of no-part, wandering excesses) cannot be properly understood without locating it with regard to the basic antagonism that cuts across the social Whole and makes it non-All ("class struggle").

Back to our basic premise: if the Real is its own impossibility, how do we pass from this level to the series of Ones, and to a surplus in excess of these Ones? From 0 to 1? The answer is that zero is already the barred One, not a primordial Void but the void of its own (One's) impossibility. Here one should supplement the argument of Badiou, for whom the primordial onto-logical space is that of a multiplicity of multiplicities against/in the Void, and then the One emerges through the operation of counting: the One *as barred* is here from the very beginning. This is also why we do not pass directly from the barred One to multiplicity, but to the Two—more precisely, to the less-than-two.

With the onset of the signifying order, the status of the One changes: if, in Life, the One is the self-positing unit of an organism, in the signifying order the One is a signifier, the signifying "unary feature," whose identity is purely differential (it is nothing but the bundle of its differences from other signi-fiers, it has no substantial identity of its own), which means that the absence of a feature also counts as a feature of its identity. For this reason a signify-ing network is never complete, and every signifying network has to include an "empty" signifier, a self-reflexive signifier which stands for the lack of the signifier. This signifier (what Lacan calls the Master-Signifier) has no counterpart, there is no signifier which could act as its differential oppo-site, since this signifier stands for the difference as such. So when the One appears, it lacks its counterpart, "binary signifier," and the multiplicity (the series of ordinary signifiers) is the filler of this missing Two. In other words, the moment we are within a signifying order, the impossibility of the One appears as the impossibility of the Two, of a signifier that would be the One's differential counterpart.

This paradoxical interplay of the One and the missing Two presupposes the minimal structure of reflexivity of every signifying network. The oppo-sition with which we began (surplus as the result/product or as the starting point) repeats itself here at another level. We either start from the series of signifiers, and the exceptional Master-Signifier fills in the gap in the series (signifier of the lack of the signifier); or the series itself fills in the lack of the binary signifier. The first option follows from Lacan's thesis according to which what is "primordially repressed" is the binary signifier (that of *Vorstellungs-Repräsentanz*): what the symbolic order precludes is the full harmonious presence of the couple of Master-Signifiers, S_1–S_2 as yin–yang, or any other two symmetrical "fundamental principles." The fact that "there is no sexual relationship" means precisely that the secondary signifier (that of the Woman) is "primordially repressed," *and what we get in the place of this repression, what fills in its gap, is the multitude of the "returns of the repressed," the series of the "ordinary" signifiers.*

The obverse aspect of this reflexivity resides in the fact that what Lacan calls "Master-Signifier" is the reflexive signifier that fills in for the very lack of the signifier. Spinoza's own supreme example, "God," is crucial here: conceived as a mighty person, God merely embodies our ignorance of true causality. Examples from the history of science abound—from phlogiston (a pseudo-concept which simply betrayed the scientists' ignorance of how light actually travels) to Marx's "Asiatic mode of production" (which is a kind of negative container: the only true content of this concept is "all the modes of production which do not fit Marx's standard categorization of the modes of production"), not to mention today's popular "postindustrial society"— notions which, while they appear to designate a positive content, merely signal our ignorance.

In the first version, the binary signifier, the symmetrical counterpart of S_1, is "primordially repressed," and it is in order to supplement the void of this repression that the chain of S_2 emerges, i.e., the original fact is the couple of S_1 and the Void at the place of its counterpart, and the chain of S_2 is secondary; in the second version, in the account of the emergence of S_1 as the "enigmatic term," the empty signifier, the primordial fact, is, on the contrary, S_2, the signifying chain in its incompleteness, and it is in order to fill in the Void of this incompleteness that S_1 intervenes. How are the two versions to be coordinated? Is the ultimate fact the vicious circle of their mutual implication?

What if, yet again, these two versions vindicate the logic of Lacan's "formulas of sexuation"? Contrary to our expectations, it is the first version—the multitude emerges in order to fill in the void of the binary signifier—which is "feminine," i.e., which accounts for the explosion of the inconsistent multitude of the feminine non-All, and the second version which is "masculine," i.e., which accounts for how a multitude is totalized into an All through the exception which fills in its void. However, the symmetry between the two versions is not complete: as in the case of Kant's antinomies of pure reason, where mathematical antinomies logically precede dynamic antinomies, the "feminine" version (multiplicity fills in the lack of the binary signifier) comes first, it accounts for the very emergence of multiplicity, of the non-totalizable series whose lack is then filled in by the reflexive Master-Signifier, the signifier of the lack of the signifier. In short, "it all begins" not simply with the multiplicity of multiplicities which "is" the Void, but with the impossible/barred One, the One which is nothing but its own impossibility.

The process to be accounted for is thus the rise of the One against the background of its own impossibility: how does the One emerge out of the multiplicity of the Real? In "dead" nature there are multiples of multiples but no Ones: the One comes to exist only where a living organism is defined by its self-relating which enables it to posit the line of delimitation between its inside and the outside of its environs. In one unexpected encounter between contemporary philosophy and Hegel, the "Christian materialist" Peter van Inwagen developed the idea that material objects like automobiles, chairs, computers, simply *do not exist*: a chair, for example, is not actually, for itself, a chair—all we have is a collection of "simples" (i.e., more elementary objects "arranged chairwise")—so, although a chair functions as a chair, it is com-posed of a multitude (pieces of wood, nails, cushions, etc.) which are, in themselves, totally indifferent toward this arrangement; there is, *stricto sensu*, no "whole" here of which a nail is a part. It is only with organisms that we have a Whole. Here, the unity is minimally "for itself"; parts effectively inter-act.[14] (So even our Earth is not One, as the Gaia hypothesis claims, although it appears to have a "dead" cold shell protecting the hot fluid core—all this remains a metaphor, the shell does not yet function as a self-referential limit.) The implications of this idea are tremendous: life is ultimately the abnormal-ity of/in dead nature, its getting captured into the dream of the One, while language (human subjectivity) is the reemergence (return) of death in life. This is why Zupančič is right to claim that

> life is but a dream of the inanimate. More precisely, it is a *nightmare* of the inanimate (its nightmarish disturbance), since the inanimate wants nothing but to be left alone. In this sense we could say that the death drive is not so much a drive as an ontological fatigue as a fundamental *affect* of life—not that it is necessarily experienced, "felt" as fatigue; it is present as a kind of "objective affect" of life. (AZ, 97)

The question here is, again: how should the inanimate be ontologically structured in order to be able to dream, to have "nightmares"? (It goes with-out saying that one should exclude all forms of animism, of the New Age spir-itualization of nature.) Dreams and nightmares are forms of appearance, they imply the gap between reality and its appearance (to itself), so the question is: how is appearing possible? Only if reality itself is not fully itself. Appear-ing fills in some primordial ontological void, so for appearing to emerge, there has to be a "negativity," a self-blockade, an immanent impossibility at work in reality itself, a split between reality and proto-reality, between reality and (not nothing but) less than nothing. In other words, what appears in the most radical sense is not the reality behind appearance but that which is excluded/occluded from reality itself, its constitutive obstacle/impossibility. This is why appearing is not a secondary effect of substantial reality but a point where, in reality itself, the causal chain breaks. In this sense, appearing is the same as the rise of subjectivity: as Kant knew, the subject's freedom equals the interruption of the natural texture of causes and effects—the subject ultimately emerges "out of nowhere." This is why a subject is by definition nontransparent to itself: because it is pure self-appearing, i.e., because the neutralization of its "natural base" (its neuronal-biological "substance") is constitutive of its functioning.

In one of the early novels about Hannibal Lecter, the claim that Hannibal's monstrosity is the result of unfortunate circumstances is rejected: "Nothing happened to him. He happened." One has to give this statement a Heideggerian reading: it's not that simply nothing happened, nothing itself happened with him. This is also how one should invert the standard notion of a traumatized subject: trauma is not something that affects the subject, the ultimate trauma is the rise/explosion of the subject itself. (This goes for humanity itself, which happened to the Earth as a traumatic emergence of the New.) Recall a scene from the middle of the second version of Hitchcock's *The Man Who Knew Too Much*: in search of "Ambrose Chappell," the hero walks along a suburban London street observing with suspicion occasional passersby who eye him with a perplexed gaze, trying to ascertain if any of them is part of the gang which kidnapped his son, till we realize that the stain in the picture, the suspicious element that sticks out, is he himself. ... It is along these lines that we should understand Lacan's surprising claim in his late work that the subject is a "cause of itself," a claim which immediately evokes German Idealism: true, the subject is "decentered," haunted by an irreducibly external object-cause; however, this object-cause does not preexist it but is in a way retroactively posited by it. The mediating element of this circularity is failure: a subject represents itself in a signifying chain, representation fails, and the subject is this failure of representation (that X which eludes representation and whose objectal counterpart is *objet a*, the *je ne sais quoi*, that which in an object is more than an object). A subject is thus the result of the failure of its own representation, it is what formally precedes representation and simultaneously what comes after—more precisely, what precedes representation is the retroactive result of its failure.

This circle of the subject as its own cause can be materially represented only as an inversion of the direction of time. Toward the end of *Superman* (1978), while the hero is busy saving others from a deadly earthquake, Lois's car falls into a crevice that opens due to an aftershock; it quickly fills with dirt and debris, and she suffocates to death. Angered at being unable to save her, Superman defies his Krypton father's earlier warning not to manipulate human history, preferring to heed his earthly father's advice that he must be on Earth for "a reason": he accelerates around the Earth, rewinding time, in order to save Lois. This acceleration is shot in a classic sci-fi way: Superman flies in a circle around the Earth, faster and faster till his flight reaches infinite speed, and then he goes even faster so that the Earth starts to turn in the opposite direction, i.e., time starts to run backward. In "nature" a thing like this cannot happen, of course: the flow of time is the basic ontological coordinate of material reality. However, life already implies a kind of retroactivity, a circle of effects retroactively positing their causes, and with the Spirit, retroactivity is even more radicalized: the process of the human Spirit is the process of a permanent rewriting of the past.

This does not mean that the subject is any way omnipotent; on the contrary, it signals its radical impotence: a subject cannot in any way control its effects on its environs, it is radically externalized, outside itself; its effects are in total discontinuity with what it experiences as its inner essence. In his book on Dostoyevsky, Rowan Williams proposes a radically new (at least to my knowledge) reading of The Idiot: in contrast to the conventional reading in which the novel's hero, Prince Myshkin, "the idiot," is perceived as a person of saintly love and goodness, "the positively good and beautiful man," as Dostoyevsky himself characterized him, a person for whom the real world of brutal power play and passions is too harsh so that, at the end, he has to withdraw into the seclusion of madness—in contrast to this reading, Williams reads Myshkin as the eye of a storm: yes, a good saintly person, but a person who, precisely as such, triggers havoc and death all around him. It is because of him, because of the role he plays in the complex network of relationships around him, that Rogozhin slaughters Nastassya Filippovna. So it's not just that Myshkin is an idiot, a naive simpleton, for those around him, while he is in himself a model of goodness: he is in effect a naive idiot, unaware of his disastrous effect on others.

1.3 MECHANISM AS A CONDITION OF FREEDOM

From here we should return to the topic of subjectivity (the spirit) as the return of death into life: within the sphere of life, "death" appears as a mechanism, which is why, as Hegel was fully aware, a "living" spirit can thrive only when it is embodied in a "dead" letter.

In his book on Hegel and mechanism, Nathan Ross sets the record straight on many crucial points.[15] His central insight concerns the link between three levels of Hegel's thought: the relationship between logic and metaphysics, the relationship between mechanism and living organism, and the relationship between civil society and state. When, in the early 1800s (in his so-called Jena period), Hegel "became Hegel," a break occurred at all three levels. Prior to this break, Hegel designated the first part of his philosophy "logic and metaphysics" (or also dialectics and speculation proper), keeping the two separate[16]—first logic, the epistemological clarification, the negative part, the critical analysis of our intellectual tools, of our Understanding, demonstrating its inadequacy, its inconsistencies, antinomies, contradictions; then metaphysics, philosophical speculation proper, the deployment of the autonomous Reason which structures all reality. The break occurs when Hegel realizes that there is no speculation beyond dialectics, no Reason beyond Understanding, no metaphysics beyond logic: speculative Reason is not a separate domain above or beyond the antinomies of Understanding, it is merely the systematic deployment of these antinomies; metaphysics is not a separate domain above logic, it is merely the systematic deployment of the antinomies of logic. Dialectical logic already is the thing itself, and we pass from logic to metaphysics when we realize that logic already is metaphysics. So, to enact this passage, we don't have to add anything to logic, we just have to get rid of the illusion that there is anything beyond.

In a way that is strictly homologous to the opposition of logic and metaphysics, Hegel also reconceives the relationship between mechanism and organism: the task is no longer to leave mechanism (the external relationship between parts) behind and replace it with a living organic Whole, but to see mechanism in its notional necessity—not only in the sense that organic relations have to be developed immanently, out of the antinomies of mechanism, but more radically, in the sense that mechanism remains the foundation of every organic relationship. And, finally, the same goes for the role of mechanism in social life: it is only in the "alienated" market society where individuals pursue their self-interest and the Whole is regulated through external mechanisms beyond subjective control that human independence and freedom can thrive; there is no return to premodern organic unity. So the task is not to "overcome" the social mechanism but to assert it as a key component of a modern free society, while regulating its excesses through state intervention.[17]

But the role of mechanism is even more basic: it concerns the very process of becoming-human. When Lacan describes the gap that separates the Symbolic from the living organism, he regularly resorts to the notion of mechanism: a signifying mechanism encroaches upon a living body, distorting its organic balance, subjecting it to an artificial order, parasitizing on it, etc. Lacan is relying here on a line of thought which is followed by Hegel. After Hegel outlines the teleological process mechanism–chemistry–life, i.e., the gradual self-overcoming of mechanism (in which parts are indifferent toward their Whole) in organic totality (in which a part is a part only insofar as it is immanently related to its Whole), how do we pass from Life to Consciousness, to Spirit? Only through a return of mechanism: Spirit, in its distance toward the immediacy of life, can assert itself only insofar as it relies on a "dead" mechanism which imposes itself on life from outside. There is a deep necessity in this reliance of the autonomous spirit on mechanism: in a mechanism, parts have an existence independently of the whole which encompasses them, they are indifferent toward their Whole (a nail is indifferent toward the fact that it holds together the leg and the surface of a wooden table)—and is not the Subject (the void of singularity) even more indifferent toward the body in which it is anchored? And let us not forget that a signifier is also arbitrary with regard to its meaning, in contrast to natural signs which maintain metaphorical or metonymic continuity with the signified (smoke as a sign of fire, etc.); Hegel himself points out that Spirit can articulate itself in speech only when signs become totally indifferent to their content.

Here we have an exquisite example of the Hegelian triad life–mechanism–spirit: mechanism reduces the complex interaction of life, but subjectivity—a still "higher" form of self-relational interaction—can emerge only as the result of this reduction. True, spirit cannot be reduced to the (mechanical) letter, but *it exists only in the interstice of the (mechanical) letter.* "Reduction" is not a good term here: the rise of "mechanism" is not just a regression from living organism to dead matter; mechanism presupposes the power of pure thought, the power of abstraction which separates what in reality belongs together[18]—or, to quote the famous passage from the foreword to Hegel's *Phenomenology of Spirit*:

> The action of separating the elements is the exercise of the force of Understanding, the most astonishing and greatest of all powers, or rather the absolute power. The circle, which is self-enclosed and at rest, and, *qua* substance, holds its own moments, is an immediate relation, the immediate, continuous relation of elements with their unity, and hence arouses no sense of wonderment. But that an accident as such, when cut loose from its containing circumference—that what is bound and held by something else and actual only by being connected with it—should obtain an existence all its own, gain freedom and independence on its own account—this is the portentous power of the negative; it is the energy of thought, of pure Self.[19]

It is precisely the much-maligned "deficiency" of "abstract Understanding" which opens up the space of lying, of falsehoods, but also of irony, of messages between the lines, of politeness, of poetry even. This is why the human spirit presupposes the non-transparency of our mind, the ultimate failure of communication: we can say something new and creative only insofar as we ultimately do not know what we are saying, insofar as talking, saying, and thinking do not coincide. This is why the idea of a direct intercommunication of minds, the idea of our thoughts directly emanating from our minds to other minds, bypassing the "mechanical" symbolic order in its autonomy—the idea that also underlies the notion of post-human Singularity—would have entailed sexuality and spirituality. Let us return here to Liu Cixin's novel about the traumatic encounter between humanity and the Trisolarians. After individuals from the two species establish communication, a problem immediately arises: Trisolarians cannot understand the difference between "think" and "say"—for the Trisolarians, they are synonymous, or, as a Trisolarian writes to its human correspondent:

> We do not have organs of communication. Our brains can display our thoughts to the outside world, thereby achieving communication. …
> The thoughts in our brain emit electromagnetic waves on all frequencies, including what is visible light to us. They can be displayed at a significant distance. … We can communicate over significant distances, not just face-to-face. The words "cheating" and "lying" are another two that we have had a hard time understanding. … Human communication organs are but an evolutionary deficiency, a necessary compensation for the fact that your brains can't emit strong thought waves. This is one of your biological weaknesses. Direct display of thought is a superior, more efficient form of communication.[20]

Predictably, the Trisolarian makes a fatal mistake here: what it dismisses as an "evolutionary deficiency" opens up the only window of hope for the human resistance to the forthcoming Trisolarian invasion. The presence of the sophons, the tiny superintelligent computers made out of protons, which allow Trisolarians instant access to all human information, means that Earth's defense plans are exposed to the enemy—but the interior of the human mind remains a secret, inaccessible to the Trisolarians.

What the young Hegel saw clearly is the link between two features which may appear opposed: he saw that "the problem of habitual or mind-numbing religion is tied to the rise of self-interest."[21] On the one hand, we have different forms of mechanism for habits which characterize modernity: in the division of labor, a worker's task is reduced to the mechanical repetition of the same gestures, with no spiritual content; in education, it all begins with the mechanical learning of grammar rules, verb conjugations, etc.; in a society where market exchange predominates, social life itself appears to be regulated by blind mechanisms out of our collective control; religion itself is reduced to an empty mechanical following of rituals and prayers without any authentic subjective engagement, without any access to the spiritual meaning of these rituals. (One finds automatic, mind-numbing repetition of empty formulas even in ancient religions, for example, in Hinduism and Tibetan Buddhism.) On the other hand, individuals focus their lives more and more on pursuing their narrow self-interest (private pleasures, isolated spiritual enlightenment, individual wealth and power), so that any pursuit of global social goals withdraws into a murky background, or is best left to blind market mechanisms which guarantee that the common good will profit from the interaction of individuals who pursue their conflicting self-interests. The key point is thus to clearly perceive the interconnection of the two features: narrow individualism focused on self-interest is the obverse of a society in which global processes run their course "mechanically," independently of subjective decisions. This point is especially pertinent today, in our societies where the anonymous reign of the market is supplemented by ideological individualism ("be truly yourself, work on yourself, actualize your potential," etc.).

However—and herein lies Hegel's genius—the moment he reaches his (philosophical) maturity, he leaves behind the Romantic opposition between this alienated/individualist universe and the nonalienated universe in which individuals directly relate to the whole of their society and their religion is a deeply felt and enacted unity, a universe projected by the Romantics back into the ancient Greek *polis*. For Hegel, there is no return to this organic unity, for two interconnected reasons: first, in ancient Greece, this unity was always-already based on an exclusion (the exclusion of slaves, women, etc.), not all the people participated in it; second, alienation (the loss of organic unity, its replacement with a "mechanical" social order) also played a positive role: it opened up the space of modern individual freedom. It is not only that alienation opens up the space for subjectivity as opposed to the objective order; in a much more precise way, the "mechanical" aspect of "drilling," mindless training, remembering and participating in rituals without understanding their meaning, enacts a kind of spiritual *kenosis* of the subject, empties it of all the false pathological "inner content" and reduces it to the void of negativity that is the core of subjectivity.

In a simple mechanism, an object is self-sufficient and indifferent to its relations to other objects; we pass into a new phase when "the object holds on to its self-sufficiency, it deprives itself of any grounded relation, but it also posits this very lack of relation as if it were a relation"[22]—the object continues to be indifferent toward other objects in its environs, but this indifference is no longer an immediate one (like the indifference of a nail toward the table whose parts it holds together), it is already mediated, i.e., indifference is a positive feature, the way an object relates to its environs; it is part of the object's identity. This mediated status of indifference is the first step toward subjectivization. This means that mechanism is not a necessary lower stage "surpassed" by later "higher" stages, but a permanent foundation of these "higher" stages—or, more precisely, as we have just seen, in order to enact the passage from a lower (organic) to a higher (spiritual) stage, this higher stage needs support in a stage which is lower than organism. If an organism is to acquire spirituality, it has to rely on nonorganic mechanisms.

Here we already encounter the minimum of "idealism" which defines the notion of Self: a Self is precisely an entity without any substantial density, without any hard kernel that would guarantee its consistency. If we penetrate the surface of an organism and look deeper and deeper into it, we never encounter some central controlling element that would be its Self, secretly pulling the strings of its organs. The consistency of the Self is thus purely virtual; it is as if it were an Inside which appears only when viewed from the Outside, on the interface-screen—the moment we penetrate the interface and endeavor to grasp the Self "substantially," as it is "in itself," it disappears like sand between our fingers. The materialist reductionists who claim "there really is no self" are therefore right, but they nonetheless miss the point. On the level of material reality (inclusive of the psychological reality of "inner experience"), there is in fact no Self: the Self is not the "inner kernel" of an organism, but a surface effect. A "true" human Self functions, in a sense, like a computer screen: what is "behind" it is nothing but a network of "selfless" neuronal machinery. Hegel's thesis that "subject is not substance" has thus to be taken quite literally: in the opposition between the corporeal-material process and the pure "sterile" appearance, the subject is appearance itself, brought to its self-reflection: it is *something that exists only insofar as it appears to itself.* This is why it is wrong to search behind the appearance for the "true core" of subjectivity: behind the appearance there is, precisely, nothing, just a meaningless natural mechanism with no "depth" to it. What we should always bear in mind is that appearance is always redoubled: it is not just that things appear different than they really are; more radically, appearance is the appearance of appearance itself, the appearance that appearance is "just an appearance," and that there is something beyond appearance, the "true state of things." Appearance thus cheats doubly, and this is why the true act of analysis not only penetrates appearances to the true state of things beneath them, but also demonstrates why this "true state of things" can reproduce itself only through deceptive appearances.

However, we have gone a little too quickly here: the Self of an organism is not yet the Self of subjectivity proper, it functions as the Aristotelian soul, as the immaterial form that holds its material components together, making them parts of a living organism. To get from Soul to subjectivity, a step further has to be taken: the circular retroactivity that characterizes life has to be brought to an extreme, and in this way self-sublated: Lacan's sign for the barred subject ($) can also be read as the barred soul, the soul reduced to the Void, cut off from the body, no longer its immanent form. This is why, in order to fill in this gap, a subject can imagine (or, rather, fantasize) another body—not the biological body, but the body divided into parts in a way different from biological anatomy. To designate this self-sublation of life in subjectivity, Hegel uses the unique term *absoluter Gegenstoß* (recoil), a withdrawal-from which creates what it withdraws from:

> Reflection therefore *finds before it* an immediate which it transcends and from which it is the return. But this return is only the presupposing of what reflection finds before it. What is thus found only *comes to be* through being *left behind*. … The reflective movement is to be taken as an *absolute recoil* [*absoluter Gegenstoß*] upon itself. For the presupposition of the return-into-self—that from which essence *comes*, and is only as this return— is only in the return itself.[23]

Absoluter Gegenstoß thus stands for the radical coincidence of opposites in which the action appears as its own counteraction, or, more precisely, in which the very negative move (loss, withdrawal) generates what it "negates." "What is found only *comes to be* through being *left behind*," and its inversion (it is "only in the return itself" that what we return to emerges, like nations who constitute themselves by "returning to their lost roots") are the two sides of what Hegel calls "absolute reflection": a reflection which is no longer external to its object, presupposing it as given, but a reflection which, as it were, closes the loop and posits its presupposition. To put it in Derridean terms, the condition of possibility is here radically and simultaneously the condition of impossibility: the very obstacle to the full assertion of our identity opens up the space for it.[24]

Everything hinges here on not missing the precise meaning of "loss" and "return": the subject is not marked by a fundamental loss ("symbolic castration"), it *is* this loss, it "only *comes to be* through being *left behind*"; the subject does not "return to itself" through the work of subjectivization, it "is only as this return," i.e., this return-to-itself constitutes what it is a return to. However, are we not thereby making two opposite claims? The subject comes to be through being left behind, i.e., through its loss, *and* the subject is the return to itself from its loss—so how does it come to be, through its loss or through returning-to-itself from its own loss? Let us recall the classic example of the constitution of nations in the great national revival of nineteenth-century Europe: when a group of people experience their national identity as something that is lost, although it forms the very core of their being, this awareness of loss is the zero-point of their national identity—prior to it, they were not yet a nation. This "pure" subjectivity of a loss is then gradually filled in through a long process of "inventing tradition," of "rediscovering" ancient roots which are effectively constructed in the very movement of returning to them. There is nothing there prior to the experience of a loss—of course there was something before the loss (in the case of India, a vast and complex tradition), but this tradition was a heterogeneous mess that has nothing to do with that to which the later national revival wants to return. This holds in general for all processes of lost and regained national identity. In the process of its revival, a nation-in-becoming experiences its present constellation as that of a loss of some precious origins, and strives to regain these origins, to return to them; however, there were no origins which were lost, the origins are constituted through the very experience of their loss and return to them. (Maybe Foucault has a point here: the discovery of what went on before is the topic of genealogy which, precisely, has nothing to do with the historicist topic of origins.) This holds for all "return to origins": when, from the nineteenth century onward, new nation-states were popping up in Central and Eastern Europe, their return to "old ethnic roots" generated these roots, producing what Eric Hobsbawm called "invented traditions."[25]

In philosophical terms, this means: it is wrong to say that the subject alienates itself in its otherness; one should, rather, say that the subject emerges through substance's self-alienation. The subject is not alienated, it *is* the alienation of Substance from the subject *and* from itself. The crucial reversal occurs when the subject, after experiencing how it is utterly alienated from the substance of its being (society, God) which appears to it as an obscure foreign power and thereby reduces it to a powerless atomic individuality, realizes that its alienation from the Substance of its being is simultaneously the alienation of the Substance from itself. That is the ultimate message of Christianity: Christ on the Cross, abandoned by God-Father, means that man's alienation from God implies God's alienation from Himself.

It may appear that the great triad of Hegel's system Logic–Nature–Spirit nonetheless confirms the conventional reading of the dialectical movement as that of alienation and return-to-oneself: does not Hegel designate logic as "the system of pure reason, as the realm of pure thought"? "This realm is truth as it is without veil and in its own absolute nature. It can therefore be said that this content is the exposition of God as he is in his eternal essence before the creation of nature and a finite mind."[26] Nature is then the self-externalization of this "realm of pure thought," and all the ensuing movement tells the story of the gradual return-to-itself from this externality, first in nature itself (where this return culminates in life), then in Spirit. But here is another key formulation by Hegel of the sphere of logic:

> The system of logic is the realm of shadows, the world of simple essentialities freed from all sensuous concreteness. The study of this science, to dwell and labor in this shadowy realm, is the absolute culture and discipline of consciousness.[27]

Note here Hegel's wonderful determination of logic, pure thinking, as "the absolute culture and discipline" of consciousness: "culture" here is used not in the sense of cultural activity, but in the strict sense of *Bildung*, of the hard work of formation/education. What makes logic so hard is not the infinite wealth of determinations that characterizes natural as well as spiritual reality, but precisely the need to abstract from this wealth and focus on pure notional determinations. Things go wrong in logic precisely when we are not ready to enforce this abstraction and imagine too much, adding to the pure notional determination the imaginary representation. (One example is the category of Becoming from the beginning of Logic: instead of a pure passage from Being to Nothing and back, we project onto it all the wealth of the natural process of becoming and growth. ...) This, however, in no way entails that Hegel's logic stands for a Platonic realm of pure Ideas freed from all sensual determinations as the ultimate Reality—the key words, repeated in the quoted passage, are "the realm of shadows" (or "this shadowy realm"): logic is a realm of shadows, of pure notional potentiality (non-actuality). The standard post-Hegelian criticism (formulated by Schelling, Feuerbach, Marx, etc.) that Hegel's logic is a mere realm of shadows lacking actuality thus misses the point, and knocks on an open door.

It is only against this background that we can properly understand Hegel's definition of light as the "existing self of matter": "As the abstract self of matter, light is absolutely lightweight, and as matter, infinite, but as material ideality it is inseparable and a simple being-outside-of-itself."[28] Should we follow the obvious path and dismiss this notion of the "selflike nature of light" as yet another example of the madness of Romantic Naturphilosophie? There is an abstract parallel: the contrast of light and darkness exists only from the standpoint of light; in darkness there is no darkness, just as there is object only in contrast to subject; but is this more than an irrelevant parallel? The true question is: is light in fact the principle of subjectivity in a lower power/potency, or is the notion of light as the first form of subjectivity in nature just a case of retroactivity, something that is discernible only when the subject is already here? In the first case, we regress into a stratified ontology in the style of Schelling: reality appears as the repetition of the same principle in a higher and higher potency—something that is utterly foreign to Hegel. But (even) if the notion of the selflike nature of light is a case of retroactivity, the question remains: how must the presubjective universe be structured to allow retroactivity? It has to be non-all, "open," ontologically not fully constituted; and this "openness" is actualized, acquires existence, in the punctuality of the subject—which is the point of impenetrable darkness. That is to say: it is crucial to remember that for Hegel (and for German Idealism in general), the ultimate core of subjectivity is impenetrable darkness (what mystics called "the night of the world").

In order fully to grasp this impenetrability, one has to perform a double turn. First, ontological impenetrability—darkness, blurred horizon—is something that appears strictly and only from the human subjective viewpoint: in the In-itself of reality, there is no impenetrability … is it not? Is not the lesson of quantum physics that reality "in itself" is impenetrable to itself (in a collapse of the wave function, superpositions become impenetrable to single reality)? This impenetrability is not just a negative feature, it has a positive function: the reduction of the complexity of a thing to its abstract essential determinations, this violent simplification which abandons the wealth of details to impenetrable background, is not just a feature of our cognition (where we have to simplify, use "abstract" concepts) but a feature at work in reality itself.

We have to reverse the standard image of subjectivity as an isolated field of light surrounded by impenetrable darkness: the impenetrable point of darkness is the subject itself qua $. To quote Hegel: "The Notion is not merely soul, but free subjective Notion that is for itself and therefore possesses personality—the practical, objective Notion determined in and for itself which, as person, is impenetrable atomic subjectivity."[29] The distinction between Soul and Subject is crucial here: Soul is the Aristotelian immanent ideal form/principle of an organism, the immaterial "life force" that keeps it alive and united, while Subject is antisoul, the point of negative self-relating which reduces the individual to the abyss of a singularity at a distance from the living substance that sustains it. That is why, for Hegel, a notion comes to exist as such, "for itself," in its opposition to its empirical instantiations, only insofar as it is located in an "impenetrable atomic subjectivity" which is not something external to the Notion, it is Notion itself in its "oppositional determination," Notion as actually existing singularity—in this sense Hegel wrote that Self is a pure Notion. The Cartesian name for this singularity is cogito: the Self reduced to the evanescent punctuality of the act of thinking.

It is at this level of evanescent punctuality that we are a priori free, and, to repeat Herbert Marcuse, this freedom is the condition of liberation: we can liberate ourselves in our actual social life only insofar as we are already free. The movie One Man's Hero (Lance Hool, 1999) tells the story of John Riley (Tom Berenger) and the Saint Patrick's Battalion, a group of Irish Catholic immigrants who deserted from the mostly Protestant US Army to the Catholic Mexican side during the Mexican–American War of 1846–1848 and fought heroically to defend the Republic of Mexico from US aggression. At the end, while working in a stone quarry for military prisoners, Riley is told by his former US commander that he has been freed, to which he responds: "I have always been free."

1.4 FROM ORGANISM TO ASSEMBLAGE

How does this punctual-evanescent subject relate to what today's theory calls "subjectivation"? The idea is to oppose subject and subjectivation along the lines of identity and becoming: subject is a preexisting universal entity exempt from ordinary reality, while subjectivation is a local process of the emergence of subjects-agents which remain particular, embedded in a specific situation. Subject is opposed to object, while subjectivation occurs as part of a complex disparate reality whose preferred name today is *assemblage*. (The link between assemblage and subjectivation becomes clear when we recall that "assemblage" is a putative English translation for Deleuze and Guattari's *agencement*—it designates not just a state of things but above all the active process of heterogeneous things-agencies coming together and building a new agency.) The notion of assemblage, which was first systematically deployed by Manuel DeLanda[30] with references to Deleuze and Guattari's *Thousand Plateaus*, was lately further developed by OOO (object-oriented ontology) theorists (Graham Harman, Levi Bryant) and others, including Jane Bennett and Judith Butler. While I am well aware of the differences between OOO and, say, Bennett's New Materialism, the fact remains that OOO—at least in Harman's version—can also be characterized as "weak panpsychism" or "terrestrial animism." When New Materialists as well as partisans of OOO oppose the reduction of matter to a passive mixture of mechanical parts, they are, of course, asserting not the old-fashioned direct teleology, but an aleatoric dynamics immanent to matter: "emerging properties" arise out of unpredictable encounters between multiple kinds of actants; the agency for any particular act is distributed across a variety of kinds of bodies. Agency thereby becomes a social phenomenon, where the limits of sociality are expanded to include all material bodies participating in the relevant assemblage. The ethical implication of such a stance is that we should recognize our entanglement within larger assemblages: we should become more sensitive to the demands of these non-human actants, and the reformulated sense of self-interest calls upon us to respond to their plight. Materiality, usually conceived as inert substance, should be rethought as a plethora of things that form assemblages of human and nonhuman actors (or actants, to use Bruno Latour's term)—humans are but one force in a potentially unbounded network of forces.

Recall Bennett's description of how actants interact in the assemblage of a polluted trash site: how not only humans but also the rotting trash, worms, insects, abandoned machines, chemical poisons, etc., each play their (never purely passive) role.[31] In a similar vein, Bryant's vision of a pluriverse without any totalizing agent which would be fully self-present is not limited to abstract ontological considerations: he derives from it a series of pertinent political insights. One of the interesting implications of his notion of a "democracy of objects"[32] concerns ecology in our capitalist societies: why do all ideologico-critical calls fail to mobilize people, why is the large majority not ready to engage in serious action? If we take into account the ideological discursive mechanisms alone, this failure becomes inexplicable and we have to invoke some deep processes of "ideological mystification." But if we widen our focus and include other actants, other processes in social reality that influence our decisions, like biased media reports, economic pressures on workers (threat of losing employment), material limitations, and so forth, the absence of engagement becomes much more understandable. ... Although there are important differences between Bennett, Bryant, and others, the common denominator among (most of) them consists of three shared and interconnected features:

• *"Flat" ontology versus the hierarchy of beings* (what Bryant calls "democracy of objects"): there are no ontologically privileged agents which can "totalize" reality: human subjects are just one in the series of disparate objects. Recall Jacques Rancière's reading of Dziga Vertov's *Man with a Movie Camera* as a practice of cinematic Communism: the affirmation of life in its multiplicity, a setting-side-by-side of a series of daily activities—washing hair, wrapping packages, playing piano, connecting phone wires, ballet dancing—which reverberate with each other on a purely formal level, through the echoing of visual and other patterns. What makes this cinematic practice Communist is the underlying assertion of the radical "univocity of being": all the displayed phenomena are equalized, all the usual hierarchies and oppositions among them, including the official Communist opposition between the Old and the New, are magically suspended.[33] While Vertov remains at the level of the ontological equalization of human activities, OOO extends it to the whole of reality: in the assemblage of things, humans are just one element among others.

• *Material versus expressive aspect of elements*: as well as acting as bearers of meaning, objects in our universe also matter and are active on account of their direct materiality. The moment we abandon anthropocentrism and locate humanity as one of the agents (albeit a privileged one) in the assemblage of things, the distinction between material and expressive level becomes necessary, since expressive level pertains only to human beings, and even in their case it is not exclusive—for example, human production is organized and kept functioning through symbolic exchange, but it also involves material processes of tremendous importance (exploiting natural resources, etc.):

> The components of social assemblages playing a material role vary
> widely, but at the very least involve a set of human bodies properly
> oriented (physically or psychologically) towards each is other. The classic
> example of these assemblages of bodies face-to-face conversations, but
> the interpersonal networks that structure communities, as well as the
> hierarchical organizations that govern cities or nation-states, can also serve
> as illustrations. Community networks and institutional organizations are
> assemblages of bodies, but they also possess a variety of other material

components, from food and physical labor, to simple tools and complex machines, to the buildings and neighborhoods serving as their physical locales.[34]

· The primacy of external over internal relations: assemblages are composed of disparate objects which are (relatively) independent of the network of their relations to other objects, and cannot be reduced to this network. Here is Bryant's recapitulation of DeLanda's arguments for giving priority to "relations of exteriority" over "relations of interiority":

> we must remove the entrenched metaphor of society as an *organism*. Within the organismic metaphor, society is compared to the human body, such that 1) all parts are *dependent* on one another, and 2) all parts (institutions) work together like organs in an organism to promote the harmony of society as a whole. Here it is notable that this conception of relations between parts is not restricted to organismic conceptions of society, but also to *structuralist* conceptions of society. The key thesis shared by these orientations is that parts have no existence or being apart from the whole to which they belong. Thus, for example, when we talk about a sound in language, we cannot say that "b" has an existence *of its own* independent of other sounds in language, but rather that "b" exists only in a *phonemic* relation with other sounds: b/p. The concept of structure is such that elements have no independent existence apart from their relations.[35]

DeLanda (and Bryant) reject this organicist thesis on the grounds that it prevents us from explaining the emergence of the New: the New arises when an element is able to extract itself from its links to a given organism and become part of another totality:

> Allowing the possibility of complex interactions between component parts is crucial to define the mechanisms of emergence, but this possibility disappears if the parts are fused together into a seamless web. Thus, what needs to be challenged is the very idea of relations of interiority. We can distinguish, for example, the properties defining a given entity from its *capacities to interact* with other entities. While its properties are given and may be denumerable as a closed list, its capacities are not given—they may go unexercised if no entity suitable for interaction is around—and form a potentially open list, since there is no way to tell in advance in what way a given entity may affect or be affected by innumerable other entities.[36]

(Incidentally, I found this opposition very problematic: why not turn it around and claim that properties are immanent and capacities relational? A hammer can be used for hitting someone on the head, or even for filling in a hole in a sink; the list is endless, and depends on the totally unpredictable relations it can enter into.) However, while the anti-organicist thrust seems totally justified, the extension of this rejection to the structuralist notion of differentiality, where the identity of every element is constituted by its differences from other elements, totally misses the point—it is difficult to imagine a stronger contrast than the one between organic unity and structural differentiality. This problematic subsumption of differential structure as a subspecies of expressive totality is a *symptom* of DeLanda's (and Bryant's) argumentation: DeLanda has to blur the key difference between the two in order to be able to ignore the radical consequences of the differentiality of the signifier spelled out by Lacan. Language (or a symbolic structure in general) is from within, necessarily, not organic, not an organic seamless Whole, but an assemblage of disparate elements, a *bricolage* full of gaps and inconsistencies—the name for this mess is *overdetermination*, a term that designates the fact of an element being caught in multiple inconsistent networks. So far from being a seamless Whole, a differential structure is by definition unbalanced, traversed by antagonisms: never the expression of an underlying "deeper" meaning but, on the contrary, structured around some fundamental impossibility.

In short, differentiality means there is no encompassing One which holds a structure together—what holds it together is ultimately just the gap of an impossibility language tries to cope with. When Lacan claims that the unconscious is structured like a language, we should bear in mind what kind of language this is—not a Habermasian ideal form of argumentation and communication but language in all its inconsistent materiality, full of overlapping, holes, and lateral links.[37] Recall the Freudian logic of pragmatic and opportunistic "compromises": something is rejected, but not quite, since it returns in a cyphered mode; it is rationally accepted, but isolated/neutralized in its full symbolic weight; etc. We thus get a mad dance of distortions which follow no clear univocal logic, but form a patchwork of improvised connections. Recall the legendary case of the forgetting of the name Signorelli from Freud's *The Psychopathology of Everyday Life*: Freud couldn't recall the name (Signorelli) of the painter of the Orvieto frescos, and produced as substitutes the names of two other painters, Botticelli and Boltraffio, and his analysis brings to light the processes of signifying associations which linked Signorelli to Botticelli and Boltraffio (the Italian village Trafoi was where he received the message of the suicide of one of his patients, struggling with sexual problems; *Herr*, the German word for Mister—*Signor*—is linked to a trip to Herzegovina, where an old Muslim told Freud that after one can no longer engage in sex, there is no reason to go on living; etc.). The complex rhizomatic texture of such associations and displacements has no clear triadic structure with a clear final resolution; the result of the tension between "thesis" (the name Signorelli) and "anti-thesis" (its forgetting) is the compromise formation of falsely remembering two other names in which (and this is their crucial feature) the dimension on account of which Freud was unable to remember Signorelli (the link between sex and death) returns in an even more conspicuous way—and there is no place for such logic in Hegel; he would have dismissed Freud's example as a game of trifling contingencies. The Freudian negation of negation is not a radical resolution of a deadlock, but, in its basic guise, the "return of the repressed" and, as such, by definition a compromise formation: something is asserted and simultaneously denied, displaced, reduced, encrypted in an often ridiculously patched-up way.

One should thus reject the OOO claim that something new can emerge only when relations between objects are external: in a differential symbolic structure, an entity defined exclusively by the network of its differential relations to others, with no internal essence independent of these relations, can also be transfunctionalized, included in a new set of relations (and, of course, this process also changes its identity). And there is a step further to be taken here. While DeLanda and Bryant talk a lot about materiality, what they seem to ignore is the weird materiality of language itself; Lacan's neologism for this materiality is *lalangue* ("llanguage"). *Lalangue* refers to two aspects of language. First, it stands for the signifying network as the "apparatus of *jouissance*," for language as the space of illicit pleasures that defy normativity: the chaotic multitude of homonyms, wordplays, "irregular" metaphorical links and resonances turns around itself in the autonomous circle of enjoy-meant (*jouis-sense*), self-referentially playing with its immanent potentials, separated from its communicational "use value" (communication, pointing toward objects and processes in reality). Insofar as *lalangue* serves nothing, merely generating meaningless enjoy-meant as its own aim, as the immanent gain of its functioning, it clearly obeys the superego injunction "Enjoy!"— and does the same not hold for capitalist self-valorization, the circular movement of money generating more money, which is also its own goal since it serves nothing, no external human need? That is why this same superego injunction "Enjoy!" sustains the capitalist drive to self-valorization. ... However, *lalangue* also stands for what we may call "really existing language" in contrast to language as a pure formal structure. Every language is embedded in a particular lifeworld, traversed by its traces: language is not a neutral transcendental frame that structures our approach to reality, it is fully penetrated/distorted by contingent historical forces, antagonisms, desires, which forever twist and pervert its purity. —Apart from this neglect of the material aspect of language itself, there is a further crucial question to be addressed here: it is easy to assert in principle the unity-in-difference of the two aspects, expressive and material, and Bryant uses it to criticize my approach, i.e., my neglect of the material aspect:

Scant attention has been devoted to this dimension of social organizations within continental social and political theory. Take the example of Žižek. Žižek focuses all of his attention on the *expressive* dimension of the social, on content, on meaning, on the signifier, yet ignores this material dimension. As a consequence, the implicit thesis seems to be that the material dimension contributes nothing to why the social is as it is. Rather, the social is to be found, according to Žižek, purely at the level of the social. And as a further result, it follows from this that Žižek holds that the only thing relevant to producing political change lies in the domain of the expressive.[38]

But how, concretely, do they combine/interact? How, exactly, is language embedded in a material lifeworld of practice? It is clear that, while it is always part of it, it cannot be simply reduced to one of its components—it always involves a gap, a distance toward it.[39] This enigmatic distance, this ambiguous position of language within and outside of reality, brings us to the crux of the matter: the ontological status of the subject. It is easy to demonstrate how what Stephen Jay Gould called "ex-aptation" is immanent to a symbolic structure (elements are continually transfunctionalized, torn out of their context, included in new totalities, retotalized into new fields of meaning); there is a key step further to be taken: the step from ex-aptation to a subjective cut. What is missing in the flat ontology of assemblages is not a seamless totality uniting them but radical discord itself—what kind of discord? Bryant inverts Badiou's formula of "objectless subject" into that of "subjectless object," claiming that his aim is not to abolish the subject but to open up a space for "a thinking of the object that isn't a correlate of the subject or the positing of the subject," and thereby to

> breach a space where we might think of the role that material beings play in social and political life, exercising all sorts of power and constraint upon us (in addition to the more traditional role that semiological agencies such as ideology, practices, and the signifier play in our life).[40]

Lacan, however, does not accept Badiou's premise; for him, there is no subject which is not correlated to an object, *objet a*—but this object is a paradoxical one, an object which fills in the void, a gap in the very texture of reality—it is this object which in effect rips the seamless texture of reality and holds the place of a gap in it. Far from just totalizing reality, "subject" can occur only when there is a radical rip in the texture of reality, when reality is not a "flat" collection of objects but implies a radical crack—ultimately, *the subject itself is the rip in reality, what tears its seamless texture apart.*
This is also why Bryant misses the point when he claims that "Žižek targets me on a point that I actually draw from him without noting that I draw

this point from him": "the barrier to knowing objects is not an *epistemological* barrier as Kant had it, but rather is a feature of objects themselves ... it seems significant that it would be here that he chooses to engage me without mentioning that it is his own move."[41] Our respective positions are by no means the same: in his version of the displacement of the epistemological obstacle into the thing itself, every object has the visible part and the hidden part of how it is in itself, outside relations with others; while in my version, the displacement of epistemological obstacle into ontological impossibility in no way implies that objects have a hidden core—quite the contrary: what is beyond the obstacle is nothing, the Void; objects are structured around their own impossibility. Here Bryant repeats Miller's mistake—recall the passage quoted above where Miller claims that when, in the formulas of sexuation, Lacan "tried to grasp the dead-ends of sexuality in a weft of mathematical logic," this was "already a secondary construction that intervenes after the initial impact of the body and *lalangue*, which constitutes a real without law, without logical rule. Logic is only introduced afterwards, with the elucubration, the fantasy, the subject supposed to know, and with psychoanalysis." The Unconscious is conceived here as a presymbolic substantial "real without law," and the symbolic texture is nothing but a series of "elucubrations" which again and again fail to recapture this "raw" real. For Lacan at his most radical, on the contrary, the Unconscious is *nothing but the texture of these "elucubrations" structured around the Real as its immanent obstacle/impossibility*: the Unconscious is not a Real that forever eludes the symbolic structure, it is this very twisted structure of failures, repetitions, and displacements. The Unconscious is not enigmatic in the sense that it remains an enigma for us who dwell in the Symbolic, it is *this very structure of an enigma*. The illusion proper to the Unconscious is not that its core eludes us forever, it is the very illusion that there is some hidden core which eludes us forever.

The moment we accept this, the entire topic of how to think our access to the In-itself, to reality existing independently of us, changes radically—neither Harman's and Bryant's flat ontology nor Badiou's notion of Event which disturbs the flat ontological order of being suffices here.

1.5 THE IN-ITSELF

One of the standard criticisms of Badiou's notions of Event and immortality is that they are clearly the secularized version of a religious event—does not Badiou himself articulate the structure of Event apropos of Saint Paul's theology? The continuous immanent flow of everyday life is all of a sudden interrupted by a call from outside, irreducible to this immanence, which introduces another (eventual) dimension, and through fidelity to this call, individuals overcome their "animal humanity" and turn into subjects. Against this criticism, one should insist that the materialist version is the "original" one, and that theology reappropriates a procedure which does not belong to it. In the materialist version, the very process of recognizing oneself in the eventual address creates (retroactively posits) the agency that enunciates it (to simplify: "God" is an effect of the believer's recognition in the divine appeal)—a process described by Althusser as that of interpellation. Furthermore, for this process of recognition in the eventual appeal to be ontologically possible, one should move beyond (or, rather, beneath) the duality of ordinary life and eventual Truth (in Badiou's terms, Being and Event): there is a third level, conceptualized by German Idealism as radical negativity and by Freud as the death drive, which precedes the duality of Being and Event. We are not, of course, dealing here with empirical history but with what one should call transcendental prehistory.

This is also the way we should reply to the standard transcendental argument against a scientific self-objectivization of humankind: against the argument which claims that every scientific self-objectivization is always-already grounded in a presupposed lifeworld of intersubjective communication and rationality which cannot be fully accounted for in terms of scientific objectivization. The Freudo-Hegelian counterargument endorses this transcendental point, but takes a step further into the domain of meta-transcendental history: lifeworld is not the ultimate horizon of our existence, it has a prehistory; many things have to happen for us to find ourselves in a lifeworld, it is itself constituted through a brutal process of "castration," repression, covering up of gaps, etc. Taken seriously with regard to its ontological implications, psychoanalytic theory is not an ontic science, it is this prehistory.[42]

From the standpoint of nature, there is no difference between nature and culture; everything is nature, and from the standpoint of culture, nature is always a social/cultural category (what we experience as nature or natural is overdetermined by a set of socially/culturally mediated premises).[43] The divide is thus thoroughly asymmetrical: on the one side, there is no divide; on the other side, the line of division is internal to one of the terms. The passage from Nature to Culture is thus profoundly "Hegelian": it is a passage from non-distinction to a distinction internal to one of the moments; we never get an "objective" distinction between the two moments. And does not the same also hold for the classic modern philosophical couple of object and subject? From the standpoint of the object, there is no subject, there are only (what will have been) objects; but once the subject emerges, every opposition between subject and object is mediated by subjectivity. Is it then possible to think "nature" prior to culture, or objectivity prior to subject? What we should bear in mind is not only that object prior to subject is not object (but some unnamable X); much more important, in order for the subject to explode out of the Real, some kind of a gap has to be there already in this Real itself, i.e., this Real already has to be traversed by an immanent impossibility. The primordial ontological fact is not the unnamable Real prior to the rise of the subject, but this Real as an immanent impossibility of itself, as a barred Real.

This is why our thesis is that of a *contingent Absolute*: once the subject emerges, it is "absolute," the point of reference of its world from which it is not possible to abstract, although its emergence is thoroughly contingent. "Absolute" does not mean omnipotent, all-knowing, or anything similar; "absolute" describes an entity whose relating to other entities is always mediated by its self-relating. What this means is that "absolute" can be said to designate the subject's self-limitation, its inability to step outside its own horizon. Derrida touched the same problem with his famous statement (from his *Grammatology*): Il n'y a pas de hors-texte (there is no outside-text), a statement often mistranslated as "There is nothing outside the text," making it appear that Derrida advocates a kind of linguistic idealism for which nothing exists beyond language. How, then, are we to read it? There is in effect a fundamental ambiguity that sticks to it: it oscillates between transcendental and ontological reading. Il n'y a pas de hors-texte can mean that all ontological claims are always-already caught in the arche-transcendental dimension of writing: they are never directly about reality out there, since they are always overdetermined by a specific texture of traces that form the impenetrable background of all our claims. But it can also be read in a directly ontological way: external reality, life, is already made up of traces, differences, i.e., the structure of *différance* is the structure of all there is. Derrida came closest to this reading in his unpublished seminar from 1975, *La vie la mort*, the first six sessions of which are devoted to biology (specifically, to François Jacob and his research on the DNA structure and the laws of heredity). Notions like "*différance*," "arche-writing," "trace," and "text" are thus not only the meta-transcendental background of our symbolic universe, they also refer to the basic structure of all living (and putatively also of all there is): "general text" is Derrida's most elementary ontological claim. (It is important to note how this ambiguity is connected with another that concerns the status of the "metaphysics of presence." Derrida abundantly varies the theme of how there is no simple Outside to the metaphysics of Presence: we can only gradually and locally deconstruct it, undermine it, expose its inconsistencies, etc.—to postulate access to a pure Outside would have meant succumbing to the ultimate trap of Presence. However, insofar as metaphysics of presence equals the history of European philosophy, a naive but pertinent problem arises: what about, say, ancient China? Were the Chinese also caught up in the "metaphysics of presence" [which then elevates "metaphysics of Presence" into a universal feature of humanity] or are they outside European metaphysics? If yes, how can we get in contact with them?)

So how are we to break out of this oscillation? Hegelian dialectics offers a way: what if the problem is its own solution? What if the oscillation ceases when we directly identify the two opposed poles? What if the very subjective-transcendental excess which prevents direct access to external reality as it is "in itself" is the site of our contact with the Real? What undermines ontology is the inscription of the subject-excess in it, i.e., the very contact with the Real.

A strictly analogous structure is at work in class struggle (or sexual difference): class struggle is never "pure," reduced to the duality of two opposed classes; there is always a third element that cannot be located in class duality, and this excessive element which "disturbs" class struggle *is* the element of class struggle: a class struggle reducible to a direct duality of classes is no longer class struggle. What we find here is the matrix of Hegel's "absolute recoil": the Real coincides with the very obstacle to itself, the very thing that obscures access to the Real is the inscription of the Real. This is why, in a proper dialectical approach, we should abandon the entire rhetoric of penetrating through deceptive appearances to the way things really are in themselves:

> Reality "such as it is" (without embellishments) appears in all these configurations—directly or indirectly—as ugly, gruesome. In other words: in order for it to "sober us up" (wake us from the illusion), it has to be perceived as *more* than it is: it has to be invested with a series of quite subjective affects—repugnance, aversion, and the like. In order to get to reality "such as it is," a (subjective) *surplus* is needed (or produced), a surplus or excess which is precisely not reducible to "reality such as it is." (The fact that rotting flesh incites affects of disgust, or at least extinguishes our desire immediately, is no less mediated by the window of [our] fantasy than what appears as sublime.) (AZ, 120)

Is this not a clear case of Hegel's point, from the Foreword to his *Phenomenology of Spirit*, that the difference between For-us and In-itself falls into For-us: the In-itself is always an In-itself for us? This does not mean just that the "true" reality independent of us is some cold indifferent mathematical constellation, but that the very subjective excess (of utter disgust) *is* our contact with In-itself, it is what inscribes us, the subject, into In-itself. The standpoint from which external reality appears as what is in "in itself," as a neutral "objective" order, exempts us from reality; this exemption is the subjective excess which opens up "objective" reality.[44]

One image of the ultimate horror is a wet, sleazy opening of the mouth of a gigantic polyp threatening to suck us in—this Otherness is radically "extimate," it not only (rather obviously) presupposes the standpoint of the threatened subject, one can even say it is nothing but the subject's objectal counterpart, the terrifying abyss of subjectivity in its "oppositional determination," as Hegel would have put it. So if all these attempts to reach the Real, from scientific objectivity through lawless chaos to the limit of imagined horror, ultimately fail, is there another way to do it? As we have already indicated, Lacan's answer is: yes, through the impasses of sexuation—which is the topic of the next chapter.

1.6 APPENDIX: A DETOUR THROUGH QUANTUM PHYSICS

As I have already indicated, quantum physics seems to provide a kind of scientific blueprint for a reality structured in this way: the passage from Einstein to Bohr repeats the logic of the passage from Kant to Hegel. For Einstein, in a thoroughly Kantian way, the "antinomy" of velocity and position as well as the contingency of the collapse of the wave function demonstrate that quantum physics does not attain the noumenal reality of things-in-themselves, i.e., that its description of reality is incomplete, that it misses some hidden components; while for Bohr, "antinomy" is the very sign that we have touched the Real. In the first case, the ontological incompleteness is transposed into an epistemological one, i.e., the incompleteness is perceived as the effect of the fact that another (secret, but fully real) agency constructed our reality as a simulated universe. The truly difficult thing is to accept the second choice, the ontological incompleteness of reality itself. (Incidentally, the same move should be accomplished apropos of object-oriented ontology, which posits a noumenal depth of objects beneath their surface displayed in their interaction with other objects: what if incompleteness is a feature of reality itself? More specifically, what if the subject is precisely an "object" which is only its own appearing? And what if the Freudian subject of the unconscious is such a subject, which means we should reject the reading of psychoanalysis as "depth psychology" trying to penetrate the substantial depth that allegedly sustains subjectivity?)

If we take the risk of proposing a formal homology between partial drives and quantum oscillations, is not the relationship between quantum proto-reality and single "full" reality homologous to that between the polymorphously perverse field of partial drives and sexual difference? The passage from quantum superpositions to single reality occurs in the form of the wave function collapse: the multiplicity of the superposed states is reduced to a single state by observation, as is made clear in the famous two-slit experiment:

> It has been known for centuries that water waves passing through a small opening create circular waves radiating outward from that opening. If there are two openings, the waves from each opening interfere with those from the other, producing waves twice as tall at the crests (or deep in the troughs)

and cancelling perfectly where a crest from one meets a trough from the other. When we send light waves through tiny slits, we see the same phenomenon: most of the light that reaches light detectors at the back lands right behind the barrier between the slits. At some places, no light appears in the interference pattern.

But light actually consists of large numbers of individual photons, quanta of light. Our experiment can turn down the amount of light so low that we know there is only a single photon, a single particle of light in the experiment at any time. What we see is the very slow accumulation of photons at the detectors, but with exactly the same interference pattern. And this leads to what Feynman called not just "a mystery," but actually "the only mystery" in quantum mechanics: how can a single particle of light interfere with itself, without going through both slits? We can see what would happen if it went through only one slit by closing one or the other slit. We get a completely different interference pattern.[45]

The paradox is best rendered by the Hegelian-sounding formulation of a single particle "interfering with itself," i.e., *self-relating*: even if we let through the slits one single particle at a time, the pattern that will form on the other side will be the interference pattern which emerges when particles interact; consequently, since at every specific moment there is only one particle (which can go through only one slit), this particle must in some way "interfere with itself, without going through both slits." The paradox is that a single particle (behaves like a wave, i.e., as if it) interferes with itself *only if it is not observed*. We should not be afraid to universalize this formula: observation of something "objectivizes" it into a positive thing, and thereby obfuscates its self-relating. And insofar as observation is usually linked to consciousness, we should further conclude that, at its most radical, self-reflexivity and consciousness exclude each other: self-reflexivity is basically unconscious. A somewhat simplified example: the basic axiom of historical dialectics is that, in order to properly grasp an event that "really happened," one has to locate it in its series of superpositions (what might have happened instead of this event, but didn't), i.e., we have to include in the event the way it "related to itself" (to other possible versions of itself).

It is therefore crucial that, in interpreting quantum physics, we do not "Deleuzianize" its implicit ontology: it is not that we first have the field of quantum oscillations and superpositions as the primordial site of production which then, through local collapses of the wave function, changes into single reality as the scene of representation. Superpositions are not the ultimate ontological fact (if they were, we would stumble upon the unresolvable problem of how/why they collapse into single reality), they are reactions to the impossibility of the One to actualize itself as One, so the collapse into One is presupposed by superpositions. The key problem is to understand how the collapse of quantum superpositions is not a secondary event but already casts a shadow on the field of quantum oscillations. Quantum waves are not functioning "in themselves," they already presuppose the "barred One," the impossibility of a single reality—they appear against the background of this impossibility, in the same way that partial drives appear against the background of the impossibility of the sexual relationship.

Our single reality emerges out of its own impossibility: single reality is impossible, it explodes into multiple superpositions, and these superpositions locally collapse into one reality. And the same goes for heterosexuality: it is also the result of its own impossibility: if heterosexuality had been directly "possible," we would have not Two Sexes but the One. In other words, it is not that the two sexes are simply impossible, they emerge out of the impossibility (of the One). This brings us to the title of this book. Merriam-Webster points out the double meaning of "incontinence": (1) failure to restrain sexual appetite, (2) inability of the body to control urination. This duality reflects in a negative way the coincidence of opposites, of the highest and the lowest, which—as Hegel noted in his *Phenomenology of Spirit*—characterizes the penis:

> The "depth" which spirit brings out from within, but carries no further than to make it a representation, and let it remain at this level—and the "ignorance" on the part of this consciousness as to what it really says, are the same kind of connection of higher and lower which, in the case of the living being, nature naïvely expresses when it combines the organ of its highest fulfilment, the organ of generation, with the organ of urination. The infinite judgment *qua* infinite would be the fulfilment of life that comprehends itself, while the consciousness of the infinite judgment that remains at the level of representation corresponds to urination.[46]

The notion of the "incontinence of the Void" is a kind of negative of this coincidence of the opposites: it brings together the double failure of the penis which leaks at the highest level (secreting sperm) and at the lowest level (secreting urine). Our ontological premise is that reality itself is not the positive outcome of some productive One but the outcome of its redoubled failure. It is not that some primordial tension/antagonism is generating the universe (this would have been a new version of ancient cosmogonies where reality is born out of the interaction between masculine and feminine principles); our universe emerges out of its own impossibility, i.e., it is the obstacle to being which sustains being.

CHAPTER 2

ANTINOMIES OF PURE SEXUATION

2.1 FROM KANT TO HEGEL

The properly philosophical outcome of chapter 1 is that everything turns around the passage from Kant to Hegel. In the predominant perception, Kant is supposed to openly admit the failure of general ontology which aims at grasping the Whole of reality: when our mind tries to do this, it inevitably gets involved in antinomies; Hegel then closes this gap, reinterpreting antinomies as contradictions whose dialectical movement enables us to grasp the Whole of reality, i.e., the return to precritical general ontology. ... But what if the actual situation is quite different? True, Kant admits antinomies, but only at the epistemological level, not as immanent features of the unreachable thing-in-itself, while Hegel transposes epistemological antinomies into the ontological sphere, and thereby undermines every ontology: "reality itself" is non-all, antinomic.

One must therefore be very precise here. When Kant deplores the fact that the thing-in-itself remains out of our reach, it is easy to detect the falsity of this deploring, clear signs of relief—thank God we escaped the danger of coming too close to it! That is why it is crucial to note that Kant does not only try to demonstrate the gap between appearances and the In-itself: Kant advocates something much stronger; his antinomies of pure reason claim to demonstrate that appearances *cannot* be the same as the In-itself, that they are necessarily mere appearances. (In an exact homology, in his *Critique of Practical Reason* Kant falsely deplores the fact that we can never be certain if our act was a truly free ethical act and not an act contaminated by pathological motivations: again, beneath this deploring, there is relief that we can forever avoid the Real of freedom.) A Hegelian critique of Kant does not simply contend that our appearances fit the In-itself; on the contrary, it fully asserts the gap between appearances and the In-itself, locating the Real in *this very gap*. In short, the very gap that seems to separate us forever from the In-itself is a feature of the In-itself; it cannot be reduced to something immanent to the sphere of phenomena.

So how are we to overcome the transcendental approach first elaborated by Kant? That is to say, how do we enact the passage from Kant to Hegel, without regressing into a precritical realist ontology? The ultimate consequence of Kant's transcendentalism is the deadlock of Reason: when it tries to overstep the boundaries of our finite experience, reason (*logos*, the symbolic order) necessarily becomes entangled in antinomies: proof that our reason cannot reach reality as it is in itself. Next step: in her epoch-making "Euthanasia of Reason," Joan Copjec linked Kant's duality of mathematical and dynamic antinomies of pure reason to Lacan's formulas of sexuation: mathematical antinomy is "feminine," while dynamic antinomy is "masculine," thereby asserting the ontological relevance of sexuality (in a way that is radically different from premodern cosmologies with their struggle of opposing principles, yin and yang, etc.).[1] But what is the exact consequence of this insight? It seems that it again asserts the transcendental agnostic hypothesis, simply providing it with a "Freudian" root—along these lines: our reason gets entangled in antinomies, it cannot gain access to reality-in-itself, because it is always (constitutively) "twisted" by sexuality (sexual difference).

The question that arises here is: how can we think this "euthanasia of reason" (reason's inevitable entanglement in radical antinomies, its inability to grasp reality in its totality, as a Whole) without positing (or presupposing; in short—in Hegelese—positing as presupposed) an In-itself out of reach of our reason? There is, of course, only one (Hegelian) way: to enact the move from epistemological deadlock to ontology, to conceive a radical antagonism (a parallax split) as immanent to reality itself. As Hegel put it, Kant displayed too much "tenderness for things" when he refused to accept that antinomy is a feature of reality itself; against Kant, we should thus grasp what he perceives as an obstacle to our cognition of the thing-in-itself, the very feature that throws us into the abyssal heart of the thing-in-itself. The fact that we cannot grasp reality as a Whole does not mean that reality as a Whole is beyond our reach, it means that reality is in itself non-all, antagonistic, marked by a constitutive impossibility—to put it succinctly, there are things because they cannot fully exist.

Imagine a gradual process of getting to know a thing, a process of approximation in which the thing ultimately always eludes us, and then imagine that this process of approaching a thing is immanent to this thing itself, so that this thing circulates around a void, an impossibility, at its very core. And this is where what Lacan calls *objet petit a*, the object-cause of desire, comes in: *objet a* gives body to this void. Kant's name for this object is "transcendental object," which is to be strictly opposed to the transcendent object (the noumenal "thing-in-itself"). The "transcendental object" is not the appearance or the remainder/trace of the noumenal Real within phenomenal reality, it is the very operator of the passage from the noumenal to the phenomenal, the operator of the emergence of phenomenal reality—something like a Kantian "Higgs particle" which renders possible the passage from the preontological real of nonsubstantial quantum oscillations to our reality of substantial particles with mass.

Some basic philosophical terms are often used in a confusing way, and one of them is definitely the term "transcendental," whose Kantian meaning tends to be overshadowed by all the talk about "transcendental meditation," where the term just designates a higher spiritual awareness no longer constrained by empirical reality. But there are more interesting cases of ambiguity; recall the double sense of "speculation": financial speculation on the market, and philosophical speculation (pure thinking unbound from empirical reality)—a nice case of what Hegel called "infinite judgment," the coincidence of opposites, of the highest and the lowest. In the same way as financial speculation deals with M-M′, money which seems to engender more money without recourse to production, philosophical speculation deals with thoughts engendering more thoughts without recourse to empirical reality. Maybe one can take the risk of drawing another such parallel, and linking Kant's notion of a transcendental object with what in mathematics is called a transcendental number:

> All transcendental numbers are irrational, but not all irrational numbers are transcendental. Not only can transcendental numbers (insofar as they are irrational) not be written as a ratio of integers; not only do their decimal forms go on forever without repeating; what further characterizes transcendental numbers is that they are numbers that can't be described by algebraic operations: there's no finite sequence of multiplications, divisions, additions, subtractions, exponents, and roots that will give you the value of a transcendental number. For example, while $\sqrt{2}$ is not transcendental, pi and e are.[2]

The feature we should bear in mind is that a transcendental number cannot be constructed by means of algebraic operations, in exactly the same way that Kant's transcendental object cannot be accounted for in the terms of transcendental categories that determine phenomenal reality—and, we may add, in the same way that Lacan's *objet a* cannot be constructed as part of the symbolic texture. However, this externality of the transcendental number to the space of algebraic operations is an immanent externality: the transcendental number is an immanent limit of the field of algebraic operations: it is its ex-timate, to use Lacan's old pun. And the same goes for the transcendental object which is *transcendental*, *not transcendent*, not the thing-in-itself: contrary to some confused and misleading formulations found in the work of Kant himself, the transcendental object is not noumenal but "nothingness," the void of the horizon of ob-jectivity, of that which stands against the (finite) subject, the minimal form of resistance that is not yet any positive determinate object that the subject encounters in the world—Kant uses the German expression *Dawider*, what is "out there opposing itself to us, standing against us."

We find the same structure in the case of Lacan's *objet petit a*, the object-cause of desire. The same object can all of a sudden be "transubstantiated" into the object of my desire: what is to you just an ordinary object is for me the focus of my libidinal investment, and this shift is caused by some unfathomable X, a *je ne sais quoi* in the object which can never be pinned down to any of its particular properties. *Objet a* is therefore close to the Kantian transcendental object, since it stands for the unknown X, for what is "in you more than yourself." *L'objet petit a* can thus be defined as a pure parallax object: it is not only that its contours change with the shift of the subject; *it exists only—its presence can be discerned only—when the landscape is viewed from a certain perspective*. Note again the coincidence of opposites at work here: *objet a* designates what is in an object more than this object itself, its unreachable core—but precisely as such, it is the very point of the inscription of subjectivity into the object. Let us take the obvious example of love: what causes love is some elusive *je ne sais quoi* in the beloved, some X that cannot be pinned down to any perceptible particular feature of the beloved; but this X does not exist in itself, it is the inscription of my desire into the object (which is why, as they say, a human being appears sublime only to the gaze of the subject in love with him/her).

There is a further paradox at work here: it is at the very point at which a pure difference emerges—a difference which is no longer a difference between two positively existing objects, but a minimal difference which divides one and the same object from itself—that this difference "as such" immediately coincides with an unfathomable object: in contrast to a mere difference between objects, *the pure difference is itself an object*. Another name for the parallax gap is therefore *minimal difference*, a "pure" difference which cannot be grounded in positive substantive properties.

We may even risk a further parallel with the "transfinite" object in Cantor's sense. Why Lacan's unexpected reference to Cantor? The distinction between "transfinite" and "infinite" elaborated by Cantor roughly fits the Hegelian distinction between "true" and "bad" (or "spurious") infinity: within the "bad infinity," we never actually reach the infinite, to every number we can add another unit, and "infinity" here refers to this very constant possibility of adding, i.e., to the impossibility of ever reaching the ultimate element in the series; but what if we treat this set of elements, which is forever "open" to addition, as a closed totality and posit the infinite as an element of its own, as the external frame of the endless set of elements it contains? The transfinite is thus a number or an element with the paradoxical property of being insensitive to addition or subtraction: if we add to it, or subtract a unit from it, it remains the same.[3] And was it not in a similar way that Kant constructed the concept of the "transcendental object"? I am tempted to risk a pun here: Cantor—Kant. The transcendental object is an object that is external to the endless series of empirical objects: we arrive at it by treating this endless series as closed, and positing outside of it an empty object, the very form of object, that frames the series.[4] It is also easy to discern the further homology with *objet petit a*, the object-cause of desire, which is also "transfinite," i.e., an empty object that frames the endless set of empirical objects. In this precise sense, Lacan's two exemplary cases of *objets a*, voice and gaze, are "transfinite": in both cases, we are dealing with an empty object that frames the "bad infinity" of the field of the visible and/or audible by giving body to what constitutively eludes this field (on that account, the object-gaze is a blind spot within the field of the visible, whereas the object-voice *par excellence*, of course, is silence).

Lacan identified *objet a* as a-sexual, which does not simply mean that it is nonsexual, external to the space of sexuality: insofar as it is the object-cause of desire; insofar as, for Freud and Lacan, desire is by definition sexual (in contrast to Jung, who asserts a nonsexual general libido, there is no general libido for Freud and Lacan), and insofar as Lacan's formula of the impossibility/void/antagonism that undermines every ontological vision of All is "there is no sexual relationship," *objet a* gives body to the impossibility of the sexual relationship. It is "a-sexual" only in this sense of giving body to the absence of the sexual relationship: if there were a sexual relationship, no *objet a* would have been needed.

Objet a is what is to be subtracted from the Real, not added to it, in order to arrive at reality. If it falls into reality, reality breaks down (for example, when gaze falls into reality, we get the paranoiac stance of "someone is watching me out there, in reality"). *Objet a* is not a something that fills in the void, it is the materialization of this void as such, its placeholder; it is not something but *less than nothing*, a "negative object": if we erase it, we do not get less but more than we had.

2.2 NO *a* WITHOUT THE PHALLUS

Does this reference to Kant's transcendentalism mean that Lacan elevates sexual difference into a kind of transhistorical a priori, a fixed frame filled in with variable content? The reply to this critical point is a double no. First, Kant's antinomies combined with Lacan's formulas of sexuation do provide the basic formal structure of sexuation, but what they provide is not simply an a priori symbolic form but a formal deadlock, a Real which undermines every permanent form of gender identity. Second, we can well imagine a human universe that leaves sexuation behind, a literally transsexual (not just transgender) universe—one that sets in motion different historical forms of sexuality. When gender theorists render the "gender binary" problematic, and emphasize the fluidity and multiplicity of sexual identities, they themselves proceed in a nonhistorical way, forgetting to historicize their own form of radical historicism: radical fluidization of the forms of sexual identity is not a transhistorical fact but a form that characterizes sexuality in the late-capitalist post-patriarchal universe. We have to accomplish here a kind of negation of negation: yes, fluidization negates all fixed forms, but we have to take a further step and "negate" (historicize) this very form of radicalized historicism, discerning in it a specific historical formation.

Furthermore, gender theory slides into ideology when it conceives the fact that gender role is not biologically predetermined but socially constructed as proof that sexual orientation is a matter of free choice, so that, ideally, subjects can play with different identities, experimenting with them, etc. What we get here is not only a denial of the Freudian Unconscious, a covert return to ego-psychology, but, even worse, a denial fully in tune with the ideology of free choice that sustains market consumerism. Yes, sexual identity is a free choice, but a choice at the level of what Schelling called the primordial decision-differentiation (Ent-Scheidung), the unconscious atemporal deed by means of which the subject chooses his eternal character which, afterward, within his conscious-temporal life, he experiences as the inexorable necessity, as "the way he always was":

> The deed, once accomplished, sinks immediately into the unfathomable depth, thereby acquiring its lasting character. It is the same with the will which, once posited at the beginning and led into the outside, immediately has to sink into the unconscious. This is the only way the beginning, the beginning that does not cease to be one, the truly eternal beginning, is possible. For here also it holds that the beginning should not know itself. Once done, the deed is eternally done. The decision that is in any way the true beginning should not appear before consciousness, it should not be recalled to mind, since this, precisely, would amount to its recall. He who, apropos of a decision, reserves for himself the right to drag it again to light, will never accomplish the beginning.[5]

A further reference to Kant imposes itself here: his notion of a primordial, atemporal, transcendental act by means of which we choose our "eternal character," the elementary contours of our ethical identity. And the link with Freud's notion of an *unconscious* decision is clear here: this absolute beginning is never made in the present, i.e., its status is that of a pure presupposition, of something which always-already took place. In other words, it is the paradox of a *passive decision*, of passively assuming the Decision that grounds our being as the supreme act of freedom—the paradox of the highest free choice which consists in assuming that one is chosen. In his *Adieu à Emmanuel Levinas*, Derrida tries to dissociate the decision from its usual metaphysical predicates (autonomy, consciousness, activity, sovereignty) and think it as the "other's decision in me": "The passive decision, condition of the event, is always, structurally, another's decision in me, a rending decision as the decision of the other. Of the absolutely other in me, of the other as the absolute who decides of me in me."[6] In psychoanalytic terms, this choice is that of the "fundamental fantasy," of the basic frame/matrix that provides the coordinates of the subject's entire universe of meaning: although I am never outside it, although this fantasy is always-already here, and I am always-already thrown into it, I have to *presuppose* myself as the one who *posited* it. Because of this radical (and radically unconscious) character of the sexual choice it is much easier to transform our body (by means of a gender-changing surgical intervention) than to undo the unconscious choice. An incident occurred recently in a Slovene high school. As part of gender education, boys in a class were asked to dress in bikinis in order to make them sensitive to the historical contingency and arbitrariness of their sexual identity—the experiment was supposed to demonstrate how our sexual identity is not biologically predetermined but constructed through the performance of social rituals. ... Such a procedure ignores the fact that although sexual identity is not biologically predetermined, it is a matter of profound unconscious choice which cannot be simply done or undone, since it is constitutive of our very identity. The approach to Lacan popular among some gay theorists is based on—let us call it, to simplify things to the utmost—the "from phallus to *objet a*" thesis. The idea is that in his late work, Lacan, with his shift of emphasis from the Symbolic to the Real, also abandoned the central role of the phallic signifier and of sexual difference, instead of which he asserted the role of *objet petit a* (or surplus-enjoyment) as more primordial, as grounding the subject's relation to enjoyment, and this object is, as Lacan wrote, "*a*-sexual."[7] From this premise, Tim Dean deploys his impersonalist theory of desire according to which we have sex not with others but with the Other. From this standpoint, of course, the phallus (the phallic signifier) has to appear as a kind of retrograde legacy: "Lacan's most profound ideological and affective convictions sometimes run counter to his most brilliant critical and analytical insights."[8] The phallic signifier is part of these "convictions" and should be reduced to a "provisional concept because so many of its functions are taken over by other concepts, in particular that of object a, which has no a priori relation to gender and, indeed, may be represented by objects gendered masculine, feminine, or neuter."[9] (Incidentally, this is always a comfortable position: when you propose a reading that obviously has to ignore some of the interpreted author's key theses, the easiest way to deal with it is to impute the inconsistency to the interpreted author him-/herself.)

With regard to sexual difference itself, Dean evokes Freud's "astonishing claim" that "the unconscious has no knowledge of sexual difference. ... Lacan maintains that there is no signifier for sexual difference in the unconscious. Hence the phallus cannot be a signifier of sexual difference. ... If there is no signifier for sexual difference in the unconscious, then as far as the unconscious is concerned heterosexuality does not exist. ... Sexual difference does not organize or determine sexual desire."[10] This is how Sam Warren Miell, in an attack on me, summarizes Dean's position:

> Our tendency to read sexual difference and sexuality in terms of each other, and to read sexual difference in terms of men and women, corresponds to a pre-Freudian, psychologistic understanding of sexuality. Worse, it endorses an identification of sexuality with the ego, with normative, idealizing results. ... The fact that the unconscious contains no signifier of sexual difference means that it is essentially bigendered/bisexual (as Freud himself already suggested), which is why Shanna T. Carlson has concluded that one way a transgendered person might be viewed in terms of psychoanalysis is as personifying "the human subject as such, the unconsciously bisexual subject for whom sexual difference is only ever an incomplete, unsatisfactory solution to the failure of the sexual relation."[11]

This entire line of thought should be rejected as an obvious misreading of Lacan. If we designate as "sexual difference" what Lacan defines with his formulas of sexuation, then sexual difference is sustained precisely by the lack of the "binary" signifier in the unconscious, by the lack of a clear symbolic opposition or couple which would determine the two sexes. Not only sexuality but human subjectivity as such is thoroughly "sexed" precisely in the sense of the trauma of sexual difference: the parallax gap between masculine and feminine positions, the two inconsistent ways to cope with—or, rather, to assume—the trauma of the impossibility of sexual relationship, is unconditional; there is no third way. Of course our position is not determined by biology, a biological man can assume a feminine position; but the choice is unconditional, there is no "bisexuality" here, the gap is parallactic, one position excludes the other, which is precisely why one should not say that "the human subject as such, the unconsciously bisexual subject for whom sexual difference is only ever an incomplete, unsatisfactory solution to the failure of the sexual relation": yes, every solution to the failure of a sexual relationship is unsatisfactory, and in this sense incomplete, but this does not mean that sexual difference is a secondary, imposed frame which can never completely capture the complexity of the unconsciously bisexual subject. There is nothing outside this failure; subject and language are themselves the outcome of this primordial failure. As Lacan put it, the Real is an impasse of formalization, and this is to be taken literally: not that the Real is an external substantive domain that resists formalization (or symbolization, although they are not the same, of course), but that the Real is totally immanent to the symbolic—it is nothing but its immanent failure.

One should note that the only "function" which operates in these formulas of sexuation is the phallic function—as Lacan emphasizes, what is "primordially repressed," what is constitutively absent even from the unconscious, is (not the signifier of sexual difference but) the "binary signifier," the signifier that would serve as the feminine counterpart to the phallic function (in the way premodern sexualized cosmology talks about masculine and feminine "principles," yin and yang, etc.). (To avoid any misunderstanding, this primordial repression of the binary signifier not only does not put women in a subordinate position; if anything, it elevates them into exemplary cases of subjectivity, since subjectivity is for Lacan defined by the missing signifier—this is how one should read Lacan's mark for the subject, $\math$, barred S, signifier.) Because the binary signifier is primordially repressed, there is no sexual relationship; sexual antagonism cannot be symbolized in a pair of opposed symbolic/differential features. However, the fact that there is no sexual relationship in no way implies that "there is no sexual difference in the unconscious," that the unconscious is beyond or beneath sexual difference, a fluid domain of partial drives which defy sexuation. One can even say that *the unconscious is thoroughly and only about sexual difference* in the sense of an antagonism impossible to symbolize that haunts the symbolic order. The impossibility of the sexual relationship does not mean that the sexual relationship is simply absent from the unconscious, it means that the very impossibility of the sexual relationship is the traumatic point of failure which structures the entire symbolic space—or, as Lacan put it in *Seminar XX*, "we take language as something that functions to compensate for the absence of ... the only part of the real that cannot manage to be formed in being, namely, the sexual relationship."[12] That is why *objet a* as a-sexual is not prior to the deadlock of sexual relationship but already mediated by it, an object which fills in the lack/void sustained by this deadlock/impossibility: there is *objet a* because there is no sexual relationship. To put it in yet another way: sexual difference is the point of failure of *logos*, of the symbolic, but this failure absolutely does not mean that there is a domain of sexuality prior to (or outside of) sexual difference and its deadlock. Sexual difference/antagonism is not just the point at which *logos*/reason fails, it is nothing but the effect of this failure. Lacan's name for this negativity is the impossibility of the sexual relationship, the impossibility formalized in his formulas of sexuation. The antagonism internal to each form of sexuation (masculine and feminine) is thus redoubled not by the antagonism between the two forms of sexuation (this would mean that the basic antagonism is some form of the "eternal struggle between the two sexes") but by the antagonism as such, the constitutive deadlock of the Real, which immediately splits into two—in exact homology with Kant's thought, where the Real that cuts across Reason immediately splits into two forms of antinomy.

Following in Dean's footsteps, Chris Coffman argues that "sexual difference is not inalterable. Rather, sexual difference is the fundamental fantasy that Lacanian psychoanalytic theory needs to traverse in order to fully register the many possible configurations of desiring subjectivities."[13] Here we have the misunderstanding at its purest: sexual difference is not the "fundamental fantasy" that obfuscates the multiplicity of desiring subjectivities, it is this proliferating multiplicity untouched by castration which is one of the fantasies that obfuscates the trauma of the nonexistence of the sexual relationship (the other fantasy being the fantasy of the sexual relationship itself).

Furthermore, far from following heterosexual normativity with his focus on sexual difference, Lacan's view on heterosexuality and homosexuality is quite unexpected: in a gay couple, the symbolic Third is the Name-of-the-Mother; moreover, Lacan's position is that only lesbians are true heterosexuals, while gays and straight heterosexuals are homosexual. To explain this last point, let us make a detour through two movies, Neil Jordan's The Crying Game and David Cronenberg's M. Butterfly. In spite of their fundamentally different character, they both tell the story of a man passionately in love with a beautiful woman who turns out to be a man dressed up as a woman and living his life as a woman (the transvestite in The Crying Game, the opera singer in M. Butterfly), and the central scene of both films is the man's traumatic confrontation with the fact that the object of his love is also a man. Here, of course, the obvious objection awaits us: does not M. Butterfly portray a tragicomic confused bundle of male fantasies about women, not a true relationship with a woman? The entire action of the film takes place among men. Does not the grotesque incredibility of the plot simultaneously mask and point toward the fact that what we are dealing with is a case of homosexual love for the transvestite? The film is simply dishonest, and refuses to acknowledge this obvious fact. This elucidation, however, fails to address the true enigma of M. Butterfly (and of The Crying Game): how can a hopeless love between the hero and his partner, a man dressed up as a woman, realize the notion of heterosexual love far more authentically than a "normal" relationship with a woman? Or, with regard to The Crying Game: why is the confrontation with the lover's body such a trauma? Not because the subject encounters something alien, but because he confronts there the core fantasy that sustains his desire. Heterosexual love of man is homosexual, sustained by the fantasy that the woman is a man dressed up as a woman. Here we can see what is meant by traversing the fantasy: not seeing through it and perceiving the reality obfuscated by it, but confronting the fantasy as such; once we do this, its hold over us (the subject) is suspended. Once the hero of *The Crying Game* or *M. Butterfly* confronts the fact, the game is over (with different results, of course: a happy ending in one case, a suicide in the other).

This brings us back to Lacan's characterization of *objet a* as "*a*-sexual": it is *a*-sexual, not simply asexual (nonsexual), where *a* obviously refers to *objet a*, so it is "sexual in the mode of *a*." In other words, the point of Lacan's pun is that there is a negative dimension in *objet a*; however, this negation is strictly immanent to sexuality, it refers to a negation constitutive of sexuality (roughly: to the nonexistence of the sexual relationship), not to a step out of its domain. How, exactly? Sexuality is in itself hindered and perverted, being simultaneously insufficient and excessive (with excess as the form of appearance of lack). On the one hand, it is characterized by the universal capacity to provide the metaphorical meaning or innuendo of any activity or object—any element, including the most abstract reflection, can be experienced as "alluding to that" (recall the proverbial example of the adolescent who, in order to forget his sexual obsessions, takes refuge in pure mathematics and physics—whatever he does here again reminds him of "that": how much volume is needed to fill out an empty cylinder? how much energy is discharged when two bodies collide?). This universal surplus—this capacity of sexuality to overflow the entire field of human experience so that everything, from eating to excretion, from beating up our fellow man (or getting beaten up by him) to the exercise of power, can acquire a sexual connotation—is not the sign of its preponderance. It is, rather, the sign of a certain structural faultiness: sexuality strives outward and overflows the adjoining domains precisely because it cannot find satisfaction in itself, because it never attains its goal. How, precisely, does an activity that is, in itself, definitely asexual acquire sexual connotations? It is "sexualized" when it fails to achieve its asexual goal and gets caught in the vicious circle of futile repetition. We enter sexuality when a gesture that "officially" serves some instrumental goal becomes an end-in-itself, when we start to enjoy the very "dysfunctional" repetition of this gesture and thereby suspend its purposefulness.

Sexuality can function as a co-sense that supplements the "desexualized" neutral-literal meaning precisely insofar as this neutral meaning is already there. As Deleuze demonstrated, perversion enters the stage as an inherent reversal of this "normal" relationship between the asexual, literal sense and the sexual co-sense. In perversion, sexuality is made into a direct object of our speech, but the price we pay for it is the desexualization of our attitude toward sexuality—sexuality becomes one desexualized object among others. The exemplary case of such an attitude is the "scientific" disinterested approach to sexuality or the Sadeian approach that treats sexuality as the object of an instrumental activity. Recall the role of Jennifer Jason Leigh in Altman's *Short Cuts*: a housewife who earns supplementary money by paid phone sex, entertaining customers with arousing talk. She is so well accustomed to her job that she can improvise into the receiver, describing, for instance, how she is all wet between her thighs, while changing her baby or preparing lunch—she maintains a wholly external, instrumental attitude toward sexual fantasies. They simply do not concern her. What Lacan aims at with the notion of "symbolic castration" is precisely this *vel*, this choice: either we accept the desexualization of the literal sense, entailing the displacement of sexuality to a "co-sense," to the supplementary dimension of sexual connotation-innuendo; or we approach sexuality "directly," we make sexuality the subject of literal speech, which we pay for with the "desexualization" of our subjective attitude to it. What we lose in every case is a direct approach, literal talk about sexuality that would remain "sexualized."

2.3 SEXUALITY, KNOWLEDGE, AND IGNORANCE

In what, then, does the link between sexuality and knowledge consist? In Longus's classic novel *Daphnis and Chloe* (from the second century AD), a young couple are passionately in love, yet they do not know how to consummate their desire—they painfully discover that lying down naked together is just not enough. Observing mating animals, the two try to imitate them, but this does not work, and they quit in frustration. Their attempts are observed, however, by the mature and sophisticated Lycaenion, who has been trying for a while to seduce Daphnis. Once she has Daphnis alone, Lycaenion offers to give him lessons; Daphnis eagerly agrees and, after the preliminaries, they have sex. After a long series of further adventures, the couple Daphnis and Chloe are married, and their love is fully consummated during a sleepless night. The lesson of *Daphnis and Chloe* is a correct one: human sexuality doesn't come naturally, it has to be learned. The naive question to be asked here is: what, exactly, is it that we have to learn in sexual education? Is it only the physical technique of performing the act, or something more?

It is not simply that while animals find the coordinates of their mating activity embedded in their natural instincts, humans lack them and therefore need their "second nature," the symbolic institution, to provide them with these coordinates. The coordinates of the symbolic order are there to enable us to cope with the impasse of the Other's desire, and the problem is that the symbolic order ultimately always fails: as Jean Laplanche points out, the traumatic impact of the "primordial scene," the enigma of the signifiers of the Other's desire, generates an excess which can never be fully "sublated" in symbolic ordering. The notorious "lack" consubstantial with the human animal is not simply negative, an absence of instinctual coordinates; it is a lack with regard to an excess, to the excessive presence of traumatic enjoyment. The paradox is that there is signification precisely because there is an excessive, nonsignifiable, erotic fascination and attachment: the condition of possibility of signification is its condition of impossibility. What if, then, the ultimate resort of the excessive development of human intelligence is the effort to decipher the abyss of *Che vuoi?*, the enigma of the Other's desire? What if that is why humans are fixated on solving tasks that cannot be solved, on trying to answer unanswerable questions? What if the link between metaphysics and sexuality (or, more precisely, human eroticism) is to be taken quite literally? Ultimately, this traumatic, indigestible kernel, as the nonsensical support of sense, is the fundamental fantasy itself. So when Freud writes: "If what [subjects] long for most intensely in their phantasies is presented to them in reality, they none the less flee from it,"[14] his point is not merely that this occurs because of censorship but, rather, because the core of our fantasy is unbearable to us.

The original site of fantasy is that of a small child overhearing or witnessing parental coitus and unable to make sense of it: what does all of this *mean*, the intense whispers, the strange sounds in the bedroom, etc.? So, the child fantasizes a scene that would account for these strangely intense fragments—recall the best-known scene from David Lynch's *Blue Velvet*, in which Kyle MacLachlan, hidden in the closet, witnesses the weird sexual interplay between Isabella Rossellini and Dennis Hopper. What he sees is a clear fantasmatic supplement destined to account for what he hears: when Hopper puts on a mask through which he breathes, is this not an imagined scene which is to account for the intense breathing that accompanies sexual activity? And the fundamental paradox of the fantasy is that the subject never reaches the moment when he can say, "OK, now I fully understand it, my parents were having sex, I no longer need a fantasy!"—this is, among other things, what Lacan meant with his *il n'y a pas de rapport sexuel*. Every *sense* has to rely on some nonsensical fantasmatic frame—when we say, "OK, now I understand it!" what this ultimately means is "Now I can locate it within my fantasmatic framework."

So when, in *Seminar XX (Encore)*, Lacan repeatedly asserts that *y a de l'un* ("there is something of the one"), this One is not the totalizing One of the Master-Signifier, but the "supplementary" partial object (organ without a body) which functions as the enabling obstacle of the sexual relationship, as its condition of (im)possibility. *Y a de l'un* is thus strictly correlative to *il n'y a pas de rapport sexuel*: the two sexual partners are never alone, since their activity has to involve a fantasmatic supplement which sustains their desire (and which can ultimately be just an imagined gaze observing them while they are engaged in sexual intercourse). *Y a de l'un* means that every erotic couple is a couple of three: 1 + 1 + a, the "pathological" stain which disturbs their pure immersion. In short, this "one" is precisely that which *prevents* the fusion of the amorous couple into One. (And one can well argue that, in the case of a lesbian couple, this "one" is none other than the phallus itself [occasionally materialized in a dildo]—so that, when Judith Butler ironically proposes the term "lesbian phallus," we should fully agree with her, simply adding that this "lesbian phallus" is the phallus *tout court*.)

In the TV series *Castle*, Richard Castle, a best-selling detective writer, collaborates with Kate Beckett, a NYPD homicide detective, in solving various murder cases in New York City. Beckett is initially infuriated at the thought of working with a writer, but the two soon start developing feelings for each other, and, as expected, the overarching plot of the series focuses on the growing romance between the two. The ongoing murder investigation is thus clearly the *objet a*, object-cause of their mutual desire, a pretext which compels them to spend a lot of time together. The problem is, of course, what will happen when they finally admit their love for each other and enter into a full erotic relationship: will they still need the pretext of murder investigations? Episode 4 ("Murder He Wrote") confronts this deadlock: Castle and Beckett decide to spend a romantic weekend in his Hamptons villa, and just as Beckett is offering herself to him by the swimming pool, dropping her bathrobe and standing naked in front of him, a dying man stumbles through the bushes behind the houses and falls dead into the pool. The precise moment of this unexpected intrusion is crucial: just before it happens, Castle looks at her naked body, obviously fascinated and full of desire, but with a slight touch of despair, as if he is secretly waiting for something to intervene and prevent the consummation of the act. The role of the body that intrudes is, of course, thoroughly ambiguous: it does not simply intervene in order to spoil the perfect weekend of lovemaking, it is simultaneously the object which sustains desire. Here we get the same body as the one mentioned by Hitchcock in his imagined perfect movie scene,[15] but in a different function: not as the surplus of production but as the surplus-object which constitutes an obstacle to the sexual relationship. All the ambiguity of the tension between Castle's object of desire (Kate) and the object-cause of his desire (a corpse that sets in motion a murder investigation) is here, perfectly exemplifying Lacan's thesis that there is no sexual relationship: the couple alone never works, it needs an obstacle as the cause of its desire.

This is why adults need sex education. The common wisdom tells us that, according to psychoanalysis, whatever we are doing, we are secretly "thinking about *that*"—sexuality is the universal hidden reference of every activity. However, the true Freudian question is: what are we thinking when we *are* "doing that"? It is real sex itself which, in order to be palatable, has to be sustained by some fantasy. The logic here is the same as that of a Native American tribe whose members have discovered that all dreams have some hidden sexual meaning—all, *except the overtly sexual ones*: here, precisely, one has to look for another meaning. Any contact with a "real," flesh-and-blood other, any sexual pleasure that we find in touching *another* human being, is not something evident, but something inherently traumatic, and can be sustained only insofar as this other enters the subject's fantasy frame.

Fantasy does not simply realize a desire in a hallucinatory way; rather, it constitutes our desire, provides its coordinates—it literally "teaches us how to desire." To put it in somewhat simplified terms: fantasy does not mean that when I desire a strawberry cake and cannot get it in reality, I fantasize about eating it; the problem is, rather, *how do I know that I desire a strawberry cake in the first place? This* is what fantasy tells me. This role of fantasy hinges on the fact that, as Lacan put it, "there is no sexual relationship," no universal formula or matrix guaranteeing a harmonious sexual relationship with one's partner: every subject has to invent a fantasy of his own, a "private" formula for the sexual relationship—for a man, the relationship with a woman is possible only inasmuch as she fits his formula.

The ultimate, properly Freudian lesson is thus that the explosion of human symbolic capacities does not merely expand the metaphorical scope of sexuality: activities that are in themselves thoroughly asexual can get "sexualized," everything can be "eroticized" and start to "mean that." … Much more importantly, this explosion *sexualizes sexuality itself*: the specific quality of human sexuality has nothing to do with the immediate, rather stupid, reality of copulation, including the preparatory mating rituals; it is only when animal coupling gets caught in a fantasmatic frame that we get what we call sexuality, i.e., that sexual activity itself gets sexualized. This, then, is why adults also need sex education—perhaps even more than children. What they have to learn is not the technique of the act, but what to fantasize while they are doing it. Each couple has to invent their specific formula. In effect, to paraphrase Dogberry's advice to Seacole from Shakespeare's *Much Ado about Nothing* to which Marx refers in *Capital*: "To be able to enjoy sex is the gift of fortune; but reading and writing comes by nature."

And this brings us back to the Hegelian reversal of epistemological obstacle into ontological impossibility: insofar as sexuality can function as actual sexual practice performed within the order of being (what we do to and with our bodies) only when its immanent impossibility (the navel of sexuality, one might say) is supplemented by fantasy, by fantasmatic coordinates, the "epistemological" void is constitutive of sexuality itself. Zupančič[16] suggests that we should read Freud's famous notion of the "dream's navel, the spot where it reaches down into the unknown,"[17] along the lines of this shift from epistemology to ontology: it is not just that the hidden core of the dream remains forever unknowable for us, the interpreters—this "primordially repressed" core is constitutive of the dream itself, more generally: of unconscious sexuality.

But why does this antagonism/impossibility actualize itself in the guise of two sexuations ("masculine" and "feminine"), why not a plurality of sexuations as the embodiment of impossibility? How does the Two emerge? The Two emerges as the positive existence of the immanent antagonism. Two is not really two, it is the One and its impossibility posited as separate. So the non-relationship between M and F is asymmetrical: it is not that each sex prevents the other from actualizing itself. Man exists insofar as he externalizes its impossibility of existing into Woman. It is not just that woman doesn't exist, woman *is* the nonexistence of man: while woman is the void ($) beneath the mask, man believes there is a positive identity of a Self beneath the mask; this is why, as Zupančič puts it, men *believe* they are men, while women *pretend* to be women. This opposition should be reflexively redoubled: women not only pretend, they also pretend to believe, and men not only believe, they also believe to pretend. To pretend to believe means that, even if belief is experienced as sincere, one wears it as a mask, one acts as if one believes; to believe to pretend means that, even if one experiences one's belief as a mere cynical game, not taking it seriously, one falls into one's own game, one in effect believes in what one thinks is only a game of pretending. And this reflexivity should be brought right up to tautology: a woman's pretending, at its purest, means that she only believes to believe (as Kierkegaard put it), while a man's belief means that he only pretends to pretend. Belief at its purest and most radical is a pretense to pretend, while pretending at its purest and most radical is believing to believe. For example, when a man believes in God, he pretends to believe, he acts as if he believes, but he is unaware of the fact that he pretends to pretend only since he fell into his own cynical game of pretending, and when a woman pretends to be religious (although she is effectively an atheist), she nonetheless believes in belief itself.

Can we link this to Pascal's formula "Act as if you believe, pretend to believe, wear a mask of belief, and you will believe, belief will gradually come to you"? Are women humans who remain stuck to the first phase? And what about the idea that pretending, acting as if, is a way to get rid of the intensity of belief? (For instance, if my love is too intense, I externalize it in rituals, I act as if I am in love, get married, etc., and in this way I acquire a distance toward it, a distance which gives me some breathing space.) Can we pretend to be men in order to transfer onto another the belief that we are men? This brings us to the situation in *General della Rovere*, Rossellini's late masterpiece, the story of a petty thief and swindler (superbly played by Vittorio de Sica) who is arrested by the Germans in the winter of 1944/45 in Genoa. The Germans propose a deal: in prison, he will pass for the legendary General della Rovere, a Resistance hero, so that other political prisoners will tell him their secrets, especially the true identity of "Fabrizio," a key Resistance leader. However, the petty thief gets so intensely caught up in the role that, at the end, he fully assumes it and prefers to be shot as the General. The petty thief pretends to be the General, but does he follow the Pascalian logic and, at the end, believe he is? Obviously not—this would have been a simple case of madness. The ethical beauty of the film is that, although the petty thief knows very well until his bitter end who he is, he is ready to risk his life as General della Rovere.

Is the gap between the petty thief and the General, then, the gap between reality and a Platonic Idea? To clarify this point, let us turn to Hitchcock's *Vertigo*, which is, in a sense, the ultimate anti-Platonic film, a systematic materialist undermining of the Platonic project, akin to what Deleuze does in the appendix to *The Logic of Sense*. The murderous fury that seizes Scottie when he finally discovers that Judy, whom he tried to make into Madeleine, is (the woman he knew as) Madeleine is the fury of the deceived Platonist when he perceives that the original he wants to remake in a perfect copy is already, in itself, a copy. The shock here is not that the original turns out to be merely a copy—a classic deception against which Platonism warns us all the time—but that (what we took to be) *the copy turns out to be the original*. Perhaps one should read *Vertigo* together with *General della Rovere*. The anti-Platonic reversal to be accomplished apropos of *General della Rovere* is the same as that of *Vertigo*: what if the "true" della Rovere was already a fake, in exactly the same way that the "true" Madeleine was already Judy faking being Madeleine? That is to say: what if he was also, as a private person, a petty swindler acting as "General della Rovere," wearing this role as a mask?

The further, even more unsettling, question here is: is such a pathetic identification with a fake role the ultimate horizon of ethical experience? Can we imagine the inverse situation: the "real" della Rovere is arrested, and the Resistance lets him know that he has to besmirch his image, to die as a miserable traitor, in order to perform one last great service for the Resistance? It is clear that sexual difference comes into this: while the petty thief acting as if he is General della Rovere had to be a man, in this second version, it would have to be a woman.

The shock of Scottie at the moment of recognition is also a Kafkaesque one. Just as, at the end of the parable on the Door of the Law in *The Trial*, the man from the country learns that the door was there only for him (that the spectacle of the magnificent Door was staged for his gaze, that the scene with regard to which he perceived himself as an accidental witness allowed to take a half-prohibited glimpse at it was entirely set up to fascinate him), in *Vertigo* also, Scottie has to accept that the fascinating spectacle of Madeleine, which he was secretly following, was staged for his gaze only, that his gaze was included in it from the very beginning. Sometimes, there is even less than a small step from the sublime to the ridiculous. *Vertigo* is definitely a sublime story, not meant to be laughed at. Yet is not its twist best encapsulated as a variation of the old Marx Brothers' joke: "this woman (Judy) looks like Madeleine and acts like Madeleine, but this should not deceive you—she *is* Madeleine!"? —And, maybe, this reversal which makes us see that the mysterious scene we are secretly witnessing is staged only for our eyes, that our gaze was from the very beginning included in it, is another way to approach the subjective reversal that characterizes the final moment of a psychoanalytic process.

In the classic patriarchal version of sexual difference, man is universal (pure universal subject, *cogito*), which is why we use the word "man" both for a masculine human being and for human beings as such, while woman stands for difference, for sex as such, for a universality polluted by particularity. Lacan's rejoinder to this *topos* is that yes, woman stands for difference, but as such she is the pure subject split from the object, a cut in the universality of substance. The male subject is the Fichtean subject: the subject as (directly) the ultimate substance, the ground-origin of all, the self-positing absolute which posits its opposite (non-I). For Hegel, on the contrary, the two aspects of "subjectivity" (the active agent *and* the agent which introduces split, partiality, appearance, illusion, as in "it's merely subjective") are inextricably linked: "to grasp substance also as subject" means that appearance, illusion, partiality, are immanent moments of substance.

If we take a quick look at Lacan's four formulas of sexuation, the first thing that strikes us is that if we read them horizontally, we get two non-contradictory pairs of formulas: (1) all *x* are subject to the phallic function; there is no *x* which is exempt from the phallic function; (2) there is one *x* which is exempt from the phallic function; non-all *x* are subject to the phallic function.[18] Lacan's ingeniously simple gesture is to posit the line of sexual difference vertically, thereby obtaining two paradoxes (universality grounded in exception: a non-all with no exception). The lesson here is that sexual difference *qua* the Real of an antagonism is not the difference between the two sexes (masculine and feminine), but a difference/antagonism which runs across (traverses) each of the two sexes, introducing a gap of inconsistency into its very heart. The difference between the two sexes is thus not sexual difference/antagonism but the difference of two ways of dealing with the antagonistic real of the Difference.

Man can appear as fully human, fully within the Symbolic, in contrast to woman, who is not fully integrated into the symbolic order. Woman can appear as the full (noncastrated) substantial Real which resists being fully caught up in the network of signifiers. Why? Because full integration needs an exception, an externality from which it delimits itself. Both these figures are fantasmatic mirages. However, if we read these two couples diagonally, we get Lacan's formulas of sexuation: man is fully integrated into the Symbolic and, as such, it needs the exception of a substantial Woman, a mythic

She of full enjoyment; there is nothing in woman that is not integrated into the Symbolic *and, as such, woman resists full integration into the Symbolic*. We can see now where the usual reading of Lacan's formulas of sexuation is misleading: it is not that a man is wholly caught up in the phallic function while part of a woman resists this inclusion, but quite the opposite—a woman is fully caught up in the phallic function (nothing of her is outside), while a man is only partially caught up in it (the exception to the phallic function grounds the male position).

2.4 FROM THE BARRED ONE TO THE BARRED OTHER

Such an approach compels us to rethink the very foundations of Freud's reading of the formations of the Unconscious: what Freud calls *Traumdeutung* (interpretation of dreams) is not a hermeneutics of dreams, a de-cyphering of their hidden meanings, but the undoing of meaning, a work of "deconstructing" meaning as a mask of negativity. Sexuality is not the ultimate meaning but the gap covered up by every meaning:

> it is as if sexual meaning, so generously produced by the unconscious, were here to mask the reality of a more fundamental negativity at work in sexuality, to separate us from it by a screen that derives its efficacy from the fact that it is itself a means of satisfaction—satisfaction through meaning, satisfaction in the production of sexual meaning, and (as the obverse of this) in the production of meaning of the sexual. Paradoxical as this might sound, one of the primary tasks of psychoanalysis is to slowly but thoroughly deactivate the path of this satisfaction, to render it useless. To produce sex as absolutely and intrinsically meaningless, not as the ultimate horizon of all humanly produced meaning. That is to say: to restore sex in its dimension of the Real. (AZ, 8)

So why is this negativity/gap the nonrelation ("there is no sexual relationship")? We should reject the standard story of the polymorphously perverse multiplicity of partial drives which are then violently totalized/normalized in the guise of subordination to the binary form of heterosexuality: a negativity is at work already in partial drives whose multiplicity proliferates against the background of the abyss/impossibility of the barred One: "the death drive is not one among the (partial) drives, but refers to an active split or declination *within every* drive. The death drive points to the negativity around which different partial drives circulate, and which they—in this sense—have in common" (AZ, 102–103).

How is every drive split? Imagine a partial oral drive caught in the endless repetitive movement of sucking: it is clear that such a circular movement presupposes an abyss around which it circulates, the abyss which makes it perform the same repetitive gesture which never reaches its goal but finds satisfaction in the very repetitive failure to do so, and this abyss that lurks in the background of the repetitive movement of a partial drive is the death drive. Is this death drive, the abyss of negativity that sustains partial drives, sexually neutral, or is it sexed? Lacan's thesis is that it is radically sexed; why? To cut a long story short: Lacan's name for the radical antagonism (impossibility) that cuts across the symbolic order is "there is no sexual relationship," and the emergence of the Symbolic is strictly linked to this impossibility: "we take language as being what functions to supply for the absence of … the only part of the real that cannot manage to be formed in being, namely, the sexual relationship."[19] One should read this claim in the strongest possible sense: language can function only against the background of the fact that *il n'y a pas de rapport sexuel*. The fact that there is no sexual relationship does not mean that there is simply no trace of sexuation in language, but quite the opposite: the impossibility of the sexual relationship, the enigma/deadlock of sexual difference that resists symbolization, haunts the symbolic order; it simultaneously sustains the effort of symbolization and prevents its conclusion. There is no neutral speaking subject indifferent toward sexual difference: the speaking subject is constitutively "sexed": "*What splits into two is the very nonexistence of the one* (that is, of the one which, if it existed, would be the Other, the radically Other). What splits in two is the very 'one that lacks,' the minus, the with-without. This is how we could read Lacan's 'formulas of sexuation': as two ways in which the constitutive minus of the signifying order is inscribed in this order itself, and dealt with" (AZ, 49).

What does it mean, precisely, this complex relationship between the One and the Other? There is no Other (binary signifier, the feminine counterpart of the phallic signifier, the signifier whose presence would ground the sexual relationship), and because of this missing Other, the One is not the One but a mark of its own (the One's) lack. A Master-Signifier is a One which fills in the lack of the One. In other words, if there were to be two sexes (each of the two clearly delimited as a positive ontic entity) they would have been the same, i.e., there would have been only one, so there are two because there is no One sex. Lacan links this primordially repressed binary signifier to Freud's concept of *Vorstellungs-Repräsentanz*.[20] Let me explain this concept apropos of how a name functions.

In contrast to the particular features of a thing, a name is a symptom of the thing it names: it stands for *objet a*, the X, the *je ne sais quoi*, which makes the designated thing a thing. This brings us to *Vorstellungs-Repräsentanz*: not simply (as Freud probably intended) a mental representation or idea which is the psychic representative of the biological instinct, but (much more ingeniously) the representative (stand-in, placeholder) of a missing representation. Every name is in this sense a *Vorstellungs-Repräsentanz*: the signifying representative of that dimension in the designated object which eludes representation, that which cannot be covered by our ideas-representations of the positive properties of this object. There is "something in you more than yourself," the elusive *je ne sais quoi* which makes you what you are, which accounts for your "specific flavor"—and the name, far from referring to the sum total of your properties, ultimately refers to that elusive X.

Does not the formula of love—"You are … you!"—rely on the split which is at the core of every tautology? You—this empirical person, full of defects—are *you*, the sublime object of love, for the tautology itself reveals the radical split or gap. This tautology surprises the lover again and again: how can you be *you*? But we should take a step further here and recall that Lacan defines *Vorstellungs-Repräsentanz* as the representative of the missing binary signifier, the feminine Master-Signifier which would be the counterpart of the phallic Master-Signifier, guaranteeing the complementarity of the two sexes, each in its own place—yin and yang, etc. Lacan's thesis is that the starting point is the self-deferral of the One, its non-coincidence with itself, and that the two sexes are two ways of dealing with this deadlock.

It is in this precise sense that one can agree with Brecht when he wrote that there is no dialectics without humor: dialectical reversals are deeply connected to comical twists and unexpected shifts of perspective. In his book on jokes, Freud refers to the well-known story of a go-between who tries to convince a young man to marry a woman he represents; his strategy is to turn every objection into a positive feature: When the man says "But the woman is ugly!" he answers: "So you will not have to worry about her deceiving you with others!" "She is poor!" "So she will be used to not spending lots of your money!" And so on until, finally, when the young man formulates a criticism that is impossible to reinterpret in this way, the middleman explodes: "What do you want? Perfection? Nobody is totally without faults!" Is it not also possible to discern in this joke the underlying structure of the legitimization of a "really existing" socialist regime? "There is too little meat and rich food in the stores!" "So you don't have to worry about getting fat and suffering a heart attack!" "There are not enough interesting films or good books available!" "So you are all the more able to cultivate a rich social life, visiting friends and neighbors!" "The secret police exert total control over my life!" "So you can just relax and lead a life safe from worries!" And so on, until: "But the air is so polluted from the nearby factory that all my children have life-threatening lung diseases!" "What do you want? No system is without its faults!" For Lacan, the phallic signifier is such a suturing element.

In Woody Allen's Tolstoy parody *Love and Death*, the first association that automatically pops up, of course, is: "If Tolstoy, where is Dostoyevsky?" In the film, Dostoyevsky (the "binary signifier" to Tolstoy) remains "repressed"—however, the price of this it is that a conversation in the middle of the film, as it were accidentally, includes the titles of all Dostoyevsky's major novels: "Is that man still in the underground?" "You mean one of the Karamazov brothers?" "Yes, that idiot!" "Well, he did commit his crime and was punished for it!" "I know, he was a gambler who always risked too much!," etc., etc. Here we encounter the "return of the repressed," i.e., the series of signifiers which fills in the gap of the repressed binary signifier "Dostoyevsky." The fact of sexual difference signals precisely the *failure* of "binary logic," the failure of the signifying couple that would "cover" sexual difference—there is sexual difference *because* the binary signifier is primordially repressed, as Lacan put it. In other words, the antagonism of/in the One does not mean the harmonious tension between the two (opposing principles, etc.), but the inner tension, the impossibility of self-coincidence, of the One itself—or, as Alain Badiou articulates it concisely, "atheism is, in the end, nothing other than the immanence of the Two."[21] This is why the standard deconstructionist criticism according to which Lacan's theory of sexual difference falls into the trap of "binary logic" totally misses the point: Lacan's *la femme n'existe pas* aims precisely at undermining the "binary" polar couple of Masculine and Feminine—the original split is not between the One and the Other, but is strictly inherent to the One; it is the split between the One and its empty place of inscription. (This is how one should read Kafka's famous statement that the Messiah will come one day after his arrival). This is also how one should conceive the link between the split inherent to the One and the explosion of the multiple: the multiple is not the primordial ontological fact; the "transcendental" genesis of the multiple resides in the lack of the binary signifier, i.e., the multiple emerges as the series of attempts to fill in the gap of the missing binary signifier. The difference between S_1 and S_2 is thus not the difference of two opposed poles within the same field, but, rather, the cut within this field—the cut of the level at which the process occurs—inherent to the one term: the original couple is not that of two signifiers, but that of the signifier and its *reduplicatio*, i.e., the minimal difference between a signifier and the place of its inscription, between one and zero.[22]

Here, Zupančič proposes a double thesis. First, sexuality is not the topic (repressed content) of the unconscious, but is at work in the very formal structure of the unconscious (of the "primordial repression"): sexuality (sexual antagonism) is grounded in the fact that the binary signifier is missing ("primordially repressed"): "the relation between the unconscious and sexuality is not that between some content and its container; *sexuality pertains to the very being-there of the unconscious, in its very ontological uncertainty*" (AZ, 12). It is this structure of "primordial repression" which sexualizes organic/biological sexuality itself. The second thesis: the subject is not only secondarily sexualized, it is sexualized in its very formal structure. The subject is represented by a signifier for other signifiers, and this signifier is the signifier of the lack of signifier—this missing signifier (a signifier whose lack is constitutive of the very order of signifiers) is the cause of the sexual "non-relationship." This brings us to the last trap to be avoided: the fact that "there is no sexual relationship" for the speaking (human) being does not mean that there is sexual relationship for animals—so what changes with the emergence of humanity?

> Whereas animal sexuality is simply inconsistent (and this is what it shares with human sexuality), *jouissance* is something like a set containing this inconsistency as its only element. ... Sexuality proper involves a further step in which the "minus," the negativity involved in sexuation and sexual reproduction, gets a positive existence in partial objects as involved in the topology of the drive. These partial objects are not just "satisfactions as objects," they function at the same time as figures or *representatives* of that negativity. It is only with this that we move from *sexuation* to *sexuality* proper (sexuality of speaking beings). (AZ, 92, 104)

The passage is thus the passage from the inconsistency of a process or object to an object that *is*—gives body to—this inconsistency, from the non-existence of the sexual relationship to the existence of a non-relationship, from an excess over objectivity to an object that is, that gives body to, this excess. *Jouissance* is never a pure excess of productivity over every object, *jouissance* is always an object; inconsistency is never only inconsistency among elements, it is always an object—therein, in this ultimate "infinite judgment," resides the Hegelian coincidence of the opposites that defines surplus-enjoyment. (A careful reader will have noted how we now arrive at the reversal of the passage from *a* as a material remainder to its purely formal status: a purely formal structure has to be materialized in an impossible object.) Consequently, the impossibility of repeating

> does not imply ... that something is "impossible to be repeated" in its unique singularity; rather, it implies the *non-being* of what is to be repeated. It is *impossible to repeat it because it is not there* in the usual sense of the term. This is the Lacanian version of the theory that what is repeated is not an original traumatic experience, interrupting whatever has taken place before, but the *interruption itself* (which he relates to the Real). And this brings us back to ... the properly psychoanalytic (Lacanian) concept of the "unbound surplus": namely, enjoyment. ... Enjoyment appears at the place of the nonexistent ("originally missing") signifier, which—with its very nonexistence—dictates the logic of the signifying chain, "declines it" in a certain way. And it declines it with the help of the enjoyment sticking to (other) signifiers. Enjoyment is the (only) "being," "substance" of that which is ontologically not, of the missing ("originally repressed") signifier. (AZ, 117)

So when, in his late work, Lacan defines *jouissance* as the only substance recognized by psychoanalysis, he is in no way advocating some kind of obscurantist pansexualism, a sexualized version of Schopenhauer where it is not the Will but sexual energy that is the ultimate ground of all being. *Jouissance* is, rather, the only positive form that what is by definition impossible ("primordially repressed") acquires, it is a "stuff of nothing," a spectral excess that positivizes the Void. Again, we are dealing here with a precise Hegelian reversal: enjoyment is not just that which interrupts the texture of signifiers (as an external substance that traumatically intervenes into it), enjoyment is engendered by *this interruption itself*. It is not a substance which resists symbolization and, as such, "curves" the symbolic texture; enjoyment is the product of this curvature itself.

2.5 THE PRODUCTION OF A NEW SIGNIFIER

Surplus-enjoyment is not just an abstract tendency of a process that cannot be contained by objects, a surplus over all objects, but is itself a pseudo-object, *objet petit a*. It is *a non-relationship which exists as an object*. One should recall here Lacan's formula: small *a* over capital Φ, i.e., surplus-enjoyment over Phallus as the signifier of (symbolic) castration; *objet a* does not simply fill in (and, in this sense, cover up) the lack opened up by castration; rather, it gives body to this lack. As such, it is not something that covers up the gap of nothing, but something which is less than nothing. Or, to put it in more speculative-Hegelian terms, *objet a* opens up the lack it fills in: if we erase *objet a* from the picture, we do not get a pure experience of lack or void before it becomes obfuscated (such authentic existential encounters are a stuff of existentialist metaphysics that Lacan avoids like the plague); if we erase *objet a* from the picture, we lose the lack itself. So when one is dealing with *objet a*, one should never forget that *objet a* is not some kind of primordial excess/surplus of creativity but an excess which emerges at the place of the primordial lack (fundamental negativity-impossibility) constitutive of the symbolic order—in short, although *objet a* is a-sexual, it already presupposes the impossibility of the sexual relationship (Lacan's name for this negativity-impossibility): "For psychoanalysis there is thus a difference between the fundamental negativity (a 'minus') and the excessive surplus (-enjoyment) that emerges at its place, and repeats the original negativity by linking, 'gluing,' the signifiers with which this negativity appears *in a certain order*" (AZ, 118). "Gluing in a certain order" and in this way providing a minimal articulation of the excessive enjoyment is, of course, precisely what Lacan designates in his late work as *sinthome* (in contrast to symptom, whose cyphered meaning has to be unraveled through interpretation). What this means is, again, that there is no (surplus-) enjoyment prior to or outside of the symbolic order: the symbolic order is constitutively twisted, structured, around some "primordially repressed" signifier, and enjoyment emerges when a group of signifiers is "glued" together in such a way that it evokes the abyss of the missing signifier.

As Zupančič points out, that is the key difference between Lacan and Deleuze, for whom "the excess/surplus is *directly* the pure productive excess of negativity (crack, Difference) repeating itself in different disguises and with different signifiers or symbols" (AZ, 118). This is also why the act of emancipation (or liberation) radically differs in the two cases: for Deleuze, the joyful assertion of the excess of productive Difference is in itself the act of liberation; while for Lacan, "the eventual tectonic shift does not take place at the level of this surplus, but thanks to the newly produced *signifier*. It is the signifier of the 'hole' at the place of which enjoyment appears that repeats this 'hole' in different disguises or signifying formations" (AZ, 127). In short, since enjoyment arises at the point where the big Other is "barred," the new signifier is S($\bar{A}$), and as such, it stops the compulsive repetition of the established form of enjoyment. In order to illustrate the emergence of this new signifier, Zupančič quotes the joke about a man who comes home from an exhausting day at work, plops down on the couch in front of the television, and tells his wife: "Get me a beer before it starts." The wife sighs, and gets him a beer. Fifteen minutes later, he says: "Get me another beer before it starts." She looks cross, but fetches another beer and slams it down next to him. He finishes that beer and a few minutes later says: "Quick, get me another beer, it's going to start any minute." The wife is furious. She yells at him: "Is that all you're going to do tonight? Drink beer and sit in front of that TV? You're nothing but a lazy, drunken, fat slob, and furthermore …" The man sighs and says, "And so it starts …" —Here is her reading of the concluding "and so it starts" as "a possible psychoanalytic intervention":

> The point of this intervention is not simply that the true hidden meaning behind the husband's repeating of the words "before it starts" is a reference to frequent domestic quarrels, but also to shift the focus to the form itself: this whole staging (the whole scene as acted out with his wife) IS *his favorite show*. And this point is made not simply so that the husband will understand what he is really saying, but also to spoil for him the symptomatic enjoyment invested in this scene of the domestic quarrel and its anticipation. In this precise sense we could say that the *form* of the symptom (the specific work of the unconscious) is "unlocked" by this intervention. (AZ, 68)

The same ambiguity is clearly discernible in Wagner's *Parsifal*, whose central problem is that of a ceremony (ritual): how is it possible to perform a ritual in conditions where there is no transcendence to guarantee it? As an aesthetic spectacle? The enigma of *Parsifal* is: what are the limits and contours of a ceremony? Is the ceremony only that which Amfortas is unable to perform, or is part of the ceremony also the spectacle of his complaint and resistance and final agreement to perform the ceremony? In other words, are Amfortas's two great complaints not highly ceremonial, ritualized? Is not even the "unexpected" arrival of Parsifal to replace him (who, nonetheless, arrives just in time, i.e., at the precise moment when the tension is at its highest) part of a ritual? This is the shift to be performed by an analytic act: the awareness that what we (mis)perceived as failed attempts to perform the ritual are in themselves already a part of the ritual. Once we become aware of this, once we perform the ritual in this extended way, its power is broken—and that is what Parsifal does: with his ascent to power the Grail remains disclosed, there is no need for the ritual. In other words, it is easy to imagine Gurnemanz (the chorus figure in *Parsifal*) observing Amfortas's lamenting his inability to perform the ritual and adding coldly: "OK, the ritual has started ..." The point being, of course, that once this shift is really assumed by the participants, the ritual can no longer go on, since "the form of the symptom (the specific work of the unconscious) is 'unlocked' by this intervention," making it clear that the whole staging of the complaint and failure of the ritual IS the heart of the ritual. It is also clear how this shift changes the subjective position of the participants: their irrelevant preparatory game changes into a full symbolic commitment, and thereby cancels it. Similarly, in Irving Winkler's *Night and the City* (1992, a remake of Jules Dassin's *noir* classic), there is a short scene in which Fabian (the main character, played by Robert De Niro) mockingly attacks one of his detractors, threatening to beat him up. As he approaches his opponent, he grabs the hand of one of his friends, who is standing at his side, and puts it in front of his neck and shoulder, as if the friend is trying to restrain him from the attack—this, of course, ironically mocks a classic detail of fight scenes when a friend tries to prevent the furious hero from beating up the enemy; by staging the whole procedure, Fabian signals its ritualized character.

This short scene also nicely illustrates the subject's inability or unreadiness to fully confront the consequences of his or her desire: in our daily lives, we (pretend to) desire things which we do not really desire, so that, ultimately, the worst thing that can happen is for us to *get* what we "officially" desire. Fabian in effect acts as an analyst: he stages the scene of wanting to attack his opponent and being prevented only by the friend's hand over his shoulder, but his staging makes it clear that he himself does not want his desire to be realized, and organizes the obstacle that restrains him from attacking his opponent. In a similar way, when today's Left bombards the capitalist system with demands that it obviously cannot fulfill (Full employment! Retain the welfare state! Full rights to immigrants!), it is basically playing a game of hysterical provocation, of addressing the Master with a demand which will be impossible for him to meet, and will thus expose his impotence. However, the problem with this strategy is not only that the system cannot meet these demands, but also that those who issue them do not *really* want them to be realized. When "radical" academics demand full rights for immigrants and the opening of borders to them, are they aware that the direct implementation of this demand would, for obvious reasons, inundate the developed Western countries with millions of newcomers, thus provoking a violent racist working-class backlash which would then endanger the privileged position of those very academics? Of course they are aware of it, but they count on the fact that their demand will not be met—in this way, they can hypocritically retain their clear radical conscience while continuing to enjoy their privileged position. In 1994, when a new wave of emigration to the United States was in the making, Fidel Castro warned the States that, if they did not stop inciting Cubans to immigrate, Cuba would no longer prevent them doing so—a threat which the Cuban authorities actually carried out a couple of days later, embarrassing the United States with thousands of unwanted newcomers. Is this not like the proverbial woman who snapped back at the man making macho advances to her: "Shut up, or you'll have to do what you're boasting about!" In both cases, the gesture is that of calling the other's bluff, counting on the fact that what the other really fears is that one will fully meet his demand. And would not the same gesture also throw our radical academics into a panic? The old '68 motto *Soyons réalistes, demandons l'impossible!* acquires here a new cynical-sinister meaning which, perhaps, reveals its truth: "Let us be realists: we, the academic Left, want to appear critical, while fully enjoying the privileges the system is offering us. So let us bombard the system with impossible demands: we all know that these demands will not be met, so we can be sure that nothing will really change, and we will maintain our privileged status quo!"

In a similar vein, I remember what happened to a colleague of mine who, after a stressful experience, went to an old and experienced Slovene psychoanalyst. Wanting to impress the analyst, he invented for him a series of obviously "Freudian" dreams staging his desire to kill his father, etc., and then pretended to "spontaneously" report them during the sessions. The analyst, who immediately saw through this deception, reacted quite ingeniously: instead of directly telling his patient to stop lying, he assumed the position of a naive traditional authority figure, and brutally scolded him: "Are you aware how much your father did for you? How dare you talk like that about him? You should respect and love him!"—this fake naivety immediately cut short the patient's game, making it clear that his "spontaneous" dreams were a calculated fake performance.

The psychoanalytic act is thus the paradox of a gesture of closure which opens up new space. If one simply asserts the openness of a situation, nothing really changes: we behave like the proverbial smoker who goes on and on smoking, sustained by the awareness that he is free to stop whenever he wants. We can conceive the repetition of a symptom as a bad joke where the speaker is unable to refrain from telling it again and again, and the psychoanalytic act is the intervention which makes it impossible for the bad joke to go on. In this sense, the psychoanalytic act is a game-spoiler: it "ruins everything," the fun (enjoyment) we were having is openly denounced in its misery. (And is not what Hegel calls "absolute knowing" also such a gesture of conclusion which opens up the space for something New?) The spurious infinity of being caught in a repetitive pleasure is thus cut short by producing its formula. This new Master-Signifier produced in the discourse of the analyst is not something already there in the Unconscious waiting to be brought out but something radically new, a new name for the antagonism, for the inconsistency of the Other; it is the outcome of a subjective intervention, a creative act, like the punch line of a joke. Let us return to the joke about a marriage broker who knows how to present each individual fault in such a way as to cause one to become reconciled to it, and then concedes that the hunchback is the one fault which cannot be excused in any way. The trick is, of course, that he acts as if he has removed each individual fault by his evasion, forgetting that each leaves behind some depreciation which is added to the next one; he deals with each factor individually, and refuses to combine them into a sum total, so that the hunchback appears as the "endearing foible" of a perfect beauty, the exception which only confirms her general attractiveness. What the broker obfuscates with his reasoning is that there is no exception, that the poor girl has only bad qualities—which is why we can also imagine the broker redeeming the hunchback as a good property ("So it will be easier for her to carry provisions from the market on her back!") and elevate another feature into the exception. Or we can even imagine elevating into the exception a single good quality: "She is really beautiful." "I admit it, this is a problem, you will have to worry a lot about her deceiving you with other men, but do you expect her to have no blemishes at all?"

Which enjoyment is lost here? The enjoyment of reinterpretation, the stupid satisfaction we get from cunningly presenting each bad feature as a good one. The concluding punch line brings out the "algorithm" of this repetitive enjoyment, and thereby prevents its further repetition. To clarify this crucial point, let us mention another example. In the 1990s, the Croatian president Franjo Tudjman was the butt of many jokes; in one of the better ones, he and his large family are in a plane cruising above Croatia. Aware of the rumors that a lot of Croats live miserable, unhappy lives, while he and his cronies amass wealth, Tudjman says: "What if I were to throw out through the window a check for one million dollars, to make at least one Croat who will catch it happy?" His flattering wife tells him: "But Franjo my dear, why shouldn't you throw out two checks for half a million each, and thus make two Croats happy?" His daughter adds: "Why not four checks for a quarter million each, and make four Croats happy?" etc., etc., until, finally, his grandson—the proverbial innocent child who unknowingly blurts out the truth—says: "But, Grandpa, why don't you simply throw yourself out of the window, and thus make *all* Croats happy?" We have it all here: the indefinite signifiers line up to approach the impossible limit by subdividing, like Achilles trying to reach the tortoise, and then this endless series caught in the logic of "spurious infinity" is totalized, closed, made complete, by the fall of the body whose Real stands for the subject itself; through the suicidal fall of the body, the subject—not: "includes itself out," but, on the contrary—totalizes the series by, as it were, excluding itself in. The body is here literally the "indivisible remainder" that fills in the gap of the endless division. Again, we can easily imagine a clinical version of this joke: a compulsive-neurotic patient complains to the analyst that he continually feels the need to sacrifice something for others so that they will love him, and the analyst tells him: "But why don't you sacrifice yourself, and make everybody happy?" Although this may sound like a call to suicide, "yourself" has to be read here as "your Self": why don't you abandon the structure of your Self, which pushes you to act like this? True, you will lose the specific enjoyment provided by your sacrificing for others, but this loss will open up the space for new forms of enjoyment. (Incidentally, what we get here is a nice case of what Lacan called "subjective destitution.")

Of all the people I have known, the greatest hero of such self-sacrificing was my mother, who literally got depressed if she wasn't able to help others by some sacrifice—the greatest hero apart from myself; and from my own experience, I can vouch for all the dirty pleasures such a stance generates. When I was doing something that I perceived as sacrificing myself for others, this act was always accompanied by fantasies of how the others for whom I sacrificed myself would first ignore my act but then, when they became aware of it, would feel terribly guilty and would abjectly apologize to me. ... Recall Lacan's famous motto from his *Four Fundamental Concepts of Psychoanalysis*: "I give myself to you, but this gift of my person—as they say—Oh, mystery! is changed inexplicably into a gift of shit."[23] This is what the analysand has to take on board: the truth of his sacrificial giving to others is that his gifts are constantly and inexplicably transformed into gifts of shit, into an imposition of unwarranted and unwanted excrement.

Jacques Rivette's *La belle noiseuse* focuses on the tense relationship between the male painter (Michel Piccoli) and his model (Emmanuelle Béart): the model resists the artist; she actively provokes him, contests his approach, and thus fully participates in the creation of the art object. In short, the model is literally "the beautiful troublemaker," the traumatic object which irritates and infuriates, rejecting its insertion into the series of ordinary objects—*ça bouge*, as they put it in French. And what is art (the act of painting) if not an attempt to *depose*, "lay down," in the painting this traumatic dimension, to exorcize it by externalizing it in the object of art? However, in *La belle noiseuse*, this pacification fails: at the end of the film, the artist immures the painting in a crack between two walls where it will stay forever, unbeknownst to future inhabitants of the house; why? The point is not that he failed to penetrate the secret of his model: he succeeded *too much*, i.e., the finished product divulges *too much* about its model, it breaks through her veil of beauty and shows her up as what she is in the Real of her being: the abhorrent cold Thing. No wonder, then, that when the model finally gets a look at the finished painting, she runs away in panic and disgust—what she sees there is the kernel of her being, her *agalma*, turned into excrement. The true victim of the operation is thus not the painter but the model herself: she was active, by means of her uncompromising attitude she provoked the artist into extracting from her and putting on the canvas the kernel of her being, and she got what she asked for, which is always precisely *more* than she asked for—she got herself *plus* the excremental excess constitutive of the kernel of her being. For precisely this reason it was necessary that the painting be concealed forever inside the wall, and not simply destroyed: any direct physical destruction would be to no avail, one can only bury it and thus keep it at bay, since what is laid down in the painting is *stricto sensu* indestructible—it has the status of what Lacan, in *The Four Fundamental Concepts*, calls *lamella*, the mythical presubjective "undead" life substance, libido as an organ.

Orson Welles was extremely sensitive to the strange logic of this "secret treasure," the hidden kernel of the subject's being which, once the subject discloses it to us, turns into a poisonous gift. It is sufficient to quote the epigraph to *Mr. Arkadin*: "A certain great and powerful king once asked a poet, 'What can I give you of all that I have?' He wisely replied, 'Anything, sir ... except your secret.'" Why? Because, to quote Lacan again: "*I give myself to you, but this gift of my person. ... Oh, mystery! is changed inexplicably into a gift of shit*"—the excessive opening up (disclosure of a secret, allegiance, obedience, etc.) of one person to another easily reverts to an excremental, repulsive intrusion. That is the meaning of the famous No Trespassing sign shown at the beginning and the end of *Citizen Kane*: it is highly hazardous to enter this domain of the utmost intimacy, as one gets more than one asked for—all of a sudden, when it is too late to withdraw, one finds oneself in a slimy obscene domain. ... Most of us know from personal experience how unpleasant it is when an authority figure we deeply admire, and even want to know more about, grants our wish and takes us into his confidence, sharing with us his greatest personal trauma: all of a sudden the charisma evaporates, and we feel the impulse just to run away. Perhaps the feature which characterizes true friendship is precisely a tactful know-how of when to stop, of not going beyond a certain threshold and "telling everything" to a friend. We do tell everything to a psychoanalyst—but precisely for that reason, he can never be our friend.

2.6   APPENDIX: VOID AND EXCESS IN MUSIC

I remember from my high-school days a rather embarrassing moment when, to keep up with the new era of sexual revolution, a sex education specialist (a fat, bald guy with thick spectacles, as unattractive as one can imagine) gave us a lesson on sex. After a lot of introductory nonsense, he finally came to the point, and did it very briefly and efficiently: he drew on the blackboard two triangles with a shared bottom line, the difference being that one of them had its high point in the middle of the board and the other toward the right edge of the board, and then he commented: "The bottom line stands for time, the first high point is the boy's climax and the second one the girl's climax; the whole problem is to bring the two climaxes as close together as possible." In my nightmares, I still remember this lesson. This stupid anecdote is nonetheless of profound theoretical interest: the gap that separates the two climaxes is a structural necessity of our sexual lives. Even when we achieve the (too-) much-celebrated simultaneous orgasm, we get something that is experienced as a lucky exception, as a momentary coincidence of two events which are structurally separated by a gap.

A nice example of this gap is provided by Wagner's *Tristan und Isolde*, an opera whose "official ideology" is completely subverted by the work's very texture. This subversion in a way revolves around the famous Mozartian irony where, while the person's words indicate a stance of cynical frivolity or manipulation, the music expresses their authentic feelings: in *Tristan*, the ultimate truth resides not in the musical message of passionate self-obliterating love fulfillment, but in the dramatic stage action itself which subverts the passionate immersion into the musical texture. The final shared death of the two lovers abounds in Romantic operas (just recall the triumphant "Moriam' insieme" from Bellini's *Norma*); against this background, one should emphasize how in Wagner's *Tristan*, the very opera which elevates this shared death into its explicit ideological goal, this, precisely, is not what actually happens—in the music, it is as if the two lovers die together, while in reality they die one *after* the other, each immersed in his/her own solipsistic dream.

Along these lines, one should read Isolde's ecstatic death at the end of *Tristan* as the ultimate operatic prosopopeia: Tristan can die only if his death is transposed onto Isolde. When Tristan repeats his claim that death cannot destroy their love, Isolde provides the concise formula of their death: "But this little word 'and'—if it were to be destroyed, how but through the loss of Isolde's own life could Tristan be taken by death?" In short, it is only in and through her death that he will be able to die. Does not Wagner's Tristan, then, offer a case of the interpassivity of death itself, of the "subject supposed to die"? Tristan can die only insofar as Isolde experiences the full bliss of lethal self-obliteration for him, in his place. In other words, what "really happens" in Act III of Tristan is only Tristan's long "voyage to the bottom of the night" with regard to which Isolde's death is Tristan's own fantasmatic supplement, the delirious construction that enables him to die in peace.

The lesson of redoubled/displaced climax in music reaches much further—let us begin with a (perhaps) unexpected example. There is a remarkable detail in the marriage sequence of (the otherwise rather dull) *You Only Live Twice*, the James Bond movie set in Japan (with a scenario written by Roald Dahl): Bond has to marry a beautiful Japanese girl from a small fishing village to provide a cover for his fight against Ernst Stavro Blofeld, and the Japanese secret service organizes the old-fashioned ceremony. The key moment of the ceremony—the arrival of the bride—is shot in two parts: in the first part, while the bride and her retinue are slowly approaching in a procession, the shots are static, as in traditional Japanese cinema, and the music is limited to "depthless" clipping string sounds; women are stepping up the stairs with their heads bowed, and when the first two raise their heads, the disappointed Bond sees that they are older ladies. When, finally, the third woman, the young beautiful bride, approaches and raises her head, and Bond sees her face for the first time, the entire tone of the scene changes: the music "takes off," the tension is released, the same tune is played by the violins as a "romantic" continuous melody, the face is displayed in a full close-up, and, when Bond and his bride are side by side, there is even a slight tracking shot forward.[24] We literally pass here from the East to the West: from the Eastern constraint, refusal of subjectivity, to the Western open display of a passion. ...[25] The first "anticolonialist" reaction here would have been that this entire opposition appears as such only from a view which is already Westernized— it would have been easy for someone attuned to Japanese spirituality to discern an "inner life" (of a different type) already in the first "static" part.[26] One should thus at least supplement our first opposition (elaborated apropos of *You Only Live Twice*) between the Eastern universe where music follows mechanical rules and the modern Western universe of expressive melodic music with the opposite (no less ideological) couple: Eastern spirituality as organic and holistic, versus the Western mechanical-scientific approach. Yes, the West is more "mechanical," reducing objects to their dead components, but it is only through this mechanization that Spirit can assert itself in contrast to Life.

However, things are much more complex.[27] The musical-libidinal shift discernible in the scene from the Bond film is characteristic of Romantic European music, and persists today—just recall rock classics like the Stones'

"Honky Tonk Woman" or Jethro Tull's "Minstrel in the Gallery," where the constraint (the self-blocked character) of the first part of the melodic line is released in the climactic part. The question here is: is this restrained/blocked character of the first part a retroactive illusion, does it already presuppose (and lay the foundations for) the melodic outburst? The answer is, of course, yes—the whole of the scene from the Bond film, visually and musically, belongs in the Western Romantic space. So when we listen, with our Western ears, to a traditional Chinese or Japanese musical piece, and we experience it as a limit that thwarts emotional release, is this lack already there in Japanese music itself, or is this music in itself "satisfied," not haunted by deprivation? The answer is that there is some lack already in the Japanese piece itself, but it simply does not function as an obstacle, and so it does not set in motion any need to release it or to fill it in.

How did this lack get experienced as an obstacle? Let us take the opposite example, that of a melody adding itself to a rhythmic background accompaniment. Today, the first notes of a popular baroque piece like Pachelbel's Canon are automatically perceived as the accompaniment, so that we wait for the moment when the melody proper will emerge; since we get no melody, but only a more and more intricate polyphonic variation of (what we perceived as) the pre-melodic accompaniment, we somehow feel "deceived." Where does this horizon of expectation, which sustains our feeling that the melody proper is missing, come from? Perhaps melody in today's accepted sense, involving the difference between the main melodic line and its background, emerges only with Viennese classicism, i.e., after the retreat of baroque polyphony. Recall the third movement of Mozart's *Gran Partita* serenade: after the first notes, whose status is uncertain (*today*, we perceive them as accompaniment preparing the way for the melody proper, while in its own time, there probably was uncertainty as to its status, i.e., it was probably perceived as already the main melodic line), there enters as if "from above," from "heavenly heights," the melody proper. … Where, then, does the melody proper end? The answer is also clear: in Beethoven's late works (especially his last piano sonatas), i.e., in Romanticism proper, whose true breakthrough resides precisely in rendering the melody proper "impossible," in marking it with a bar of impossibility (the flowering of "beautiful Romantic melodies" is nothing but the kitschy obverse of this fundamental impossibility).[28] So we have an apparently universal phenomenon (melody) which is, "as such," nonetheless constrained, limited to a precisely defined historical period. What is perhaps the ultimate achievement of late Romantic expressionism is precisely the notion of the melodic line, of the main theme, as something which has to be "wrought out," sculptured, extracted from the inertia of vocal stuff by means of painful labor: far from functioning as a starting point for a series of variations which then form the main part of the piece, the main musical theme results from the painful perlaboration of the musical matter which forms its main body.

In short, complementary to this emergence of the melody is its gradual disappearance signaled by the often observed fact that, a decade after Beethoven's death, a long, "beautiful," self-enclosed melody all of a sudden becomes "objectively impossible"; this observation provides the proper background to the well-known vicious quip that Mendelssohn's melodies usually begin well but finish badly, losing their drive and ending in a "mechanical" resolution (his *Fingal's Cave* overture, or the beginning of the violin concerto which marks a clear melodic regression with regard to Beethoven's violin concerto). Far from being a simple sign of Mendelssohn's weakness as a composer, this failure of the melodic line rather bears witness to his sensitivity toward the historical shift; those who were still able to write "beautiful melodies" were kitsch composers like Tchaikovsky. On the other hand, Mendelssohn was, precisely for that reason, not yet a full Romantic: Romanticism "arrives at its notion" (to put it in Hegelese) only when this failure is included in, and becomes a positive factor of, the desired effect. César Franck's Prelude, Choral and Fugue, the supreme example of religious kitsch, nonetheless provides a nice example of "impossible longing" in the guise of the melody which endeavors to reach the climax, but is again and again forced to abandon its effort and, as it were, to fall back.

Back to Pachelbel's Canon: we can experience the historical cut we are dealing with at its purest if we compare the canon with an old European pop music kitsch, "Rain and Tears" (Demis Roussos, Aphrodite's Child), whose beginning closely resembles the beginning of the canon—however, the melody then explodes pathetically, and we are deep in kitsch. So where does musical kitsch begin? The original sin was committed by Beethoven, whose music undoubtedly often verges on kitsch—one need only mention the over-repetitive exploitation of the "beautiful" main theme in the first movement of his Violin Concerto, or the rather tasteless climactic moments of the *Leonore* 3 overture. How vulgar are the climactic moments of *Leonore* 3 (and 2, its even worse, utterly boring version) in comparison with Mozart's overture to *The Magic Flute*, where Mozart still retains what one cannot but call a proper sense of musical *decency*, interrupting the melodic line before it reaches the full orchestral climactic repetition and, instead, jumping directly to the final staccatos! Can one imagine this overture rewritten in Beethoven's *Leonore* 3-style, with the bombastic repetition of the melodic line? Perhaps Beethoven himself sensed it, writing another, final, overture, the Opus 72c *Fidelio*—brief and concise, sharp, the very opposite of *Leonores* 2 and 3. (The true pearl, however, is the undeservedly underestimated *Leonore* 1 Opus 138, whose very date is not certain—it is Beethoven at his best, with the beautiful rise to a climax without any embarrassing excesses.)

In this passage from Mozart to Beethoven we find another surprising case of the dialectics of lack and surplus: the strict correlation between the thwarted melodic culmination (the blocked climax) in Mozart, and one of his most beautiful signature specialties—when the deployment of a musical piece seems to be over and one expects only the final cadenza, a surprising addition comes along: joy exploding in wild rhythm, from the finale of *The Abduction from the Seraglio* to *The Magic Flute*, where the tender music of the "water and fire trials" is supplemented by an explosive fast conclusion sung by the chorus. These explosive surpluses express the excess of energy thwarted by the restraint that prevents the full climax of the main development—the thwarted energy is displaced onto this excess. This means that once we follow Beethoven, and allow full climax, these excesses are no longer possible.[29]

The climax displaced from its "proper" place to the appended surplus provides the minimal structure of subjective representation: the subject thwarted from its "proper" expression at the climactic moment of the melodic deployment returns in a supplementary moment which represents it for the main body of the musical piece. What happens in Romanticism, which opts for the full melodic deployment up to its climax, is the attempt to *subjectivize* the "pure" empty subject, to identify the subject with the wealth of inner subjective life striving to express itself. The modern subject proper (the Cartesian *cogito*, the Kantian transcendental subject, etc.) is, of course, not the Romantic expressive subject, the "person" trying to express all its inner richness; it is, rather, the abyss of a self-referential void internally excluded from every signifying structure, the void which can be registered/represented only through a thwarted structure.

CHAPTER 3

TOWARD A UNIFIED THEORY OF
FOUR DISCOURSES AND SEXUAL DIFFERENCE

3.1 FORMULAS OF SEXUATION

One of the crucial differences between psychoanalysis and philosophy concerns the status of sexual difference: for philosophy, the subject is not inherently sexualized, sexualization occurs only at the contingent, empirical level; whereas psychoanalysis promulgates sexuation into a kind of formal, a priori condition of the very emergence of the subject. (It is homologous with the notion of desire: in Kant's philosophy, the faculty of desire is "pathological," dependent on contingent objects, so there can be no "pure faculty of desiring," no "critique of pure desire," while for Lacan, psychoanalysis precisely is a kind of "critique of *pure* desire." In other words, desire *does* have a non-pathological ("a priori") object-cause: the *objet petit a*, the object which overlaps with its own lack.) For that precise reason, the Lacanian problematic of sexual difference—of the unavoidability of sexuation for human beings ("beings of language")—has to be strictly distinguished from the (de)constructionist problematic of the "social construction of gender," of the contingent discursive formation of gender identities which emerge by being performatively enacted. In order to grasp this crucial distinction, the analogy with class antagonism may be of some help: class antagonism (the unavoidability of the individual's "class inscription" in a class society, the impossibility of staying beyond, remaining unmarked by class antagonism) also cannot be reduced to the notion of the "social construction of class identity," since every determinate "construction of class identity" is already a "reactive" or "defense" formation, an attempt to "cope with" (to come to terms with, to pacify) the trauma of class antagonism. Every symbolic "class identity" already displaces class antagonism by translating it into a positive set of symbolic features: the conservative organicist notion of society as a collective Body, with different classes as bodily organs (the ruling class as the benevolent and wiser "head," workers as "hands," etc.) is only the most obvious case of it. And, for Lacan, things are the same with sexuation: it is impossible to "stay outside," the subject is always-already marked by it, it always-already "takes sides," it is always-already "partial" with regard to it. The paradox of the problematic of the "social construction of gender" is that, although it presents itself as a break out of "metaphysical" and/or essentialist constraints, it implicitly accomplishes the return to the pre-Freudian philosophical (i.e., nonsexualized) subject: the problematic of the "social construction of gender" presupposes the subject as given, it presupposes the space of contingent symbolization, while for Lacan, "sexuation" is the price to be paid for the very constitution of the subject, for its entry into the space of symbolization.

One should insist here on the adequate reading of Freud's infamous statement concerning the status of sexual difference: "Anatomy is destiny." This statement should be read as a Hegelian "speculative judgment" in which the predicate "passes over" into the subject. That is to say: its true meaning is not the obvious one, the standard target of the feminist critique ("the anatomical difference between the sexes directly founds, is directly responsible for, the different sociosymbolic roles of men and women"), but rather the opposite one: the "truth" of anatomy is "destiny," i.e., a symbolic formation. In the case of sexual identity, an anatomical difference is "sublated," turned into the medium of appearance/expression—more precisely, into the material support—of a certain symbolic formation. So, in Hegelese, we should read Freud's "anatomy is destiny" as a speculative judgment in which it is not only a predicate (being-destiny) that is added to the same subject (anatomy)—it is the predicate (destiny) which becomes subject of the process, and subordinates to itself as its predicate what was previously the subject.

In short, what sustains the difference between the two sexes is not the direct reference to the series of symbolic oppositions (masculine Reason versus feminine Emotion, masculine Activity versus feminine Passivity, etc.), but a different way of coping with the necessary inconsistency involved in the act of assuming one and the same universal symbolic feature (ultimately that of "castration"). It is not that man stands for *Logos* as opposed to the feminine emphasis on Emotions; it is rather that, for man, *Logos* as the consistent and coherent universal principle of all reality relies on the constitutive exception of some mystical, ineffable X ("there are things one should not talk about"), while, in the case of woman, there is no exception, "one can talk about everything," and, for that very reason, the universe of *Logos* becomes inconsistent, incoherent, dispersed, "non-all." Or, with regard to the assumption of a symbolic title, a man who tends to identify with his title absolutely, to put everything at stake for it (to die for his cause), nonetheless relies on the myth that he is not only his title, the "social mask" he is wearing, that there is something beneath it, a "real person"; in the case of a woman, on the contrary, there is no firm, unconditional commitment, everything is ultimately a mask, but, for that very reason, there is nothing "behind the mask." Or, with regard to love: a man in love is ready to give everything for it, the beloved is elevated into the absolute, unconditional Object, but, for that very reason, he is compelled to sacrifice her for the sake of his public or professional cause; a woman is entirely, without restraint or reserve, immersed in love, there is no dimension of her being which is not permeated by love—but, for that very reason, "love is not-all" for her, it is forever accompanied by an uncanny fundamental indifference. To quote Byron: "Man's love is of man's life a thing apart,/'Tis woman's whole existence" (*Don Juan*).

3.2 THE WELLESIAN LARGER-THAN-LIFE

How is this notion of sexual difference to be connected to the matrix of four discourses?[1] Let us begin with an author whose entire work is focused on the inherent deadlock of male subjectivity: Orson Welles. As James Naremore has shown,[2] the trajectory of a typical Welles film runs from the initial "realist," ironic, sociocritical depiction of a social milieu, to focusing on the tragic fate of a larger-than-life central character (Kane, Falstaff, etc.). This shift from a social-realist commentary (the liberal, gently critical, "social democratic" depiction of everyday life) to a morbid obsession with its Gothic excess, the prodigious individual and the tragic outcome of his hubris (which, incidentally, also provides the background for the shift from Marion to Norman in Hitchcock's *Psycho*), is the central unresolved antagonism of the Welles universe, and, as Adorno would have put it, Welles's greatness resides in the fact that he does not resolve or dissimulate this antagonism.

The first thing to take note of here is the allegorical character of Welles's obsession with such larger-than-life characters: their ultimate failure is clearly a stand-in, within the diegetic space of his films, for Welles himself, for the hubris of his own artistic procedure and its ultimate failure. The second thing to take note of is the way in which these excessive characters unite two opposite features: they are simultaneously aggressive, proto-Fascist, permeated by a ruthless lust for power, and quixotic, ridiculous, out of contact with real social life, living in their dream world. This ambiguity is grounded in the fact that they are figures of "vanishing mediators": they clearly undermine the old balanced universe for which Welles has such a nostalgic fondness (the old small-town idyll of the Ambersons destroyed by industrial progress, etc.), yet they unknowingly lay the ground for their own demise, i.e., there is no place for them in the new world they helped to create.

Moreover, this tension between realist social satire and the hubris of the larger-than-life character is materialized in the radical ambiguity of the Wellesian trademark formal procedure, his manipulation of deep focus, achieved by a wide-angle lens. On the one hand, the depth of field, of course, perfectly conveys the immersion of the individual into a wider social field—individuals are reduced to one of the many focal points in a paratactic social reality; on the other hand, however, deep focus "subjectively" distorts the proper perspective by "curving" the space, and thus confers on it a dream-like "pathological" quality—in short, deep focus registers at the formal level the split between the excessive main figure and the "ordinary" people in the background:

> while there has been a great deal of theoretical discussion about depth of field in the film [*Kane*], rather little has been said about forced depth of perspective. ... Again and again Welles uses deep focus not as a "realistic" mode of perception, but as a way of suggesting a conflict between the characters' instinctual needs and the social or material world that determines their fate. ... The short focal-length of the lens enables him to express the psychology of his characters, to comment upon the relation between character and environment, and also to create a sense of barely contained, almost manic energy, as if the camera, like one of his heroes, were overreaching.[3]

The wide-angle lens thus produces the effect which is the exact opposite of what was celebrated by André Bazin, i.e., of the harmonious realist immersion of the main character into his environs, as one of the focal points of the multilayered reality: the wide lens, rather, emphasizes the gap between the hero and his environs, simultaneously revealing the way in which the hero's excessive libidinal force almost anamorphically distorts reality. The depth of field—which, by way of the wide-angle lens, distorts reality, curves its space by pathologically exaggerating the close-up of the main character, and bestows on the reality which stretches behind a strange, dreamlike quality—thus accentuates the gap that separates the main character from social reality; as such, it directly materializes Wellesian "larger-than-life" subjectivity in all its ambiguity, oscillating between excessive, superman power and pathological ridicule.

One can thus see how the Bazinian notion of the use of depth of field is not simply wrong: it is as if the very distance between the two uses of depth of field in Welles—the Bazinian-realist in which the individual is embedded in the multilayered social reality, and the "excessive" which emphasizes the rift between the individual and his social background—articulates the tension in Welles's work between the liberal-progressive collectivist attitude and the focus on the larger-than-life individual. (A further point to be made about the Wellesian use of depth of field is that it confers a kind of positive ontological density on darkness and shades: when, in an "expressionistic" shot, we perceive in the background an overilluminated object, surrounded on both sides by impenetrable dark shades, this darkness is no longer simply the negative of the positively existing things, but in a way "more real than real objects themselves"—it stands for the dimension of primordial density of matter, out of which definite objects [temporarily] emerge.)

Welles's basic theme—the rise and fall of the larger-than-life character who finally gets his "comeuppance"—allows for different readings. One is the Truffaut reading:

> As [Welles] himself is a poet, a humanist, a liberal, one can see that this good and non-violent man was caught in a contradiction between his own personal feelings and those he has to portray in the parts given him because of his physique. He has resolved the contradiction by becoming a moralistic director, always showing the angel within the beast, the heart in the monster, the secret of the tyrant. This has led him to invent an acting style revealing the fragility behind power, the sensitivity behind strength. ... The weakness of the strong, this is the subject that all of Orson Welles's films have in common.[4]

The obvious problem with this reading is that it romanticizes the monster who is discovered, deep in his heart, to have a fragile, gentle nature—the standard ideological legitimization up to Lenin who, in Stalinist hagiography, was always depicted as deeply moved by cats and children, and brought to tears by Beethoven's *Appassionata*. (The ultimate version of this procedure is to feminize masculinity: a true man is in a passive-feminized relationship toward the divine Absolute whose will he actualizes.) However, Welles does not fall into this ideological trap: for him, the essential "immoral" goodness (life-giving exuberance) of his larger-than-life characters is consubstantial with what their environs perceive as their threatening, "evil," "monstrous" dimension.

The other, opposite reading is the Nietzschean one: the larger-than-life hero is "beyond good and evil" and as such essentially good, life-giving; he is broken by the narrowness and constraints of the self-culpabilizing morality which cannot stand life-asserting Will. The fragility and vulnerability of the Wellesian hero directly follows from his absolute innocence, which remains blind to the twisted ways by means of which morality strives to corrupt and destroy life. (Is not another aspect of this Nietzscheanism Welles's growing fascination with the status of semblance, of a "fake," of the truth of the fake as such, etc.?) This larger-than-life character is exuberant with his generosity, his "beyond-pleasure-principle" and utilitarian considerations.

I am thus tempted to repeat once again, apropos of Welles, Adorno's thesis according to which the truth of Freudian theory resides in the very unresolved contradictions of his theoretical edifice: the inner contradiction of Wellesian subjectivity is irreducible, one cannot assert one side of it as the "truth" of the other side and, say, posit the generous Life-substance as authentic, disclaiming the moral person as an expression of the mediocre crowd intended to suffocate the primordial Goodness beyond good and evil; or, on the contrary, conceive the primordial Life-substance as something which has to be gentrified through the intervention of *logos*, in order to prevent it from turning into a destructive unruliness. Welles himself was clearly aware of this undecidability: "All the characters I've played are various forms of Faust. I hate all forms of Faust, because I believe it's impossible for man to be great without admitting there is something greater than himself—either the law or God or art—but there must be something greater than man. I have sympathy for those characters—humanly but not morally."[5] Welles's terms here are misleading: his larger-than-life figures are in no way "more human" but on the contrary inhuman, foreign to "humanity" in terms of the normal meaning of mediocre human existence with its petty joys, sorrows, and weaknesses. Furthermore, these larger-than-life figures are distributed along the axis which reaches from Falstaff, for Welles the embodiment of essential goodness and life-giving generosity, to Kindler in *The Stranger*, a cruel murderous Nazi (not to mention Harry Lime in Reed's *The Third Man*); in one of his interviews for *Cahiers du Cinéma*, Welles includes in this series even Goering, as opposed to the bureaucratic-mediocre Himmler. How these larger-than-life figures subvert the standard ethico-political oppositions is clear from Thompson's (Kane's collaborator in the film) description of Kane to the reporter, included in the final script but not in the film itself:

> He was the most honest man who ever lived, with a streak of crookedness a yard wide. He was a liberal and a reactionary. He was a loving husband—and both wives left him. He had a gift of friendship such as few men have—and he broke his oldest friend's heart like you'd throw away a cigarette you were through with. Outside of that ...[6]

A simplified Heideggerian reading, which would conceive the Wellesian larger-than-life figure as the purest exemplar of the hubris of modern subjectivity, is also out of place here: the problem is that if subjectivity is to assert itself fully, this excess has to be suppressed, "sacrificed." We are dealing here with the inner split of subjectivity into the larger-than-life excess and its subsequent "normalization," which subordinates it to cold power calculation—it is only by means of this self-suppression or, rather, self-renunciation, this self-imposed limitation, that the hubris of subjectivity loses its extreme vulnerability. Only as such, by means of this self-limitation, can it elude the "comeuppance" waiting for it at the end of the road, and thus truly take over—the move from Falstaff to Prince Hal. Another way to put it is to say that this Faustian larger-than-life figure is a kind of "vanishing mediator" of modern subjectivity, its founding gesture which has to withdraw into its result. (A raw and massive historical analogy to this withdrawal is the way the Renaissance larger-than-life character, with his attitude of excessive generosity and free expenditure, acts as a necessary mediator between hierarchized medieval society and the calculating utilitarian attitude of the modern "disenchanted" world; in this precise sense, Welles himself is a "Renaissance figure.")

3.3 FIGURES OF FATHER-*JOUISSANCE*

The Wellesian antagonism between normal and larger-than-life characters thus cannot be directly translated into a symbolic opposition; the only way to describe it is by means of a repetitive self-referential procedure in which the "higher" pole of the first determination changes its place and becomes the "lower" pole of the next determination. On account of his generosity and life-affirming attitude, the larger-than-life figure is "human," in contrast to the stiff "normal" figure, yet it is simultaneously monstrously excessive with regard to the "humanity" of ordinary men and women. In its self-referential repetition, the "higher" symbolic feature is self-negated: the Wellesian hero is "more human" than ordinary people, yet this very excess of humanity makes him no longer properly "human"—as with Kierkegaard, in whose œuvre the Ethical is the truth of the Aesthetical, yet the very dimension of the Ethical, brought to its extreme, involves its own religious suspension. Welles's ultimate topic, which he approaches again and again from different perspectives, is thus the Real, the impossible kernel, the antagonistic tension, at the very heart of modern subjectivity. This same undecidability is also at work in the Wellesian formal tension between the realistic depiction of community life, and the "expressionistic" excesses of the depth of field: these "expressionistic" excesses (uncanny camera angles, play with light and shadow, etc.) are simultaneously a self-referential excess of form, with regard to the calm and transparent rendering of "social reality," and much closer to the true impetuses and generative forces of social life than the stiff conventions of realism. It is thus not merely that Welles's formal excesses and inconsistencies reveal or stage the inherent inconsistencies of the depicted content; rather, they function as the "return of the repressed" of the depicted content, i.e., their excess is correlative to a hole in the depicted content. The point is not only that the ambiguous use of deep focus and depth of field indexes the ambiguity of the Wellesian ideological project, i.e., Welles's ambivalent attitude toward the larger-than-life Faustian figures which are simultaneously condemned from the liberal-humanist progressive standpoint and function as the obvious object of fascination: if this were so, we would have a simple relation of reflection/mirroring between the formal excess and the content's ideological inconsistency. The point is, rather, that the formal excess reveals the "repressed" truth of the ideological project: Welles's libidinal identification with what his official liberal-democratic view rejects.

In this sense, I am tempted to speak about the Wellesian obscenity of form. That is to say: insofar as the autonomized form is to be conceived as the index of some traumatic repressed content, it is easy to identify the repressed content which emerges in the guise of Welles's formal extravaganzas and the excesses which draw attention to themselves (in *Kane*, in *Touch of Evil*, etc.): the obscene, self-destructive *jouissance* of the noncastrated larger-than-life figure. When, in Welles's later films (notably in *Chimes at Midnight*, although this tendency is already discernible in *Ambersons*), this excess of form largely disappears in favor of a more balanced and transparent narrative, this change bears witness to a shift of emphasis in the structural ambiguity of the larger-than-life figure from its destructive and evil aspect (Quinlan in *Touch of Evil*) to its aspect of pacifying, life-giving goodness (Falstaff in *Chimes*)—the Wellesian formal extravaganzas are at their strongest when the larger-than-life figure is perceived in its destructive aspect.

The central necessity around which the tragic dimension of this Wellesian larger-than-life hero turns is his necessary betrayal by his most devoted friend or successor, who can save his legacy and become "the one who will follow you" only by organizing his downfall. The exemplary case of this fidelity-through-betrayal occurs when the only way for a son to remain faithful to his obscene father is to betray him, as in the turbulent relationship between Falstaff and Prince Hal in Welles's *Chimes at Midnight* where Falstaff is clearly the obscene shadowy double of Hal's official father (King Henry IV). In *Chimes at Midnight*, the most poignant scene is undoubtedly that of renunciation, when Prince Hal, now the newly invested King Henry V, banishes Falstaff: the intense exchange of gazes belies the explicit content of the king's words, and bears witness to a kind of telepathic link between the two, to an almost unbearable compassion and solidarity; the implicit message delivered by the king's desperate gaze is "Please, understand me, I am doing this for the sake of my fidelity to you!"[7] Prince Hal's betrayal of Falstaff as the supreme act of fidelity is furthermore grounded in the concrete political stance of the new king: as is well known, Henry V was a kind of royal counterpoint to Joan of Arc, the first "patriotic" proto-bourgeois king to use wars to forge national unity, appealing to the national pride of ordinary people in order to mobilize them—his wars were no longer the conventional feudal games fought with mercenaries. One could thus claim that Prince Hal "sublated" (in the precise Hegelian sense of *Aufhebung*) his socializing with Falstaff, his mixing with the lower classes, his feeling the pulse of the ordinary people with their "vulgar" amusements: his message to Falstaff is thus: "Only by betraying you can I transpose/integrate what I got from you into my function as king." Even in *Touch of Evil*, one cannot avoid the impression that when the honest Vargas (Charlton Heston) successfully entraps the corrupt Quinlan (Orson Welles), he somehow betrays him. (It is the same with the betrayal of the father: only by betraying him can one assume the paternal symbolic function.)

This trauma of the excessively enjoying father who must be betrayed is at the very root of neurosis: neurosis always involves a perturbed, traumatic relationship to the father: in neurosis, the "sublation" of Father-Enjoyment into the paternal Name fails, the figure of the Father remains marked with a traumatic stain of *jouissance*, and one of the traumatic scenes which brings such a distasteful *jouissance* to the neurotic is the scene of the father either caught "with his pants down," i.e., in an act of excessive, obscene enjoyment, or being humiliated (in both cases, the father is not "at the level of his symbolic mandate"). Such a scene transfixes the hysteric's gaze, it paralyzes him: the encounter with the Real of the paternal *jouissance* turns the hysteric into an immobilized, frozen gaze, like Medusa's head. In Dostoyevsky's *The Brothers Karamazov*, we find both versions of this trauma: the Karamazov father himself is the obscene father, an embarrassing figure indulging in excessive enjoyment; furthermore, we have a scene in which, when Dimitri attacks a poor man, his son, observing them, approaches Dimitri, pulls his sleeve to divert his attention from beating his father, and gently entreats him: "Please, do not beat my father ..."

This is how one is to read the triad Real–Symbolic–Imaginary with regard to the father: the symbolic father is the Name of the Father; the imaginary father is the (respectful, dignified) "self-image" of the father; the real father is the excess of enjoyment whose perception traumatically disturbs this "self-image." The encounter with this trauma can set in motion different strategies to cope with it: the death wish (would that the father die, to stop being such an embarrassment to me—the ultimate source of embarrassment is the very fact that the father is alive); assuming the guilt, i.e., sacrificing myself in order to save the father; etc. The hysterical subject tries to locate the lack in the father that would weaken him, while the obsessional neurotic, who perceives the father's weakness and feels guilty for it, is ready to sacrifice himself for him (and thus to obfuscate his desire to humiliate the father).

Do we not encounter both versions of the obscene father in Wagner? Let us recall the traumatic relationship between Amfortas and Titurel, a true counterpart to the dialogue between Alberich and Hagen from *Twilight of Gods*. The contrast between the two confrontations of father and son is clear: in *Twilight*, the dynamic (nervous agitation, most of the talking) is on the side of the father, with Hagen for the most part merely listening to this obscene apparition; in *Parsifal*, Titurel is an immobile, oppressive presence who barely breaks his silence with the superego injunction "Reveal the Grail!" whereas Amfortas is the dynamic agent giving voice to his refusal to perform the ritual. Is it not clear, if one listens very closely to this dialogue from *Parsifal*, that the truly obscene presence in *Parsifal*, the ultimate cause of the decay of the Grail community, is not Klingsor, who is evidently a mere small-time crook, but rather Titurel himself, an obscene undead apparition, a dirty old man who is so immersed in his enjoyment of the Grail that he perturbs the regular rhythm of its disclosure? The opposition between Alberich and Titurel is thus not the opposition between obscene humiliation and dignity, but rather between the two modes of obscenity itself: between the strong, oppressive father-*jouissance* (Titurel) and the humiliated, agitated, weak father (Alberich).

Is not the ultimate example of the obscene father provided by the Bible itself?

> Noah, a man of the soil, proceeded to plant a vineyard. When he drank some of its wine, he became drunk and lay uncovered inside his tent. Ham, the father of Canaan, saw his father's nakedness and told his two brothers outside. But Shem and Japheth took a garment and laid it across their shoulders; then they walked in backwards and covered their father's nakedness. Their faces were turned the other way, so that they would not see their father's nakedness.
>
> When Noah awoke from his wine and found out what his youngest son had done to him, he said, "Cursed be Canaan! The lowest of slaves will he be to his brothers. (Genesis 9:20–26)

Apart from the enigmatic fact that Noah did not curse Ham directly, but rather Ham's offspring (his son), the fact referred to by some interpretations as the legitimization of slavery (Canaan is often referred to as "black"), the key point is that this scene clearly stages the confrontation with the helpless obscene *Père-Jouissance*: the good sons respectfully look away, cover their father, and thus protect his dignity, while the evil son maliciously trumpets forth his father's helpless obscenity. Symbolic authority is thus grounded in voluntary blindness, it involves a kind of will-not-to-know, the attitude of *je n'en veux rien savoir*—that is to say, about the obscene side of the father.

Where are we today concerning this Wellesian antagonistic tension? In Bryan Singer's *The Usual Suspects*, the tension is no longer the one between the multilayered tapestry of social reality and the hubris of unbridled subjectivity; we are dealing, rather, with the surface of the dispersed series of contingent, meaningless encounters, cynical jokes, and improvisations *à la* Tarantino, beneath which one can gradually discern the paranoiac narrative frame—what is "larger than life" is the conspiracy of the invisible Master who pulls the strings behind the contingent and inconsistent tapestry of our everyday experience. (Or, to put it in a different way: the key to the analysis of *The Usual Suspects* lies in the answer to the question "Why is Kevin Spacey, not Gabriel Byrne, the mysterious Keyser Söze?" Within the Wellesian universe, the mysterious Keyser Söze would undoubtedly have to be Keaton [Gabriel Byrne]—the Wellesian "monster with a heart," and the traditional spectator [myself among them] cannot escape the feeling of disappointment when it is finally revealed that Keyser Söze is the Kevin Spacey character.) An alternative displacement of the Wellesian tension is provided by the films of David Lynch, where the "larger-than-life" dimension is no longer embodied in the pre-Oedipal paternal hero, but is directly portrayed as the horror of the presymbolic spectral life-substance threatening to invade (symbolized) reality.

One can thus see the common feature which links three such seemingly disparate figures as the Wellesian larger-than-life hero, Roark from Ayn Rand's *The Fountainhead*, and Bobby Peru from *Wild at Heart*. All three give body to the excessive nature of drive (signaled in Welles by his oft-repeated story of the scorpion who bites the frog carrying it over the water, although he knows this will mean his death too—he cannot but follow his drive; signaled in Rand by the unconditional character of Roark's insistence on his architectural vocation; signaled in Lynch by Peru's assertion of life in the very act of self-annihilation); in all three, this excess is signaled by a series of features which bear witness to their "autonomy," i.e., independence from petty considerations of profit and other narrow human concerns: after firing his closest collaborator and almost-friend Leland for writing a bad review of Susan's operatic debut, Kane nonetheless finishes this review in the disparaging tone of Leland; when Toohey provokes Roark into telling him what he really thinks about him, Roark retorts that he does not think about him at all; after extorting from Laura Dern her consent, Bobby Peru does not act on it but, in a supreme sovereign gesture, lets her go.[8]

3.4 RANDIAN "SUBJECTIVE DESTITUTION"

What we find in Welles is thus the fundamental tension of male subjectivity, its constitutive oscillation between the Master's excessive expenditure and the subject's attempt to "economize" this excess, to normalize it, to contain it, to inscribe it into the circuit of social exchange, the oscillation best expressed by Bataille's opposition of autonomous sovereignty and economizing heteronomy. It is also easy to discern how this tension refers to Lacan's two matrixes: with regard to the matrix of the four discourses, we are clearly dealing with its upper level, with the shift from the Master to the University discourse; with regard to the formulas of sexuation, we are dealing with the masculine side, with the tension between the universal function (epitomized by the "knowledge" embodied in the agent of the University discourse) and its constitutive exception (the Master's excess). In what, then, would consist the feminine counterpoint to this tension of male subjectivity? Let us elaborate this point apropos of an author who is all too easily dismissed as "phallocratic," Ayn Rand. Rand, who wrote the two absolute bestsellers of the twentieth century, *The Fountainhead* (1943) and *Atlas Shrugged* (1957), yet was (deservedly) ignored and ridiculed as a philosopher, shared with Welles the obsession with larger-than-life figures: her fascination for male figures displaying absolute, unswayable determination of their Will seems to offer the best imaginable confirmation of Sylvia Plath's famous line, "Every woman adores a Fascist." Although it is easy to dismiss the very mention of Rand alongside Welles as an obscene extravaganza—artistically she is, of course, worthless—the properly subversive dimension of her ideological procedure is not to be underestimated: Rand fits into the line of "overconformist" authors who undermine the ruling ideological edifice by their very excessive identification with it. Her over-orthodoxy was directed at capitalism itself, as the title of one of her books (*Capitalism: The Unknown Ideal*) tells us; according to her, the truly heretical thing today is to embrace the basic premise of capitalism without its communitarian, collectivist, welfare, etc., sugarcoating. So what Pascal and Racine were to Jansenism, what Kleist was to German nationalist militarism, what Brecht was to Communism, Rand is to American capitalism.

It was perhaps her Russian origins and upbringing which enabled her to formulate directly the fantasmatic kernel of American capitalist ideology. The elementary ideological axis of her work consists in the opposition between the prime movers, "men of mind," and the second-handers, "mass men." The Kantian opposition between ethical autonomy and heteronomy is here brought to its extreme: the "mass man" is searching for recognition outside himself, his self-confidence and assurance depend on how he is perceived by others; while the prime mover is fully reconciled with himself, relying on his creativity, selfish in the sense that his satisfaction does not depend on getting recognition from others or on sacrificing himself, his innermost drives, for the benefit of others. The prime mover is innocent, delivered from the fear of others, and for that reason without hatred even for his worst enemies (Roark, the "prime mover" in *The Fountainhead*, doesn't actively hate Toohey, his great opponent, he simply doesn't care about him; here is the famous dialogue between the two: "Mr. Roark, we're alone here. Why don't you tell me what you think of me? In any words you wish. No one will hear us." "But I don't think of you."). On the basis of this opposition, Rand elaborates her radically atheistic, life-affirming, "selfish" ethics: the "prime mover" is capable of love for others, this love is even crucial for him since it does not express his contempt for himself, his self-denial, but, on the contrary, the highest self-assertion: love for others is the highest form of properly understood "selfishness," i.e., of my capacity to realize through my relationship with others my own innermost drives. On the basis of this opposition, *Atlas Shrugged* constructs a purely fantasmatic scenario: John Galt, the novel's mysterious hero, assembles all prime movers and organizes their strike—they withdraw from the collectivist oppression of bureaucratized public life. As a result of their withdrawal, social life loses its impetus, social services, from stores to railroads, no longer function, global disintegration sets in, and the desperate society calls the prime movers back; they accept, but on their own terms. What we have here is the fantasy of a man finding the answer to the eternal question "What moves the world?"—the prime movers—and then being able to "stop the motor of the world" by organizing the prime movers' retreat. John Galt succeeds in *suspending* the very circuit of the universe, the "run of *things*," causing its symbolic death and the subsequent rebirth of the New World. The ideological gain of this operation resides in the reversal of roles with regard to our everyday experience of the strike: it is not the workers but the capitalists who go on strike, thus proving that they are the truly productive members of society who do not need others to survive. The hideout to which the prime movers retreat, a secret place in the midst of the Colorado mountains accessible only via a dangerous, narrow passage, is a kind of negative version of Shangri-La, a "utopia of greed": a small town in which unbridled market relations reign, in which the very word "help" is prohibited, in which every service has to be reimbursed by true (gold-covered) money, in which there is no need for pity and self-sacrifice for others.

The Fountainhead gives us a clue to the matrix of intersubjective *relations* which sustains this myth of prime movers. Its four main male characters constitute a kind of Greimasian semiotic square: the architect Howard Roark is the autonomous creative hero; Wynand, the newspaper tycoon, is the failed hero, a man who could have been a "prime mover"—deeply akin to Roark, he got caught in the trap of crowd manipulation (he was not aware of how his media manipulation of the crowd actually makes him a slave who follows the crowd's whims); Keating is a simple conformist, a wholly externalized, "other-oriented" subject; Toohey, Roark's true opponent, is the figure of diabolical Evil, a man who never could have been a prime mover and knows it—he turns his awareness of his worthlessness into the self-conscious hatred of prime movers, i.e., he becomes an Evil Master who feeds the crowd with this hatred. Paradoxically, Toohey is the point of self-consciousness: he is the only one who knows it all—who, even more than Roark, who simply follows his drive, is fully aware of the true state of things. We thus have Roark as the being of pure drive in no need of symbolic recognition (and as such uncannily close to the Lacanian saint—only an invisible line of separation distinguishes them), and the three ways to compromise one's drive: Wynand, Keating, Toohey. The underlying opposition here is that of desire and drive, as exemplified in the tense relationship between Roark and Dominique, his sexual partner. Roark displays perfect indifference toward the Other characteristic of drive, while Dominique remains caught in the dialectic of desire which is the desire of the Other: she is gnawed by the Other's gaze, i.e., by the fact that others, the common people totally insensitive to Roark's achievement, are allowed to stare at it and thus spoil its sublime quality. The only way for her to break out of this deadlock of the Other's desire is to destroy the sublime object in order to save it from becoming the object of the ignorant gaze of others: "You want a thing and it's precious to you. Do you know who is standing ready to tear it out of your hands? You can't know, it may be so involved and so far away, but someone is ready, and you're afraid of them all. ... I never open again any great book I've read and loved. It hurts me to think of the other eyes that have read it and of what they were."[9]

These "other eyes" are the Evil Gaze at its purest, which grounds the paradox of property: if, within a social field, I am to possess an object, this possession must be socially acknowledged, which means that the big Other who vouchsafes this possession of mine must in a way possess it in advance in order to let me have it. I thus never relate directly to the object of my desire: when I cast a desiring glance at the object, I am always-already gazed at by the Other (not only the imaginary other, the competitive-envious double, but primarily the big Other of the symbolic Institution which guarantees property), and this gaze of the Other which oversees me in my desiring capacity is in its very essence "castrative," threatening. That is the elementary castrative matrix of the dialectics of possession: if I am truly to possess an object, I have first to lose it, i.e., to concede that its primordial owner is the big Other. In traditional monarchies, this place of the big Other is occupied by the king, who in principle owns all the land, so that whatever individual landowners possess was given, granted, to them by the king; this castrative dialectic reaches its extreme in the case of the totalitarian leader who, on the one hand, emphasizes again and again how he is nothing in himself, how he only embodies and expresses the will, creativity, etc., of the people, but, on the other hand, gives us everything we have, so we must be grateful to him for everything we have, right down to our meager daily bread and our health. At the level of drive, however, immediate possession is possible, one can dispose of the Other, in contrast to the everyday order of desire in which the only way to remain free is to sacrifice everything one cares for, to destroy it, never to have a job one wants and enjoys, to marry a man one absolutely despises. ...

So, for Dominique, the greatest sacrilege is to throw pearls to swine: to create a precious object and then expose it to the Other's evil Gaze, i.e., to let it be shared with the crowd. And she treats herself in precisely the same way: she tries to resolve the deadlock of her position as a desired object by willingly embracing, even searching for, the utmost humiliation—she marries the person she most despises and tries to ruin the career of Roark, the true object of her love and admiration. Roark, of course, is well aware of how her attempts to ruin him result from her desperate strategy to cope with her unconditional love for him, to inscribe this love in the field of the big Other; so, when she offers herself to him, he repeatedly rejects her and tells her that the time is not yet ripe: she will become his true partner only when her desire for him is no longer bothered by the Other's gaze—in short, when she accomplishes the shift from desire to drive. The (self-)destructive dialectics of Dominique, as well as of Wynand, bears witness to the fact that they are fully aware of the terrifying challenge of Roark's position of pure drive: they want to break him down in order to deliver him from the clutches of his drive.

This dialectics provides the key to what is perhaps the crucial scene in *The Fountainhead*: Dominique, while riding a horse, encounters Roark on a lonely country road, working as a simple stonecutter in her father's mine; unable to endure the insolent way he looks back at her, the look which attests to his awareness of her inability to resist being attracted to him, Dominique furiously whips him (in the film version, this violent encounter is rendered as the archetypal scene of the mighty landlord's lady or daughter secretly observing the attractive slave: unable to admit to herself that she is irresistibly attracted to him, she acts out her embarrassment in a furious whipping of the slave). She whips him, she is his Master confronting a slave, but her whipping is an act of despair, an awareness of *his* hold over *her*, of her inability to resist him—as such, it is already an invitation to brutal rape. So the first act of love between Dominique and Roark is a brutal rape done with no compassion:

> He did it as an act of scorn. Not as love, but as defilement. And this made her lie still and submit. One gesture of tenderness from him—and she would have remained cold, untouched by the thing done to her body. But the act of a master taking shameful, contemptuous possession of her was the kind of rapture she had wanted.[10]

This scorn is paralleled by Dominique's unconditional willingness to destroy Roark—the willingness which is the strongest expression of her love for him; the following quote bears witness to the fact that Rand is in effect a kind of feminine version of Otto Weininger:

> I'm going to fight you—and I'm going to destroy you—and I tell you this as calmly as I told you that I'm a begging animal. I'm going to pray that you can't be destroyed—I tell you this, too—even though I believe in nothing and have nothing to pray to. But I will fight to block every step you take. I will fight to tear every chance you want away from you. I will hurt you

through the only thing that can hurt you—through your work. I will fight to starve you, to strangle you on the things you won't be able to reach. I have done it to you today—and that is why I shall sleep with you tonight. ... I'll come to you whenever I have beaten you—whenever I know that I have hurt you—and I'll let you own me. I want to be owned, not by a lover, but by an adversary who will destroy my victory over him, not with honorable blows, but with the tough of his body on mine.[11]

The woman strives to destroy the precious *agalma* which is what she doesn't possess in her beloved man, the spark of his excessive autonomous creativity: she is aware that only in this way, by destroying his *agalma* (or, rather, by making him renounce it), will she own him, only in this way will the two of them form an ordinary couple; yet she is also aware that in this way, he will become worthless. Therein lies her tragic predicament. Is then, *in ultima analisi*, the scenario of *The Fountainhead* not that of Wagner's *Parsifal*? Roark is Parsifal the saint, the being of pure drive; Dominique is Kundry in search of her deliverance; Gail is Amfortas, the failed saint; Toohey is Klingsor, the impotent evil magician. Like Dominique, Kundry wants to destroy Parsifal, since she has a foreboding of his purity; like Dominique, Kundry simultaneously wants Parsifal not to give way, to endure his ordeal, since she is aware that her only chance of redemption lies in Parsifal's resistance to her seductive charms.

Parsifal resists Kundry's advances by means of his identification with Amfortas's wound: at the very moment of Kundry's kiss, he retreats from her embrace, shouts "Amfortas! The wound!" and seizes his thigh (the site of Amfortas's wound); as Elisabeth Bronfen has demonstrated in a penetrating analysis, this comically pathetic gesture by Parsifal is that of hysterical identification, i.e., a step into the hysterical theater.[12] The true hysteric of the opera, of course, is Kundry, and it is as if Parsifal's very rejection of her contaminates him with hysteria. The main weapon and index of Kundry's hysteria is her laughter, so it is crucial to probe its origins: the primordial scene of laughter is the Way of the Cross, where Kundry was observing the suffering Christ and laughing at him. This laughter then repeats itself again and again apropos of every master Kundry serves (Klingsor, Gurnemanz, Amfortas, Parsifal): she undermines the position of each of them by means of the surplus-knowledge contained in her hysterical, obscene laughter which reveals the fact that the master is impotent, a semblance of himself. This laughter is thus profoundly ambiguous: it stands not only for making a mockery of the other, but also for despair at herself, i.e., for her repeated failure to find a reliable support in the Master. The question that one should raise here is that of the parallel between Amfortas's and Christ's wounds: what do the two have in common? In what sense is Amfortas (who was wounded when he succumbed to Kundry's temptation) occupying the same position as

Christ? The only consistent answer, of course, is that Christ himself was not pure in his suffering: when Kundry observed him on the Way of the Cross, she detected his obscene *jouissance*, i.e., the way he was "turned on" by his suffering. What Kundry is desperately searching for in men is, on the contrary, somebody who would be able to resist the temptation of converting his pain into a perverse enjoyment.

Back to Rand: the true conflict in the universe of her two novels is thus not between the prime movers and the crowd of second-handers who parasitize on the prime movers' productive genius, with the tension between the prime mover and his feminine sexual partner being a mere secondary subplot of this principal conflict. The true conflict runs within the prime movers themselves: it resides in the (sexualized) tension between the prime mover, the being of pure drive, and his hysterical partner, the potential prime mover who remains caught in the deadly self-destructive dialectic (between Roark and Dominique in *The Fountainhead*, between John Galt and Dagny in *Atlas Shrugged*). When, in *Atlas Shrugged*, one of the prime-mover figures tells Dagny, who unconditionally wants to pursue her work and keep the transcontinental railroad company running, that the prime movers' true enemy is not the crowd of second-handers but herself, this is to be taken literally. Dagny herself is aware of it: when prime movers start to disappear from public productive life, she suspects a dark conspiracy, a "destroyer" who forces them to withdraw and thus gradually brings the whole of social life to a standstill; what she does not yet see is that the figure of "destroyer" that she identifies as the ultimate enemy is the figure of her true Redeemer. The solution occurs when the hysterical subject finally gets rid of her enslavement and recognizes in the figure of the "destroyer" her Savior. Why? Second-handers possess no ontological consistency of their own, which is why the key to the solution is not to break them, but to break the chain which forces the creative prime movers to work for them—when this chain is broken, the second-handers' power will dissolve by itself. The chain which links a prime mover to the perverted existing order is none other than her attachment to her productive genius: a prime mover is ready to pay any price, up to the utter humiliation of nourishing the very force which works against her, i.e., which parasitizes on the activity she officially endeavors to suppress, just to be able to continue to create.

What the hystericized prime mover must accept is thus the fundamental existential indifference: she must no longer be willing to remain the hostage of the second-handers' blackmail ("We will let you work and realize your creative potential, on condition that you accept our terms"); she must be ready to give up the very kernel of her being, that which means everything to her, and to accept the "end of the world," the (temporary) suspension of the very flow of energy which keeps the world running. In order to gain everything, she must be ready to go through the zero-point of losing everything. And, far from indicating the "end of subjectivity," this act of assuming existential indifference is, perhaps, the very gesture of absolute negativity which gives birth to the subject. What Lacan calls "subjective destitution" is thus, paradoxically, another name for the subject itself, i.e., for the void beyond the theater of hysterical subjectivizations.

3.5 THE UNIFIED THEORY

The reference to *Parsifal* brings us back to the matrix of the four discourses: Wynand, the failed Master; Toohey, the corrupted agent of Knowledge; the hysterical Dominique; and Roark the analyst, i.e., the subject who assumed subjective destitution. This matrix provides the two versions of everyday subjectivity, the subject of the University discourse ("instrumental reason," the self-effacing manipulator)[13] and the hysterical subject (the subject engaged in the permanent questioning of her being), as well as the two versions of the "larger-than-life" subjectivity: the (masculine) Master who finds fulfillment in gestures of excessive expenditure, and the (feminine) desubjectivized being of pure drive. One can also see, now, how the matrix of the four discourses is to be sexualized: its upper level (Master–University) reproduces the constitutive tension of masculine subjectivity, while its lower level (Hysteric–Analyst) reproduces the constitutive tension of feminine subjectivity. Welles's films focus on the shift from Master to University, from the constitutive Excess to the series this excess grounds, i.e., on the traumatic necessity of the Master's betrayal; while Rand's universe is centered on the shift from the hysterical ambivalence of desire (the need to destroy what one loves, etc.) to the self-contained circuit of drive. The hysteric's logic is that of the non-All (for a hysteric, the set is never complete—there is always something missing, although one can never pinpoint what, exactly, is missing), while drive involves the closure of a circular movement with no exception (the space of drive is like that of the universe in relativity theory: it is finite, although it has no external boundary).

The matrix of the four discourses thus contains two radically different narratives which are not to be confused: the standard masculine narrative of the struggle between the exceptional One (Master, Creator) and the "crowd" which follows the universal norm, as well as the feminine narrative of the shift from desire to drive, i.e., from the hysteric's entanglement in the deadlocks of the Other's desire to the fundamental indifference of the desubjectivized being of drive. For that reason, the Randian hero is not "phallocratic"; rather, the figure of the failed Master (Wynand in *The Fountainhead*, Stadler in *Atlas Shrugged*) is phallocratic: paradoxical as it may sound, with regard to the formulas of sexuation, the being of pure drive that emerges once the subject "goes through the fantasy" and assumes the attitude of indifference toward the enigma of the Other's desire is a feminine figure. What Rand was not aware of was that the upright, uncompromising masculine figures with a will of steel with which she was so fascinated are in effect figures of the feminine subject liberated from the deadlocks of hysteria.[14] It is thus a thin, almost imperceptible line that separates Rand's ideological and literary trash from the ultimate feminist insight.

Such a reading of the feminine "formulas of sexuation" also enables us to draw a crucial theoretical conclusion about the limits of subjectivity: hysteria is not the limit of subjectivity, there is a subject beyond hysteria. What we get after "traversing the fantasy," i.e., the pure being of drive that emerges after the subject undergoes "subjective destitution," is not a kind of subjectless loop of the repetitive movement of drive, but, on the contrary, the subject at its purest: I am almost tempted to say, the subject "as such." Saying "Yes!" to the drive, i.e., precisely to that which can never be subjectivized, freely assuming the inevitable, i.e., the drive's radical closure, is the highest gesture of subjectivity. It is thus only after assuming a fundamental indifference toward the Other's desire, getting rid of the hysterical game of subjectivizations, after suspending the intersubjective game of mutual (mis)recognition, that the pure subject emerges. The answer to the question: Where, in the four subjective positions that I have elaborated, do we encounter the Lacanian subject, the subject of the unconscious? is thus, paradoxically: in the very discourse in which the subject undergoes "subjective destitution" and identifies with the excremental remainder which forever resists subjectivization.

3.6 APPENDIX: HISTORY AND SEXUAL NON-RELATIONSHIP

The ultimate obstacle to the sexual relationship is, of course, history itself, history at its most radical—not just a combination of narratives (stories), but the dense inertia and opacity of the Real. This is how history is presented in Rossellini's *Voyage in Italy*: as the traumatic Third, the Real which lurks in the background, going its own way, indifferent to the plight of individuals. The ideological traps that lurk here are best represented by the gap that separates the two versions of *Solaris*, Stanisław Lem's classic science-fiction novel and Andrei Tarkovsky's cinema version. *Solaris* is the story of a space-agency psychologist, Kelvin, sent to a half-abandoned spaceship above a newly discovered planet, Solaris, where, recently, strange things have been taking place (scientists going mad, hallucinating and killing themselves). Solaris is a planet with an oceanic fluid surface which moves incessantly and, from time to time, imitates recognizable forms—not only elaborate geometric structures, but also gigantic child bodies or human buildings; although all attempts to communicate with the planet fail, scientists entertain the hypothesis that Solaris is a gigantic brain which somehow reads our minds. Soon after his arrival, Kelvin finds by his side in his bed his dead wife, Hari, who, years ago on Earth, killed herself after he had abandoned her. He is unable to shake Hari off, all attempts to get rid of her fail miserably (after he sends her into space with a rocket, she rematerializes the next day); analysis of her tissue demonstrates that she is not composed of atoms like normal human beings—beneath a certain microlevel, there is nothing, just a void. Finally, Kelvin grasps that Hari is a materialization of his own innermost traumatic fantasies. Solaris, this gigantic Brain, directly materializes our innermost fantasies which support our desire; it is a machine that generates/ materializes in reality itself my ultimate fantasmatic objectal supplement/ partner that I would never be ready to accept in reality, although my entire psychic life turns around it.

Read in this way, the story is really about the hero's inner journey, about his attempt to come to terms with his repressed truth—or, as Tarkovsky himself put it in an interview apropos of Solaris: "Maybe, effectively, the mission of Kelvin on Solaris has only one goal: to show that love of the other is indispensable to all life. A man without love is no longer a man. The aim of the entire 'solaristic' is to show humanity that there must be love." In clear contrast to this, Lem's novel focuses on the inert external presence of the planet Solaris, of this "Thing which thinks" (to use Kant's expression, which is a perfect fit here): the point of the novel is precisely that Solaris remains an impenetrable Other with no possible communication with us— true, it returns to us our innermost disavowed fantasies, but the Che vuoi? beneath this act remains thoroughly impenetrable (why does It do it? As a purely mechanical response? To play demonic games with us? To help us— or compel us—to confront our disavowed truth?). It would thus be interesting to include Tarkovsky's in the series of Hollywood commercial rewritings of novels that have served as the basis for a movie: Tarkovsky does exactly the same as the most lowly Hollywood producer, reinscribing the enigmatic encounter with Otherness into the framework of the production of the couple. In contrast to Tarkovsky's regressive gesture, Lem's novel remains faithful to the minimal frame best encapsulated by "Knock," the shortest story ever told, Fredric Brown's "sweet little action story that is only two sentences long": "The last man on Earth sat alone in a room. There was a knock on the door." This is the situation of a subject at its minimal, ontologically prior to every intersubjectivity: the sudden intrusion of an otherness which is not yet another One.

A different, less ideological, way to relate the vicissitudes of sexual lives to history is illustrated in one of the masterpieces of contemporary Chinese cinema, Jia Zhangke's Still Life, which can be said to reinvent Rossellini and

Antonioni in a Chinese mode, providing a Chinese non-Hollywood twist to the "production of the couple." The irony is that the building of the Three Gorges dam, this brutal and gigantic human intervention into the natural environment, the embodiment of collective human activity, is depicted as the inert Real which provides the background to the couple's vicissitudes, like the ancient ruins in Rossellini's *Voyage to Italy*. The film can in effect be designated an exercise in "socialist formalism": its beauty resides in its "time image," not "time movement": the protracted moments when, narratively, "nothing happens," the camera just wanders around the background of decay, flood, and buildings falling apart—the looming presence of the dam is the film's "situation." ... Although the historic Real in the background is the social and ecological nightmare of the biggest dam ever blocking natural water flow, the film wisely abstains from direct sociocritical commentary, limiting itself to showing its "apolitical" effects.

Still Life takes place in what is left of Fengjie, a ghost town in the process of being drowned because of the Three Gorges dam—when one of the heroes asks where a certain street is, someone points to the middle of the river; higher on the banks, deserted buildings rot in the summer heat; except for the elderly, who are too tired to move, and the groups of workmen slowly demolishing the remaining buildings with hand tools, just about everyone has vanished. The film's (and town's) time is the empty time between the socialist past and the capitalist future: as far as we can see, there is no social structure or authority, and the commercial life of capitalism has not taken hold. Inanition and mere things have overwhelmed the human presence, as in Antonioni's empty urban landscapes of the Po Valley.

Two individual stories are set against this background. Sanming, a coal miner from Shanxi, arrives in Fengjie in search of the wife and daughter he lost sixteen years ago; the address given to him is now a strip of grass in the vast body of water created by the dam. To earn money, he participates in the very destruction that consumed his old home, helping to tear down buildings earmarked for demolition; however, despite being a willing agent in the destruction of his country's memory, his endeavor to connect his past and his future places him in sharp contrast to this rush to destroy centuries of culture in order to pursue an insanely rapid pace of prosperity. The death of one of the men he befriends leads directly to his own symbolic rebirth, when at the conclusion of his story he returns to Shanxi with a renewed life purpose. In the second story, Shen Hong, a nurse, searches for her husband who abandoned her two years before. The husband also works on demolishing buildings; however, in contrast to Sanming, he is in a much higher social class, overseeing a large staff; he also hires local thugs to persuade those reluctant to leave their homes to make way for the demolition. Shen Hong's story also ends with a subjective decision: when she is reunited with her husband, she asks him for a divorce. In both stories, the inert background of the "situation" (the flooded city, i.e., culture being overtaken by nature) is contrasted with subjective acts at the individual level.

Although Sanming and Shen Hong never meet, their stories are connected by visual tropes which counteract the downbeat realism of the story. More generally, the whole of Still Life is characterized by the properly dialectical tension between form and content, a tension which brings to mind not so much Rossellini and Antonioni as, rather, Robert Altman. Altman's universe, best exemplified by his masterpiece Short Cuts, is that of contingent encounters between a multitude of series, a universe in which different series communicate and resonate on the level of what Altman himself refers to as "subliminal reality" (meaningless mechanical shocks, encounters, and impersonal intensities which precede the level of social meaning). So, when, in Nashville, violence explodes at the end (the murder of Barbara Jean at the concert), this explosion, although unheralded and unaccounted for on the level of the explicit narrative line, is nonetheless experienced as fully justified, since the ground for it was laid at the level of signs circulating in the film's "subliminal reality." This also means that one should avoid the temptation of reducing Altman to a poet of American alienation, depicting the silent despair of everyday lives: there is another Altman, the Altman of opening oneself to joyful contingent encounters. Along the same lines as Deleuze and Guattari's reading of Kafka's universe of the Absence of the inaccessible and elusive transcendent Center (Castle, Court, God) as the Presence of multiple passages and transformations, I am tempted to read Altmanian "despair and anxiety" as the deceptive obverse of the more affirmative immersion into the multitude of subliminal intensities.

Mutatis mutandis, the same goes for Still Life. Despite the obvious desolation and depression engendered by the film's content, the underlying mood, expressed by its formal texture, is one of melancholic beauty and an affirmation of life: the river and the green mountains on both sides of the dam extend into the distance in majestic panoply; gray clouds hang over the scene like painted backdrops; the air is moist and palpable; even the thick rusted pipes of abandoned factories seem to breathe. This aesthetic evokes another name: Tarkovsky, in whose films, exemplarily in his masterpiece Stalker, postindustrial wasteland abounds, with wild vegetation growing over abandoned factories, concrete tunnels and railroads full of stale water, and wild overgrowth in which stray cats and dogs wander. Nature and industrial civilization are overlapping again here, but through a common decay— civilization in decay is in the process of again being reclaimed (not by idealized harmonious Nature, but) by nature in decomposition. The ultimate Tarkovskyan landscape is that of humid nature: a river or pool close to some forest, full of the debris of human artifice (old concrete blocks or pieces of rusting metal).

We should thus distinguish three levels in *Still Life*: the individual one (the stories of the two heroes), the particular one (the social content, the process of human industrial activity), and the universal one (the image of the universe presented by the cinematic form itself). The dialectics of the film resides in the complex interactions of these three levels, with all possible "strategic alliances" of the two terms against the third one: individuals as agents of the Social opposed to Nature; individuals in solidarity with decaying Nature against the devastating social process; Nature and the Social blended together into an objectivized Substance opposing individuals.

It is in this respect that *Still Life* is superior to Kim Ki-duk's much more popular *Spring, Summer, Fall, Winter ... and Spring*. Feminists were, for once, right to protest against this film—the "natural cycle" it presents is worth a closer look: we are deep in Wagnerian-Weiningerian waters. First, we have a wise Buddhist monk and a small innocent boy who is playing around, his only sin being that he likes to tie small stones to animals. Then, a couple of years later, a young woman arrives to be healed, and chaos is unleashed: the boy—now an adolescent—and the woman copulate, and the boy follows her to the city, abandoning his lonely dwelling on a raft that floats on a mountain lake. A few years afterward, the boy, now a man in his early thirties, returns, pursued by two detectives: out of jealousy, he killed the woman, thus realizing the prophecy of the old monk who had warned him that love for a woman leads to attachment, which ends in killing the object of attachment. A decade or more later, after the monk's ritual suicide, the man returns (he has served his prison term for murder) and takes over the lake dwelling, becoming a monk. Later, in winter, a young woman, her face completely covered with a transparent cloth, brings to his dwelling a small boy and leaves him there, falling through cracking ice as she is leaving. So we are again in spring where we started: a monk with a young boy pupil. ... The role of woman here fits the coordinates of Kundry in *Parsifal*: either an object of lust, causing man's fall and her own death, or a faceless/nameless mother whose fate is to deliver her child and then erase herself from the picture—the good old duality of whore and mother has rarely been presented in such a pure form.

The first thing to do here is to take the film's cycle more literally than it takes itself: why does the young man kill his love when she abandons him for another man? Why is his love so possessive? An average man in secular life would have accepted it, however painful it would have been for him. What if it is his very Buddhist-monk upbringing that made him do it? That is to say: what if woman appears only as an object of lust and possession, which ultimately provokes the man to kill her *from the Buddhist position of detachment*? So the whole "natural cycle" that the film deploys, murder included, is internal to the Buddhist universe. Although it may appear that *Still Life* also flirts with this "oriental" notion of the life cycle that transcends human concerns, the three-level dialectic undermines the stability of each level, so that the natural cycle itself loses its "eternal" character of the "big Other" and gets caught up in historical dynamics: it is implicitly denounced as what individuals melancholically imagine in order to be able to endure the traumatic impact of history.

CHAPTER 4

TRANSREAL, TRANSHUMAN, TRANSGENDER

4.1 UPS, AGAIN

We have now reached the vantage point from which we can return to the point of departure, the triad of UPS: the "universal" Void (the impossibility of One) constitutive of the order of Being as such; the impossibility of the sexual relationship constitutive of sexual difference; the impossibility of the social relationship constitutive of capitalism. At each level, the Void of impossibility is correlative to a surplus (paradoxical elements like the Higgs particle in quantum ontology, *objet a* in sexuality, "rabble" in modern society). The main danger to be avoided here at any price is the transposition of this triad into an ontological classification, as if the barred One grounds universal ontology, the inexistence of sexual relationship grounds the human sphere as one of the particular regions of being, and the Void around which capital circulates grounds the capitalist social order in its singularity. The triad of UPS is, rather, reflected into each level: the impossibility of One underlies the universal order of being; the impossibility of sexual relationship grounds sexual particularization, the allotment to each individual of a particular sexual position; capitalism is a singularity among modes of production, not just one particular mode among others but the exception, the symptomal point at which the antagonism proper to class societies appears at its purest. But, even more radically, from our singular standpoint, the three levels are telescoped into the capitalist singularity so that we cannot analyze the ontological impossibility of One independently of sexual difference, and we cannot analyze sexual difference independently of experiencing the capitalist singularity. It is only the capitalist experience that—precisely insofar as it dissolves not only estates and other forms of social hierarchy, but also sexual hierarchy— enables us to grasp the impossibility of the sexual relationship (in homology to class struggle); the process of capitalist self-reproduction also enables us to perceive the basic ontological paradox of the Void generating excess. What this means is that, as Lacan put it, there is no metalanguage; Mao was wrong when he deployed his Olympian vision reducing human experience to a tiny unimportant detail: "The United States cannot annihilate the Chinese nation with its small stack of atom bombs. Even if the US atom bombs were so powerful that, when dropped on China, they would make a hole right through the earth, or even blow it up, that would hardly mean anything to the universe as a whole, though it might be a major event for the solar system."[1]

There is an "inhuman madness" in this argument: is not the fact that the destruction of planet Earth "would hardly mean anything to the universe as a whole" a rather poor solace for extinguished humanity? The argument works only if, in a Kantian way, one presupposes a pure transcendental subject unaffected by this catastrophe—a subject which, although nonexistent in reality, is operative as a virtual point of reference (recall Husserl's dark dream, from his *Cartesian Meditations*, of how the transcendental *cogito* would remain unaffected by a plague that annihilated the whole of humanity). In contrast to such a stance of cosmic indifference, we should act as if the entire universe was created as a background for the struggle of emancipation, in exactly the same way as, for Kant, God created the world in order to serve as the battleground for the ethical struggle of humanity—it is as if the fate of the entire universe is decided in our singular (and, from the global cosmic standpoint, marginal and insignificant) struggle.

This paradox enables us to formulate the ultimate line of demarcation between ontology and its beyond: it is not enough to say that the subject can emerge only if the Void itself is "barred" by impossibility—such a view remains within the space of general ontology, where the subject appears as a specific case of the barred Void. But if we reject a "general ontology" of less-than-nothing (or even of the "impossible-barred One") which then, applied to humanity, gives us an antagonistic subject, how, then, can we avoid a relapse into subjectivism (subject as the unsurpassable horizon)?

The paradox is that, although (human) subjectivity is obviously not the origin of all reality, although it is a contingent local event in the universe, the path to universal truth does not lead through abstraction from it in the well-known sense of "let's try to imagine how the world is independently of us," the approach which brings us to some "gray" objective structure—such a vision of a "subjectless" world is by definition just a negative image of subjectivity itself, its own vision of the world in its absence. (The same holds for all the attempts to picture humanity as an insignificant species on a small planet on the edge of our galaxy, i.e., to view it in the same way as we view a colony of ants.) Since we are subjects, constrained to the horizon of subjectivity, we should instead focus on what the fact of subjectivity implies for the universe and its structure: the event of the subject derails the balance, it throws the world out of joint, but such a derailment *is* the universal truth of the world. And, insofar as the subject is in its very core sexed, the only access to the Real for us is through the impasse of sexuation—through the *impasses* of sexuation, which have nothing whatsoever to do with traditional sexualized cosmologies (the universe as the eternal struggle between masculine and feminine principles).

What this also implies is that the access to "reality in itself" does not demand from us that we overcome our "partiality" and arrive at a neutral vision elevated above our particular struggles—we are "universal beings" only in our full partial engagements. This contrast is clearly discernible in the case of love: against the Buddhist love of All, or any other notion of harmony with the cosmos, we should assert the radically exclusive love for the singular One, a love which throws out of joint the smooth flow of our lives.

The most elementary form of this partiality is the symbolic order itself, which always and by definition provides a partial/twisted view of reality: the reality we see and interact with is always and by definition "augmented" by our virtual supplements, and these supplements, instead of separating us from the Real, are the very site of the inscription of the Real. Let me make this key point somewhat clearer by (yet again) referring to one of my standard examples: Lévi-Strauss's analysis, from his *Structural Anthropology*, of the spatial disposition of buildings in the Winnebago, one of the Great Lakes tribes. The tribe is divided into two subgroups ("moieties"), "those who are from above" and "those who are from below"; when we ask an individual to draw on a piece of paper, or on sand, the ground plan of his/her village (the spatial disposition of cottages), we obtain two quite different answers, depending on his/her membership of one or the other subgroup. Both perceive the village as a circle; but for one subgroup, there is within this circle another circle of central houses, so that we have two concentric circles, while for the other subgroup, the circle is split into two by a clear dividing line. In other words, a member of the first subgroup (let us call it "conservative-corporatist") perceives the ground plan of the village as a ring of houses more or less symmetrically disposed around the central temple, whereas a member of the second ("revolutionary-antagonistic") subgroup perceives his/her village as two distinct heaps of houses separated by an invisible frontier.[2] The point Lévi-Strauss wants to make is that this example should in no way entice us into cultural relativism, according to which the perception of social space depends on the observer's group-belonging: the very splitting into the two "relative" perceptions implies a hidden reference to a constant—not the objective, "actual" disposition of buildings but a traumatic kernel, a fundamental antagonism the inhabitants of the village were unable to symbolize, to account for, to "internalize," to come to terms with, an imbalance in social relations that prevented the community from stabilizing itself into a harmonious whole. The two perceptions of the ground plan are simply two mutually exclusive endeavors to cope with this traumatic antagonism, to heal its wound via the imposition of a balanced symbolic structure. It is here that one can see in what precise sense the Real intervenes through anamorphosis. We have first the "actual," "objective," arrangement of the houses, and then its two different symbolizations which both distort, in an anamorphic way, the actual arrangement. However, the "real" here is not the actual arrangement, but the traumatic core of the social antagonism which distorts the tribe members' view of the actual antagonism.

The Real is thus the disavowed X on account of which our vision of reality is anamorphically distorted. It is simultaneously the Thing to which direct access is not possible *and* the obstacle which prevents this direct access; the Thing which eludes our grasp *and* the distorting screen which makes us miss the Thing. More precisely, the Real is ultimately the very shift of perspective from the first to the second standpoint: the Lacanian Real is not only distorted, but *the very principle of the distortion* of reality. And—back to our starting point—it is in this reflexive reversal, in this properly speculative coincidence ("identity") of what is distorted and the principle of distortion, that the passage from Kant to Hegel resides. This structure of distortion deserves a closer look.

4.2   ANTI-SEMITISM AND OTHER POKÉMON GAMES

Released in July 2016, Pokémon Go is a location-based, augmented-reality game for mobile devices, typically played on mobile phones; players use the device's GPS and camera to capture, battle, and train virtual creatures ("Pokémon") who appear on the screen as if they were in the same real-world location as the player: as players travel the real world, their avatar moves along the game's map. Different Pokémon species reside in different areas—for example, water-type Pokémon are generally found near water. When a player encounters a Pokémon, AR (Augmented Reality) mode uses the camera and gyroscope on the player's mobile device to display an image of a Pokémon as though it were in the real world.[3] This AR mode is what makes Pokémon Go different from other PC games: instead of taking us out of the real world and drawing us into the artificial virtual space, it combines the two; we look at reality and interact with it through the fantasy frame of the digital screen, and this intermediary frame supplements reality with virtual elements which sustain our desire to participate in the game, push us to look for them in a reality which, without this frame, would leave us indifferent. Sound familiar? Of course it does. What the technology of Pokémon Go externalizes is simply the basic mechanism of ideology—at its most basic, ideology is the primordial version of "augmented reality."

The first step in this direction of technology imitating ideology was taken a couple of years ago by Pranav Mistry, a member of the Fluid Interfaces

Group at the MIT Media Lab, who developed a wearable "gestural interface" called "SixthSense."[4] The hardware—a small webcam which dangles from one's neck, a pocket projector, and a mirror, all connected wirelessly to a smartphone in one's pocket—forms a wearable mobile device. The user begins by handling objects and making gestures; the camera recognizes and tracks the user's hand gestures and the physical objects using computer-vision-based techniques. The software processes the video stream data, reading it as a series of instructions, and retrieves the appropriate information (texts, images, etc.) from the Internet; the device then projects this information onto any physical surface available—all surfaces, walls, and physical objects around the wearer can serve as interfaces. Here are some examples of how it works: In a bookstore, I pick up a book and hold it in front of me; immediately, I see projected onto the book's cover its reviews and ratings. I can navigate a map displayed on a nearby surface, zoom in, zoom out, or pan across, using intuitive hand movements. I make a sign of @ with my fingers and a virtual PC screen with my email account is projected onto any surface in front of me; I can then write messages by typing on a virtual keyboard. And one could go much further here—just think how such a device could transform sexual interaction. (It suffices to concoct, along these lines, a sexist male dream: just look at a woman, make the appropriate gesture, and the device will project a description of her relevant characteristics—divorced, easy to seduce, likes jazz and Dostoyevsky, good at fellatio, etc., etc.) In this way, the entire world becomes a "multi-touch surface," while the whole Internet is constantly mobilized to supply additional data allowing me to orient myself.

Mistry emphasized the physical aspect of this interaction: until now, the Internet and computers have isolated the user from the surrounding environment; the archetypal Internet user is a geek sitting alone in front of a screen, oblivious to the reality around him. With SixthSense, I remain engaged in physical interaction with objects: the alternative "either physical reality or the virtual screen world" is replaced by a direct interpenetration of the two. The projection of information directly onto the real objects with which I interact creates an almost magical and mystifying effect: things appear to continuously reveal—or, rather, emanate—their own interpretation. This quasi-animist effect is a crucial component of the IoT: "Internet of things? These are nonliving things which talk to us, although they really shouldn't talk. A rose, for example, which tells us that it needs water."[5] (Note the irony of this statement: it misses the obvious fact: a rose is alive.) But, of course, this unfortunate rose does not do what it "shouldn't" do: it is merely connected with measuring apparatuses which let us know that it needs water (or they just pass this message directly to a watering machine). The rose itself knows nothing about it; everything happens in the digital big Other, so the appearance of animism (we communicate with a rose) is a mechanically generated illusion.

However, this magic effect of SixthSense does not simply represent a radical break with our everyday experience; rather, it openly stages what was always the case. That is to say: in our everyday experience of reality, the "big Other"—the dense symbolic texture of knowledge, expectations, prejudices, and so on—continuously fills in the gaps in our perception. For example, when a Western racist stumbles upon a poor Arab on the street, does he not "project" a complex of such prejudices and expectations onto the Arab, and thus "perceive" him in a certain way? This is why SixthSense presents us with another case of ideology at work in technology: the device imitates and materializes the ideological mechanism of (mis)recognition which overdetermines our everyday perceptions and interactions.

And does not something similar happen in Pokémon Go? To simplify things to the utmost, did Hitler not offer the Germans the fantasy frame of Nazi ideology which made them see a specific Pokémon—"the Jew"—popping up all around, and providing the clue to what one has to fight against? And does the same not hold for all other ideological pseudo-entities which have to be added to reality in order to make it complete and meaningful? One can easily imagine a contemporary anti-immigrant version of Pokémon Go where the player wanders about a German city and is threatened by Muslim immigrant rapists or thieves lurking everywhere.

Here we encounter the crucial question: is the form the same in all these cases, or is the anti-Semitic conspiracy theory which makes us see the Jewish plot as the source of our troubles formally different from the Marxist approach which observes social life as a battleground of economic and power struggles? There is a clear difference between these two cases: in the second case, the "secret" beneath all the confusion of social life is social antagonisms, not individual agents which can be personalized (in the guise of Pokémon figures), while Pokémon Go does inherently tend toward the ideologically personalized perception of social antagonisms. In the case of bankers threatening us from all around, it is not hard to see how such a figure can easily be appropriated by a Fascist populist ideology of plutocracy (as opposed to "honest" productive capitalists). ... The point of the parallel between Nazi anti-Semitism and Pokémon Go is thus a very simple and elementary one: although Pokémon Go presents itself as something new, grounded in the latest technology, it relies on old ideological mechanisms. Ideology is the practice of augmenting reality.

The general lesson from Pokémon Go is that, when we deal with the new developments in Virtual Reality (VR) technology, we usually focus on the prospect of full immersion, thereby neglecting the much more interesting possibilities of Augmented Reality (AR) and Mixed Reality (MR):

· In VR, you wear something on your head (currently, a head-mounted display that can look like a boxy set of goggles or a space helmet) that holds a screen in front of your eyes, which in turn is powered by a computer. Thanks to specialized software and sensors, the experience *becomes* your reality, filling your vision; at the high end, this is often accompanied by 3D audio that feels like a personal surround-sound system on your head, or controllers that let you reach out and interact with this artificial world in an intuitive way. The forthcoming development of VR will heighten the level of immersion so that it will feel as if we are fully present in it: when VR users look (and walk) around, their view of that world will adjust in the same way as it would if they were looking or moving in *real* reality.

· AR takes our view of the real world and adds digital information, from simple numbers or text notifications to a complex simulated screen, making it possible to augment our view of reality with digital information about it without checking another device, leaving both our hands free for other tasks. We thus immediately see reality plus selected data about it that provide the interpretive frame of how to deal with it—for example, when we look at a car, we see the basic data about it on screen.

· But the true miracle is MR: it lets us see the real world and, as part of the same reality, "believable" virtual objects which are "anchored" to points in real space, and thus enable us to treat them as "real." Say, for example, that I am looking at an ordinary table, but see interactive virtual objects (a person, a machine, a model of a building) sitting on top of it; as I walk around, the virtual landscape holds its position, and when I lean in close, it gets closer in the way a real object would. To some degree, I can then interact with these virtual objects in such a "realistic" way that what I do to them has effects in non-virtual reality (for example, I press a button on the virtual machine and the air-conditioning starts to work in reality).[6]

We thus have four levels of reality: RR ("real" reality which we perceive and interact with), VR, AR, MR; but is RR really simply reality, or is even our most immediate experience of reality always mediated and sustained by some kind of virtual mechanism? Today's cognitive science definitely supports the second view—for example, the basic premise of Daniel Dennett's "heterophenomenology"[7] is that subjective experience is the theorist's (interpreter's) symbolic fiction, his supposition, not the domain of phenomena directly accessible to the subject. The universe of subjective experience is reconstructed in exactly the same way as we reconstruct the universe of a novel from reading its text. In a first approach, this seems innocent enough, self-evident even: of course we do not have direct access to another person's mind, of course we have to reconstruct an individual's self-experience from his external gestures, expressions and, above all, words. However, Dennett's point is much more radical; he pushes the parallel to the extreme. In a novel, the universe we reconstruct is full of "holes," not fully constituted; for example, when Conan Doyle describes Sherlock Holmes's apartment, it is in a way meaningless to ask exactly how many books there were on the shelves—the writer simply did not have an exact idea of it in his mind. And, for Dennett, it is the same with another person's experience in "reality": what one should not do is to suppose that, deep in another's psyche, there is a full self-experience of which we get only fragments. Even the appearances cannot be saved.

This central point of Dennett can be nicely explained if one contrasts it with two standard positions which are usually opposed as incompatible, but are in effect solidary: first-person phenomenalism and third-person behavioral operationalism. On the one hand, the idea that, even if our mind is merely software in our brains, nobody can take from us the full first-person experience of reality; on the other hand, the idea that, in order to understand the mind, we should limit ourselves to third-person observations which can be objectively verified, and not accept any first-person accounts. Dennett undermines this opposition with what he calls "first-person operationalism": the gap is to be introduced into my very first-person experience—the gap between content and its registration, between represented time and the time of representation. A nice proto-Lacanian point of Dennett (and the key to his heterophenomenology) is this insistence on the distinction, in homology with space, between the time of representation and the representation of time: they are not the same, i.e., the loop of flashback is discernible even in our most immediate temporal experience—the succession of events ABCDEF ... is represented in our consciousness so that it begins with E, then goes back to ABCD, and, finally, returns to F, which in reality directly follows E. So even in our most direct temporal self-experience, a gap akin to that between signifier and signified is already at work: even here, one cannot "save the phenomena," since what we (mis)perceive as a directly experienced representation of time (the phenomenal succession ABCDEF ...) is already a "mediated" construct from a different time of representation (E/ABCD/F ...).

"First-person operationalism" thus emphasizes how, even in our "direct (self-)experience," there is a gap between content (the narrative inscribed into our memory) and the "operational" level of how the subject constructed this content, where we always have a series of rewritings and tinkerings: "introspection provides us—the subject as well as the 'outside' experimenter—only with the content of representation, not with the features of the representational medium itself."[8] In this precise sense, the subject is his own fiction: the content of his own self-experience is a narrativization in which memory traces already intervene. So when Dennett makes "'writing it down' in memory criterial for consciousness; that is what it is for the 'given' to be 'taken'—to be taken one way rather than another," and claims that "there is no reality of conscious experience independent of the effects of various vehicles of content on subsequent action (and, hence, on memory),"[9] we should be careful not to miss the point: what counts for the concerned subject himself is the way an event is "written down," memorized—memory is constitutive of my "direct experience" itself, i.e., "direct experience" is what I memorize as my direct experience. Or, to put it in Hegelian terms (which would undoubtedly appall Dennett): immediacy itself is mediated, it is a product of the mediation of traces. One can also put this in terms of the relationship between direct experience and judgment on it: Dennett's point is that there is no "direct experience" prior to judgment, i.e., what I (re)construct (write down) as my experience is already supported by judgmental decisions.

For this reason, the whole problem of "filling in the gaps" is a false problem, since there are no gaps to be filled in. Let us take the classic example of our reading a text which contains a lot of printing errors: most of these errors pass unnoticed, i.e., since, in our reading, we are guided by an active attitude of recognizing patterns, we, for the most part, simply read the text as if there were no mistakes. The usual phenomenological account of this would be that, owing to my active attitude of recognizing ideal patterns, I "fill in the gaps" and automatically, even prior to my conscious perception, reconstitute the correct spelling, so that it appears to me that I am reading the correct text, without mistakes. But what if the actual procedure is different? Driven by the attitude of actively searching for known patterns, I quickly scan a text (our actual perception is much more discontinuous and fragmentary than it may appear), and this combination of an active attitude of searching and fragmented perception leads my mind directly to the conlcusion that, for example, the word I just read is "conclusion," not "conlcusion," as it was actually written? There are no gaps to be filled in here, since there is no moment of perceptual experience prior to the conclusion (i.e., judgment) that the word I have just read is "conclusion": again, my active attitude drives me directly to the conclusion.

Back to VR, AR, and MR: is not the conclusion that imposes itself that our "direct" experience of "real" reality is already structured like a mixture of RR, AR, and MR? It is thus crucial to bear in mind that AR and MR "work" because they do not introduce a radical break into our engagement in reality, but mobilize a structure which is already at work in it. There are arguments (drawn from the brain sciences) that something like ideological confabulation is proper to the most elementary functioning of our brain; recall the famous split-brain experiment:

The patient was shown 2 pictures: of a house in the winter time and of a chicken's claw. The pictures were positioned so they would exclusively be seen in only one visual field of the brain (the winter house was positioned so it would only be seen in the patient's left visual field [LVF], which corresponds to the brain's right hemisphere, and the chicken's claw was placed so it would only be seen in the patient's right visual field [RVF], which corresponds to the brain's left hemisphere).

A series of pictures was placed in front of the patient who was then asked to choose a picture with his right hand and a picture with his left hand. The paradigm was set up so the choices would be obvious for the patients. A snow shovel is used for shoveling the snowy driveway of the winter house and a chicken's head correlates to the chicken's claw. The other pictures do not in any way correlate with the 2 original pictures. The patient chose the snow shovel with his left hand (corresponding to his brain's right hemisphere) and his right hand chose the chicken's head (corresponding to the brain's left hemisphere). When the patient was asked why he had chosen the pictures he had chosen, the answer he gave was astonishing: "The chicken claw goes with the chicken head, and you need a snow shovel to clean out the chicken shed."

Why would he say this? Wouldn't it be obvious that the shovel goes with the winter house? For people with an intact corpus callosum, yes it is obvious, but not for a split-brain patient. Both the winter house and the shovel are being projected to the patient from his LVF, so his right hemisphere is receiving and processing the information and this input is completely independent from what is going on in the RVF, which involves the chicken's claw and head (the information being processed in the left hemisphere). The human brain's left hemisphere is primarily responsible for interpreting the meaning of the sensory input it receives from both fields, however the left hemisphere has no knowledge of the winter house. Because it has no knowledge of the winter house, it must invent a logical reason for why the shovel was chosen. Since the only objects it has to work with are the chicken's claw and head, the left hemisphere interprets the meaning of choosing the shovel as "it is an object necessary to help the chicken, which lives in a shed, therefore, the shovel is used to clean the chicken's shed." Gazzaniga famously coined the term "left brain interpreter" to explain this phenomenon.[10]

It is crucial to note that the patient "wasn't 'consciously' confabulating": "The connection between the chicken claw and the shovel was an honest expression of what 'he' thought."[11] And is not ideology, at its most elementary, such an interpreter confabulating rationalizations in the conditions of repression? A somewhat simplified example: Let's imagine the same experiment with two pictures shown to a subject fully immersed in ideology, a beautiful villa and a group of starving miserable workers; from the accompanying cards, he selects a fat rich man (inhabiting the villa) and a group of aggressive policemen (whose task is to squash the workers' eventual desperate protest). His "left brain interpreter" doesn't see the striking workers, so how does it account for the aggressive policemen? By confabulating a link such as: "Policemen are needed to protect the villa with the rich man from robbers who break the law." Were not the (in)famous nonexistent WMD which justified the US attack on Iraq precisely the result of such a confabulation, which had to fill in the void of the true reasons for the attack?

4.3 FROM BIT TO IT

This intertwinement of Real, Symbolic, and Imaginary in the constitution of what we experience as reality confronts us with the old problem of the passage "from bit to it": what is the X that has to be added to the network of symbolic features so that we get the "real thing," not just a symbolic fiction? The old, stupid wisdom quoted by Engels says: "The proof of the pudding is in the eating." But is it? Do we not, rather, need the proof of eating itself? A friend (whom I will leave anonymous, of course) recently wrote me:

> I had a dream in which I was caught in a stressful situation that dragged on and on—in a tense personal conflict, I failed again and again to make a decision and act, and this protraction filled me with anxiety experienced as strong chest pressure and pain. Then a reflexive moment appeared in the dream: I became aware that I am dreaming, and decided to awaken, to step out of the dream, in order to also get rid of the chest pain, presuming that the chest pain was the somatic effect of the stressful content of the dream. So I awakened, the dream dispelled—but the chest pain remained, I found myself in the midst of a strong panic attack. In short, it was not my dream which triggered chest pain, I rather invented the dream with me in a stressful situation in order to make the real bodily pain part of the dream narrative and in this way derealize it, making it part of a dream. I still remember the terrifying feeling when I was forced to accept that chest pain as real—for a second, I even played with the idea of escaping into a dream again ...

Chest pain here clearly played the role similar to that of a phone ringing which I quickly include in a dream in order to prolong my sleep—it was obviously a kind of Real which could not have been "sublated" into a moment of the dream narrative; it was the "it" whose raw, factual nature resisted full integration into (narrative, informational) bits. This experience may be taken to provide a clear example of how we cannot directly pass "from bit to it," from symbolic reasoning or telling stories to raw reality. And is not Hegel's idealism precisely a desperate attempt to perform such an impossible passage from notion to reality? He does this in a couple of places in his system:

the passage from logic to philosophy of nature; within logic itself, the passage from (subjective) syllogism to (objective) mechanism; plus Hegel's reaffirmation of the ontological proof of God. The underlying structure is always the same: when the process of logical mediation reaches its completion, we pass into objectivity, logical mediation collapses into positive reality. The impenetrable material density of "it" is thus an effect of its opposite, of total transparency achieved by conceptual mediation/internalization of every positivity.

An example from cinema can serve as a metaphor here. The only interesting feature of *Adventurers* (a 1970 trash movie based on a Harold Robbins novel) are its credits: first a simple line, then other lines out of which the drawing of a landscape gradually emerges, and when the drawing is completed and colored, it passes into a shot of the depicted reality itself. Therein lies the big problem: is such a passage immanent, or does it involve the intervention of an external element (as in Plato, who posited *chōra* as the formless recipient of ideal forms)? More precisely, this problem has two aspects. First, there is the ontological dimension: is there something that we have to add to conceptual determinations to get a real entity? (It is for this reason that Kant claimed that being is not a predicate: it is pure positedness that has to be added to the series of predicates that characterize a thing.) Then, there is the epistemological dimension best illustrated by the famous example of Mary imagined by Thomas Nagel: Let's say that Mary has never seen a red object, although she has full scientific knowledge about the color red; when she finally sees an actual red object for the first time, will she learn anything new? Is there something in the specific experience of a color, a kind of irreducible "thusness," which cannot be reduced to or generated from its conceptual determinations? Is "red" an example of qualia, ineffable and immediately apprehensible "raw feels"? (In his *Consciousness Explained*, Dennett provides a [sometimes] almost Hegelian critique of the notion of qualia, demonstrating how seeing and/or recognizing an object is never a direct act of apprehending an entity but involves a complex set of mental operations—what we "see out there" is a combination of perceptive details, mental conclusions, and generalizations, as well as spontaneous reasoning and application of concepts.)

We should note that the status of "it" changes here from objective to subjective: from "What makes reality beyond our notions of it?" to "Is the specific way a thing or one of its properties appears to us reducible to the objective existence of this thing (as it is formulated by science)?" The next step in this direction was accomplished by Nagel in his famous paper "What Is It Like to Be a Bat?," where he claims that consciousness has an essentially subjective character, a what-it-is-like aspect, and that this subjective aspect of the mind may never be sufficiently accounted for by the objective methods of reductionist science. It is interesting to note that this thesis also has an identity politics version: "No one but a black lesbian (victim of rape, blind person, etc.) really knows what it is to be a black lesbian!" The point made is that appearance is irreducible to the mechanism that generates it.

David Chalmers[12] brought this line of argumentation to its extreme when he formulated the so-called "hard problem" of consciousness: in contrast to the "easy problems" (explaining specific activities of our mind like calculating, focusing attention, perceiving external reality) which are easy because we can solve them by specifying the mechanism which can perform the function, i.e., by applying to them the materialist scientific conception of natural phenomena, the bare fact of experience, of "being aware" of a state of things, will "persist even when the performance of all the relevant functions is explained." From the "it" that accounts for the reality of things, we thus pass through the "it" of qualia and the "it" of self-experience, to the "it" of the very raw fact of self-awareness.

But what if we turn around this notion of the insufficiency of conceptual mediation to account for the reality of a thing? What if there is more in the concept of a thing than in its immediate reality? "Notion" has to be understood here in a very specific way: not as a Platonic abstraction (the abstract concept of a table in contrast to individual tables), but more in the sense of what Deleuze called "transcendental empiricism," as the dense web of virtual variations that surround the reality of a thing. With regard to this dense transcendental field, reality is the result of its reduction to one version, like the collapse of wave function in quantum physics. (It is in this sense that one should talk about the ontological proof of God: "God" stands for the entire hyperdimensional field of multiverse realities.) Let me make this point somewhat clearer through an example from art: a good painting of, say, a woman supplements the woman's photographic reality with its transcendental field of virtualities: all the layers of potentialities that underlie the actual existence of a woman, the potential aggressiveness or threat of libidinal explosion that may lurk beneath her gentle appearance, her vulnerability and exposure to male violence, the melancholy that often brands the existence of a woman, up to the disparity of the composure of the feminine body which may all of a sudden strike an external gaze. All these virtualities (which, in a painting, are directly inscribed into the feminine figure and distort its "realist" shape) are not just subjective misperceptions of the "objective reality" of the body, they bring out potentialities inscribed into the thing itself. Recall "A Woman Throwing a Stone," a lesser-known painting by Picasso from his surrealist period in the 1920s: the distorted fragments of a woman on a beach throwing a stone are, of course, a grotesque misrepresentation, measured by the standard of realist reproduction; however, in their very plastic distortion, they immediately/intuitively render the Idea of a "woman throwing a stone," the "inner form" of such a figure.

From here, we can return to the topic of a dream as a way to derealize the Real (of a disturbance in external reality) through its inclusion in the dream narrative. As is well known, Lacan introduces an additional twist here: yes, we construct a dream to prolong our sleep by integrating into its texture the external disturbance; but we awaken not when this external disturbance gets too strong—we awaken in order to escape the horror of some traumatic Real upon which we stumble in the dream, which means that there is an "it" that resists symbolization also in the dream. Reality itself (awakening into reality) can be an escape from the Real that we encounter in the dream.

The ontology implied by this intertwinement of real, reality, and dream is a kind of Platonic materialism one can nicely exemplify by *The Man in the High Castle*, Philip K. Dick's alternate-history classic from 1963, which takes place in 1962, fifteen years after an alternate ending to World War II in which the war lasted until 1947, when the victorious Axis powers—Imperial Japan and Nazi Germany—rule over the former United States. The novel features a "novel within the novel" which describes an alternate history within this alternate history wherein the Allies defeat the Axis. ... We can read this double reversal as a dark allegory of our own time in which, although Fascism was defeated in reality, it is triumphing more and more in fantasy.[13] However, such a reading neglects the fact that the alternate reality described in the "novel within the novel" is not simply our reality but differs from it in many crucial details.[14] If we follow Lacan's claim that the Real as a rule appears in the guise of a fiction within a fiction, we should thus conceive alternate reality (depicted in the novel) and our reality as two realities, two variations of reality, while the Real is the fiction (the novel within the novel, or, in the TV series version, the film within the film) which is neither of the two realities—our reality is one of the alternate realities with reference to the Real of the Truth-Fiction. What this means is that there are fictions which should be taken more seriously than reality precisely because they are "mere fictions." In order to understand our reality, we should first imagine the possible alternate realities, and then construct the "impossible Real" which serves as their secret point of reference, as their "hard core." What we have here is a kind of Freudian version of phenomenological eidetic variation: in Husserl, we vary the empirical content of, say, a table in order to arrive at what unites all empirical variations, the absolutely necessary and invariable components that make a table what it is, the *eidos* of table; in psychoanalysis, one collects all variations in order to reconstruct their "absent center," a purely virtual (inexistent in reality) form negated (distorted, displaced, etc.) in a specific way by every variation given in reality.

And, in a political discourse, are not human rights the same virtual point of reference? Yes, one can convincingly demonstrate the particular content that gives the specific ideological spin to the notion of human rights; yes,

universal human rights are in effect the rights of white male property own-
ers to exchange freely on the market and exploit workers and women, as well
as exert political domination. However, this is only half the story: when we
experience the gap between the false universality of human rights and the
particular injustices this universal form justifies, this gap should not push us
to renounce human rights and freedoms as a fake, but to begin to struggle for
their content. Is not the entire struggle for human rights also the struggle for
this content? First, women (beginning with Mary Wollstonecraft) demanded
these rights, then the slaves in Haiti did it in the first successful black uprising
(for which they are punished even today), and so on.

But is not such a notion of universality all too Eurocentric? Are not all
other emancipatory movements compelled to repeat the European original?
We should bear in mind here that the Hegelian repetition which sublates a
contingency into universal necessity thereby changes the past (not factually,
of course, but in its symbolic status). The French Revolution became a world-
historical event with a universal significance only through its repetition in
Haiti, where the black slaves led a successful rebellion with the goal of estab-
lishing a free republic like the French one; without this repetition, the French
Revolution would have remained a local idiosyncratic event. The same holds
today for the Syriza government in Greece: it will become a universal event
only if it triggers a process of its "repetitions," of similar movements taking
over in other countries; otherwise, it will just remain a local Greek idiosyncrasy. What this means is that, in both cases, a repetition did (or will) retroactively change the event from a particular idiosyncrasy into a universal
truth-event.

One can criticize this notion of repetition for remaining racist: the first
gesture was the French one, and all the Haiti slaves could have done was to
repeat the French events, to follow the white men's lead. However, this criticism misses the retroactivity of the event: the French Revolution became a
universal historical event only through its repetition in Haiti. What this means
is that one should adopt here a shamelessly naive Platonic perspective: the
Haiti revolutionaries did not copy the French revolutionaries, they both copied the Idea of a radical emancipatory revolution, and the Haiti revolutionaries were not only "copying" (imitating, realizing) it better, more faithfully,
but it was only through their "copying" that what they copied (the Idea) came
to be, arrived at its truth.

4.4   LALANGUE

The same parallax intertwinement of the internal and the external is at work
in the very core of what Lacan calls *lalangue* ("llanguage") which, as we have
already seen,[15] stands for the signifier as the "apparatus of *jouissance*," for language as the space of illicit pleasures that defy normativity; but it also stands

for "really existing language" in contrast to language as a pure formal structure. Recall Walter Benjamin's essay "On Language in General and Human Language in Particular," in which the point is not that human language is a species of some universal language "as such" which also comprises other species: there is no actually existing language other than human language—but, in order to comprehend this "particular" language, one *has* to introduce a minimal difference, conceiving it with regard to the gap which separates it from language "as such."

This, however, is not all—and we should give this "not all" all the weight of the Lacanian *pas-tout*. The fact that not-all of language is traversed by social antagonisms, scarred by traces of social pathology, does not mean that there is an exception, an aspect of language (in this case, its form) which cannot be reduced to social reality and its antagonisms, since it provides the a priori frame through which we relate to reality. It is precisely because there is nothing which escapes social mediation that not-all of language is socially mediated: *what escapes social mediation is not something exempted from it but the meta-transcendental social mediation of the very linguistic frame through which we perceive and relate to reality.* When we conceive language as a mirror which is always-already distorted/traversed by the pathology of social antagonisms, we ignore *the way this mirror is itself included in reality as a mode of its distortion.* Language is not only traversed by antagonisms/traumas—the supreme trauma is that of language itself, of how language brutally destabilizes the Real. The same goes for an individual's relation to language: we usually take a subject's speech, with all its inconsistencies, as an expression of his/her inner turmoil, ambivalent emotions, etc.; this holds even for a literary work of art: the task of psychoanalytic reading is supposed to be to unearth the inner psychic turmoil which found its coded expression in the work of art. Something is missing in such a classic account: speech does not only register or express a traumatic psychic life; the entry into speech is in itself a traumatic fact ("symbolic castration"). What this means is that we should include, in the list of traumas speech tries to cope with, the traumatic impact of speech itself. The relationship between psychic turmoil and its expression in speech should thus also be turned around: speech does not simply express/articulate psychic turmoil; at a certain key point, psychic turmoil itself is a reaction to the trauma of dwelling in the "torture-house of language."

This, then, is how the two sides of the parallax structure of *lalangue* function. The exclusion (exemption) from social reality is one side of *lalangue*, i.e., *lalangue* emerges when language acquires autonomy, since it is uncoupled from external reality; but the other side of *lalangue* is the exclusion of formal language, i.e., *lalangue* emerges when language loses its formal autonomy and is totally extro-verted, traversed by the contingent pathologies of social life. When we link the four terms (autonomous apparatus of enjoy-meant;

tool of communication and reference; autonomous formal structure; total extro-version, openness to social pathology) diagonally, it is not difficult to discern in this parallax the structure of masculine and feminine formulas of sexuation. The "masculine" side is composed of language as formal structure and its relating to external reality through its (communicational, referential, expressive) use, while the "feminine" side is composed of the two aspects of "non-all," no exception (autonomous self-propelling circulation with no external reference) and no totality, no "whole" (language pulverized by antagonisms, inconsistencies and perversions). It is crucial to maintain this radical ambiguity of *lalangue* which is simultaneously without a relation to outside *and* thoroughly "out of itself," with no "internal structure" as a point from which it could relate to externality.

4.5 HUMAN, POST-HUMAN

The big historical question is, of course, how this twisted relationship between Outside and Inside is affected by the ongoing digital revolution. According to the predominant *doxa*, cyberspace explodes, or at least potentially undermines, the reign of Oedipus: it involves the "end of Oedipus," i.e., what occurs in it is the passage from the structure of symbolic castration (the intervention of the Third Agency which prohibits/disturbs the incestuous dyad, and thus enables the subject's entry into the symbolic order) to some new, post-Oedipal libidinal economy. Of course, the mode of perception of this "end of Oedipus" depends on the standpoint of the theoretician: first, there are those who see in it a dystopian prospect of individuals regressing to presymbolic psychotic immersion, losing the symbolic distance which sustains the minimum of critical/reflective attitude (the idea that the computer functions as a maternal Thing which "swallows" the subject who entertains toward it an attitude of incestuous fusion)—in short, today, in the digitized universe of simulation, the Imaginary overlaps with the Real, at the expense of the Symbolic (Jean Baudrillard, Paul Virilio).

This position is at its strongest when it insists on the difference between appearance and simulacrum: "appearance" has nothing in common with the postmodern notion that we are entering the era of universalized simulacra in which reality itself becomes indistinguishable from its simulated double. The nostalgic longing for the authentic experience of being lost in the deluge of simulacra (detectable in Virilio), as well as the postmodern assertion of a Brave New World of universalized simulacra as the sign that we are finally getting rid of the metaphysical obsession with authentic Being (detectable in Vattimo)—both miss the distinction between simulacrum and appearance: what gets lost in today's digital "plague of simulations" is not the firm, true, nonsimulated Real, but *appearance itself*. So what is appearance? In a sentimental answer to a child asking him what God's face looks like, a priest answered that, whenever the child encounters a human face radiating benev-olence and goodness, whomsoever this face belongs to, he gets a glimpse of His face. The truth of this sentimental platitude is that the suprasensible (God's face) is discernible as a momentary, fleeting appearance, a "grimace," of an earthly face. It is *this* dimension of "appearance" which transubstanti-ates a piece of reality into something which, for a brief moment, radiates the suprasensible Eternity that is missing in the logic of simulacrum: in simu-lacrum which becomes indistinguishable from the Real, everything is here, and no other, transcendent dimension actually "appears" in/through it. Here we are back at the Kantian problematic of the sublime: in Kant's famous reading of the enthusiasm evoked by the French Revolution in the enlight-ened public around Europe, the revolutionary events functioned as a sign through which the dimension of transphenomenal Freedom, of a free soci-ety, *appeared*. "Appearance" is thus not simply the domain of phenomena, but those "magic moments" in which the other, noumenal, dimension momen-tarily "appears" in ("shines through") some empirical/contingent phenom-enon. That is also the problem with cyberspace and virtual reality: what VR threatens is not "reality" which is dissolved in the multiplicity of its simula-cra, but, on the contrary, appearance itself. To put it in Lacanian terms: simu-lacrum is imaginary (illusion), while appearance is symbolic (fiction); when the specific dimension of symbolic appearance starts to disintegrate, imagi-nary and real become more and more indistinguishable. The key to today's universe of simulacra, in which the Real is less and less distinguishable from its imaginary simulation, lies in the retreat of "symbolic efficiency." This crucial distinction between simulacrum (overlapping with the Real) and appearance is easily discernible in the domain of sexuality, as the distinction between pornography and seduction: pornography "shows it all," "real sex," and for that very reason produces the mere simulacrum of sexuality, while the process of seduction consists entirely in the play of appearances, hints, and promises, and thereby evokes the elusive domain of the suprasensible sublime Thing.

On the other hand, there are those who emphasize the liberating poten-tial of cyberspace: cyberspace opens up the domain of shifting multiple sex-ual and social identities, potentially at least liberating us from the hold of the patriarchal Law; it as it were realizes, in our everyday practical experi-ence, the "deconstruction" of old metaphysical binaries ("real Self" versus "artificial mask," etc.). In cyberspace, I am compelled to renounce any fixed symbolic identity, the legal/political fiction of a unique Self guaranteed by my place in the sociosymbolic structure—in short, according to this sec-ond version (Sandy Stone, Sherry Turkle), cyberspace announces the end of the Cartesian *cogito* as the unique "thinking substance." Of course, from this second point of view, the pessimistic prophets of the psychotic "end of

Oedipus" in the universe of simulacra simply betray their inability to imagine an alternative to Oedipus. What we have here is another version of the standard postmodern deconstructionist narrative according to which, in the bad old patriarchal order, the subject's sexual identity was predetermined by his/her place and/or role within the fixed symbolic Oedipal framework; the "big Other" took care of us and conferred on us the identity of either a "man" or a "woman," and the subject's ethical duty was limited to the effort to succeed in occupying the preordained symbolic place (homosexuality and other "perversions" were perceived as simply so many signs of the subject's *failure* to succeed in going through the Oedipal path, and thus achieving "normal"/"mature" sexual identity). Today, however, as Foucault allegedly demonstrated, the legal/prohibitive matrix of Power which underlies the Oedipal functioning of sexuality is in retreat, so that, instead of being interpellated to occupy a preordained place in the sociosymbolic order, the subject has gained the freedom (or at least the promise, the prospect of freedom) to shift between different sociosymbolic sexual identities, to construct his/her Self as an aesthetic *œuvre*—the theme at work from Foucault's late notion of the "care of the Self" up to deconstructionist feminist emphasis on the social formation of gender. It is easy to perceive how the reference to cyberspace can provide an additional impetus to this ideology of aesthetic self-creation: cyberspace delivers me from the vestiges of biological constraints and elevates my capacity to construct my Self freely, to let myself adopt a multitude of shifting identities.

However, opposed to both versions of "cyberspace as the end of Oedipus" are some rare, but nonetheless penetrating, theoreticians who assert the continuity of cyberspace with the Oedipal mode of subjectivization:[16] cyberspace retains the fundamental Oedipal structure of an intervening Third Order which, in its very capacity as the agent of mediation/mediatization, sustains the subject's desire, while simultaneously acting as the agent of Prohibition which prevents its direct and full gratification; on account of this intervening Third, every partial gratification/satisfaction is marked by a fundamental "this is not *that*." The notion that cyberspace as the medium of hyperreality suspends the symbolic efficiency and brings about the false total transparency of the imaginary simulacra coinciding with the Real, this notion, while effectively expressing a certain "spontaneous ideology of cyberspace" (to paraphrase Althusser), dissimulates the actual functioning of cyberspace which not only continues to rely on the elementary structure of the symbolic Law, but even renders it more palpable in our everyday experience. Suffice it to recall the conditions of our surfing the Internet or participating in a virtual community: first, there is the gap between the "subject of enunciation" (the anonymous X who does it, who speaks) and the "subject of the enunciated /of the statement" (the symbolic identity I assume in cyberspace, which can be and in a sense always is "invented"—the signifier which marks my identity in cyberspace is never directly "myself"); the same goes for the other side, for my partner(s) in cyberspace communication—here, the undecidability is radical, I can never be sure who they are: are they "really" the way they describe themselves, is there any "real" person at all behind a screen persona, is the screen persona a mask for a multiplicity of persons, does the same "real" person possess and manipulate more screen personas, or am I simply dealing with a digitized entity which does not stand for any "real" person? In short, *inter-face* means precisely that my relationship to the Other is never *face-to-face*, that it is always mediat(iz)ed by the interposed digital machinery which stands for the Lacanian "big Other" as the anonymous symbolic order whose structure is that of a labyrinth: I "browse," I wander around in this infinite space where messages circulate freely without fixed destination, while the Whole of it—this immense circuitry of "murmurs"—remains forever beyond the scope of my comprehension. (In this sense, I am tempted to propose the proto-Kantian notion of the "cyberspace Sublime" as the magnitude of messages and their circuits which even the greatest effort of my synthetic imagination cannot encompass/comprehend.) Furthermore, does not the a priori possibility of viruses disintegrating the virtual universe point toward the fact that, in the virtual universe also, there is no "Other of the Other," that this universe is a priori inconsistent, with no last guarantee of its coherent functioning?

The conclusion thus seems to be that there is a properly "symbolic" functioning of cyberspace: cyberspace remains "Oedipal" in the sense that, in order to circulate freely in it, one must assume a fundamental prohibition and/or alienation—yes, in cyberspace, "you can be whatever you want," you're free to choose *a* symbolic identity (screen persona), but you must choose *one* which will always in a way betray you, which will never be fully adequate; you must accept being represented in cyberspace by a signifying element which runs around in the circuitry as your stand-in. ... Yes, in cyberspace, "everything is possible," but at the price of assuming a fundamental *impossibility*: you cannot circumvent the mediation of the interface, its "bypass," which separates you (as the subject of enunciation) forever from your symbolic stand-in.

In the last decade, however, radical digitization combined with scanning our brain (or tracking our bodily processes with implants) has opened up the prospect of so-called post-humanity, which in effect poses a threat to the twisted relationship between Inside and Outside: we are confronting the realistic possibility of an external machine that will know us, biologically and psychically, much better than we know ourselves; registering what we eat, buy, read, watch, and listen to, our moods, fears, and satisfactions, this external machine will get a much more accurate picture of ourselves than our conscious Self which, as we know, doesn't even exist as a consistent entity.[17] Our "Self" is composed of narratives which retroactively try to impose some consistency on the pandemonium of our experiences, obliterating experiences and memories which disturb these narratives. Ideology does not reside primarily in stories invented (by those in power) to deceive others, it resides in stories invented by subjects to deceive themselves. But the pandemonium persists, and the machine will register the discords, and will maybe even be able to deal with them in a much more rational way than our conscious Self. For instance, when I have to decide to marry or not, the machine will register all the shifting attitudes that haunt me, the past pains and disappointments that I prefer to sweep under the carpet.

And why not extend this prospect even to political decisions? While my Self can be easily seduced by a populist demagogue, the machine will take note of all my past frustrations, it will register the inconsistency between my fleeting passions and my other opinions—so why should the machine not vote on my behalf? So while the brain sciences confirm the "poststructuralist" or "deconstructionist" idea that we are stories we tell ourselves about ourselves, and that these stories are a confused *bricolage*, an inconsistent multiplicity of stories with no single Self totalizing them, it seems to offer (or promise, at least) a way out which is thanks to its very disadvantage: precisely because the machine which reads us all the time is "blind," without awareness, a mechanical algorithm, it can make decisions which are much more adequate than those made by human individuals, much more adequate not only with regard to external reality but also and above all with regard to these individuals themselves, to what they really want or need:

> Liberalism sanctifies the narrating self, and allows it to vote in the polling stations, in the supermarket, and in the marriage market. For centuries this made good sense, because though the narrating self believed in all kinds of fictions and fantasies, no alternative system knew me better. Yet once we have a system that really does know me better, it will be foolhardy to leave authority in the hands of the narrating self. ... Liberal habits such as democratic elections will become obsolete, because Google will be able to represent even my own political opinions better than myself.[18]

One can make a very realist case for this option: it is not that the computer which registers our activity is omnipotent and infallible, it is simply that, on average, its decisions work substantially better than the decisions of our mind: in medicine, it makes better diagnoses than the average doctor, etc., up to the exploding algorithmic trading on stock markets, where programs that one can download for free already outperform financial advisers. One thing is clear: the liberal "true Self," the free agent which enacts what I "really want," simply doesn't exist, and fully endorsing this inexistence means abandoning the basic individualist premise of liberal democracy. The digital machine is the latest embodiment of the big Other, the "subject supposed to know," which operates as a field of knowledge (a chain of signifiers) without S_1, without a Master-Signifier which "represents the subject for other signifiers" by adding a specific "spin" or bias to a particular narrative. There is, of course, a whole series of questions that persist here. Is the function of the Master-Signifier just a negative one (imposing on a field of knowledge a subjective spin) or does it play a positive role? Harari is aware of this ambiguity: "In the past, censorship worked by blocking the flow of information. In the twenty-first century, censorship works by flooding people with irrelevant information. ... In ancient times having power meant having access to data. Today having power means knowing what to ignore." [19] Can this ignoring be done by a "blind" machine, or does it require a minimal form of subjectivity?

So where, in the space of a digital machine, is there an opening for subjectivity? Is the vision of post-humanity an actual threat to subjectivity, a real danger that subjectivity will disappear, so that the only way to retain subjectivity is to block the passage to post-humanity, or is there still a subject in the post-human condition, which means that the vision of post-humanity is ultimately an ideological fantasy? One can in fact claim that the vision of post-humanity relies on an inadequate notion of human subjectivity: when cognitivists speak about humanity, they mean the standard, naive notion of an individual who experiences him-/herself as a free, responsible agent—the Freudian subject is nowhere to be seen here. On the other hand, Jacques-Alain Miller's attempt to save subjectivity (and therewith the space for psychoanalysis) in the ongoing onslaught of cognitivism and biogenetics rehashes the standard hermeneutic operation: even if we are totally objectivized in the eyes of science, we still have to adopt a subjective stance toward this objectivization, i.e., it matters how we subjectivize or experience our situation, and this mode of subjectivization is the space of psychoanalytic intervention.

If the (almost) omnipotent digital big Other stands for our radical alienation (our truth located outside ourselves, inaccessible to us), what then would "separation" (Lacan's name for the operation that counters alienation) mean here? Separation is not the separation of the subject from the Other but an operation that takes place within the Other itself, exposing the Other as "barred," divided from itself, marked by an antagonism; and is not the digital big Other also prone to its own glitches, inconsistencies? And does not this imperfection/inconsistency of the big Other open up a space for subjectivity, even for subjective freedom? One should be careful here not to confuse freedom and randomness: even if a process is not fully determined but depends on genuinely random processes like the decay of uranium atoms, it is in no sense free but merely determined by meaningless randomness.

We can discern yet another opening for subjectivity. There is a long tradition, in philosophy and in the sciences, of denying free will, but doubts about free will "don't really change history unless they have a practical impact on economics, politics, and day-to-day life. Humans are masters of cognitive dissonance, and we allow ourselves to believe one thing in the laboratory and an altogether different thing in the courthouse or in parliament."[20] Harari points out how even popular champions of the new scientific world like Dawkins or Pinker, after writing hundreds of pages which debunk free will and freedom of choice, end up supporting political liberalism. However, today, "liberalism is threatened not by the philosophical idea that 'there are no free individuals,' but rather by concrete technologies. We are about to face a flood of extremely useful devices, tools and structures that make no allowance for the free will of individual humans. Can democracy, the free market and human rights survive this flood?"[21] So if development renders *Homo sapiens* obsolete, what will follow it? A post-human *Homo deus* (with abilities that are traditionally identified as divine) or a quasi-omnipotent digital machine? Singularity (global consciousness) or blind intelligence without awareness?

With regard to the possibility of new forms of awareness emerging, one should bear in mind Metzinger's warning. While he considers artificial subjectivity possible, especially in the direction of hybrid biorobotics, and, consequently, an "empirical, not philosophical" issue, he emphasizes its ethically problematic character: "it is not at all clear if the biological form of consciousness, as so far brought about by evolution on our planet, is a *desirable* form of experience, an actual *good in itself*."[22] This problematic feature concerns conscious pain and suffering: evolution "has created an expanding ocean of suffering and confusion where there previously was none. As not only the simple number of individual conscious subjects but also the dimensionality of their phenomenal state spaces is continuously increasing, this ocean is also deepening."[23] And it is reasonable to expect that new, artificially generated forms of awareness will create new, "deeper" forms of suffering.

Second option: if machines win, then "humans are in danger of losing their value, because intelligence is decoupling from consciousness."[24] This decoupling of intelligence and consciousness confronts us again with the enigma of consciousness: in spite of numerous rather desperate attempts, evolutionary biology can offer no clear definition of the evolutionary function of awareness/consciousness. Consequently, now that intelligence is decoupling from consciousness, "what will happen to society, politics and daily life when nonconscious but highly intelligent algorithms know us better than we know ourselves?"[25]

Third and most realistic option: a radical division, much stronger than the class division, within human society itself. Among the best Soviet jokes is the one about a debate in the Politburo about money: will there be money in Communism or not? Leftists claim there will be no money, since money belongs to capitalist alienation, and Rightists claim there will be money to facilitate exchange of products. Stalin rejects both views as wrong, as a Rightist and Leftist deviation, and proposes a dialectical synthesis: there will be money and there will not be money. How? ask the surprised members of the Politburo, and Stalin calmly answers: "Some will have money and others will not have it." We should reply in the same way to the dilemma: will the future, totally digitized society still allow human freedom, or will we all be just elements controlled by the digital machine? The answer is, of course, both at the same time: some will still have freedom, while others will be totally regulated by digital machinery. In the near future, biotechnology and computer algorithms will combine their powers in producing "bodies, brains and minds," with the gap exploding "between those who know how to engineer bodies and brains and those who do not": "those who ride the train of progress will acquire divine abilities of creation and destruction, while those left behind will face extinction."[26] The main threat, therefore, is that of the rise of a "small and privileged elite of upgraded humans. These superhumans will enjoy unheard-of abilities and unprecedented creativity, which will allow them to go on making many of the most important decisions in the world. … However, most humans will not be upgraded, and they will consequently become an inferior caste, dominated by both computer algorithms and the new superhumans. … Splitting humankind into biological castes will destroy the foundations of liberal ideology."[27]

4.6   THE TRANSGENDER DEADLOCK OF CLASSIFICATION

One thing is certain: from the psychoanalytic standpoint, what the shift to the post-human amounts to at its most fundamental is the overcoming (leaving behind) of the sexual in its most radical ontological dimension—not just "sexuality" as a specific sphere of human existence but the Sexual as an antagonism, the bar of an impossibility, constitutive of being-human in its finitude. And the issue carefully avoided by partisans of the new asexual man is: to what extent are many other features usually identified with being-human, features such as art, creativity, consciousness, dependent on the antagonism that constitutes the Sexual? This is why the addition of "asexual" to the series of positions that compose LGBT+ is crucial and unavoidable: the endeavor to liberate sexuality from all "binary" oppressions in order to set it free in its entire polymorphous perversity necessarily ends up in the abandoning of the very sphere of sexuality—the liberation of sexuality has to end up in the liberation (of humanity) from sexuality.

The deadlock of classification is clearly discernible in the need to expand the LGBT formula: the basic LGBT (Lesbian, Gay, Bisexual, Transgender) becomes LGBTQIA (Lesbian, Gay, Bisexual, Transgender, Questioning, Inter-sex, Asexual) or even LGBTQQIAAP (Lesbian, Gay, Bisexual, Transgender, Queer, Questioning, Intersex, Asexual, Allies, Pansexual). To resolve the prob-lem, one often simply adds a "+" which serves to include all other communi-ties associated with the LGBT community, as in LGBT+. This, however, raises the question: is "+" just a stand-in for the missing positions like "and others," or can one be directly a +? The properly dialectical answer is: yes—in the series, there is always one exceptional element which clearly does not belong to it, and thereby gives body to +. It can be "allies" ("honest" non-LGBT indi-viduals), "asexuals" (negating the entire field of sexuality), or "questioning" (floating around, unable to adopt a determinate position).[28]

In order to protect the rights of LGBTQ+ people, the City of New York offers its residents thirty-one categories from which to choose when they want to describe their identity. Here is the complete list: Bi-gendered, Cross-dresser, Drag King, Drag Queen, Femme Queen, Female-to-Male, FTM, Gender Bender, Genderqueer, Male-to-Female, MTF, Non-Op, HIJRA, Pan-gender, Transexual/Transsexual, Trans Person, Woman, Man, Butch, Two-Spirit, Trans, Agender, Third Sex, Gender Fluid, Non-Binary Transgender, Androgyne, Gender Gifted, Gender Blender, Femme, Person of Transgen-der Experience, Androgynous. However, a spokesman for the New York City Commission on Human Rights confirmed that the list is "not exhaustive." Furthermore, failure to comply with the NYCCHR's regulations on gender identity by committing what it deems to be "gender identity"-based dis-crimination can be punished with a fine of up to $250,000.[29] Protection of minorities thereby turns into punitive legal regulation which goes right up to prohibiting theoretical debate: during a recent debate about gender-neutral third-person-singular pronouns on Canadian TV, a partisan of transgender rights directly claimed that those who disagree with the legal enforcement of multiple gender identities should not be allowed to participate in public debates, since their attitude amounts to violation of basic human rights and hate speech—they should be prosecuted. It is weird to see how people who are usually radical critics of legal regulation and normativity (in Foucault's sense of modern power as an exercise of biopolitical regulation) all of a sud-den turn into ferocious advocates of such regulation.

Furthermore, the obvious surplus-pleasure generated by the classification of thirty-one identities resides in the humiliation (devaluation) of Woman and Man which are reduced to two elements with equal status as Butch or Drag King, reminding us of the famous claim of Montenegrins (a nation of half a million people): "We and the Russians together comprise more than one hundred million people." Isn't it clear that, without any denigration of the rights of transgender people, one should accept that "Butch" is one of the positions in a lesbian relationship and, as such, not on the same categorial level as Woman? And why should this claim be stigmatized as diminishing the dignity of a Butch? Why should the fact that one belongs to a small subcategory not make one's position even more precious? Why should the overwhelming fact that the large majority of people are heterosexual men or women in any way diminish the status of others? Why should the fact that heterosexuality has—in some sense, at least—a more "natural" foundation (insofar as sexuality is in some way linked to human reproduction) not render those forms of sexual identity and activity which diverge from this function even more properly "human" in the sense of creatively overcoming natural limitations? Isn't the fact that homosexuality is in some basic sense "unnatural" precisely what makes it specifically human (although there are also cases of homosexuality among higher primates)? What comes out in homosexuality is a "denaturalization," implicitly at work in human sexuality as such, which can be defined precisely by its divergence from its natural goal—human sexuality turns an activity biologically destined for reproduction into an end-in-itself.

Does something similar not hold also for the "class binary"? Many people whom I have met, from different levels of the social scale, energetically claimed that they don't fit the simple class binary—so should we also multiply the names here? Bi-class (a Proletarian subemploying and exploiting other Proletarians), Masturbatory Cross-class (a small self-employed company owner exploiting himself), Class Queen (a motherly Capitalist who takes care of her workers but tolerates no trade unions), Proletarian-to-Capitalist (PTC), Capitalist-to-Proletarian (CTP), Class Bender, Classqueer, Panclass, Proletarian, Capitalist, Non-Class, Transclass, Aclass, Third Class, Class Fluid, Non-Binary Transclass, Class Gifted, Person of Transclass Experience, Two-Spirit Capitalist (a perfect designation for people like Bill Gates and George Soros: half-time ruthless manipulators, half-time generous humanitarians), Precarious Proletarian, Digital Capitalist, CEC Butch (a Capitalist brutally Exploiting another Capitalist). ... As they say in Gilbert and Sullivan's *The Mikado*, they are all on the list and none of them would be missed—the renamed capitalists, not transgender people. Why? The right of each person to be called what this person wants, since it feels hurt if it is referred to by a different designation, is not an unconditional right. A slave owner may perceive himself to be a benevolent and caring paternal figure, and he can insist on being called by a name that implies this, otherwise he will feel hurt; but we should of course reject this demand. There are people who absolutely deserve to be addressed in a way that degrades and humiliates them.

So how are we to translate this multiplicity into our everyday speech? Since it would be too much to demand specific pronouns for each of the thirty-one identities, the need for a gender-neutral third-person-singular pronoun arises, and the proposed solutions are *ne, ve, ze (zie)* with hir ("ze washed hir hair"), plus *they* used as a singular pronoun (with the justification that centuries ago it was sometimes used like this). But the problem with this solution is that one cannot expect this artificially created neutral-universal pronoun actually to be used by the majority—consequently, there is only one solution to this deadlock, the one we find in another field of disposing of waste: that of trash bins. Public trash bins are more and more differentiated today: there are special bins for paper, glass, metal cans, cardboard packaging, plastic, etc. Here already, things sometimes get complicated: if I have to dispose of a paper bag or a notebook with a tiny plastic band, where does it belong, in paper or in packaging? No wonder we often get on the bins detailed instructions beneath the general designation: PAPER—books, newspapers, etc., but not hardcover books or books with plasticized covers, etc. In such cases, to properly dispose of one's waste would take up to half an hour or more of detailed reading and tough decisions. To make things easier, we then get a supplementary trash bin for GENERAL WASTE where we throw everything that does not meet the specific criteria of other bins—again, as if, apart from paper trash, plastic trash, etc., there is trash as such, universal trash. And should we not do the same with pronouns? Since no classification can satisfy all identities, should we not add to the standard "she" and "he" whatever we decide (*ne, ve, ze* ...) as a general container for all those who do not recognize themselves in the first two slots? With regard to toilets, we should do the same and add to the two usual gender slots (MEN, WOMEN) a door for GENERAL GENDER. Is this not the only way to inscribe into an order of symbolic differences its constitutive antagonism? Lacan pointed out that the "formula" of the sexual relationship as impossible/real is $1 + 1 + a$, i.e., the two sexes plus the "bone in the throat" that prevents its translation into a symbolic difference. This third element does not stand for what is excluded from the domain of difference, it stands for (the Real of) the difference as such.

The reason for this failure of every classification that tries to be exhaustive is not the empirical wealth of identities that defy classification but, on the contrary, the persistence of sexual difference as real, as "impossible" (defying every categorization) and simultaneously unavoidable. The multiplicity of gender positions (male, female, gay, lesbian, bi-gender, transgender, etc., etc.) circulates around an antagonism that forever eludes it. Gays are masculine, lesbians feminine, transsexuals enforce a passage from one to another, cross-dressing combines the two, bi-gender floats between the two ... whichever way we turn, the Two lurks beneath. This deadlock of exhaustive classification is nicely expressed in the famous song from Act I of *The Mikado* where

Ko-Ko, the Lord High Executioner, enumerates the list of those who "won't be missed":

> As someday it may happen that a victim must be found,
> I've got a little list—I've got a little list
> Of society offenders who might well be underground,
> And who never would be missed—who never would be missed!

There are literally hundreds of actualized versions of this list, predominantly referring to contemporary and local nuisances, but what is missing (in view of the ominous Stalinist resonance of the notion of the list of those to be liquidated) is a nice Stalinist version listing all the usual candidates for the title "enemy of the people" (those of bourgeois origins, Trotskyites, rich kulaks, formalist artists, etc.). I am also no less tempted to add a list of those who certainly would not be missed by any authentic Leftist today: liberals who transform any properly political crisis into a humanitarian problem, "orthodox" Communists who await the true working-class Revolution, identity-politicians for whom class struggle is just one in the series of antisexist, antiracist, etc., struggles, those who think that today is the time for concrete action and not for "pure," useless theory, etc. But what interests us more here are the concluding lines of the song:

> And apologetic statesmen of a compromising kind,
> Such as—What d'ye call him—Thing'em-bob, and likewise—Never-mind,
> And 'St—'st—'st—and What's-his-name, and also You-know-who—
> The task of filling up the blanks I'd rather leave to you.
> But it really doesn't matter whom you put upon the list,
> For they'd none of 'em be missed—they'd none of 'em be missed!

After the narrator gets confused and cannot go on with the list ("What d'ye call him ... Never-mind ... What's-his-name"), he concludes the series with an exemplary empty signifier, the proverbial "You-know-who," who can stand for anyone up to the Queen, which already indicates the fact that "it really doesn't matter whom you put upon the list" (and, incidentally, this brings us close to Hegel's theory of monarchy, where it explicitly doesn't matter who is King). We find exactly the same paradox in the most famous classification song of all, the "catalogue aria" from Mozart's *Don Giovanni*. As Leporello, Don Giovanni's servant, explains to Elvira, in this catalogue, all of his master's conquests are classified according to three different criteria: by their country (which concludes with "in Spain alone one thousand and three"), their social status (peasant girls, city girls, baronesses ...), and their physical properties (subdivided into color of their hair, weight ...). At the end of the list, however, he adds the opposition old/young, which functions in a different way: his master most enjoys young ones, and he seduces the old ones "for the pleasure of adding to the list." This last opposition does not refer to any specific features of the seduced women (country, external look, social status ...); it mobilizes only the abstract opposition between direct physical pleasure (which is provided in the greatest amount by making love to a young girl) and the pure signifier's pleasure, the pleasure of adding another name to the list (an act done by Leporello, which means that Leporello's keeping the list is an essential component of Don Giovanni's sexual pleasure). This last pleasure is clearly a reflexive pleasure, not a direct pleasure but a pleasure to register pleasures, to add them to a list; as such, it provides a perfect example of what Freud called *Mehrgenuss*, and what Lacan called surplus-enjoyment. And, exactly as in the list song from *Mikado*, the concluding point that follows the assertion of the reflexive Master-Signifier is the indifference of all elements (people to be liquidated in *Mikado*, women in *Don Giovanni*): "It doesn't matter if she's rich, / Ugly or beautiful; / If she wears a skirt, / You know what he does." It is crucial to bear in mind that this violent abstraction from particular properties (*vulgari eloquentia*: it doesn't matter whom Don Giovanni fucks, they are all the same) can be asserted as such only through Leporello, through the signifying dimension, through the fact that the ultimate pleasure is not that of the direct sexual act but that of its registering— they are "all the same" as items on the list.

This deadlock of classification brings us back to what one could call the primal scene of anxiety that defines transgenderism: I stand in front of the standard bi-gender toilets with two doors, LADIES and GENTLEMEN, and I am caught in anxiety, not recognizing myself in either of the two choices. Again, do "normal" heterosexuals not have a similar problem: do they also not often find it difficult to recognize themselves in prescribed sexual identities? Which man has not caught himself in a momentary doubt: "Do I really have the right to enter GENTLEMEN? Am I really a man?" We can now see clearly what the anxiety when confronted with the choice LADIES or GENTLEMEN really amounts to: the anxiety of (symbolic) castration. Whatever choice I make, I will lose something, and this something is *not* what the other sex has—both sexes together do not form a Whole, since something is irretrievably lost by the very division of sexes. We can even say that, in making the choice, I assume *the loss of what the other sex doesn't have*, i.e., I have to renounce the illusion that the Other has that X which would fill in my lack. And one can well guess that transgenderism is ultimately precisely an attempt to avoid (the anxiety of) castration: a flat space is created in which the multiple choices I can make do not bear the mark of castration.

It is this play between series of "normal" signifiers and a reflexive "empty" signifier which a subjectless digital machine cannot include: it can register the incompleteness of the series, but it cannot invert this incompleteness into a new reflexive signifier. Or, to put it in yet another way, the ultimate difference between the digital universe and the symbolic space proper concerns the status of counterfactuals. Recall the famous joke from Lubitsch's *Ninotchka*: "'Waiter! A cup of coffee without cream, please!' 'I'm sorry, sir, we have no cream, only milk, so can it be a coffee without milk?'" At the factual level, coffee remains the same coffee, but what we can change is to make the coffee without cream into a coffee without milk—or, more simply even, to add the implied negation and to make the plain coffee into a coffee without milk. The difference between "plain coffee" and "coffee without milk" is purely virtual, there is no difference in the real cup of coffee, and exactly the same goes for the Freudian unconscious: its status is also purely virtual, it is not a "deeper" psychic reality—in short, the unconscious is like "milk" in "coffee without milk." And there is the catch: can the digital big Other which knows us better than we know ourselves also discern the difference between "plain coffee" and "coffee without milk"? Or is the counterfactual sphere outside the scope of the digital big Other, which is confined to facts in our brain and social environs that we are unaware of? The difference we are dealing with here is the difference between the "unconscious" (neuronal, social, etc.) facts that determine us and the Freudian "unconscious," whose status is purely counterfactual.

This domain of counterfactuals can be operative only if subjectivity is involved, since the basic twist of every signifying structure (the "primordial repression" of the binary signifier) implies a subject, or, as Lacan, put it, a signifier is that which represents a subject for another signifier. Back to our example: in order to register the difference between "plain coffee" and "coffee without milk," a subject has to be operative.

*

So what was this chapter, which seems to jump from one domain to another totally different one (virtual reality, post-humanity, proliferation of gender identities), really about? Attentive readers could not miss what holds it together: discussion of a unique process—the gradual disintegration of our most basic sense of reality, and of our lives in it, that is taking place today before our eyes. This process is occurring on three different levels, which again relate to each other as a new version of UPS: the *universal* level of the undermining of our basic stance toward reality through the impact of virtual reality (and its offspring, augmented reality and mixed reality); the *particular* level of the threat to the very core of being human that announces itself in the guise of the passage to a trans- or post-human dimension; the *singular* level of human sexuality, which is leaving behind its predominant binary form and approaching a transgender state. In what is this entire process rooted? To find an answer, we have to include yet another, fourth, level: that of the impact of global capitalism, which is the topic of the critique of political economy.

4.7 APPENDIX: THE POST-HUMAN DISORDER

It is interesting to note that Badiou, otherwise Miller's great opponent, follows Miller's path in interpreting our present as the age of the formless Real. His *The True Life*,[30] written in an unashamed Maoist-Platonic pathos—for instance, the second chapter ends with "Long live our daughters and our sons!"[31]—opens with the provocative claim that, from Socrates onward, the function of philosophy has been to corrupt the youth, to alienate (or, rather, estrange) them from the predominant ideologico-political order, to sow radical doubts and enable them to think autonomously. No wonder Socrates, the "first philosopher," was also its first victim, ordered by the democratic court of Athens to drink poison. Today, however, the task of a philosopher is no longer to undermine the hegemonic hierarchical symbolic edifice which grounds social stability, but to make the young aware of the dangers of the growing post-patriarchal nihilist order which presents itself as the domain of new freedoms. We live in an extraordinary era when there is no tradition on which we can base our identity, no frame of meaningful life which would enable us to live a life beyond hedonistic reproduction.[32] This New World Disorder, this gradually emerging worldless civilization, particularly affects the young, who oscillate between the intensity of completely burning out (sexual enjoyment, drugs, alcohol, even up to violence) and the endeavor to succeed (study, forge a career, earn money, etc., within the existing capitalist order), the only alternative being a violent retreat into some artificially resuscitated Tradition. There are attempts to assert a social form of radical negativity (unconstrained expenditure in Bataille's sense of sovereignty) as the only thing that can really undermine the smooth flow of capitalist reproduction. Along these lines, Lee Edelman has developed the notion of homosexuality as involving an ethics of "now," of unconditional fidelity to *jouissance*, of following the death drive by totally ignoring any reference to the future or engagement with the practical complex of worldly affairs. Homosexuality thus stands for the thorough assumption of the negativity of the death drive, of withdrawing from reality into the Real of the "Night of the World." Edelman opposes the radical ethics of homosexuality to the predominant obsession with posterity (i.e., children): children are the "pathological" moment which binds us to pragmatic considerations, and thus compels us to betray the radical ethics of *jouissance*.[33] However, if we follow Badiou, there is a suspicion that the unleashing of such radical negativity is merely the obverse of the capitalist manipulative calculation, its own nihilistic self-destructive aspect.[34]

No wonder, then, that a capitalist total mobilization tends to turn into its opposite, the "irrational" explosion of deadly consumption—both together constitute the two facets of the disintegration of our shared ethical Substance, which affects the two sexes differently: boys are gradually turning into perpetual adolescents, with no clear initiation rites that would enact their entry into maturity (military service, acquiring a profession, even education, no longer play this role). No wonder then, that, in order to supplant this lack, youth gangs proliferate, providing ersatz initiation and social identity. In contrast to boys, girls today are more and more precociously mature, treated as miniature adults, expected to control their lives, to plan their career. ... What, then, is happening to sexual difference today? Traditionally, men were perceived as the bearers of the One (the monotheist God, patriarchal power, stable social hierarchy), while women were associated with the Two, their position being that of "between-the-Two," between mother and whore, lover and saint. Badiou sees in this between-the-Two something much deeper than an after-effect of patriarchy: "a woman is the overcoming of the One in the guise of a passage of between-the-Two. Such is my speculative definition of femininity." The conclusion he draws from this is surprising, but pertinent: by virtue of their very existence women are atheists, they embody resistance to One-God, denouncing it as fiction:

> A woman is always by herself the terrestrial proof that God doesn't exist, that God doesn't have to exist. It is sufficient to look at a woman, to do what is called to take a look, to be immediately convinced that one can well do without God. This is why in traditional societies women are hidden. Things are here more serious than a vulgar sexual jealousy. Tradition knows that, in order to keep God alive in whatever way, women have to be kept absolutely invisible.[35]

Today, however, when the reign of the symbolic One is weakened, the hierarchy of roles and places under a divine Name-of-the-Father is becoming largely irrelevant. To fill this void, a new One is emerging: a hedonistic consumer caught up in market competition, enjoying life and simultaneously a ruthless manipulator in how he/she does it. Here, unexpectedly, sexual difference enters the frame: men are ludic adolescents, out-Laws, while women are "hard, mature, serious, legal and punitive." "This is why there is a bourgeois feminism bent on domination."[36] Women today are not called by the ruling ideology to be subordinated, they are called—interpellated, solicited, expected—to be judges, administrators, ministers, CEOs, teachers, even policewomen and soldiers. A paradigmatic scene occurring daily in our security institutions is that of a female teacher/judge/psychologist taking care of an immature asocial young male delinquent. ... A new figure of the One is thus arising: a cold competitive agent of power, seductive and manipulative, attesting to the paradox that "in the conditions of capitalism women can do better than men."[37]

The ultimate dream of this post-patriarchal feminine society is, of course, that of reproduction without men, of a society reproducing itself principally through the artificial insemination of women: "for the first time in the entire history of humanity, the disappearance of the male sex is really possible."[38] Badiou's solution to this predicament is the creation of a new symbolic space for men and women, beyond traditional patriarchal hierarchy, but also beyond the capitalist nihilism of the Real outside the Law. (Here Badiou comes unexpectedly close to Miller, for whom today's capitalism also functions as a Real outside the symbolic Law.) Such a new symbolic space can arise only by means of a properly philosophical gesture of the creation of new basic Signifiers, of a new symbolization through which both sexes are reinvented: a new space where women are also scientists, politicians, artists, where men also deal with reproduction.[39] Here again Badiou is unexpectedly close to Miller, who sees in today's "postmodern" global society a direct passage from Tradition to Disorder, from symbolized sexuality to the Real of enjoyment outside (symbolic) Law: it is not necessary to wait for a new symbolization of sexuality since, just as today's global capitalism is not a chaotic Real outside the Law but continues to be traversed by antagonisms, sexual difference also persists as the Real, as the bar of an impossibility which outlives its patriarchal symbolization. The first thing to do is thus not to search for the traces of some new symbolization of sexual difference, but to interrogate what is in sexuality here and now more than its patriarchal traditional symbolization. Without this interrogation, the dream of a new symbolic space of sexuality is just that, an empty dream, an ideological mirage that enables us to avoid the antagonism constitutive of human sexuality.

Philosophically, the "woman question" (to use this old, totally inappropriate designation) is thus resolvable neither through a new symbolization, as Badiou proposes, nor through the elevation of woman into an entity which resists symbolization, into the "indivisible remainder" of the process of symbolization. This second path was taken by Schelling, who "knew that one cannot derive an expression like 'woman' from principles. What cannot be derived one should narrate."[40] Schelling's break out of the logical structure of reality (which can be presented as a notional system) into the Real of primordial drives (where there is no deduction, one can only tell a story), i.e., his move from logos to mythos, is thus also an assertion of the Feminine. Schelling extrapolated this line of thought to its extreme: his premise (or, rather, Sloterdijk's premise imputed to Schelling)[41] is that female orgasm, this most ecstatic moment of sexual pleasure (as the ancient Greeks already knew), is the high point of human evolution. Sloterdijk even claims that its experience plays the role of the ontological proof of God: in it, we, humans, come in contact with the Absolute. Schelling tried to break out of the idealist closed circle, bringing in matter, organism, life, development, so he was attentive not only to the pure logical mind but also to what goes on in the bodily sphere, sexuality, with human evolution: bliss is not just the Aristotelian thought thinking itself, but also a body enjoying itself to the almost unbearable maximum.

If, then, female orgasm functions as a new version of the ontological proof of God, as a new version of the One, and if, as Badiou claims, woman always stands for the Two, for a passage, an in-between, a split in the One-God, does atheism imply that we have to denounce full female orgasm as a male fantasy? Definitely yes, which is why the one good thing one can say about the ongoing rise of techno-sex, the process of techno-gadgets replacing human partners, is that it enables us to get rid of the mythic One-Woman, the embodiment of full sexual pleasure. Lacan proposed the neologism *lathouses* as the name for "things that did not exist" prior to the scientific intervention into the Real, from mobile phones to remote-controlled toys, from air-conditioners to artificial hearts: "for the tiny little *a*-objects that you are going to encounter when you leave, on the pavement at every street corner, behind every shop window, in the superabundance of these objects designed to cause your desire in so far as it is now science that governs it, think of them as *lathouses*. I notice a bit late since I invented it not too long ago that it rhymes with *ventouse* [windy]."[42] (And it echoes *vente*, sale, we might add, to bring out the link to capitalism.) But it also rhymes with *partouze* (a slang expression for gangbang), the message of this rhyme being: *lathouse* is the reality of *partouze*, i.e., pleasure administered by gadgets is the reality of full Enjoyment.

As such, *lathouse* is to be opposed to symptom (in the precise Freudian sense of the term): *lathouse* is knowledge embodied (in a new "unnatural" object), while symptom is the subject's ignorance embodied. Now we can see why, apropos of *lathouses*, we have to include capitalism—we are dealing with a whole chain of surpluses: scientific technology, with its surplus-knowledge (a knowledge beyond mere *connaissance* of already existing reality, a knowledge which gets embodied in new objects); capitalist surplus-value (the commodification of this surplus-knowledge in the overflow of gadgets); and, last but not least, the surplus-enjoyment (gadgets as forms of *objet a*) which accounts for the libidinal economy of the hold of *lathouses* over us.

However, although *lathouse* dispels the myth of full feminine enjoyment, it does not resolve the status of the feminine Other: the mythic Woman as the bearer of full orgasm, and *lathouses* that provide supplementary pleasures to men, are merely two ways of avoiding the "woman question." This is why, insofar as philosophers are the thinkers of the One, woman is a scandal for them, and, as Nietzsche noted, a married philosopher is a figure that belongs to comedy—just recall Socrates and his Xanthippe, characterized by

Xenophon as "the hardest to get along with of all the women there are." Even before Socrates, a woman was placed in a similar role in the well-known anecdote about Thales, the first philosopher, told, among others, by Plato in his Theaetetus: while focused on observing the stars, Thales of Miletus failed to see a well directly in his path and fell into it, and a Thracian servant girl laughed, amused by the fact that, while he sought to understand what was above him, he was not mindful of what was right in front of him.[43] But Aristotle provided a counter-story:

> Thales grew weary of the taunts and laughter of his "hard-headed" business acquaintances, who chided him for wandering aimlessly, looking at flowers and clouds, and wasting his time "just thinking," whereas everyone else was industriously making money. So Thales decided to show how knowledge could be the basis for making money. Knowing that olives and olive oil were major commodities of the area, Thales carefully observed the weather, sunshine, rainfall, the growth of crops, and so on. Based on his observations, he predicted a superior olive crop for that year and, without telling anyone, he quietly bought up all the options on the olive presses. When the huge harvest came in just as he had predicted, the farmers, olive oil producers, and merchants, as they did every year at harvest time, tried to contract for use of the olive presses before their crops spoiled. To their surprise and chagrin, they found that Thales had already purchased the options, and they had to pay him high fees or lose their crops.[44]

Much more interesting than the obvious point of this story (a philosopher can earn money—if he is interested in it, which he is not insofar as he is a true philosopher) is the fact that, already at the very beginning of philosophy, a link between philosophical speculation (about stars, about the ultimate reality) and financial speculation is established, a link which culminates in Marx's claim that Hegelian speculation (the self-movement of the Concept) provides the clue to financial speculation (in which money seems to engender more money). (One should note that, in Aristotle's anecdote, Thales is not "practical" in a direct sense—for example, inventing a new, better olive press—but "practical" in the sense of profiting in a totally non-productive way from a clever speculation.) And, perhaps, the couple of Plato and Aristotle that appears here is relevant for the topic we are dealing with—recall Raphael's famous fresco The School of Athens: in the center stand Plato on the left and Aristotle on the right. In a wonderful anachronism, each of the two holds a modern (of Raphael's time) bound copy of a work of his in his left hand, while gesturing with his right (Plato holds Timaeus and Aristotle his NicomacheanEthics). The two figures "gesture along different dimensions: Plato vertically, upward along the picture-plane, into the beautiful vault above; Aristotle on the horizontal plane at right-angles to the picture-plane (hence in strong foreshortening), initiating a powerful flow of space toward viewers. It is popularly thought that their gestures indicate central aspects of their philosophies, for Plato, his TheoryofForms, and for Aristotle, his empiricist views, with an emphasis on concrete particulars. Many interpret the painting to show a divergence of the two philosophical schools. Plato argues a sense of timelessness whilst Aristotle looks into the physicality of life and the present realm."[45]

Is the couple of Plato and Aristotle, then, implicitly sexualized: is Plato presented as masculine and Aristotle as feminine? In short, is Aristotle himself Plato's Thracian servant girl? But is not this notion of women as bearers of ordinary pragmatic common sense, bringing men down to earth from their heaven of pure thinking, all too simple? Our tradition is full of similar notional couples aimed at capturing one aspect of the difference between men and women, and even Badiou is not providing a strict theory of sexual difference; he is simply mobilizing the predominant ideological coordinates that fix the traditional meaning of sexual difference. At this level, one should perhaps supplement him: it is not so much that man and woman are opposed as One and between-the-Two; there is a split that characterizes the ideological coordinates of each of the two sexes. Men are supposed to be subjects of a (given) Word, sticking to principles, while women are prone to empty chatter and lying; plus men are supposed to be adventurous, venturing outside their narrow home domain, while women are more conservative, confined to this domain. A man is thus simultaneously principled and more adventurous, while a woman is more fluid/flirtatious and more stable/conservative ... this inconsistent list goes on and on. But what if all these stories are nothing but desperate attempts to deal with the deadlock of femininity? What if men tell stories about women, what if they concoct myths about the Feminine, in order to obfuscate the logical paradox that constitutes femininity? What if *mythos* is a male attempt to normalize a logical deadlock embodied in a woman? What if "woman" is a logical paradox, not a dark sphere beyond *logos* accessible only through mythic narratives? In short, what if Woman stands neither for the hidden core of the Real beneath the curtain of the symbolic texture, nor for ordinary earthly reality, but for a crack in this reality, for the void or gap which is then filled in with myths and fantasies? Recall how, in his *Phenomenology*, Hegel describes the passage from Consciousness to Self-Consciousness:

> Raised above perception, consciousness reveals itself united and bound up with the supersensible world through the mediating agency of the realm of appearance, through which it gazes into this background that lies behind appearance. The two extremes, the one that of the pure inner region, the other that of the inner being gazing into this pure inner region, are now merged together; and as they have disappeared qua extremes, the middle

term, the mediating agency, qua something other than these extremes, has also vanished. This curtain [of appearance], therefore, hanging before the inner world is withdrawn, and we have here the inner being [the self] gazing into the inner realm—the vision of the undistinguished selfsame reality, which repels itself from itself, affirms itself as a divided and distinguished inner reality, but as one for which at the same time the two factors have immediately no distinction; what we have here is Self-Consciousness. It is manifest that behind the so-called curtain, which is to hide the inner world, there is nothing to be seen unless we ourselves go behind there, as much in order that we may thereby see, as that there may be something behind there which can be seen.[46]

Hegel seems to be saying something relatively simple here: in its last and highest stage of development, Consciousness is looking for the suprasensible truth beyond the "curtain" of our phenomenal reality, and it arrives at this truth when it finds (only) itself beyond the curtain, i.e., when it discovers that the only suprasensible agent is consciousness itself as the dynamic power that undermines the stability of phenomenal reality. … However, such a reading misses the crucial mediating role of failure: Consciousness reaches Self-Consciousness through the experience of the utter failure to discern any content in the Beyond hidden by the curtain of phenomena. More precisely, consciousness does not directly find itself behind the curtain; it finds nothing, a void, it stumbles upon an impossibility, and it become Self-Consciousness only through identifying with this failure/impossibility.

Hegel repeats exactly the same move when he describes how Catholic Crusaders naively believed that they would find in Jerusalem the corpse of Jesus, like a dried-up mummy in a grave, so that they would then be able to bring it back to Europe and display it as a relic in Rome or Paris. The grave of Christ has to be empty, and it is through this traumatic disappointment, through confronting this crying/gaping void, that the spirit of Europe comes to itself. This correlation of spirit and missing object is crucial, and what Lacan adds to it is only that this missing object, this lack of object, has to be embodied in an object which is nothing but the positivization of a lack.

And this brings us back to the "woman question": philosophers of the One were right, "woman" is in effect an ontological scandal, also in the original sense of the Greek skandalon (a snare, trap, offense, stumbling block). And since the philosophical name for this scandal of ontology, for an entity which can never be located in the order of being, is subject, we should draw the conclusion that subject is, at its most radical level, feminine. Feminine failure is the (back)ground of all masculine conquests and achievements. Woman is not a failed subject (as if only a man can be a full subject), woman is the ontological failure which opens up the space for subjectivity. Woman is a subject which precedes subjectivity.

PART II

THE BELATED ACTUALITY OF MARX'S
CRITIQUE OF POLITICAL ECONOMY

In his conversations with Truffaut, Hitchcock recalls the quintessential scene that he wanted to insert into *North by Northwest*—the scene was never shot, undoubtedly because it reveals all too directly the basic matrix of his work, so that its actual filming would have produced the effect of an almost indecent obviousness:

> I wanted to have a long dialogue between Cary Grant and one of the factory workers [at a Ford automobile plant] as they walk along the assembly line. Behind them a car is being assembled, piece by piece. Finally, the car they've seen being put together from a simple nut and bolt is complete, with gas and oil, and all ready to drive off the line. The two men look at each other and say, "Isn't it wonderful!" Then they open the door of the car and out drops a corpse.[1]

What we would have seen in this long shot is the elementary unity of the *production process*—is not the corpse that mysteriously drops out from nowhere, then, the perfect stand-in for the surplus-value that is generated "out of nowhere" through the production process? This corpse is the surplus-object at its purest, the objectal counterpoint to the subject, the surplus-product of the subject's activity. If we are to grasp this link between subject and object (which totally subverts the conventional philosophical notion of this couple) properly, it is crucial to avoid the equally conventional modern opposition of production and representation, i.e., the (Deleuzian and poststructuralist) assertion of the site of production which is reflected in a constrained/distorted way in the scene of re-presentation as its pale shadow. Already Lacan's definition of the signifier gives clear guidance on this point: he asserts the priority of representation—a subject is what is represented in a signifier, not the productive force that generates signifiers. It is against the background of this rejection of the centrality of production that one should read the parallax between subject of (signifying) representation and object (of production), between lack and surplus. I must be precise here: the surplus-object emerges as the result (product) of the very process of representation; it is the embodiment of its failure. (Note how, in Marx also, surplus originates from the failure of the value of the labor force to include the value of its product.) Production occurs at the point of the failure of representation: the surplus is produced, emerges, only through representation/exchange, i.e., production (of surplus-enjoyment) is a process which takes place within the sphere of representation, there is no "presubjective" acephalous production of *jouissance* or flow of desire or whatever, so we are as far as possible from the Deleuzian vision of some primordial productivity secondarily constrained by the scene of representation.

Insofar as the object arises through the failure of representation, the surplus that emerges in the process of production cannot be thought without the subject: the surplus-object is the site of the inscription of the subject into the process of production. This same formal structure is at work at different levels, which is why Marxian surplus-value is to be included in the series with surplus-enjoyment and (the oft-neglected) surplus-knowledge. Surplus-knowledge is a knowledge in excess of ordinary knowledge, a pseudo-knowledge, a specter of "deeper" knowledge which fills in the gap of the lack of knowledge: a knowledge of "something more," not just our ordinary reality, in all the multiplicity of its versions, from gnostic "higher" truths and New Age speculations to conspiracy theories.

And the subject? The subject is the ultimate surplus, an empty surplus site filled in by the surpluses of knowledge, enjoyment, etc.: the ultimate effect without cause.

5.1 THE PARADOX OF *LUSTGEWINN*

Lacan begins the eleventh week of his seminar *Les non-dupes errent* (1973–1974) with a straight question directed back at himself: "what was it that Lacan, who is here present, invented?" He answers the question "like that, to get things going: *objet a*."[1] So it is not "desire is the desire of the Other," "the unconscious is structured like a language," "there is no sexual relationship," or any other from the list of usual suspects: Lacan immediately emphasizes that his choice is not just one among the possible ones, but *the* choice.

Objet a has a long history in Lacan's teaching; it precedes by decades his systematic references to the analysis of commodities in Marx's *Capital*. But it is undoubtedly this reference to Marx, especially to Marx's notion of surplus-value (*Mehrwert*), that enabled Lacan to deploy his "mature" notion of *objet a* as surplus-enjoyment (*plus-de-jouir*, *Mehrlust*): the dominant theme which permeates all his references to Marx's analysis of commodities is the structural homology between Marx's surplus-value and what Lacan baptized surplus-enjoyment, the phenomenon called by Freud *Lustgewinn*, a "gain of pleasure," which designates not a simple stepping up of pleasure but the additional pleasure provided by the very formal detours in the subject's effort to attain pleasure. Think about Brecht's *Me-Ti* which, in its retelling of the history of revolutionary movements in Europe, transposes them into an imaginary China (Trotsky becomes To-tsi, etc.): our retranslation of pseudo-Chinese names back into their European original ("Aha, To-tsi is Trotsky!") makes the text much more pleasurable—just imagine how much *Me-Ti* would have lost if it had been written as a direct report on European history. Or—the most elementary example—how much a process of seduction gains with its intricate innuendos, false denials, etc.: these detours are not just cultural complications or sublimations circulating around some hardcore Real—this hardcore Real is retroactively constituted through secondary detours; "in itself" it remains a fiction.

Samo Tomšič is right to draw from this logic of surplus the radical conclusion: just as, in libidinal economy, there is no "pure" pleasure principle undisturbed by the perversities of compulsion-to-repeat which cannot be accounted for in terms of the pleasure principle, in the sphere of the exchange of commodities there is no direct closed circle of exchanging a commodity for money in order to buy another commodity, a circle not yet corroded by the perverse logic of buying and selling commodities in order to get more money: the logic in which money is no longer just a mediator in the exchange of commodities but becomes an end-in-itself. The only reality is the reality of spending money in order to get more money, and what Marx calls C-M-C, the closed exchange of a commodity for money in order to buy another commodity, is ultimately a fiction whose function it is to provide a "natural" foundation for the process of exchange ("It's not just about money and more money, the whole point of exchange is to satisfy concrete human needs!"): "C-M-C is not more immediate, not an authentic exchange that is later corrupted by profit-oriented M-C-M′, but an inner fiction of the circulation (M-C-M′)."[2] In other words, M-C-M′ is the symptomal point at which a gap or reversal which was operative from the very beginning, even in the simplest commodity exchange, breaks out into the open:

> Lustgewinn is the first sign that the homeostasis of the pleasure principle is mere fiction. Nevertheless it demonstrates that no satisfaction of needs can produce more pleasure, just as no surplus-value can logically follow from the circulation (C-M-C). Surplus-jouissance, the connection of pleasure with profit making, does not simply undermine the supposedly homeostatic character of the pleasure principle; it shows that the homeostasis is a necessary fiction, which structures and supports unconscious production, just as the imaginary achievement of worldview mechanisms consisted in providing an enclosed whole, without cracks in its overall construction. Lustgewinn is Freud's first conceptual confrontation with what will later be situated beyond the pleasure principle, the compulsion to repeat, and what will introduce the psychoanalytic equivalent to the circulation (M-C-M′).[3]

In short, just as better is the enemy of good, more pleasure is the enemy of pleasure. The process of the "gain-of-pleasure" (Lustgewinn) operates through repetition: one misses the goal and repeats the movement, trying again and again, so that the true aim is no longer the intended goal but the repetitive movement of attempting to reach it. One can also put it in terms of form and content, where "form" stands for the form, the mode, of approaching the desired content: while the desired content (object) promises to provide pleasure, a surplus-enjoyment is gained by the very form (procedure) of pursuing the goal. This is the classic example of how oral drive functions:

while the goal of sucking a breast is to get fed by milk, the libidinal gain is provided by the repetitive movement of sucking, which thus becomes an end-in-itself. Is not something similar going on in a (dubious) story about Robespierre often mentioned by critics of Jacobinism? When one of Robespierre's allies was accused of acting in an illegitimate way, he demanded (to the surprise of those close to him) that the charges be taken seriously, and proposed the immediate constitution of a special commission to examine the allegations; when one of his friends expressed his worry about the fate of the accused (what if he is found guilty? Will this not be bad news for the Jacobins?), Robespierre calmly smiled back: "Don't worry about that, somehow we'll save the accused ... but now we have the commission!" The commission which will remain at the disposal of the Jacobins to purge their enemies—this was for Robespierre the true gain in what appeared to be a concession to his enemies. Another figure of *Lustgewinn* is the reversal that characterizes hysteria: renunciation of pleasure reverts to a pleasure of/in renunciation, repression of desire reverts to a desire for repression, etc. In all these cases, gain occurs on a "performative" level: it is generated by the very performance of working toward a goal, not by reaching the goal.

After a Walmart store closes in the evening, many shopping carts full of items thrown into them are found among the shelves; they were mostly abandoned there by members of the newly impoverished middle-class families who are no longer able to buy things, so they—usually the whole family—visit the store, go through the ritual of shopping (throwing things they needed or desired into a cart), and then just abandon the full cart and leave the store. In this sad way, they obtain the surplus-enjoyment of shopping in its pure isolated form, without buying anything. And are we not often engaged in similar activities, even if their "irrationality" is not so directly visible? We do something—including shopping itself—with a clear purpose, but we are really indifferent toward this purpose, since the true satisfaction is brought about by the activity itself. The example of Walmart merely lays bare something that is already at work in "real" shopping. This example also enables us to perceive clearly the link between *Lustgewinn* and surplus-value: with *Lustgewinn*, the aim of the process is not its official goal (satisfaction of a need), but the expanded self-reproduction of the process itself—as we saw in our example of oral drive, the true aim of sucking the mother's breast is not to get fed by milk but the pleasure brought by the activity of sucking itself—and in an exactly homologous way, with surplus-value, the true aim of the process of exchange is not the appropriation of a commodity that would satisfy a need of mine, but the expanded self-reproduction of capital itself. This process is by definition infinite, without a final point.

And does not exactly the same hold for bureaucracy? There are two memorable scenes in Terry Gilliam's movie *Brazil* which perfectly stage the crazy excess of bureaucratic *jouissance* perpetuating itself in its autocirculation. After the hero's plumbing breaks down, and he leaves a message to the official repair service for urgent help, Robert De Niro enters his apartment, a mythical-mysterious criminal whose subversive activity is that he listens in on emergency calls and then immediately goes to the customer, repairing his plumbing for free, bypassing the inefficient state repair service's paperwork. Indeed, in a bureaucracy caught in this vicious cycle of *jouissance*, the ultimate crime is to simply and directly do the job one is supposed to do—if a state repair service actually does its job, this is (at the level of its unconscious libidinal economy) considered an unfortunate byproduct, since the bulk of its energy goes into inventing complicated administrative procedures that enable it to invent ever-new obstacles, and thus postpone the work indefinitely. In a second scene, we meet—in the corridors of a vast government agency—a group of people permanently running around, a leader (big-shot bureaucrat) followed by a bunch of lower administrators who shout at him all the time, asking him for a specific opinion or decision, and he nervously spurts out fast, "efficient" replies ("This is to be done by tomorrow latest!" "Check that report!" "No, cancel that appointment!"). This appearance of nervous hyperactivity is, of course, a staged performance which masks a self-indulgent, nonsensical spectacle of imitating, of playing "efficient administration"—again, a case of *Mehrgenuss*, of the surplus-pleasure brought by the very unending bureaucratic performance.

We find an even more unexpected example of this surplus-enjoyment in Thomas Aquinas's *Summa Theologica*, where he draws the conclusion that the blessed in the Kingdom of Heaven will see the punishments of the damned in order that their bliss be more delightful for them (and St. John Bosco drew the same conclusion in the opposite direction: the damned in Hell will also be able to see the joy of those in Heaven, which will add to their suffering). Here are Aquinas's two formulation of this claim:

> Nothing should be denied the blessed that belongs to the perfection of their beatitude. ... Wherefore in order that the happiness of the saints may be more delightful to them and that they may render more copious thanks to God for it, they are allowed to see perfectly the sufferings of the damned.[4]

> That the saints may enjoy their beatitude more thoroughly, and give more abundant thanks for it to God, a perfect sight of the punishment of the damned is granted them.[5]

Aquinas, of course, is careful to avoid the obscene implication that good souls in Heaven can find pleasure in observing the terrible suffering of other souls. He proceeds in two moves. He begins with the thesis that, in Heaven, the blessed will enjoy full illumination of their minds, and that knowledge is also a blessing and perfection that should not be denied to the saints. If the saints in Heaven were to be ignorant of the damned, this would be a denial of the blessing of knowledge. Consequently, the saints in Heaven will possess a greater knowledge, including a greater knowledge of Hell, even seeing it. Next problem: good Christians should feel pity when they see suffering—will the blessed in Heaven also feel pity for the torments of the damned? Aquinas's no is grounded in a rather flimsy hair-splitting argumentation:

> Seeing the punishment of the wicked, the righteous have no pity: Whoever pities another shares somewhat in his unhappiness. But the blessed cannot share in any unhappiness. Therefore they do not pity the afflictions of the damned.[6]

Aquinas's second line of argumentation tries to refute the notion that the blessed in Heaven gain joy from the punishment of the damned in a direct obscene way—he does this by introducing a distinction between two modes of enjoying a thing:

> A thing may be a matter of rejoicing in two ways. First directly, when one rejoices in a thing as such: and thus the saints will not rejoice in the punishment of the wicked. Secondly, indirectly, by reason namely of something annexed to it: and in this way the saints will rejoice in the punishment of the wicked, by considering therein the order of Divine justice and their own deliverance, which will fill them with joy. And thus the Divine justice and their own deliverance will be the direct cause of the joy of the blessed: while the punishment of the damned will cause it indirectly.[7]

The problem of this last explanation is, of course, that the relationship between the two levels would have been, in effect, turned around: enjoying Divine Justice would have functioned as the rationalization, the moral cover-up, for sadistically enjoying the neighbor's eternal suffering. What makes Aquinas's formulation suspicious is the surplus-enjoyment it introduces: as if the simple pleasure of living in the bliss of Heaven is not enough, and has to be supplemented by an additional surplus-enjoyment of being allowed to take a look at another's suffering—only in this way may the blessed souls "enjoy their beatitude more thoroughly." ... Here we can easily imagine the appropriate scene in Heaven: when some blessed souls complain that the nectar served was not as tasty as it was last time, and that blissful life up there is rather boring after all, angels serving the blessed souls would snap back: "You don't like it here? So take a look at how life is down there, at the other end, and maybe you will learn how lucky you are to be here!" And the corresponding scene in Hell should also be imagined as totally different from St. John Bosco's vision: far away from the Divine gaze and control, the damned souls enjoy an intense and pleasurable life in Hell—only from time to time, when the Devil's administrators of Hell learn that the blessed souls in Heaven will be allowed briefly to observe life in Hell, they kindly implore the damned souls to stage a performance and pretend to suffer terribly in order to impress the idiots from Heaven. ... In short, the sight of the other's suffering is the *objet a*, the obscure cause of desire which sustains our own happiness (bliss in Heaven)—if we take our sight of the other's suffering away, our bliss appears in all its sterile stupidity.

This inherently boring aspect of Paradise justifies Sloterdijk's simple but correct reproach to the Muslim notion of paradise as a place where 70 virgins are awaiting a hero, offering themselves to be copulated again and again: "Nowhere on the earth one dies in order to copulate on the other side. ... Every meaningful version of paradise is based on the motif of a deep relaxation which, however, one should not equate with the construct of death drive in psychoanalysis."[8]

But if one wants to see a much more radical, clinically clear case of the opposition of pleasure and enjoyment, it is enough to take a look at Joseph Goebbels's (in)famous speech on total war, "Wollt ihr den totalen Krieg?" (Do you want a total war?), delivered in the Sportpalast in Berlin on February 18, 1943. Goebbels addresses a public shocked by the Stalingrad defeat: he freely admits the difficult (if not desperate) situation, then asks the public ten questions (and, of course, gets to each of them an enthusiastic yes). Here are some fragments:

> I ask you: Are you, and the German nation, resolved to work ten, twelve, and if need be fourteen or sixteen hours a day, if the Führer should command it, and to give your all for victory? ... I ask you: Do you want total war? Do you want it, if need be, even more total and radical than we are capable of imagining it today? ... I ask you: Is your confidence in the Führer more passionate, more unshakable than ever? Is your readiness to follow him on all his paths, and to do whatever is necessary to bring the war to a successful conclusion, absolute and unlimited? ... As my tenth and last question I ask you: Is it your wish that even in wartime, as the party program commands, equal rights and equal duties shall prevail, that the home front shall give evidence of its solidarity and take the same heavy burdens of war upon its shoulders, and that the burdens be distributed equitably, whether a person be great or small, poor or rich? ... I have asked you. You have given me your answers. You are a part of the nation; your response has thus shown the attitude of the German people. You have told our enemies what they must know lest they abandon themselves to illusions and misinformation. ... Now, people, rise up, and let the storm break loose![9]

What these questions demand is a gigantic renunciation of pleasure, and more sacrifice, even sacrifice brought to an extreme, "absolute and unlimited"; Goebbels promises a war "even more total and radical than we are capable of imagining it today," with civilians working up to sixteen hours a day … and yet, his ecstatically shouting voice and weirdly grimacing face at the climactic moments of this speech bear witness to a *jouissance* in renunciation itself, which reaches beyond imagination and approaches the absolute. In these moments, his outward-directed rage subtly turns into passivity, as if his face is twisted in an orgasmic way, passively experiencing a painful lust—a case of "pleasure in pain" if ever there was one, an expression of a distorted Kantian sublime in which the pain of renunciation coincides with an ecstatic witnessing of a noumenal dimension.

This is why we should apply to the humanitarians who bemoan "the end of Europe" the great Hegelian lesson: when someone paints a picture of Europe's absolute and utter moral degeneration, the question to be raised is in what way such a stance is complicit in what it criticizes. No wonder that, with the exception of humanitarian appeals to compassion and solidarity, the effects of such compassionate self-flagellation are null. If we in the West really want to overcome racism, the first thing to do is to leave behind this politically correct process of endless self-culpabilization. Although Pascal Bruckner's critique of today's Left often approaches ridicule, that does not prevent him from occasionally generating pertinent insights—one cannot but agree with him when he detects in European politically correct self-flagellation an inverted clinging to one's own superiority. Whenever the West is attacked, its first reaction is not aggressive defense but self-probing: What did we do to deserve it? We are ultimately to blame for the evils of the world; Third World catastrophes and terrorist violence are merely reactions to our crimes. … The positive form of the White Man's Burden (responsibility for civilizing the colonized barbarians) is thus merely replaced by its negative form (the burden of the white man's guilt): if we can no longer be the benevolent masters of the Third World, we can at least be the privileged source of evil, patronizingly depriving them of their responsibility for their fate (if a Third World country engages in terrible crimes, it is never their own responsibility, but always an aftereffect of colonization: they are merely imitating what their colonial masters did, etc.). This privilege is the *Mehrgenuss* earned by self-culpabilization.

Along these lines, politically correct logic often mobilizes the mechanism of what one could call "delegated sensitivity":[10] its line of argumentation is often "I am tough enough, I am not hurt by sexist and racist hate speech or by making fun of minorities, but I am speaking for all those who may be hurt by it"—the points of reference are thus the presupposed naive Others, those who need protection because they will miss the irony or cannot stand attacks. This is yet another case of what Robert Pfaller called "interpassivity":[11] I delegate the passive experience of a hurt sensitivity onto a naive other, thereby enacting the other's infantilization. That is why we should ask ourselves if political correctness is really something that belongs to the Left—is it not a strategy of defense against radical Leftist demands, a way to neutralize antagonisms instead of openly confronting them? Many of the oppressed feel clearly how the PC strategy often just adds insult to injury: while oppression remains, they—the oppressed—now even have to be grateful for the way liberals try to protect them.

One of the most deplorable byproducts of the wave of refugees that entered Europe in the winter of 2015/2016 was the explosion of moralist outrage among many Left liberals: "Europe is betraying its legacy of universal freedom and solidarity! It has lost its moral compass! It treats war refugees like infesting intruders, preventing their entry with barbed wire, locking them up in concentration camps!" Such abstract empathy, combined with calls to open up the borders unconditionally, deserves the great Hegelian lesson of the Beautiful Soul—but what if the authors of such appeals knew very well that they would contribute nothing to the terrible plight of the refugees, that the ultimate effect of their interventions is just to feed anti-immigrant resentment? What if secretly they know very well that what they are demanding will never happen, since it would trigger an instant populist revolt in Europe? Why, then, are they doing it? There is only one consistent answer: the true aim of their activity is not really to help the refugees but the *Lustgewinn* brought about by their accusations, the feeling of their own moral superiority over others—the more refugees are rejected, the more anti-immigrant populism grows, the more these Beautiful Souls feel vindicated: "You see, the horror goes on, we are right!" …

5.2 SURPLUS-POWER

The next step to be taken here is to grasp the link between this surplus and lack: it is not just that a surplus fills in a lack; surplus and lack are two sides of the same coin. Hegel produces the exact formula of this paradoxical relationship between lack and surplus apropos of the "rabble":

> § 245 When the masses begin to decline into poverty, (a) the burden of maintaining them at their ordinary standard of living might be directly laid on the wealthier classes, or they might receive the means of livelihood directly from other public sources of wealth (e.g. from the endowments of rich hospitals, monasteries, and other foundations). In either case, however, the needy would receive subsistence directly, not by means of their work, and this would violate the principle of civil society and the feeling of individual independence and self-respect in its individual members.
> (b) As an alternative, they might be given subsistence indirectly through

being given work, i.e. the opportunity to work. In this event the volume of production would be increased, but the evil consists precisely in an excess of production and in the lack of a proportionate number of consumers who are themselves also producers, and thus it is simply intensified by both of the methods (a) and (b) by which it is sought to alleviate it. It hence becomes apparent that despite an excess of wealth civil society is not rich enough, i.e. its own resources are insufficient to check excessive poverty and the creation of a penurious rabble.[12]

So it is the very surplus that (re-)creates the lack it is supposed to fill in, so that we should even radicalize Hegel's formulation: it is not only that "despite an excess of wealth civil society is not rich enough," it is *the very excess of wealth that makes it not rich enough* (to get rid of poverty). In other words, the key question is: if there is a surplus (excessive wealth) on the one side, and a lack (poverty) on the other side, why can't we reestablish the balance by simple redistribution (taking the wealth from the excessively rich and giving it to the poor)? The formal answer: because lack and surplus are not located within the same space where they are just unequally distributed (some people lack things, others have too much). The paradox of wealth resides in the fact that the more you have, the more you feel the lack—it is again the superego paradox (the more you follow the injunction, the more guilty you are), discernible also in the paradox of anti-Semitism (the more Jews are destroyed, the more powerful are those who remain).

A different version of this same logic of lack and its surplus was also at work in the everyday experience of life in so-called Really Existing Socialism. Despite the oppressiveness of the political regime, and the profound distrust of the majority of the population toward the ruling power, a kind of unspoken pact held between those in power and their subjects. Most of the time, the basic feature of life was, of course, lack in the guise of shortages—something was always unavailable in the stores and in general in public services: not enough meat or milk products, not enough detergent, no beds in hospitals, not enough apartments, etc., etc. In order to survive, the majority of people had to turn to petty violations of the law (bribery, personal connections, moonlighting, black market, and other forms of cheating), which were discreetly tolerated by those in power—while people were aware that everyone could be prosecuted, almost no one really was, so although people lived in relative poverty, almost everyone felt that he was at an advantage, that he somehow got more than his due. This situation gave rise to a unique combination of cynical distance and an obscene solidarity in guilt: people were grateful for not being prosecuted, they were satisfied by gaining small illegal profits. ... This perception of getting more than one's due was literally the obverse of the life of shortages; it was what made this life bearable.

The same codependence between surplus (of power) and its lack (impotence) characterizes the functioning of political power. For a somewhat simplified example of the excess constitutive of the functioning of an actual power, recall the traditional liberal notion of representative power: citizens transfer (part of) their power to the state, but under precise conditions (this power is constrained by law, limited to very precise conditions of its exercise, since the people remain the ultimate source of sovereignty, and can repeal power if they so decide). In short, the state, with its power, is the minor partner in a contract which the major partner (the people) can at any point repeal or change, basically in the same way as each of us can change the contractor which takes care of our waste or our health. However, the moment one takes a close look at an actual state power edifice, one can easily detect an implicit but unmistakable signal: "Forget about our limitations—ultimately, we can do whatever we like with you!" This excess is not a contingent supplement spoiling the purity of power, but its necessary constituent—without it, without the threat of arbitrary omnipotence, state power is not a true power, it loses its authority.

The "subject-supposed-to-be-in-power" is a structural illusion immanent to the functioning of power: the illusion that there is a bearer/agent of power, an entity which pulls the strings. Le Gaufey's formula for overcoming this mirage is *la toute-puissance sans tout-puissant*:[13] omnipotence is a fact of the symbolic universe in which we can retroactively change the past. According to the standard view, the past is fixed, what happened happened, it cannot be undone, and the future is open, it depends on unpredictable contingencies. What we should propose here is a reversal of this standard view: the past is open to retroactive reinterpretations, while the future is closed, since we live in a determinist universe (see Frank Ruda's defense of determinism).[14] This does not mean that we cannot change the future; it just means that, in order to change our future, we should first (not "understand" but) change our past, reinterpret it in a way that opens up toward a different future from the one implied by the predominant vision of the past.

The proper atheist/materialist position is thus not to deny omnipotence but to assert it without an agent that sustains it (God or another omnipotent Entity)—but is this enough? Do we not have to take a further step and assert the thwarted (inconsistent, constrained) character of the big Other *qua* depersonalized structure? And it is precisely this inconsistency/limitation of the big Other that resubjectivizes it in the sense of raising the question "But what does the Other want?" And, of course, in a Hegelian way, this enigma of the Other's desire is an enigma for the Other itself. Only at this level do we reach "symbolic castration," which does not stand for the subject's "castration," for his/her being at the mercy of the big Other, for his/her depending on its whims, but for the "castration" of this Other itself. The barred Other is thus not just the depersonalized Other but also the bar which cracks this depersonalized Other itself.

Furthermore, the specter of omnipotence arises when we stumble upon the limitation of the Other's potency: *toute-puissance* (omnipotence) is *toute-en-puissance* (all-in-potentiality), the actualization of its power/potency is always constrained: "Omnipotence is for Lacan not a kind of maximum, apex, or even infinitization of potency—to which one often reduces it in order to deny its actual existence—but a beyond of potency which appears only in the latter's failure. It does not appear on the slope of impotence but on the slope of what remains 'all-in-potentiality,' without ever passing over into the dimension of an act which belongs to the domain of some determinate potency/power."[15]

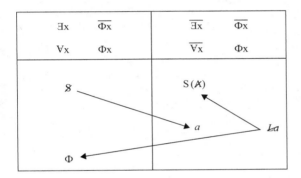

A reference to Lacan's formulas of sexuation may be of some help here—it is crucial how we read here the double line that points from $\not{La}$ to $S(\not{A})$ and to Φ: we should not read it as a substantial division between two options (part of woman is subordinated to castration, caught in the phallic economy of the symbolic order, while another part is outside, immersed in the unspeakable *jouissance féminine*). We should bear in mind that in both cases, Φ and $S(\not{A})$, we are dealing with the same logic of the reflexive reversal of the lack of a signifier into a signifier of a lack—we are dealing with the same element in a different modality, maybe a little bit like the (in)famous soft-porn postcards from the predigital era with a woman who, when you look at the postcard from a certain edge, is wearing a T-shirt, but when you twist it around a tiny bit, her breasts appear to be bare. ... Do we not get the same shift in Lacan's scheme? The capitalized Φ is the fascinating quasi-divine presence, and just a slight shift in perspective makes it appear as the signifier of a lack. This brings us back to the link between omnipotence and impotence: the divine Omnipotence is, as Lacan saw clearly, a twisted mode of appearance of the divine impotence.

5.3 SURPLUS-KNOWLEDGE AND SCIENCE

And does not exactly the same hold for knowledge? Is not "higher" meta-physical knowledge a form of appearance of its opposite, ignorance? More precisely, surplus-knowledge has two forms, masculine and feminine. The masculine form supplements ordinary knowledge of reality with another, higher knowledge as the exception (gnosis), while the feminine form is that of modern science, where surplus is inscribed into normal scientific knowledge, which is constantly transforming/overcoming itself.[16] There is a homology between the surplus-knowledge of modern science and capitalist surplus-value: both are appropriated by the capitalist master. Before capitalism, knowledge was on the side of the servant—a master gave the order and the artisan servant was supposed to have the practical knowledge to execute it, a farmer was supposed to know how to grow crops, etc. With capitalism, the production process gets split from within, its scientific foundation and the organizational knowledge that regulates it is on the side of the capitalist and turned against the worker.

> I would call the state of knowledge before Descartes pre-accumulative. With Descartes knowledge, scientific knowledge, is constituted on the mode of production of knowledge. Just as an essential stage of our structure that one calls social but is in fact metaphysical, and which is called capitalism, is accumulation of capital, the relation of the Cartesian subject to this being, which is affirmed in it, is founded on the accumulation of knowledge. After Descartes knowledge is what serves to make knowledge grow.[17]

If, then, the moment of Descartes stands for the "primordial accumulation of knowledge," one should immediately raise the question: accumulated from where? Not from ancient traditions: the new capitalist master appropriates it from the worker's artisanal *savoir-faire* and integrates it into science. Ancient wisdoms and teachings transferred to the initiated belong to masters and priests to whom operational expert knowledge appears too lowly to care about, better left to the subordinated, while capitalists take expert knowledge from their servants/workers. The master's wisdom is repetitive, it functions as a fidelity to established tradition (if a revolution occurs, it has to appear as a return to true origins, as in Protestantism), it lacks the drive to self-renovation and expansion. In contrast, modern science is split between university and hysteria: like capitalism, which can reproduce itself only through permanent expansion, scientific knowledge's mode of existence is self-expansion, permanent discovery, the search for more knowledge, and this modality of knowledge is properly hysterical, a permanent experience of "This is not (yet) that!," a permanent search for more knowledge to be found elsewhere. I am tempted to propose here, in homology with the formula M-C-M', the formula of the self-propelled accumulation of knowledge K-T-K'—in both cases, we have the same self-propelling circularity: money begets more money, knowledge begets more knowledge. In terms of discourses, this means that the University discourse in itself is not able to generate more knowledge out of itself, following its own logic—it has to make a detour through the discourse of hysteria, the product of which is (new) knowledge:

> Something changed in the master's discourse at a certain point in history. We are not going to break our backs finding out if it was because of Luther, or Calvin, or some unknown traffic of ships around Genoa, or in the Mediterranean Sea, or anywhere else, for the important point is that on a certain day surplus-*jouissance* became calculable, could be counted, totalized. This is where what is called the accumulation of capital begins.[18]

This shift is the shift from the auratic *je ne sais quoi*, what Plato called *agalma*, what is in a charismatic person "more than him- or herself," the surplus over measurable qualities, the mysterious ingredient which by definition cannot be measured (the X that makes a master a master, a star a star … or, for anti-Semites, a Jew a Jew), to a purely quantified surplus, a surplus that can be measured in the guise of profit.

For Lacan, modern science is defined by two concomitant foreclosures: the foreclosure of the subject and the foreclosure of truth as cause. A scientific text is enounced from a desubjectivized "empty" location, it allows for no references to its subject of enunciation, it is supposed to deliver the impersonal truth which can be repeatedly demonstrated, "anyone can see and say it," i.e., the truth should be in no way affected by its place of enunciation. We can already see the link with the Cartesian *cogito*: is not the "empty" enunciator of scientific statements the subject of thought reduced to a vanishing punctuality, deprived of all its properties? This same feature also accounts for the foreclosure of truth as cause: when I commit a slip of the tongue and say something other than what I wanted to say, and this other message tells a truth about me that I am often not ready to recognize, then one can also say that in my slips the truth itself spoke, subverting what I wanted to say. There is truth (a truth about my desire) in such slips, even if they contain factual inexactitude—to take an extremely simple example, when the moderator of a debate, instead of saying "I am thereby opening the session!" says "I am thereby closing the session!" he obviously indicates that he is bored and considers the debate worthless. "Truth" (of my subjective position) is the cause of such slips; when it operates, the subject is directly inscribed into its speech, disturbing the smooth flow of "objective" knowledge.

How, then, can Lacan claim that the subject of psychoanalysis—the divided subject, the subject traversed by negativity—is the subject of modern science (and the Cartesian *cogito*)? Is it not that, by foreclosing truth and subject, modern science also ignores negativity? Is science not a radical attempt to construct a (literally) truthless discourse of knowledge? Modern science breaks with the traditional universe held together by a deeper meaning (like a harmony of cosmic principles—yin and yang, etc.), a universe which forms a teleologically ordered Whole of a multiplicity of hierarchically ordered spheres, a Whole in which everything serves a higher purpose. In the philosophical tradition, the major vestige of the traditional view is Aristotle: Aristotelian Reason is organic-teleological, in clear contrast to the radical contingency of modern science. No wonder today's Catholic Church attacks Darwinism as "irrational" in comparison with the Aristotelian notion of Reason: the "reason" of which the Church speaks is a Reason for which Darwin's theory of evolution (and, ultimately, modern science itself, for which the assertion of the contingency of the universe, the break with Aristotelian teleology, is a constitutive axiom) is "irrational."

Freud's arch-opponent Jung is on the side of this traditional universe: his approach to psychic phenomena is effectively that of "depth psychology," his vision is that of a closed world sustained by deeper archetypal meanings, a world permeated by spiritual forces which operate at a level "deeper" than that of "mechanical" sciences, a level at which there are no contingencies, where ordinary occurrences partake in a profound spiritual meaning to be unearthed by self-exploration; life has a spiritual purpose beyond material goals, and our task is to discover and fulfill our deep innate potential by embarking on a journey of inner transformation which brings us in contact with the mystical heart of all religions, a journey to meet the self and at the same time to meet the Divine. Rejecting (what he perceived as) Freud's scientific objectivism, Jung thus advocates a version of pantheism which identifies individual human life with the universe as a whole.

In clear contrast to Jung, Freud emphasizes the lack of any harmony between a human being and its environs, any correspondence between human microcosm and natural macrocosm, accepting without any reserve the fact of a contingent meaningless universe. That is Freud's achievement: psychoanalysis is not a return to a new kind of premodern hermeneutics in search of the unknown deep layers of meaning which regulate the apparently meaningless flow of our lives, it is not a new version of the ancient interpretation of dreams searching for deeper messages hidden in them; our psychic life is thoroughly open to unexpected traumatic encounters, its unconscious processes are a domain of contingent signifying displacements; there is no inner truth at the core of our being, only a cobweb of *proton pseudos*, primordial lies called "fundamental fantasies"; the task of the psychoanalytic process is not to reconcile ourselves with the fantasmatic core of our being but to "traverse" it, to acquire a distance toward it. This brief description explains how psychoanalysis relates to modern science: it tries to resubjectivize the universe of science, to discern the contours of a subject that fits modern science, a subject that fully participates in the contingent and meaningless "gray world" of the sciences. The question that arises here is: how does capitalism fit into this passage to modern science? "Capitalism then needs to be thought of as the restoration of pre-modernity within modernity, a counter-revolution that neutralizes the emancipatory political potential of scientific revolution."[19] Although capitalism is intimately linked to the rise of modern science, its ideologico-political and economic organization (liberal egotist individuals pursuing their interests, their messy interaction secretly regulated by the big Other of the Market) signals a return to the premodern universe—but does this mean that Communism extends the logic of modern science also to the ethico-political sphere? Kant's goal was to do exactly this, to elaborate an ethico-political edifice that would be on the level of modern science—but did he in fact achieve this, or is his theoretical edifice a compromise? Did he not openly say that his goal was to limit knowledge in order to make space for belief? And are not Habermasians doing the same when they exempt intersubjectivity from the domain of objective science? (And, in this vein, does not Hegel stand for a return to the Aristotelian organic-teleological view of reality as a rational Whole? Is his thought not marked by a rejection of the universe of modern science characterized by meaningless contingency?) Which, then, is the ethico-political space that fits modern science, Kant's or a new one to be invented (for example, the one proposed by brain scientists like Patricia and Paul Churchland)? What if the two are necessarily nonsynchronous, i.e., what if modernity itself *needs* a premodern ethico-political foundation, what if it cannot stand on its own, what if fully actualized modernity is an exemplary ideological myth?

The return of the traditional order in capitalism is thus not simply an indication that the logic of science is somehow constrained in capitalism, it is an indication that this containment is immanent to the universe of modern science, implied by the foreclosure of the subject. To put it bluntly: science cannot stand completely on its own, it cannot account for itself (no matter how much positivist accounts try to do so), i.e., the universality of science is based on an exception.

When and how, then, will politics be synchronized with modern science? It is not that the universe of modern science should directly impose itself onto the sphere of politics, so that social life will be regulated by the insights based on the cognitivist/biogenetic naturalization of human life (the tech-gnostic vision of society regulated by the digital big Other). It is simply that the subject engaged in politics should no longer be conceived as the liberal free agent pursuing its interests but as the subject of modern science, the Cartesian *cogito*, which, as Lacan said, is the subject of psychoanalysis. Therein lies the problem: can we imagine an emancipatory politics whose agent is the empty Cartesian subject? Jacques-Alain Miller's answer is that the domain of politics is by definition the domain of imaginary and symbolic collective identifications, so that all that psychoanalysis can do is to retain a healthy cynical distance toward the sphere of politics—psychoanalysis cannot ground a specific form of political engagement. The wager of the Communist hypothesis is, on the contrary, that there is a politics based on the empty Cartesian subject: the political name of the empty Cartesian subject is a proletarian, an agent reduced to the empty point of substanceless subjectivity. A politics of radical universal emancipation can be grounded only on the proletarian experience.

5.4 USE VALUE, EXCHANGE VALUE, CULT VALUE

Hitherto, we have resorted to the homology between different forms of surplus without questioning its foundation or its limitation, as well as the intertwinement of different surpluses. For example, what makes the homology between the logic of commodities and the logic of the signifier problematic is that the signifying dimension is inscribed into the sphere of commodities in the guise of something that is missing in Marx's conceptualization, although it is its constitutive part from the very beginning. Marx's starting point is the dual nature of a commodity, the division between use value and exchange value; however, the couple use value and exchange value does not cover the entire field: another dimension of value is needed, called by Lacan "cult value." Let us take a commodity like stone-washed jeans: they have a use value (we can wear them as trousers) and an exchange value (expressed in the price), but also a third value that cannot be reduced to the first two, a dense web of meanings that sticks to a commodity as its aura: what "way of life" do stone-washed jeans imply; what stance toward reality, what image of myself do I present when I wear them? In our PC times, environmental cult value is gaining prominence: who really believes that half-rotten and expensive "organic" apples are really healthier? The point is that, in buying them, we do not just buy and consume a product—we simultaneously do something meaningful, show our care for the environment and our global awareness, participate in a large collective project. ... Lacan called this dimension "cult value," while Thomas Presskorn-Thygesen and Ole Bjerg call it simply "sign value."[20] They argue that "enjoyment plays a crucial role when symbolic identity is created through consumption of commodities with certain sign values. In order for the consumer to redeem the commodity's sign value she must be able to enjoy its use value. The compulsive buyer lacks this ability to enjoy, causing a fundamental disturbance in her identity as consumer."[21] The term "enjoyment" is to be opposed here to "pleasure": pleasure is experienced when, in consuming a commodity, its use value satisfies a (socially constructed, not merely natural, of course) need of mine, while enjoyment is generated by the effect on the consumer of commodity's sign value—for example, in the case of stone-washed jeans, it is pleasurable to wear them, and what I enjoy is the way wearing them shapes and asserts my self-identity as a certain type of person:

> The structuring of desire in the symbolic order is also at the same time a construction of the subject's social identity. By consuming different commodity-objects of desire, the consumer positions herself in a symbolic system of signs thereby attaining a particular identity. The sign-value of the commodity signals a particular social meaning of the commodity and the consumer gets a share of this meaning through her consumption. In short, commodities shape the way we think and feel about ourselves.[22]

The catch here is that it is not possible for a consumer to keep use value and sign value apart, since sign value is experienced as an organic component of the commodity's use value: I desire stone-washed jeans because, when I wear them, I experience myself, my identity, the way I want to: "The commodity's use-value serves the ideological function as the material correlate to the subject's true self."[23] This overlapping of use value and sign value is not immediate, it has to be enforced, and the active moment in this enforcing is sign value, which exerts pressure on the consumer to convince himself that he really needs the commodity in question as the "material correlate" of his true self:

> If the sign-value of the commodity is to function as a marker and creator of identity, the buyer has to be able to muster a need for the use-value of the commodity, and has to be able to retain this need in her relationship to herself as well as to others. The higher the sign-value, the greater the demand on the buyer to be able to expand her needs and her capacity for consumption. In other words, she must be able to convince herself and the world around her that she needs this particular commodity. This conviction must be not only intellectual but also habitual.[24]

What clearly comes in here is the superego dimension in the guise of the injunction to enjoy the commodity in question. One should note the inversion characteristic of the superego which is at work here: the injunction does not enjoin us to follow our duty against the temptation of succumbing to the pleasure provided by the use value of a commodity ("Do not buy stone-washed jeans—even if they are comfortable to wear, you are thereby endorsing imperialist ideology!"); on the contrary, the commodity's sign value, the ideology associated with it, enjoins us to enjoy its use value even if we really do not feel any need for it: "The acquisition of a commodity must be followed by a sense of enjoyment that functions as evidence of the consumer's urgent need for the commodity. The compulsive buyer suffers from being unable to produce this kind of evidence. This does not mean that the compulsive buyer has no desire for the commodity, but her desire is only directed at the sign-value of the commodity."[25]

The tension that emerges here unavoidably results in what Baudrillard called "the falling rate of enjoyment": with each further commodity that I buy, more effort is needed to find enjoyment in its consumption. My spontaneous reaction to this deadlock is simply to dismiss the commodity at hand as unsatisfactory and go on buying more and more new commodities (whose rate of enjoyment just goes on falling, of course): "Each commodity only satisfies us for a moment. The real thing always eludes us. This tragic suffering of *jouissance* is perhaps nowhere clearer exhibited than in the case of the compulsive buyer, who restlessly strives for the objects prescribed by the capitalist symbolic order—hoping for enjoyment while merely and tragically being deferred from one sign-value to the next in a compulsion to repeat."[26] The truth of this entire movement is, of course, the properly dialectical reversal that characterizes the compulsive buyer: the libidinal investment is displaced from the alleged goal (consuming the object) to the mediating activity (buying), i.e., the true source of joy becomes the act of buying itself; the bought commodities are indifferent, they are mostly left unused (for example, men often go on buying basically useless gadgets as extensions of their PCs). This reversal is not a pathology that distorts the "normal" buying process; it is, on the contrary, something that lurks in the most rudimentary act of buying: "What is found in the compulsive buyer is merely an exaggerated form of what is already present in the normal consumer to a lesser degree."[27] Just as the repression of desire turns into the desire for repression, or the punishment for an illicit desire turns into the desire for punishment, here, the act of buying with the aim of satisfying a desire turns into a desire for the act of buying.

So, back to Marx and Lacan: does this mean that Marx missed a dimension of commodities? Things are more complex: the overlooking of sign value, the coalescence of sign value and use value, is a necessary illusion of the sphere of commodities itself.

5.5 BEYOND HOMOLOGY

We have thus the surpluses of knowledge, of enjoyment, of value, and of power—and one can argue that we should add to the subject-supposed-to-know,[28] subject-supposed-to-believe, and subject-supposed-to-enjoy, the subject-supposed-to-be-in-power. But how far can we push the homology between these couples: pleasure–enjoyment, use value–value, meaning–sense, power–excess power? When the very renunciation of (or postponement of) pleasure can bring a surplus-pleasure; when the very consummation of use value, the "official" goal of producing commodities, becomes a means (or a subordinate moment) in the expanded self-reproduction of value; when the breakdown of meaning (explicit referential sense), and the ensuing nonsense, give rise to the specter of a "deeper" sense; when the exercise of power pushed to the extreme of impotence gives birth to the mirage of omnipotence; are we in all these cases really dealing with the same matrix? The ultimate horizon of a truly materialist approach is never formal homology—that is the limitation of the Marxist approaches of Alfred Sohn-Rethel (who deploys the homology between the universe of commodities and Kant's transcendentalism) or Lucien Goldmann (who deploys the parallel between early capitalism and Jansenist theology). (An extreme version of this parallelism is found in Ferruccio Rossi-Landi's *Language as Work*, in which he develops the notion of modes of linguistic production, proposing terms like linguistic capital, linguistic exploitation, etc.) One should pass from metaphor to metonymy, from homology to the immanent deduction of the very multiplicity of levels—for example, it is not enough to articulate the homology between the universe of commodities and a certain (Christian, usually) theology, one has also to consider why the universe of commodities can function only if it redoubles itself in theology, why it cannot stand on its own. Marx wrote somewhere that it is not enough to reduce superstructural phenomena to their material base, one has also to deduce the need for superstructural phenomena from the antagonisms of the material base. To do this, one should enact a transposition from metaphor to metonymy, something that Benjamin does apropos of translation: instead of conceiving translation as a metaphorical substitute for the original, as something that should render as faithfully as possible the meaning of the original, both original and translation are posited as belonging to the same level, parts of the same field. The gap that, in the traditional view, separates the original from its (always imperfect) translation is thus transposed back into the original itself: the original itself is already the fragment of a broken vessel, so that the goal of the translation is not to achieve fidelity to the original but to supplement the original, to treat the original as a broken fragment of the "broken vessel," and to produce another fragment which will not imitate the original but fit it as one fragment of a broken Whole may fit another. The same move is enacted by the early Hegelian Marxists (Lukács, Korsch) in their critique of the orthodox Marxist "theory of reflection" approach to knowledge (our knowledge mirrors external reality, asymptotically approaching it), so that the problem is how faithfully does the cognitive reflection mirror objective reality: for Lukács and Korsch, reality and cognition relate as a Whole and its part, i.e., the focus should be on the immanently practical aspect of cognition: the way in which cognition itself is part of the process it mirrors (for example, how does class awareness transform its bearer into an actual revolutionary agent?).

Here, a truly dialectical-materialist approach should nonetheless go a step further than Lukács and Korsch. Acts of exchange (of products) cannot be confined to the mediated satisfaction of needs (I give you what you need in exchange for getting what I need from you—wheat for salt, etc.). Anthropologists like Lévi-Strauss demonstrated long ago that there is always a "phatic" dimension at work in the exchange of commodities: an act of exchange is always minimally self-reflexive; its goal is (also) to establish a social link between agents of exchange. But which excess is primordial, the excess of production (over the utility of products) or the excess of exchange (over the need for exchanged objects, but also the excess of symbolic exchange over the communicated content)? The obvious answer is, of course, that we have here a parallax structure: there is no choice to be made, the split between production and (symbolic) exchange is irreducible and constitutive for both of them; we are dealing with the same excess in its two forms, with the same entity inscribed into two different topologies. ... Nevertheless, such a solution is all too easy—it leaves unexplained how the gap between production and exchange arises; ultimately, it leaves us in a position not unlike that of Habermas, who distinguishes between work (instrumental reason led by the norm of efficiency of domination and control) and language interaction (led by the emancipatory norm of free argumentation and mutual recognition). The conventional Marxist solution is, of course, to assert the primacy of production, and to account for different modes of exchange in terms of different social organizations of production. Ultimately, the very appearance of the autonomy of exchange is the outcome of an immanent antagonism ("alienation") in production.

Here, however, things get complicated. How does economic exchange relate to *symbolic* exchange? Can symbolic exchange also be grounded in social relations of production? While Marx's position is clearly the predominance of production, Hegel—in the famous passage from his *Phenomenology*—conceives human labor as the outcome of the struggle for recognition, i.e., he asserts the primacy of intersubjectivity. Furthermore, there are some other options which should also be rejected, among them the thesis (popular in the heyday of discourse theory) that speech and labor are both processes of production (of meaning, of objects), and the fetishist effect is crucial in both domains (the product obfuscates the production process); however, without specifying the precise difference between speech and labor, this homology is all too abstract.

The notion of *praxis*, of engaged activity that sustains a collective lifeworld, also remains rooted in the Aristotelian unity of soul and body. Recall the notion (elaborated by different authors from Bakhtin to late Wittgenstein) of language as an organic moment of social praxis, as an active moment of a lifeworld. The critical target of this approach is the allegedly "idealist" notion of language as a medium of the designation of reality: as its mirroring, not a part of it and an active intervention into it. Language is primarily a way to interact in the world, to achieve something—for example, to seduce a love partner, to exert domination, to regulate collaboration, to convince others—not just a passive medium designating it. Language, labor, and other forms of human interaction all together form the living Whole of praxis. But, again, from a strictly Lacanian standpoint, the alternative of language which serves to talk about reality from a distance and of language as an organic moment of life-practice misses (or, rather, presupposes) something: the very opening of the gap that (potentially) separates words from things. In other words, the true question is: how does the gap that allows a speaking being to acquire a distance toward reality arise within reality itself? Prior to functioning as a mode of active intervention into reality, language enacts a withdrawal from direct immersion in lifeworld activity. Prior to the safe distance there is thus a violent process of acquiring-a-distance, of tearing reality apart—this is what Lacan focuses on when he talks about "symbolic castration," and what Deleuze is dealing with when he tries to discern the contours of the process by means of which the child-subject enters the order of sense proper, of the *abstraction* of sense, gaining the capacity to abstract a quality from its embeddedness in a bodily Whole, to conceive of it as a becoming no longer attributed to a certain substance—as Deleuze would have put it, "red" no longer stands for the predicate of the red thing, but for the pure flow of becoming-red. So, far from tying us down to our bodily reality, "symbolic castration" sustains our very ability to "transcend" this reality and enter the space of immaterial Becoming. Does not the autonomous smile which survives on its own when the Cheshire Cat's body disappears in *Alice in Wonderland* also stand for an organ "castrated," cut off from the body? This is why "quasi cause," the operator of this abstraction, is Deleuze's name for the Lacanian "phallic signifier": the quasi cause "*extracts singularities from the present, and from individuals and persons which occupy this present,*"[29] and, in the same movement, provides them with their relative autonomy with regard to the intensive processes as their real causes, endowing these impassive and sterile effects with their morphogenetic power—is not this double movement *exactly* that of "symbolic castration" (whose signifier is the phallus)? First, the impassive-sterile Event is cut off, extracted, from its virile, corporeal, causal base (if "castration" means anything at all, it means this). Then, this flow of Sense-Event is constituted as an autonomous field of its own, the autonomy of the incorporeal symbolic order with regard to its corporeal embodiments. "Symbolic castration," as the elementary operation of the quasi cause, is thus a profoundly *materialist* concept, since it answers the basic need of any materialist analysis: "If we are to get rid of essentialist and typological thought we need some process through which virtual multiplicities are derived from the actual world and some process through which the results of this derivation may be given enough coherence and autonomy."[30]

For decades, we have heard how language is an activity: not a medium of representation which denotes an independent state of things, but a life-practice which "does things," which constitutes new relations in the world. Has the time not come to ask the obverse question? How can a practice which is fully embedded in a lifeworld start to function in a representative way, subtracting itself from its lifeworld entanglement, adopting a distanced position of observation and denotation? Hegel praised this "miracle" as the infinite power of Understanding, the power to separate—or, at least, treat as separated—what in real life belongs together. Mystics celebrate the inner peace we achieve when we withdraw from immersion in the eternal crazy dance of reality, where everything is caught in an incessant movement; Hegel and Lacan reveal the violent obverse of this inner peace. Language never "fits" reality, it is the mark of a radical imbalance which forever prevents the subject from locating itself within reality.

As much as the symbolic order is included in social practice as its imma-nent moment, as much as we should understand language as a moment of the totality of social practice, we should always bear in mind that language never fully fits social reality, that there is no common space of social reality which encompasses language as one of its moments. There is no common denomi-nator between language and reality, no matter how much language is "prac-tical," embedded in social practice, traversed by social antagonisms, power plays, passions, etc. This is why the three levels of situating language with regard to reality do not suffice: (1) language as (imperfectly) mirroring/reflecting the reality it designates from an unspecified external position; (2) language as an immanent moment of social practice, as a medium of our interaction with which we "do things"; (3) language in its transcendental role, as the medium of the constitution of reality ("house of being," as Hei-degger put it). To these three levels, a fourth should be added: language as something that can occur only if there is a crack in reality to which it relates. That is to say: language is excluded from reality, at a distance from it, but this exclusion is strictly internal: language holds the place of what is excluded from reality itself, of the Real that has to be "primordially repressed" so that reality can emerge. In other words, language implies a minimal gap between (symbolically constituted) reality and the Real whose ex-sistence is signaled by the cracks in in reality.

So when we are dealing with four levels or spheres of surpluses—enjoyment, value, knowledge, power (which means that we should sup-plement Lévi-Strauss's idea of the three spheres of exchange—exchange of women, signs, products—with another sphere, the sphere of power rela-tions)—the first thing to do is to search for the modes of intermingling of these four levels: the sign value of a commodity always interposes itself between its use value and its exchange value (according to some anthropologists, the very clumsiness of the most "primitive" prehistoric stone axe already makes it clear that the axe functioned also as the sign of its owner's strength); the gap that separates pleasure and *jouissance* already presupposes the dimension of the signifier, i.e., there is no surplus-enjoyment without signifying repetition; the intricacies of meaning and sense are sustained by the dimension of enjoy-meant (*jouis-sense*), etc. While for Marx the basic dimension is clearly that of production, and the social dimension is at its most basic that of a social mode of production, Hegel (in his *Phenomenology*) takes the opposite path and deploys the social (libidinal, even) mediation of labor: in order for a human being to become a worker, a complex social process of recognition (the "struggle for life or death") has to take place; in addition, the outcome of this struggle introduces a profound libidinal shift, transforming desire into a thwarted one (*gehemmtes Begehren*), the one whose satisfaction is forever postponed, with the implied libidinal inversion (the postponement of pleasure turning into the pleasure found in the postponement of direct satisfaction itself).

Is not capitalism itself a case of such intermingling? In capitalism, domination is transposed from relations between people to relations between things: relations between people can appear democratic, egalitarian, with no direct domination, no fetishization of the other into a charismatic Master, since domination is reproduced at the level of relations between things (commodities). What one should add here is, of course, that there is a short circuit between the two levels: the proletarian who sells his labor-power is doubly inscribed: he is a subject, a free agent, and at the same time a "thing," a commodity sold on the market.

CHAPTER 6

IN DER TAT: THE ACTUALITY OF FANTASY

6.1 THE INTRICACIES OF THE LABOR THEORY OF VALUE

The question of the continuing relevance of Marx's critique of political economy in our era of global capitalism has to be answered in a properly dialectical way: as Badiou repeatedly emphasizes, not only is Marx's critique of political economy, his outline of the capitalist dynamics, still absolutely relevant, one should even take a step further and claim that it is only today, with global capitalism, that—to put it in Hegelese—reality arrives at its notion. However, a properly dialectical reversal intervenes here: at this very moment of full actuality the limitation has to appear, the moment of triumph is that of defeat, after overcoming external obstacles the new threat comes from within, signaling immanent inconsistency. When reality fully reaches its notion, this notion itself has to be transformed. So let us begin our analysis with the deceivingly commonsense definition of labor as such at the beginning of chapter 7 of *Capital*:

> The labour-process, resolved as above into its simple elementary factors, is human action with a view to the production of use-values, appropriation of natural substances to human requirements; it is the necessary condition for effecting exchange of matter between man and Nature; it is the everlasting Nature-imposed condition of human existence, and therefore is independent of every social phase of that existence, or rather, is common to every such phase. It was, therefore, not necessary to represent our labourer in connection with other labourers; man and his labour on one side, Nature and its materials on the other, sufficed.[1]

Something is wrong with the process of abstraction here: "man and his labour on one side, Nature and its materials on the other, sufficed"—really? Is not *every* production process by definition social? If we want to grasp the labor process in general, should we not link it to "society in *general*"? This abstraction of labor into the asocial is ideological in the strict sense: it misrecognizes its own sociohistorical conditions: it is only with capitalist society that the Robinsonian category of abstract labor as asocial emerges. It is not an innocent conceptual mistake, but has a crucial social content: it directly grounds Marx's technocratic vision of Communism as a society in which the production process is dominated by the "general intellect." Marx's vision here is that of a fully automated production process in which the human being (worker) "comes to relate more as watchman and regulator to the production process itself." Marx's systematic use of the singular ("man," "worker") is a key indicator of how "general intellect" is not intersubjective, it is "monological." It is as if in Communism, with its rule of "general intellect," this asocial character of labor is directly realized.

This brings us to the crucial question raised by any revival of the Marxist critique of political economy: the question of the so-called labor theory of value, usually considered the weakest link in the chain of Marx's theory. Marx first criticizes the idea (the ideological illusion which imposes itself "at first sight") that exchange value is a purely relational term, the result of comparing one commodity with another, not the intrinsic property of a commodity:

> Exchange value, at first sight, presents itself as a quantitative relation, as
> the proportion in which values in use of one sort are exchanged for those
> of another sort, a relation constantly changing with time and place. Hence
> exchange value appears to be something accidental and purely relative, and
> consequently an intrinsic value, i.e., an exchange value that is inseparably
> connected with, inherent in commodities, seems a contradiction in
> terms.[2]

If this is a false appearance, what, then, is the true status of exchange value? Here comes the surprise: although it is not relational but intrinsic, it is not intrinsic in the sense of a natural property of the commodity as object:

> the exchange values of commodities must be capable of being expressed
> in terms of something common to them all, of which thing they represent
> a greater or lesser quantity. This common "something" cannot be a
> geometrical, a chemical, or any other natural property of commodities. Such
> properties claim our attention only insofar as they affect the utility of those
> commodities, make them use values. But the exchange of commodities is
> evidently an act characterized by a total abstraction from use value. ... As use
> values, commodities are, above all, of different qualities, but as exchange
> values they are merely different quantities, and consequently do not contain
> an atom of use value. If then we leave out of consideration the use value
> of commodities, they have only one common property left, that of being
> products of labor.[3]

Is not this strange universal intrinsic value, which is nonetheless of a totally different nature from all the natural (physical) properties of the commodity as an object, a purely meta-physical (spiritual) property? When we look at commodities as products of abstract labor, "there is nothing left of them in each case but the same phantom-like objectivity." "As crystals of this social substance, which is common to them all, they are values—commodity values." "Not an atom of matter enters into the objectivity of commodity as values; in this it is the direct opposite of the coarsely sensuous objectivity of commodities as physical objects." "Commodities possess an objective character as values only insofar as they are all expressions of an identical social substance, human labour, that their objective character as value is purely social."[4]

So what is the exact status of this "phantom-like objectivity"? Is Marx here not an ontological realist in the medieval Thomist sense, claiming that the universal has an autonomous existence within the object, beyond its physical properties? Furthermore, does he not commit again here a blatant *petitio principii*? The passage from use value to exchange value (based exclusively in the labor time spent on it) is not the passage from particular to universal: if we abstract from the concrete properties which account for the use value of a commodity, what remains is obviously usefulness (utility) as such, as an abstract property that all commodities share; and, in an exactly symmetrical way, being-the-product-of-labor as the common property of all commodities is an abstraction from concrete particular labor which provided a particular commodity with its use value.

The reply to this is that (exchange) value is a social category, the way the social character of production is inscribed into a commodity: the relationship between use value and (exchange) value is not that between particularity and universality, but that between the different uses of the same commodity, first as an object that satisfies some need, then as a social object, as a token of relations between subjects. Value concerns products (commodities) as social entities, it is the imprint of the social character of a commodity, and this is why labor is its only source—once we see that value concerns "relations between people," the claim that its source is labor becomes almost a tautology. In other words, the only source of value is human labor, because value is a social category which measures the participation of each individual laborer in the totality of social labor; to claim that capital and labor material are also "factors" which create value is the same as claiming that they are also members of human society.

We can now see clearly the origin of Marx's confusion: when he grounds his labor theory of value in the claim that, if we abstract from the concrete properties of a commodity which satisfy some human need, the only common feature that remains is that they are all products of human labor, he forgets to add that it is social labor, labor in its social dimension, and he thereby opens up the path to the "logical" critique of his "mistake." The reason he forgets to add this is because his abstract notion of labor is asocial (single worker confronting tools and material), and, again, he thereby opens up the path to the "realist" misunderstanding of value as an immanent property of a commodity.

The labor theory of value faces a further problem: if the value of a commodity is determined by the labor time needed to produce it, how do we explain the differences in skill between laborers, i.e., the obvious fact that an hour of a doctor's labor produces more value than an hour of an unskilled factory worker's? In order to resolve this problem, Marx introduces the distinction between "simple labor" and "complex labor" (the work of highly trained workers), where complex labor counts as "multiples of simple labor." In this way, complex labor can be reduced to simple labor, and this reduction is an objective social process which goes on "behind the backs of the producers." One should not accuse Marx here of being guilty of a vulgar naturalization: he is well aware that what counts as "simple labor" is not a transhistorical constant but depends on a specific historical situation:

> Of course, human labour-power must itself have attained a certain level of development before it can be expended in this or that form. But the value of a commodity represents human labour pure and simple, the expenditure of human labour in general. ... It is the expenditure of simple labour-power, i.e. of the labour-power possessed in his bodily organism by every ordinary man, on the average, without being developed in any special way. *Simple average labour*, it is true, varies in character in different countries and at different cultural epochs, but in a particular society it is given.[5]

Is not the distinction between "simple labor" and "complex labor" deeply problematic from Marx's own standpoint? Marx repeatedly insists that abstract labor which generates value is just that: an abstraction, the reduction of labor to the pure abstract flow of labor time, the obliteration of all particular qualities—so why should the quality of the performed labor determine the value it generates? Marx's point is that, within each "cultural epoch" (it is worth noting that Marx evokes culture here, not just history), "simple average labor" functions as a zero-level standard to which all its more complex forms can be reduced (and *are* reduced in the social practice of exchange):

> More complex labour counts only as *intensified*, or rather *multiplied* simple labour, so that a smaller quantity of complex labour is considered equal to a larger quantity of simple labour. Experience shows that this reduction is constantly being made. A commodity may be the outcome of the most complicated labour, but through its value it is posited as equal to the

product of simple labour, hence it represents only a specific quantity of simple labour. The various proportions in which different kinds of labour are reduced to simple labour as their unit of measurement are established by a social process that goes on behind the backs of the producers; these proportions therefore appear to the producers to have been handed down by tradition.[6]

The key, enigmatic term here is "experience": as David Harvey noted in his classic commentary, "Marx never explains what 'experience' he has in mind, making this passage highly controversial."[7] The least one can add is that this "experience" has to be conceived as referring to a specific historical situation: not only what counts as simple labor, but the very practice of reducing complex to simple labor, is something historically specific and not a universal feature of human productivity, limited not only to capitalism but to classic industrial capitalism. As Anson Rabinbach has demonstrated, it is operative only within the nineteenth-century break with Hegel, the assertion of the thermodynamic engine as a paradigm of how labor-power operates, the paradigm which replaces the Hegelian paradigm of labor as the expressive deployment of human subjectivity still operative in the texts of the young Marx:

The thermodynamic engine was the servant of a powerful nature conceived as a reservoir of undiminished and inexhaustible motivating power. The laboring body, the steam engine and the cosmos were connected by a single and unbroken chain, by an indestructible energy, omnipresent in the universe and capable of infinite mutation, yet immutable and invariant. … This discovery also had a profound, game changing effect on Marx's thinking about labor. After 1859, Marx increasingly regarded the distinction between concrete and abstract labor in the language of labor power, as an act of *conversion* rather than *generation*. Marx credited early nineteenth century French engineers—Navier, Coriolis, Poncelet—who analyzed steam engines and the discoveries of Lord Kelvin and von Helmholtz, who first used the concept of *Arbeitskraft* to describe how energy is converted into work. Put in another way, Marx superimposed a thermodynamic model of labor onto the ontological model of labor he inherited from Hegel. As a result, for Marx labor power became quantifiable and equivalent to all other forms of labor power (in nature or in machines). Marx thus shifted his focus from the emancipation of mankind *through* labor, to emancipation *from* productive labor by an even greater productivity, since the productivity of the machine is measured by the extent to which it replaces human labor power. Marx became a "productivist," when he no longer considered labor to be simply an anthropologically "paradigmatic" mode of activity, and when, in harmony with the new physics, he saw labor power as an abstract magnitude (a measure of labor-time) and a natural force (a specific set of energy equivalents located in the body). ... Though worlds apart ideologically, Helmholtz's characterization of the universe as *Arbeitskraft*, Marx's theory of the relentless transformation of labor power into the powerful engine of capital, and Frederick Winslow Taylor's utopia of the worker's body subordinated to the rational intelligence of the engineer, were all variations on the theme of the metaphor of the human motor, of the working body as a medium for converting energy into work.[8]

The question that arises here is: is this paradigm which relies on the mechanical, linear flow of time (of labor) as a measure of value still applicable in our late-capitalist postindustrial societies? This question has to be answered precisely to avoid the attempts of the ruling ideology to dismiss Marx's critique of political economy as belonging to another era, and to celebrate the potential of today's post-Fordist capitalism to use labor-power in a much more creative and cooperative way:

> An intellectually vigorous new discourse of 'antidisciplinarity' has found a niche in the boardrooms of corporations and on the editorial pages of influential newspapers and periodicals. Take for example that journal of post-Marxist studies, the *Wall Street Journal*, which in the 1990s campaigned against the lingering consequences of the Taylorist-Fordist workplace, e.g. firms sticking to an outdated model in which management distrusts the autonomy of workers, prescribes dull routinized tasks, curbs creativity, and creates a workplace ill-suited to 'literate, independent-minded workers.'[9]

Along similar lines, David Harvey[10] recently made a series of important points about Marx's labor theory of value. His starting point is the well-known fact whose implications are often ignored: value for Marx is a social relation which, as such, is *immaterial* ("not an atom of matter" enters into it) but *objective*. Marx, who is often criticized for his vulgar economic materialism, here makes a very refined, non-reductionist point. Critics who are aware of this "objective immateriality" accuse Marx of a neo-Thomist realism (objective idealism), as if "value" for Marx is an objective ideal entity that resides somewhere deep in a commodity. The answer to this reproach is that, for Marx, the value of a commodity is purely relational: it does not exist somewhere deep in a commodity independently of its relations to other commodities, it is "actualized" only through acts of exchange. All the "contradictions" of the expression of value in money stem from the fact that an immaterial social relation has to be expressed in a concrete material object which, in this way, "becomes the form of manifestation of its opposite, abstract human labour." As a material object, money "becomes a commodity, an external object capable of becoming the private property of any individual. Thus the social power that derives from social labour becomes the private power of private persons."[11] We have here yet another version of what Hegel called "infinite judgment": social relation appears as an object which is privately owned and can be treated as just another object to be sold or otherwise exchanged.

Marx's so-called labor theory of value is thus a kind of misnomer: it should in no way be read as claiming that one should discard exchange, or its role in the constitution of value, as a mere appearance which obscures the key fact that labor is the origin of value. One should, rather, conceive the emergence of value as a process of mediation by means of which value "casts off" its use—value is surplus-value over use value. The general equivalent of use values had to be deprived of use value, it had to function as a pure potentiality of use value. Essence is appearance as appearance: value is exchange value as exchange value—or, as Marx put it in a manuscript version of the changes to the first edition of *Capital*: "The reduction of different concrete private labours to this abstraction [*Abstraktum*] of the same human labour is accomplished only through exchange which effectively posits the products of different labours as equal to each other."[12] In other words, "abstract labor" is a value relationship which constitutes itself only in exchange, it is not the substantial property of a commodity independently of its relations with other commodities. For orthodox Marxists, such a "relational" notion of value is already a compromise with "bourgeois" political economy which they dismiss as a "monetary theory of value"; however, the paradox is that these very "orthodox Marxists" themselves in effect regress to the "bourgeois" notion of value: they conceive of value as being immanent to the commodity, as its property, and thus naturalize its "spectral objectivity" which is the fetishized appearance of its social character.

We are not dealing here with mere theoretical niceties: the precise determination of the status of money has crucial economic-political consequences. If we consider money as a secondary form of expression of value which exists "in itself" in a commodity prior to its expression—that is, if money is for us a mere secondary resource, a practical means that facilitates exchange—then the door is open to the illusion, succumbed to by Leftist followers of Ricardo, that it would be possible to replace money with simple notes designating the amount of work done by their bearer and giving him or her the right to the corresponding part of the social product—as if, by means of this direct "work money," one could avoid all "fetishism" and ensure that each worker is paid their "full value." The point of Marx's analysis is that this project ignores the formal determinations of money which make fetishism a necessary effect. In other words, when Marx defines exchange value as the mode of appearance of value, one should mobilize here the entire Hegelian weight of the opposition between essence and appearance: essence exists only insofar as it appears, it does not preexist its appearance. In the same way, the value of a commodity is not its intrinsic substantial property which exists independently of its appearance in exchange.

This is also why we should abandon the attempt to expand value so that all kinds of labor will be recognized as a source of value—recall the great feminist demand in the 1970s to legalize housework (from cooking and maintaining the household to caring for children) as productive of value, or some contemporary eco-capitalist demands to integrate the "free gifts of nature" into value production (by trying to determine the costs of water, air, forests, and all other commons). All these proposals are "nothing more than a sophisticated green-washing and commodification of a space from which a fierce attack upon the hegemony of the capitalist mode of production and its (and our) alienated relation to nature can be mounted":[13] in their attempt to be "just" and to eliminate or at least constrain exploitation, such attempts simply enforce an even stronger all-encompassing commodification. Although they try to be "just" at the level of content (what counts as value), they fail to problematize the very form of commodification, and Harvey is right to propose instead to treat value in dialectical tension with non-value, i.e., to assert and expand spheres not caught up in the production of (market) value (like household work or "free" cultural and scientific work) in their crucial role. Value production can thrive only if it incorporates its immanent negation, the creative work that generates no (market) value, it is by definition parasitic on it.

A further challenge to market economy comes from the exploding virtualization of money, which compels us to thoroughly reformulate the standard Marxist topic of "reification" and "commodity fetishism," insofar as this topic still relies on the notion of fetish as a solid object whose stable presence obfuscates its social mediation. Paradoxically, fetishism reaches its acme precisely when the fetish itself is "dematerialized," turned into a fluid "immaterial" virtual entity; money fetishism will culminate with the passage to its electronic form, when the last traces of its materiality disappear—electronic money is the third form, after "real" money, which directly embodies its value (gold, silver), and paper money which, although a "mere sign" with no intrinsic value, still clings to its material existence. And it is only at this stage, when money becomes a purely virtual point of reference, that it finally assumes the form of an indestructible spectral presence: I owe you $1,000, and no matter how many material notes I burn, I still owe you $1,000; the debt is inscribed somewhere in virtual digital space. It is only with this thorough "dematerialization," when Marx's famous old thesis from *The Communist Manifesto*—that in capitalism, "all that is solid melts into air"—acquires a much more literal meaning than the one Marx had in mind, when not only is our material social reality dominated by the spectral/speculative movement of Capital, but this reality itself is progressively "spectralized" (the "Protean

Self" instead of the old self-identical Subject, the elusive fluidity of its experiences instead of the stability of the owned objects)—in short, when the usual relationship between firm, material objects and fluid ideas is turned around (objects are progressively dissolved in fluid experiences, while the only stable things are virtual symbolic obligations)—it is only at this point that what Derrida called the spectral aspect of capitalism is fully actualized.

However, as is always the case in a properly dialectical process, such a spectralization of the fetish contains the seeds of its opposite, of its self-negation. Imagine the endpoint of this process of spectralization: the self-overcoming of commodification into its full naturalization, a point at which money in a way "falls into the Real"—for instance, when I enter a store, a scanning machine just identifies me and checks my database (bank and police records, etc.), so that I do nothing, there is no specific act of buying on my part, I just take the things I want out of the store and the digital network registers it (and endorses it if I met the financial and legal requisites) without any symbolic act of recognition. … (One can easily imagine a similar procedure in going to a restaurant or theater: I simply do what I want there; the financial aspect remains fully in the virtual background.)

6.2 THE UNCONSCIOUS STRUCTURED LIKE A HEGELIAN SPECULATION

But is this spectral domain simply an effect of the actual material process of production, or does it have an actuality of its own? If we adopt the first stance, we find ourselves in pragmatism, which perceives itself as an attitude of taking into account the complexity of actual life processes: a pragmatist does not blindly cling to abstract principles, he is flexible, ready to accommodate principles to the incessant change of reality. A properly dialectical answer to pragmatism is not to accuse it of being too conformist and fluid, i.e., to claim that, despite the complexity of real life, we have to follow some firm principles; even less is it a proper dialectical answer to propose some kind of "synthesis" between abstract principles and complex reality, a kind of proper measure or balance between the two extremes. The best properly dialectical answer to pragmatism would rather be something like: "Pragmatism is good enough for theory, but not good enough for practice." In short, the criticism of pragmatism should not be that it is too opportunist and unprincipled but that it is too principled, elevating its pragmatic stance into a fixed principle and thereby forgetting the extent to which even those who, in their conscious attitude, follow pragmatic flexibility, in fact obey in their actual activity a much more "principled" attachment to fixed rules.

For Marx, a typical capitalist considers himself utterly "practical," flexible, pragmatic, but the actuality of his life is "abounding in metaphysical subtleties and theological niceties."[14] It is not that we are actually much more pragmatic than our principles allow, it is rather that we are actually much more dogmatic and principled than our pragmatic stance allows. In other words, what a pragmatic stance ignores is the fact clearly stated in the very first sentence of the famous section 4 of the first chapter of *Capital*, "The Fetishism of Commodities and the Secret Thereof": "A commodity appears, at first sight, a very trivial thing, and easily understood. Its analysis shows that it is, in reality, a very queer thing, abounding in metaphysical subtleties and theological niceties."[15] In short, it is not that we officially follow theology while we privately mock it or treat it in a pragmatic way; it is in our private (and public) lives that we are pragmatic, while in our unconscious we are much more "principled," obeying theological niceties. But what, precisely, is the status of this "unconscious"? It is not located in our psychic depth, it is out there, practiced, embodied in our social activity, in its formal determinations: "Whence, then, arises the enigmatical character of the product of labor, as soon as it assumes the form of commodities? Clearly from this form itself."[16] This is why Marx's criticism of the classic bourgeois political economy is not that it remained caught in the intricacies of form and missed some hidden content, but, on the contrary, that it missed the dialectical necessity of the form itself:

> Political Economy has indeed analyzed, however incompletely, value and its magnitude, and has discovered what lies beneath these forms. But it has never once asked the question why labor is represented by the value of its product and labor time by the magnitude of that value. It is one of the chief failings of classical economy that it has never succeeded, by means of its analysis of commodities, and, in particular, of their value, in discovering that form under which value becomes exchange value. Even Adam Smith and Ricardo, the best representatives of the school, treat the form of value as a thing of no importance, as having no connection with the inherent nature of commodities. The reason for this is not solely because their attention is entirely absorbed in the analysis of the magnitude of value. It lies deeper. The value form of the product of labor is not only the most abstract, but is also the most universal form, taken by the product in bourgeois production, and stamps that production as a particular species of social production, and thereby gives it its special historical character.[17]

Marx is at his most antireductionist here: the task of a dialectical theory is not to reduce a phenomenon to its material base but the exact opposite, to inquire into how this phenomenon arose out of the antinomies of its base; it is not to bring out the content hidden by deceiving form, but to inquire into why this content articulated itself in this form. Conceived in this way, Marx's "labor theory of value" displays an unexpected homology with the key ingredient of Freud's theory, the "labor theory of the unconscious":[18]

the unconscious "value" of a dream is exclusively the product of "dream-work," not of the dream-thoughts on which dream-work exercises its transformative activity, just as the value of a commodity is the product of the work expended on it. The paradox here is that it is the very cyphering (obfuscation) of the dream-thought, its translation into the dream texture, that engenders the properly unconscious content of a dream. Freud emphasizes that the true secret of the dream is not its content (the "dream-thoughts"), but the form itself:

> The latent dream-thoughts are the material which the dream-work transforms into the manifest dream. ... The only essential thing about dreams is the dream-work that has influenced the thought-material. ... Analytic observation shows further that the dream-work never restricts itself to translating these thoughts into the archaic or regressive mode of expression that is familiar to you. In addition, it regularly takes possession of something else, which is not part of the latent thoughts of the previous day, but which is the true motive force for the construction of the dream. This indispensable addition is the equally unconscious wish for the fulfillment of which the content of the dream is given its new form. A dream may thus be any sort of thing in so far as you are only taking into account the thoughts it represents—a warning, an intention, a preparation, and so on; but it is always also the fulfillment of an unconscious wish and, if you are considering it as a product of the dream-work, it is only that. A dream is therefore never simply an intention, or a warning, but always an intention, etc., translated into the archaic mode of thought by the help of an unconscious wish and transformed to fulfill that wish. The one characteristic, the wish-fulfillment, is the invariable one; the other may vary. It may for its part once more be a wish, in which case the dream will, with the help of an unconscious wish, represent as fulfilled a latent wish of the previous day.[19]

The key insight is, of course, the "triangulation" of latent dream-thought, manifest dream content, and the unconscious wish, which limits the scope of—or, rather, directly undermines—the hermeneutic model of the interpretation of dreams (the path from the manifest dream content to its hidden meaning, the latent dream-thought), which travels in the opposite direction to the path of the formation of a dream (the transposition of the latent dream-thought into the manifest dream content by the dream-work). The paradox is that this dream-work is not merely a process of masking the dream's "true message": the dream's true core, its unconscious wish, inscribes itself only through this process of masking, so that the moment we retranslate the dream content back into the dream-thought expressed in it, we lose the "true motive force" of the dream—in short, it is the process of masking itself which inscribes into the dream its true secret. One should therefore reverse the standard notion of penetrating deeper and deeper into the core of the dream: it is not that we first move from the manifest dream content to the first-level secret, the latent dream-thought, and then, taking a step further, go even deeper, to the dream's unconscious core, the unconscious wish. The "deeper" wish is located in the very gap between the latent dream-thought and the manifest dream content. It is only this "labor theory of the unconscious" that enables us to read correctly Freud's comparison of the dream-work with the capitalist production process. In order to explain the distinction between the (conscious) wish encoded in a dream and the dream's unconscious desire, Freud compares the wish to the contractor (manager, entrepreneur) and the unconscious desire to the capital that finances (covers the libidinal expenses of) the translation of this wish into a dream:

> To speak figuratively, it is quite possible that a day thought plays the part of the contractor (*entrepreneur*) in the dream. But it is known that no matter what idea the contractor may have in mind, and how desirous he may be of putting it into operation, he can do nothing without capital; he must depend upon a capitalist to defray the necessary expenses, and this capitalist, who supplies the psychic expenditure for the dream, is invariably and indisputably *a wish from the unconscious*, no matter what the nature of the waking thought may be.[20]

In a superficial reading, it may appear that the work proper (dream-work) is just a mediator between the conscious wish and the unconscious capital: the contractor (conscious wish) borrows from the unconscious the capital to finance its translation into the dream language. Here, however, we have to take into account Freud's insistence on how the unconscious desire "infects" the dream only through the dream-work: the exclusive source of the unconscious desire is the work of encoding/masking the dream-thoughts, it does not have a substantial existence outside this work. This primacy of form over content also accounts for the paradox of perversion in the Freudian theoretical edifice: perversion demonstrates the insufficiency of the simple logic of transgression. The conventional wisdom tells us that perverts practice (do) what hysterics only dream about (doing), i.e., "everything is allowed" in perversion, perverts openly actualize all repressed content—nonetheless, as Freud emphasizes, *nowhere is repression as strong as in perversion*, a fact more than confirmed by our late-capitalist reality in which total sexual permissiveness causes anxiety and impotence or frigidity instead of liberation.

There is a nice detail in *Ball of Fire* (directed by Howard Hawks, screenplay by Billy Wilder): when one of the professors wants to mention the name of a woman whose presence was traumatic for them, his colleague immediately interrupts him by pointing out that there are names which not only should not be mentioned, they should even not be omitted too obviously. One should go a step further here: true repression does not reside in not mentioning a name, but in openly talking about it in such a way that its traumatic effect is suspended. When, in February 2003, Colin Powell addressed the UN General Assembly in order to argue for the attack on Iraq, the US delegation asked that the large reproduction of Picasso's *Guernica* on the wall behind the speaker's podium should be covered by a different visual ornament. Although the official explanation was that *Guernica* did not provide the adequate optical background for the televised transmission of Powell's speech, it was clear to everyone what the US delegation was afraid of: that *Guernica*, the painting supposed to be a depiction of the catastrophic results of the German aerial bombing of the Spanish city in the Civil War, would give rise to the "wrong kind of associations" if it were to serve as the background to Powell advocating the bombing of Iraq by the far superior US Air Force. This is what Lacan means when he claims that repression and the return of the repressed are one and the same process: if the US delegation had abstained from demanding that *Guernica* be covered up, probably no one would have associated Powell's speech with the painting displayed behind him; the very change, the very gesture of concealing the painting, drew attention to it and imposed the wrong association, confirming its truth.

This compels us to draw a distinction between the repressed content and the form of repression, where the form remains operative even after the content is no longer repressed—in short, the subject can fully appropriate the repressed content, but repression remains. Why? Commenting on a short dream of one of his patients (a woman who first refused altogether to tell Freud the dream "because it was so indistinct and muddled") which revealed itself to refer to the fact that the patient was pregnant but was in doubt as to who the baby's father was (i.e., the parenthood was "indistinct and muddled"), Freud draws a key dialectical conclusion: "the lack of clarity shown by the dream was a part of the material which instigated the dream: part of this material, that is, was represented in the form of the dream. The form of a dream or the form in which it is dreamt is used with quite surprising frequency for representing its concealed subject-matter."[21] The gap between form and content is properly dialectical here, in contrast to the transcendental gap whose point is that every content appears within an a priori formal frame, and we should always be aware of the invisible transcendental frame which "constitutes" the content we perceive—or, in structural terms, we should distinguish between elements and the formal places these elements occupy. We attain the level of the proper dialectical analysis of a form only when we conceive a certain formal procedure not as expressing a certain aspect of the (narrative) content, but as marking/signaling the part of content that is excluded from the explicit narrative line, so that—and this is the properly theoretical point—if we want to reconstruct "all" of the narrative content, we must reach beyond the explicit narrative content as such, and include some formal features which act as the stand-in for the "repressed" aspect of the content. It is in this form (which cannot be simply reduced to its content, since it stands for what is "repressed" from this content itself), in its dialectical deployment, that we encounter the "capitalist unconscious" as the "objective" illusion constitutive of social reality itself.

Marx describes the passage from money to capital in the Hegelian terms of the passage from substance to subject (capital as the self-deploying and self-differentiating substance, a substance-money made subject): with capitalism, value is not a mere abstract "mute" universality, a substantive link between the multiplicity of commodities; from the passive medium of exchange, it turns into the "active factor" in the entire process. Instead of only passively assuming the two different forms of its actual existence (money–commodity), it appears as the subject "endowed with a motion of its own, passing through a life-process of its own": [22] it differentiates itself from itself, positing its otherness, and then again overcomes this difference, i.e., the movement is its own movement. In this precise sense, "instead of simply representing the relations of commodities, it enters … into private relations with itself": [23] the "truth" of its relating to its otherness is its self-relating, i.e., in its self-movement, capital retroactively "sublates" its own material conditions, changing them into subordinate moments of its own "spontaneous expansion"—in pure Hegelese, it posits its own presuppositions.

Hegel's proposition "Substance is subject" is also an infinite judgment in which opposites coincide: it does not directly identify the two, or characterize Substance as subject (in the sense of "the substance of all being is really a subjective agent who dynamically creates and regulates all of reality, like a personal God or another form of an absolute I"). For Hegel, "subject" remains a principle of division, limitation, finitude, appearance, a power which disrupts the unity of Substance, so that "Substance is subject" means something like "Substance is divided from within, thwarted, caught in illusions, alienated from itself." It is not enough to say that Substance is dynamic, a conflict of opposing forces, etc.; Substance itself is caught up in this process, it turns into a subordinate moment of one of its moments. In the self-reproduction of capital, money (which first appears as a subordinate instrument enabling the exchange of commodities) becomes subject, subordinating to itself the entire sphere of exchange, reducing it to a moment of its self-reproduction. This notion of Hegelian speculation as the mystified expression of the speculative (self-)movement of capital is clearly expressed in this passage:

This inversion [*Verkehrung*] by which the sensibly-concrete counts only as the form of appearance of the abstractly general and not, on the contrary, the abstractly general as property of the concrete, characterizes the expression of value. At the same time, it makes understanding it difficult. If I say: Roman Law and German Law are both laws, that is obvious. But if I say: Law [*Das Recht*], this abstraction [*Abstraktum*] *realizes itself* in Roman Law and in German Law, in these concrete laws, the interconnection becomes mystical.[24]

But, again, one should be very careful here: Marx is not simply criticizing the "inversion" that characterizes Hegelian idealism (in the style of his youthful writings, especially *The German Ideology*). His point is not that, while "in effect" Roman Law and German Law are two kinds of law, in idealist dialectics the Law itself is the active agent—the subject of the entire process—which "realizes itself" in Roman Law and German Law. Marx's point is that this "inversion" characterizes reality itself:

If now we take in turn each of the two different forms which self-expanding value successively assumes in the course of its life, we then arrive at these two propositions: Capital is money: Capital is commodities. In truth [*In der Tat*: actually], however, value is here the active factor in a process, in which, while constantly assuming the form in turn of money and commodities, it at the same time changes in magnitude, differentiates itself by throwing off surplus-value from itself; the original value, in other words, expands spontaneously.[25]

The unexpected appearance of the words "*in der Tat* [actually]" indicates Marx's break with every form of empiricism or vulgar materialism: the "actuality" Marx refers to here is *the actuality of the ideological fantasy itself*—in social reality, the only true "active factor" in the process of production and exchange are workers themselves and their social relations, and "objectively" the self-movement of Value is the ideological chimera which reflects, in a mystifying way, the reality of social production and relations. But Marx insists that such a direct reduction of ideological chimeras to social reality is wrong: it misses the "actuality" of these chimeras. It is "in truth" ("actually") that the relations are "inverted," i.e., that the universality of value realizes itself in its two species, as money and as commodities: as in Hegelian dialectics, the universality of value is here "the active factor" (the subject). This is why we should distinguish between the way reality appears to the everyday consciousness of the individuals caught in the process, and the way reality appears "objectively," without the individuals being aware of it: this second, "objective" mystification can be articulated only through theoretical analysis. And this is why Marx wrote that "the relations connecting the labour of one individual with that of the rest appear, not as direct social relations between individuals at work, but as what they really are, material relations between persons and social relations between things"[26]—the paradoxical claim that, in commodity fetishism, social relations appear *"as what they really are"* (as social relations between things). This overlapping of appearance and reality does not mean (as it does for common sense) that we have no mystification, since reality and appearance coincide, but, on the contrary, that mystification is redoubled: in our subjective mystification, we adequately follow a mystification inscribed into our social reality itself. It is from this insight that one should reread the following well-known passage from *Capital*:

> It is *a definite social relation of the producers* in which they *equate* [*gleichsetzen*] their different types of labour *as human labour*. It is not less a *definite social relation of producers*, in which they *measure* the magnitude of their labours *by the duration of expenditure of human labour-power*. But *within our practical interrelations* these social characters of their own labours *appear* to them *as social properties pertaining to them by nature*, as *objective* determinations [*gegenständliche* Bestimmungen] of *the products of labour themselves*, the equality of human labours as a *value-property* of the products of labour, the *measure* of the labour by the socially necessary labour-time as the *magnitude of value* of the products of labour, and finally the social relations of the producers through their labours appear as a *value-relation* or *social relation of these things*, the products of labour. Precisely because of this the products of labour *appear* to them as *commodities*, sensible-supersensible [*sinnlich übersinnliche*] or *social things*.[27]

The crucial words here are *"within our practical interrelations"*: Marx locates the fetishist illusion not into thinking, into how we misperceive what we do and are, but into our social practice itself. (He uses the same words a couple of lines below: "Therefore, *within our practical interrelations, to possess the equivalent-form* appears as the *social natural property* [*gesellschaftliche Natureigenschaft*] of a thing, as a property pertaining to it *by nature*, so that hence it appears to be *immediately exchangeable* with other things just as it exists for the senses [*so wie es sinnlich da ist*].") This is exactly how we should read Marx's general formula of the fetishist mystification ("*sie wissen das nicht, aber sie tun es*"—they don't know it, but they are doing it): what individuals don't know is the fetishist "inversion" they obey "within their practical interrelations," i.e., in their social reality itself.[28]

So when we are dealing with the breathtaking dynamic of capitalism, its self-propelling proliferation, we should bear in mind that what pushes capitalism toward incessant proliferation is the very fact of being stuck, caught in a closed cycle of its reproduction. Capitalism is in fact not like other modes of production which fall into crisis when they encounter their limitation: the limitation of capitalism is the ground of its strength, since the more it is in "crisis," the more it mobilizes its dynamic to get over it. One cannot but recall here the ambiguity of the term *stasis*, which means a state of equilibrium, a cessation of flow, and (in Thucydides and Flavius Josephus) a civic strife (based on *stasis* as in "to make a stand," to stand up against)—and does not this double meaning perfectly encapsulate the tension of the Freudian drive? Drive intervenes in the continuous flow of life as a moment of stasis, of fixation on a partial object around which drive circulates; it is thus the interruption of the organic flow of life, it "makes a stand" against it. In a strictly homologous way, capitalism "makes a stand" by getting fixated on its object-cause, surplus-value. There is a well-known anecdote about an American philosopher who rebutted a colleague arguing that, while a double negation means affirmation, a double affirmation never amounts to a negation, with a simple remark: "Yeah, yeah ..." Maybe the Freudian drive stands for something similar: a double yes signaling the fixation on some particular moment which interrupts the smooth flow of life. In one of his deplorable regressions into historicist evolutionism, Marx himself misses this exceptional status of capitalism:

> The mode of production of material life conditions the general process of social, political and intellectual life. It is not the consciousness of men that determines their existence, but their social existence that determines their consciousness. At a certain stage of development, the material productive forces of society come into conflict with the existing relations of production or—this merely expresses the same thing in legal terms—with the property relations within the framework of which they have operated hitherto. From forms of development of the productive forces these relations turn into their fetters. Then begins an era of social revolution. The changes in the economic foundation lead sooner or later to the transformation of the whole immense superstructure.[29]

This holds for all modes of production *except for capitalism*, where the material productive forces of society are in conflict with the existing relations of production from its very inception, and it is this very contradiction which pushes it to constant self-revolutionization. This is why capitalism is the symptomal point of exception at which the truth of all other modes of production breaks out into the open. This means that the reading of Hegel's dialectic as an idealistic formulation of the process of capital's self-propelling circulation does not suffice. What, in this view, Hegel deploys is the mystified expression of the *mystification* immanent to the circulation of capital, or, in Lacanian terms, of its "objectively-social" fantasy; to put it in somewhat naive terms, for Marx, capital is not "really" a subject-substance which reproduces itself by positing its own presuppositions, etc.; what this Hegelian fantasy of capital's self-generating reproduction obliterates is workers' exploitation, i.e., how the circle of capital's self-reproduction draws its energy from the external (or, rather, "ex-timate") source of value, how it has to parasitize on workers. So why not pass directly to the description of workers' exploitation, why bother with fantasies which sustain the functioning of capital? It is crucial for Marx to include in the description of capital this intermediary level of "objective fantasy" which is neither the way capitalism is experienced by its subjects (they are good empirical nominalists unaware of the "theological niceties" of capital) nor the "real state of things" (workers exploited by capital).

Crucial here is the reversal of C-M-C (individuals produce commodities in excess of their needs, they exchange them, and money is just a mediating moment for the producer to exchange his excessive product for a product that he needs) into M-C-M' (with my money, I buy a commodity and then sell it in order to gain more money). The second operation works, of course, only if the commodity that I buy can be used to produce more value than it is worth, and this commodity is labor-power. In short, the condition of M-C-M' is that, in a self-referential twist, labor-power which produces commodities itself becomes a commodity. (Another twist is added here by the explosive development of biogenetics: the prospect of scientifically producing a commodity that produces commodities. ...) The temptation to be resisted here is to conceive the passage from C-M-C to M-C-M' as a kind of alienation or denaturalization of a more elementary process: it seems natural and appropriate to exchange what one can produce but doesn't need for what one needs but is produced by others, the entire process is regulated by my actual needs, but things take a weird turn when what should be only a mediating moment (money) turns into an end-in-itself, so that the goal of the entire movement loses its moorings in my actual needs and turns into endless self-multiplication of what should have been secondary means.

Against this temptation, one should emphasize that the reversal of C-M-C into M-C-M' (i.e., the emergence of the specter of self-propelling money) is, already for Marx, a perverted expression of self-propelled human productivity. From the Marxist standpoint, the true aim of human productivity is not the satisfaction of human needs; it is, rather, the satisfaction of needs which, in a kind of cunning of reason, is used in order to motivate the expansion of human productivity. The reversal of C-M-C into M-C-M' thus echoes the more primordial gap between production and the use value of the produced objects: production can never be confined to the satisfaction of needs, a fact clearly signaled by the practice of sacrifice (purposeless destruction of products). We should thus avoid here the young Marx's "instead of" rhetoric of alienation ("instead of money serving as a means of exchanging useful products, satisfaction of human needs serves as a means for the multiplication of money").

6.3 FROM SPECULATIVE NOTION TO SPECULATIVE CAPITAL

It is against this background that one should approach the key question: is not Hegel's speculative dialectics secretly modeled upon the speculative movement of Capital? Is not the illusion the same in both cases, that of the self-enclosed circular expansive movement of M-M′ (money which begets more money) or C-C′ (concept which begets more concepts)? For this reason, Kojin Karatani insists that, although Marx's *Darstellung* of the self-deployment of capital is full of Hegelian references, the self-movement of Capital is far from the circular self-movement of the Hegelian Notion (or Spirit): the point of Marx is that this movement never catches up with itself, that it never recovers its credit, that its resolution is postponed forever, that crisis is its innermost constituent (the sign that the Whole of Capital is the non-True, as Adorno would have put it), which is why the movement is that of "spurious infinity," forever reproducing itself: "The end of *Capital* is never the 'absolute Spirit.' *Capital* reveals the fact that capital, though organizing the world, can never go beyond its own limit. It is a Kantian critique of the ill-contained drive of capital/ reason to self-realize beyond its limit."[30] However, first, Hegel's Absolute is also not "absolute" in the naive sense of achieving its full self-identity, it never ends but is forever caught in its eternally repeated circle of self-reproduction; recall Hegel's repeated image of the Idea enjoying its eternal cycle of losing itself and reappropriating its otherness. Second, Marx's critique is precisely *not* Kantian, since he conceived the notion of limit in the properly Hegelian sense—as a *positive* motivating force which pushes capital further and further in its ever-expanding self-reproduction, not in the Kantian sense of a negative limitation. In other words, what is not visible from the Kantian standpoint is how "the ill-contained drive of capital/reason to self-realize beyond its limit" is totally consubstantial with this limit. The central "antinomy" of Capital is its driving force, since the movement of capital is ultimately motivated not by the endeavor to appropriate/penetrate all empirical reality external to itself, but by the endeavor to resolve its inherent antagonism. In other words, capital "can never go beyond its own limit," but not because some noumenal Thing resists its grasp; it "can never go beyond its own limit" because, in a sense, it is blind to the fact that *there is nothing beyond this limit*, just a specter of total appropriation generated by this very limit.

Consequently, one must again be very precise here: what is excluded in both cases (self-reproducing circulation of money and of concepts) is not simply and primarily the external reality which cannot be reduced to its notional mediation; it is, rather, the specific symptomal point (of subjectivity, of labor-power) at which *internality is inscribed into externality, not the other way round*. The ambiguity of the notion of suture can be of some help here. Suture is usually conceived as the mode in which the exterior is inscribed in the interior, thus "suturing" the field, producing the effect of self-enclosure with no need for an exterior, effacing the traces of its own production: traces of the production process, its gaps, its mechanisms, are obliterated, so that the product can appear as a naturalized organic whole (as with identification, which is not simply full emotional immersion into the quasi-reality of the story, but a much more complex split process). Suture is thus somewhat like the basic matrix of Alistair MacLean's adventure thrillers from the 1950s and 1960s (*The Guns of Navarone, Ice Station Zebra, Where Eagles Dare*): a group of dedicated commandos on a dangerous mission all of a sudden discover that there must be an enemy agent among them, i.e., that their Otherness (the Enemy) is inscribed *within* their set. However, the much more crucial aspect is the obverse one: not only "no interior without exterior," but also "no exterior without interior." That is the lesson of Kant's transcendental idealism: in order to appear as a consistent Whole, external reality has to be "sutured" by a subjective element, an artificial supplement that has to be added to it in order to generate the effect of reality, like the painted background that confers on a scene the illusory effect of "reality." And interface takes place at this level: it is the internal element that sustains the consistency of "external reality" itself, the artificial screen that confers on what we see the effect of reality. This is the *objet petit a* for Lacan: the subjective element constitutive of objective-external reality.

The matrix of an external site of production that inscribes itself into the domain of illusions it generates has thus to be supplemented: this matrix simply does not account for the emergence of the *subject*. According to the standard (cinematic) suture theory, the "subject" is the illusory stand-in, *within* the domain of the constituted-generated, for its absent cause, for its production process: the "subject" is the imaginary agent which, while dwelling inside the space of the constituted phenomena, is (mis)perceived as their generator. This, however, is not what the Lacanian "barred subject" is about: in the standard suture theory, the subject is that which represents, within the constituted space, its absent cause/outside (production process), while the Lacanian subject can be conceptualized only when we take into account how the very externality of the generative process ex-sists only insofar as the stand-in of the constituted domain is present in it.

This is what Lacan aims at in his persistent reference to torus and other variations of the Möbius-strip-like structures in which the relationship between inside and outside is inverted: if we want to grasp the minimal structure of subjectivity, the clear-cut opposition between inner subjective experience and outer objective reality is not sufficient—there is an excess on both sides. On the one hand, we should accept the lesson of Kant's transcendental idealism: out of the confused multitude of impressions, "objective reality" emerges through the intervention of the subject's transcendental act.

In other words, Kant does not deny the distinction between the multitude of subjective impressions and objective reality; his point is merely that this very distinction results from the intervention of a subjective gesture of transcendental constitution. In a homologous way, Lacan's "Master-Signifier" is the "subjective" signifying feature which sustains the very "objective" symbolic structure: if we abstract this subjective excess from the objective symbolic order, the very objectivity of this order disintegrates.

In this sense, the Marxian symptom—labor-power—is a commodity whose use value is to generate value: not a point at which use value is inscribed into value, but a point at which (*generating*) *value is directly inscribed into use value*, as one of the species of use value. The false appearance of M-M', of money engendering out of itself more money, obfuscates the fact that the detour through use value is necessary in order to generate the surplus. Similarly, the false appearance of C-C', of concept engendering out of itself more concept, obfuscates the fact that the detour through subjectivity is necessary for the notion's self-generation—but which subject? Here we encounter the limit of the standard Feuerbachian and materialist critique of Hegel's idealism ("thought doesn't think itself, there must be an actual subject who is doing the thinking"): "The Notion is not merely *soul*, but free subjective Notion that is for itself and therefore possesses *personality*—the practical, objective Notion determined in and for itself which, as person, is impenetrable atomic subjectivity. ... It contains *all* determinateness within it."[31] The distinction between Soul and Subject is crucial here: Soul is the Aristotelian immanent ideal form/principle of an organism, the immaterial "life force" that keeps it alive and united, while subject is anti-soul, the point of negative self-relating which reduces the individual to the abyss of a singularity at a distance from the living substance that sustains it. That is why, for Hegel, a notion comes to exist as such, "for itself," in its opposition to its empirical instantiations, only insofar as it is located in an "impenetrable atomic subjectivity." His point here is not the commonsense vulgarity according to which, in order for universal thoughts to exist, there has to be an empirical subject that does the thinking (this is the endlessly boring theme of Hegel's critics, from the young Marx onward: "thoughts don't think themselves, only concrete living subjects can think ..."). While Hegel is fully aware of this dependence of thoughts on a thinking subject, his point is a more precise one: what kind of subject can do this "abstract" thinking (in the common sense of the term: thinking formal thoughts purified of their empirical wealth—for example, thinking of a "horse" in abstraction from the wealth of content of empirical horses)? His answer is: a subject which is itself "abstract," deprived of the wealth of empirical features, reduced to its "impenetrable atomic" singularity. In other words, universal form can emerge as such only in an entity which is for itself reduced to the impenetrable abyss of pure singularity. More precisely, this impenetrable atomic singularity is not something external to the Notion, it is Notion itself in its "oppositional determination," Notion as actually existing singularity. It is in this sense that Hegel wrote that Self is a pure Notion. The Cartesian name for this singularity is *cogito*: the Self reduced to the evanescent punctuality of the act of thinking.

Back to the circulation of Capital: we can see now why characterizing the passage from M-C-M' to M-M' as "rejection of negativity" is deeply misleading. The reason for this characterization is obvious: C stands for the mediation through use value that introduces a discordant moment into the self-identical complicity of the realm of pure value. However, such an external intrusion is not enough to isolate the place of negativity: the external intruder occupies a gap which opens up and introduces a discord into the very domain of value, and this discord, this immanent distance of value from itself, this "castration," defines (or, rather, directly is) the subject. (In this sense, Jean-Claude Milner was right: [exchange] value [not use value] represents the subject for another [exchange] value.) The subject is the distance of value from itself—also at the level of political economy, where the subject (labor-power) is not only a commodity with a value but also the source of value, i.e., that which, through its use, enriches value by adding surplus-value to it. It is crucial to locate the subject at this "abstract" level of value, not simply at the level of use value—if we do the latter, we reduce the subject to an empirical entity.

Is then the passage from M-C-M' to M-M'—the exclusion of C, the last remainder of the external reality which cannot be reduced to its notional mediation—not the most radical act of negativity, of adopting a negative attitude toward reality? M-M' is not just the ultimate speculative illusion, exclusion of negativity, but at the same time the self-split of negativity which cannot be reduced to an effect of external actual life. In other words, the very gesture of excluding negativity is, in its form, the purest act of negativity.

What this means with regard to capitalism is that the basic illusion of the capitalist universe is not that it appears to itself as a speculative circle of self-propagation detached from reality (M-M'), but rather the opposite: not too much speculative fiction, but too rooted in reality—the reference of the capitalist process of self-reproduction has to remain the fiction that this entire process is grounded in concrete human needs, that it is a complex way in which actual individuals satisfy their actual needs.

CHAPTER 7

CAPITALIST DISCOURSES

7.1 CAN ONE EXIT FROM THE CAPITALIST DISCOURSE WITHOUT BECOMING A SAINT?

In *Television*, Lacan talks about the "exit from the capitalist discourse," but the context in which he does it is crucial: he posits the psychoanalyst "in relation to what was in the past called: being a saint,"[1] and, after some descriptions of the excremental subjective position of a saint, he concludes: "The more one is a saint, the more one laughs; that's my principle, to wit, the way out of capitalist discourse—which will not constitute progress, if it happens only for some."[2] What characterizes a saint is thus not his high moral stance (Lacan explicitly mentions his rejection of distributive justice) but his distance from every symbolic identity, his withdrawal from the domain of exchange, of reciprocity, of the word's bond. What this means is that one should not make too much of Lacan's "anticapitalism": exit from capitalist discourse is clearly reserved "only for some," it is the exception which seems to prove the universal rule. (Furthermore, one can also argue that the saintly exit is an immanent part of the capitalist machine: we need to step out from time to time in order to recharge our batteries.) But is this all, or can we use Lacan's theory to draw more radical conclusions for the emancipatory struggle? Let us begin with a brief account of what one might clumsily call the "libidinal economy" of today's global capitalism.

The first thing to note is that, in the opposition between law and mercy, today's capitalism is on the side of mercy. It is easy to oppose the domains of law and mercy: law implies equitable exchange, tit for tat, repaying a debt, adequate punishment for a crime, while mercy is an excessive act that disturbs the symmetry of law—an act of mercy literally breaks the law (it gives its recipient something he/she doesn't deserve, it erases a punishment he/she is obliged to endure). That is why mercy imposes a debt on its subjects: the undeserved erasure of debt makes the recipient forever indebted toward his/her benefactor, it burdens him/her with an infinite/irrecoverable debt. In psychoanalytic terms, mercy obeys the logic of the superego—the more our debt is erased, the more we owe. (This is why it is so humiliating when an injustice is corrected by means of an act of mercy—for instance, when slaves are given freedom by a merciful act of a Master. The only mercy acceptable here is the mercy of the ex-slaves toward their ex-Masters.) Mercy is a gesture of sovereignty: paraphrasing Carl Schmitt, who wrote that the sovereign is one who can suspend the rule of law and introduce a state of exception, we can say that the sovereign is one who can suspend the law and grant mercy. Consequently, mercy is a form of the state of exception, an exception to the rule of law.

The task of a critical analysis is therefore to examine how the purity of what may look like mercy is already stained by narcissistic calculations. *Magnificent Obsession* (a Douglas Sirk melodrama from 1954, a remake of an earlier one from 1935) proposes a notion of goodness as giving (helping others in distress), but in such a way that nobody knows about it (except, obviously, the one who receives the gift). It tells the story of a spoiled rich playboy, Robert Merrick, who is saved through the use of a hospital's only resuscitator, but because the medical device cannot be in two places at once, it results in the death of Dr. Phillips, a selfless, brilliant surgeon and generous philanthropist. Helen, Phillips's young widow, receives a flood of calls, letters, and visitors all offering to pay back loans that Phillips refused to accept repayment of during his life. Many claimed he refused by saying "it was already used up." Merrick falls in love with Helen, though she holds him responsible for her husband's demise. One day, he insists on driving her home and makes a pass at her; she gets out and is hit by another car, losing her sight. Merrick confronts a friend of Helen's husband, wanting to know why a beautiful young woman like her would marry a middle-aged man, and is told that Phillips had a philosophy: to help people, but never let it be known that you are the one helping them—only then, he believed, could there be true reward in life. Merrick watches over Helen, and visits her during her recuperation, concealing his identity and calling himself Dr. Robert. When he finds out that she is nearly penniless, he secretly pays for specialists to try to restore her vision. She travels to Zurich and is told that her eyesight is gone forever. Merrick follows her, confesses his true identity, and proposes. She forgives him, but goes away, not wanting to be a burden to him. Years later, Merrick, who has become an outstanding brain surgeon, learns that Helen urgently needs an operation, which he performs. When she wakes up, her sight has miraculously returned; his debt to her thereby repaid, the lovers are finally united.

Does Merrick thereby also not get back his invested goodness? Therein lies the film's libidinal manipulation: he acts out of pure goodness, without expecting any return, keeping it secret, but it is as if there is some "big Other" who nonetheless notices his acts and regulates the flow of things so that good deeds are properly rewarded—one gets a reward on condition that one doesn't count on it. But would not a more authentic dénouement be for Merrick to save Helen—make her see—knowing full well that by restoring her sight he will lose her?

Law and mercy are not just externally opposed, they immanently pass into each other. In the beginning there was no pure symmetrical exchange which was then supplemented by acts of mercy; it was not the rule of law which was then supplemented by acts of mercy. Prior to the exchange of goods was potlatch, in which equivalent exchange and mercy coincide: in it, acts of mercy (or, rather, gifts) themselves are put in a relation of exchange: I first invite you to a feast, the feast is a pure gift, an excess of my generosity, but I then expect you to also organize a feast as a pure gift. In such a constellation, the act of subversion would have been not to return the gift (or, even worse, to return the gift immediately, so that the appearance of a free gift would have been dispelled, replaced by a cold exchange, a tit for tat). With regard to the rule of law, it also needs exceptions, and that is why the figure of Shylock is so subversive: he undermines the rule of Law by sticking to it without exception. The cruel irony of the history of relations between capitalist-colonialist nations (whose basic principle was legal equivalent exchange) and the colonized (who were not yet fully within the market economy of exchange) is that it is a long history of broken laws/treaties, from the US treatment of Native Americans to the Israeli treatment of Palestinians, which is why the role of Shylock (who simply demands what the law gives him) is played by Palestinians. Recently a Palestinian lawyer in the West Bank made a quite logical, Shylockian demand on the State of Israel:

> A lawyer for the family of a Palestinian teen whose 2014 murder was part of a chain of events that sparked the Gaza war says he wants Israel to punish the teenager's killers in the same way it does Palestinian militants. Lawyer Mohannad Jubara is petitioning Israel's Supreme Court to demolish the family homes of the three Israeli men who abducted 16-year-old Mohammed Abu Khdeir and burned him to death in 2014.[3]

Since Israel carries out demolitions of militants' homes to deter future attacks, is not this demand perfectly logical? (Recall also the outcry after the adolescents responsible for this attack were arrested—rumors spread that they were tortured by the Israeli police, and the public protested … against what? Against the fact that they appeared to have been treated in the same way as Palestinian adolescents suspected of terrorism!) Golda Meir allegedly said that, after the Holocaust (or, according to another version, after the Eichmann trial), Israel can do whatever it likes—although Jews allegedly live according to the strict rule of Law, the State of Israel exploited the Holocaust as the ground for a superego exception from the law.

Shylock wants his pound of flesh, but this pound of flesh should not be confused with Marxian surplus-value: surplus-value is precisely not a pound of flesh but a fleshless spectral excess that disturbs the equivalent exchange of flesh, violates it as its internal excess and condition (as Marx put it, the appropriation of surplus-value occurs in the very form of equivalent exchange), and Shylock wants precisely to reinscribe this excess back into flesh, to get back what he loses in the equivalent exchange of flesh.

7.2 CAPITALIST PERVERSION

Within these coordinates of the hegemonic ideology, global capitalism appears as a limitless cycle of expanded self-reproduction that threatens to swallow everything in its crazy dance, undermining all traditional fixed forms of social life; in psychoanalytic terms: as a libidinal regime which suspends the rule of law/castration. A multiplicity of ideological forms then impose themselves which promise to constrain the socially destructive effects of this dynamic, i.e., to enable us to have our cake (of capitalist dynamics) and eat it, from traditional religious and moral systems ("Asian values," etc.) to ecology. This opposition—limitless capitalist expansion versus its external limits—is, however, a false one: it ignores the limit (antagonism) that is immanent to the capitalist system, and propels its very limitless expansion. From the libidinal standpoint, capitalism is a regime of perversion, not psychosis: it disavows castration, it does not exclude or suspend it:

> capitalism entails a generalization of the perverse *jouissance* at the level of the social link, an insurmountable horizon, in which a thousand perversions may blossom, while the general social framework remains unchangeable: the closed world of commodity form, whose polymorphous nature enables the processing, integration and neutralization of all forms of antagonism. The capitalist subject mocks castration, declares it an anachronism and a remainder of the phallocentric universe that the postmodern has overcome once and for all. Castration, and consequently psychoanalysis, is considered to be merely one of those famous grand narratives, whose end needs to be acknowledged. In the end, this position conceives capitalism as a vicious circle, from which it is impossible to break out.[4]

One has to make a choice here—generalized perversion or psychosis? Perversion is not psychotic, it does not rely on autism of *jouissance*: in perversion, castration is disavowed, not excluded/suspended; it remains operative as the absent point of reference; the more the subject disavows it, the more its weight is felt. Unfortunately, Lacan himself seems to oscillate here, sometimes talking about capitalism as perversion, sometimes as a psychotic "foreclosure," as in the following Deleuzian-sounding lines: "What distinguishes the capitalist discourse is this—*Verwerfung*, rejection from all the fields of symbolic, with all the consequences that I have already mentioned. Rejection of what? Of castration. Every order, every discourse that aligns itself with capitalism leaves aside what we will simply call the matters of love."[5] This is why global consumerist capitalism is in its basic structure Spinozan, not Kantian: it actually appears as a flow of absolute immanence in which multiple effects proliferate, with no cuts of negativity/castration interrupting this flow: "Capitalism rejects the paradigm of negativity, castration: the symbolic operation that constitutes the subject as split and decentralized."[6] It is in this sense that contemporary capitalism is "postpolitical," and, consequently, the "return of negativity, in the guise of castration, can serve as a minimal localization of the political dimension of psychoanalysis."[7]

However, "autism of *jouissance*" is definitely not the norm in contemporary permissive-hedonistic capitalism, but rather its excess, a surrender to unconstrained consumption whose exemplary cases are drug addiction and alcoholism. The impasses of today's consumerism provide a clear case of the Lacanian distinction between pleasure and enjoyment: what Lacan calls "enjoyment" (*jouissance*) is a deadly excess over pleasure, i.e., its place is beyond the pleasure principle. In other words, the term plus-de-jouir (surplus- or excess enjoyment) is a pleonasm, since enjoyment is in itself excessive, in contrast to pleasure, which is by definition moderate, regulated by a proper measure. We thus have two extremes: on the one hand the enlightened hedonist who carefully calculates his pleasures to prolong his fun and avoid getting hurt; on the other hand the *jouisseur* proper, ready to consume his very existence in the deadly excess of enjoyment—or, in terms of our society, on the one hand the consumerist calculating his pleasures, well protected from all kinds of harassments and other health threats; on the other hand the drug addict (or smoker, or ...) bent on self-destruction. Enjoyment serves nothing, it is of no use whatsoever, and the great effort of the contemporary hedonistic-utilitarian "permissive" society is to incorporate this un(ac)countable excess into the field of (ac)counting. One should thus reject the commonsense opinion according to which in a hedonistic-consumerist society we all enjoy: the basic strategy of enlightened consumerist hedonism is, on the contrary, to deprive enjoyment of its excessive dimension, of its disturbing surplus, of the fact that it serves nothing. Enjoyment is tolerated, solicited even, but on condition that it is healthy, that it doesn't threaten our psychic or biological stability: chocolate yes, but fat-free; Coke yes, but diet; coffee yes, but decaffeinated; beer yes, but alcohol-free; mayonnaise yes, but without cholesterol; sex yes, but safe sex, etc. We are here in the domain of what Lacan calls the discourse of the University, as opposed to the discourse of the Master: a Master goes to the limit in his consumption, he is not constrained by petty utilitarian considerations (which is why there is a certain formal homology between the traditional aristocratic master and a drug addict focused on his deadly enjoyment), while the consumerist's pleasures are regulated by scientific knowledge propagated by the University discourse. The decaffeinated enjoyment we thus obtain is a semblance of enjoyment, not its Real, and it is in this sense that Lacan talks about the imitation of enjoyment in the discourse of the University. The prototype of this discourse is the multiplicity of reports in popular magazines which advocate sex as good for our health: the sexual act works like jogging, strengthens the heart, relaxes our tensions; even kissing is beneficial. The basic feature of subjectivity that fits global capitalism is total mobilization in the service of efficiency. The idea of a new "post-Fordist" workplace which takes workers' needs into account relies on the spirit of total mobilization where even relaxation serves to recharge us for work—in the same way that we speak about power breakfasts, etc., we already have companies which help us to enjoy power napping:

> According to Christopher Lindholst, CEO of Restworks—a company
> that provides workplace rest and napping installations for corporations,
> hospitals, and universities—napping at work could actually be key to
> helping employees reach their full potential. So, it's no wonder that some
> big, well-known companies—think Google, NASA, and Zappos—are
> implementing these mid-day snoozes to help give their team members a
> boost. And, they aren't just expecting employees to slouch in their own desk
> chairs. No, brief naps have become a key part of their company cultures,
> meaning they give their teams the appropriate spaces and atmospheres
> (from comfy chairs to dedicated nap rooms) to catch a few z's when they
> feel the need to recharge at work.[8]

It may appear that this is a humane measure: workers should not be active continuously, they need time to relax. However, we should always bear in mind that this inclusion of rest into work time implies (and relies on) exactly what it says: rest itself becomes part of our work, it is subordinated to its demands. And we can easily guess what awaits us at the end of this road: power sex. What about preparing small rooms with a bed and shower for quickies where employees can "catch a few Ooh! Yes! More!'s when they feel the need to recharge at work"?

Gaze and voice are inscribed into the field of normative social relations in the guise of shame and guilt. Shame is obviously linked to the Other's gaze: I am ashamed when the (public) Other sees me in my nudity, when my dirty intimate features are publicly disclosed, etc. Guilt, on the contrary, is independent of how others see me, what they say about me: I am guilty in myself, the pressure of guilt comes from within, emanating from a voice that addresses me from the core of my being and makes me guilty. The opposition gaze/voice is thus to be linked to the opposition shame/guilt as well as to the opposition Ego Ideal / superego: superego is the inner voice which haunts me and makes me guilty, while Ego Ideal is the gaze in view of which I feel ashamed. These couples of oppositions enable us to grasp the passage from traditional capitalism to its hedonistic-permissive version that predominates today: the hegemonic ideology no longer functions as the Ego Ideal whose gaze makes me ashamed when I am exposed to it, the Other's gaze loses its castrative power; it functions as an obscene superego injunction which makes me guilty (not when I violate symbolic prohibitions but) for not fully enjoying, for never enjoying enough.

When, exactly, does the *objet a* function as the superego injunction to enjoy? When it occupies the place of the Master-Signifier, i.e., as Lacan formulated it in the last pages of *Seminar XI*, when the short circuit between S_1 and a occurs.[9] The key move to be accomplished in order to break the vicious cycle of the superego injunction is thus to enact the separation between S_1 and a. Consequently, would it not be more productive to follow a different path: to start with the different modus operandi of *l'objet a* which in psychoanalysis no longer functions as the agent of the superego injunction—as it does in the discourse of perversion? This is how Jacques-Alain Miller's claim of the identity of the Analyst's discourse and the discourse of today's civilization[10] should be read: as an indication that this latter discourse (social link) is that of perversion. That is to say: the fact that the upper level of Lacan's formula of the discourse of the Analyst is the same as his formula of perversion ($a–\$$) opens up a possibility of reading the entire formula of the discourse of the Analyst also as a formula of the perverse social link: its agent, the masochist pervert (the pervert *par excellence*), occupies the position of the object-instrument of the other's desire, and, in this way, through serving his (feminine) victim, he posits her as the hystericized/divided subject who "doesn't know what she wants"—the pervert knows it for her, i.e., he pretends to speak from the position of knowledge (about the other's desire) which enables him to serve the other; and, finally, the product of this social link is the Master-Signifier, i.e., the hysterical subject elevated to the role of the master (dominatrix) whom the pervert masochist serves.

In contrast to hysteria, the pervert knows perfectly well what he is for the Other: a knowledge supports his position as the object of his Other's (divided subject's) *jouissance*. For that reason, the formula of the discourse of perversion is the same as that of the Analyst's discourse: Lacan defines perversion as inverted fantasy, i.e., his formula of perversion is $a–\$$, which is precisely the upper level of the Analyst's discourse. The difference between the social link of perversion and that of analysis is grounded in the radical ambiguity of *objet petit a* in Lacan, which stands simultaneously for the imaginary fantasmatic lure/screen and for that which this lure is obfuscating, for the void behind the lure. Consequently, when we pass from perversion to the analytic social link, the agent (analyst) reduces himself to the void which provokes the subject into confronting the truth of his desire. Knowledge in the position of "truth" below the bar under the "agent," of course, refers to the supposed knowledge of the analyst, and, simultaneously, signals that the knowledge gained here will not be the neutral "objective" knowledge of scientific adequacy, but the knowledge which concerns the subject (analysand) in the truth of his subjective position. Recall, again, Lacan's outrageous statement that even if what a jealous husband claims about his wife (that she sleeps around with other men) is all true, his jealousy is still pathological; along the same lines, one could say that even if most of the Nazi claims about the Jews were true (they exploit Germans, they seduce German girls, etc.), their anti-Semitism would still be (and was) pathological—because it represses the true reason *why* the Nazis *needed* anti-Semitism in order to sustain their ideological position. So, in the case of anti-Semitism, knowledge about what the Jews "really are" is fake, irrelevant, while the only knowledge at the place of truth is the knowledge about why a Nazi *needs* the figure of the Jew to sustain his ideological edifice.

But is not perversion, for this very reason, closer to the University discourse? For Lacan, a pervert is not defined by the content of what he does (his weird sexual practices). Perversion, at its most fundamental, resides in the formal structure of how the pervert relates to truth and speech: the pervert claims direct access to some figure of the big Other (from God or history to the desire of his partner), so that, dispelling all the ambiguity of language, he is able to act directly as the instrument of the big Other's will. In this sense, both Osama bin Laden and President Bush, although political opponents, share the structures of a pervert. They both act upon the presupposition that their acts are directly ordered and guided by divine will. And Stalin is to be added to this series: a Bolshevik is not a subject but an object-instrument of historical necessity. It is the sadistic pervert himself who occupies the place of the object, i.e., who assumes the position of the pure object-instrument of the Other's *jouissance*, displacing the division constitutive of subjectivity onto the other, onto his victim.[11] (In this respect, sadistic perversion is very close to obsessional neurosis, with the only [yet crucial] difference that the sadistic pervert is active in order to generate the Other's *jouissance*, while the obsessional neurotic is active for precisely the opposite reason, i.e., in order to prevent the Other's enjoyment—*pour que ça ne bouge pas dans l'autre*, as they put it in French.) Such a position of the agent's knowledge is what defines the University discourse, so if we are to understand the libidinal economy of capitalism, it is crucial to raise the question of the link between capitalism and the University discourse.

The thesis on "inherent transgression" does not amount to a simple commonsense point that a set of values, laws, etc., in order to survive, must accommodate itself to the complexity of real life, tolerate compromises, etc. What distinguishes shadowy superego rules from this kind of worldly "wisdom" is that (1) the superego paralegal network is experienced as obscene, permeated with enjoyment; and (2) for that reason, it must remain publicly unacknowledged, i.e., its public revelation disintegrates the system. Or, to put it in yet another way, shadowy unwritten superego rules are the remainder of the original lawless violence which founded the rule of Law itself—this violence is not something present only at the beginning, it must be there all the time in order for the rule of law to maintain itself. Unwritten superego rules are the synchronic aspect of the diachronic process of the imposition of law through the lawless act of violence—or, rather, this diachronic process, the story of the "original crime," is the narrativization of the necessary, structural, synchronic incoherence of the law.

The unique impact of *The Matrix* derives not so much from its central thesis (what we experience as reality is an artificial virtual reality generated by the "Matrix," the megacomputer directly attached to all our minds), but from its central image of the millions of human beings leading a claustrophobic life in a water-filled cradle, kept alive in order to generate the energy (electricity) for the Matrix. So when (some of these) people "awaken" from their immersion in the Matrix-controlled virtual reality, this awakening is not an opening into the wide space of external reality, but first a horrible realization of this enclosure, where each of us is in effect merely a fetus-like organism, immersed in the amniotic fluid. This utter passivity is the foreclosed fantasy that sustains our conscious experience as active, self-positing subjects—it is the ultimate perverse fantasy, the notion that we are ultimately instruments of the Other's (Matrix's) *jouissance*, sucked out of our life substance like batteries. That is the true libidinal enigma of this situation: why does the Matrix need human energy? The purely energy-related solution is, of course, meaningless: the Matrix could easily have found another, more reliable source of energy which would not have demanded the extremely complex arrangement of the virtual reality coordinated for millions of human units. The only consistent answer is: the Matrix feeds on the humans' *jouissance*—so here we are back at the fundamental Lacanian thesis that the big Other itself, far from being an anonymous machine, needs a constant influx of *jouissance*. This is how we should turn around the state of things presented by the film: what the film presents as the scene of our awakening into our true situation is in fact its exact opposite, the very fundamental fantasy that sustains our being.

The intimate connection between perversion and cyberspace is a commonplace today. According to the conventional view, the perverse scenario stages the "disavowal of castration," and is not cyberspace also a universe unencumbered by the inertia of the Real, constrained only by its self-imposed rules? And is it not the same with virtual reality in *The Matrix*? The "reality" in which we live loses its inexorable character, it becomes a domain of arbitrary rules (imposed by the Matrix) that one can violate if one's Will is strong enough. However, according to Lacan, what this conventional notion leaves out of consideration is the unique relationship between the Other and the *jouissance* in perversion. What, exactly, does this mean? Recall Marie Jean Pierre Flourens's claims that the anesthetic works only on our memory's neuronal network: unknowingly, we are our own greatest victims, butchering ourselves alive. ... Is it not also possible to read this as the perfect fantasy scenario of interpassivity, of the Other Scene in which we pay the price for our active intervention in the world? There is no active free agent without this fantasmatic support, without this Other Scene in which he is totally manipulated by the Other. A sadomasochist willingly assumes this suffering as the access to Being. That is the correct insight of *The Matrix*: in its juxtaposition of the two aspects of perversion—on the one hand, reduction of reality to a virtual domain regulated by arbitrary rules that can be suspended; on the other hand, the concealed truth of this freedom, the reduction of the subject to absolute instrumentalized passivity.[12] It is only against this background that we can properly understand how the late-capitalist permissive-hedonistic discourse motivates subjects:

> demand for *jouissance* without castration—*vivre sans temps mort, jouir sans entraves*, to recall the famous graffiti from 1968—is the productive ground for the *jouissance* of the system. Life without boredom (dead time) and enjoyment without restriction (or without castration) inaugurate a new, more radical and invisible form of exploitation. Of course, the inevitable truth of creativity, mobility and flexibility of labour is the creativity, mobility and flexibility of the capitalist forms of domination.[13]

One should note how this stance of constant "creativity, mobility and flexibility" in which work and enjoyment coincide is shared by late-capitalist subjectivity as well as by the Deleuzian and other grassroots direct democracy movements. YouTube is full of sites in which ordinary people present a recording (usually an hour long) of themselves accomplishing some ordinary chore like baking a cake, cleaning a bathroom, or painting their car—nothing extraordinary, just a regular activity whose predictable rhythm engenders a soothing effect of peace in the viewer. It is easy to understand the attraction of watching such recordings: they enable us to escape the vicious cycle of the oscillation between nervous hyperactivity and bouts of depression. Their extraordinary nature resides in their very ordinariness: such totally predictable everyday chores are becoming rarer and rarer in our frantic daily rhythm.

One has to take a step further here and raise a more specific question: if "the inevitable truth of creativity, mobility and flexibility of labour is the creativity, mobility and flexibility of the capitalist forms of domination," how, precisely, are the two identified (or, rather, mediated)? We are dealing with permissive capitalism focused on intense, untrammeled enjoyment, a capitalism whose libidinal economy disavows castration, i.e., a capitalism which no longer relies on the paternal Law and is celebrated by its apologists as the reign of generalized perversion. Consequently, since the core of perversion is defined by the couple of sadism and masochism, the question to be raised is: how does the libidinal economy of permissive hedonistic capitalism relate to this couple? In general terms, the difference between sadism and masochism concerns the status of shame: the goal of the sadist's activity is not just to make the victim suffer but to cause shame in the victim, to make him/her ashamed of what is happening to him/her. In masochism, on the contrary, the victim no longer experiences shame, he/she openly displays his/her *jouissance*. So even if in a masochist performance the same thing goes on as in a sadist exercise—say, a master beating his victim—the line separating the two gets blurred, since "behind its contract a subversion of domination took place. The subject, who can enjoy in the position of the object, is the only true master, while the apparent executor is merely a prop, a subject for whom the contract presupposes not to enjoy. The contract demands a castrated master, deprived of the power to cause shame."[14] In short, the gaze of the Master (big Other) no longer gives birth to shame and is no longer castrative but itself gets castrated: impotent, unable to control or prevent the servant/victim's *jouissance*. However, this impotence is deceptive:

> subjects offer themselves to the regime's gaze and shamelessly exhibit *jouissance*, not knowing that the regime in the position they assume establishes the continuity between *jouissance* and labour. Once in the position of surplus-object, the students are themselves studied by the regime's gaze.[15]

Is it true, then, that "the masochist would indeed be the perfect subject of capitalism, someone who would enjoy being a commodity among others, while assuming the role of surplus labour, the position of the object that willingly satisfies the systemic demands"?[16] Is it true that "the capitalist regime demands from everyone to become ideal masochists and the actual message of the superego's injunction is: 'enjoy your suffering, enjoy capitalism'"?[17] The problem here is: can the contract between capitalist and worker really be compared with the masochistic contract? The first and obvious big difference is that in the labor contract, the capitalist pays the worker (in order to extract from him surplus-value), while in the masochistic contract, the victim pays the "master" to do the work, i.e., to stage the masochistic performance which produces surplus-enjoyment in the victim. Is the proletarian masochist, then, the secret master who binds the Master-capitalist by a contract to torture him in order to gain his own surplus-enjoyment? While this version has to be rejected, one should nonetheless assert its underlying principle: *jouissance is* suffering, a painful excess of pleasure (pleasure in pain), and, in this sense, *jouissance is* in effect masochistic. (Recall that one of Lacan's definitions of *jouissance* is precisely "pleasure-in-pain": the surplus that transforms pleasure into *jouissance* is that of pain.) However, one should also recall that the masochistic contract sets a limit to the excess, thereby reducing the masochistic spectacle to a sterile theatrical performance (in an endless circular movement of postponement, the spectacle never reaches a climax)—in this sense, the masochistic spectacle is rather a kind of "pleasurization" of *jouissance*, in contrast to sadism, which goes to the very limit in brutality (although, again, there are also masochists who go to the very limit in torture …).

7.3 MASTER, HYSTERIC, UNIVERSITY, ANALYST

Furthermore, how does class antagonism inscribe itself into the capitalist discourse? Insofar as it functions as University discourse, things are clear: the capitalist is the agent of knowledge who dominates workers, and the product of this domination is $, the proletarian pure subject deprived of all substantial content. However, what happens insofar as it functions as the Hysteric's discourse? To put it bluntly, what is the class determination of the hysteric as the agent of capitalist discourse? Is the hysteric the proletarian as the product of the University discourse? And is the Master, then, he (the hysteric) who provokes the capitalist (who pretends to act as a bearer of knowledge, a rational manager organizing production, but whose truth is being the Master who exerts domination)? But what if the obverse also holds—i.e., what if the capitalist is a hysteric caught in the infernal self-perpetuating cycle of extended reproduction, provoking his own true Master, Capital itself? And what if the true agent of knowledge is the worker who keeps running the production process through his know-how? In short, what if the tension between the University discourse and the Hysteric's discourse runs diagonally across both poles of class antagonism, dividing each of the two?

Consequently, when we talk about "capitalist discourse," we should bear in mind that this discourse (social link) is split from within, that it functions only if it constantly oscillates between two discourses, discourse of University and discourse of Hysteria. Lacan did propose a specific formula for capitalist discourse: in Seminar XVIII ("Le savoir du psychanalyste," 1970–1971, unpublished), he plays with the idea of taking the discourse of the Master, but with the first (left) couple exchanging places: $ occupies the place of the agent and the Master-Signifier the place of truth:

$$\left\downarrow \frac{\$}{S_1} \times \frac{S_2}{a} \right\downarrow$$

The connecting lines remain as with the Master's discourse ($\$$–a, S_1–S_2), but they run diagonally: while the agent is the same as in the discourse of the Hysteric, the (divided) subject, it addresses itself not to the Master, but to surplus-enjoyment, the "product" of capitalist circulation. As in the discourse of the Master, the "other" here is the Servant's Knowledge (or, more and more, scientific knowledge), dominated by the true Master, capital itself.[18] But it would be easy to show that this discourse cannot stand on its own, that it cannot deliver what it promises (the formula of the eternal self-perpetuating circulation of capital). It should, rather, be taken as an indicator of the impossible fantasy of capitalism, of the spin capitalism introduces into the Master's discourse; since this spin cannot stand on its own, it triggers the split of the Master's discourse into the discourse of Hysteria and the discourse of the University as the two facets of the capitalist social link.

Therein lies the parallax of capitalism, which can also be expressed in terms of the opposition between desire and drive: hysterical desire and perverse drive. The overlapping element of the two is $\$$ (subject), the product of the University discourse and the agent of the Hysteric's discourse, and, simultaneously, S_2 (knowledge), the product of the Hysteric's discourse and the agent of the University discourse. Knowledge works on its other, the object, and the product is the subject, $\$$; the axis of the impossible is the way this subject relates to its Master-Signifier, which would define its identity. In the reversal to the discourse of Hysteria, the agent is now the subject who addresses its other as the Master-Signifier, and the product is knowledge about what the subject is as an object; but since this knowledge is again impossible, we get a reversal into the discourse of the University, which addresses the object. This is the twisted structure of the Möbius strip, of course: progressing to the end on one side, we all of a sudden find ourselves on the other side. (And is the other axis not the axis of Master and Analyst, with *objet a* and S_1 as the overlapping elements? One should also note that each of these two couples combines a masculine and a feminine sexual logic: masculine university versus feminine hysteria; masculine master versus feminine analyst.) Does not this intertwining of two discourses provide the underlying discursive structure of the double aspect of modernity: the hysterical logic of incessant expanded subjective productivity and the university logic of domination through knowledge? That is to say: what we perceive as "modernity" is characterized by two different topics. First, it is the notion of subjectivity as a destabilizing force of incessant self-expansion and self-transcending, as the agent possessed by an insatiable desire; then, there is the specifically modern form of control and domination whose first embodiment is the baroque absolutist state, and which culminated in the twentieth-century "totalitarian" state analyzed by Foucault (discipline and punish), Adorno and Horkheimer (instrumental reason, administered world), etc., the form which entered a new stage with the prospect of digital control and the biogenetic manipulation of human beings. In its ideological aspect, this duality appears in terms of the opposition between individualist libertarianism and state control. It is crucial not to abolish this parallax structure by reducing one topic to the other—for example, by dismissing self-expanding subjectivity as an ideological illusion that obfuscates the truth of total control and domination, or simply combining the two topics (the self-expanding subject asserts its power through control and domination).

One has to take a step further here. The parallax split of capitalist discourse is grounded in the fact that capitalism remains a master discourse, but a master discourse in which the structure of domination is repressed, pushed beneath the bar (individuals are formally free and equal, domination is displaced onto relations between things-commodities). This detour in no way implies that the capitalist is in some way less a master than a premodern "true" Master—the proper gesture of a Master is just to "give a sign" (to enunciate his [Master-]Signifier, not to regulate and control its execution): "it is effectively impossible that there be a master who makes the entire world function. Getting people to work is even more tiring, if one really has to do it, than working oneself. The master never does it. He gives a sign, the master signifier, and everybody jumps." [19] And it is precisely by renouncing this direct position of a Master that the capitalist can in effect "make the world function," that he in effect organizes things. To recapitulate: the underlying structure is that of a capitalist Master pushing his other (worker) to produce surplus-value that he (the capitalist) appropriates. But since this structure of domination is repressed, its appearance cannot be a(nother) single discourse: it can only appear split into two discourses. Both university discourse and hysterical discourse are the outcome of the failure of the Master's discourse: when the Master loses his authority and becomes hystericized (which is another name for questioning his authority, experiencing it as fake), authority reappears in a displaced way, desubjectivized, in the guise of the authority of neutral expert knowledge ("It's not me who exerts power, I just state objective facts and/or knowledge").

Now we come to an interesting conclusion: if capitalism is characterized by the parallax of Hysteria and University discourses, is resistance to capitalism then characterized by the opposite axis of Master and Analyst? Some old-fashioned orthodox Leftists would even maintain that—insofar as, as Miller claimed, capitalist discourse displays the structure of the Analyst's discourse—the passage from capitalism to Communism should be conceived as the passage from Analyst's discourse back to Master's discourse. The recourse to

Master does not necessarily designate the conservative attempt to counteract capitalist dynamics with a resuscitated figure of traditional authority; rather, it points toward the new type of Communist master (Leader) emphasized by Badiou, who is not afraid to oppose the necessary role of the Master to our "democratic" sensitivity: "I am convinced that one has to reestablish the capital function of leaders in the Communist process, whichever its stage."[20] A true Master is not an agent of discipline and prohibition; his message is not "You cannot!" nor "You have to ... !" but a releasing "You can!"—what? Do the impossible, i.e., what appears impossible within the coordinates of the existing constellation—and today, this means something very precise: you can think beyond capitalism and liberal democracy as the ultimate framework of our lives. A Master is a vanishing mediator who gives you back to yourself, who delivers you to the abyss of your freedom: when we listen to a true leader, we discover what we want (or, rather, what we always-already wanted without knowing it). A Master is needed because we cannot accede to our freedom directly—to gain this access we have to be pushed from outside, since our "natural state" is one of inert hedonism, of what Badiou called "human animal." The underlying paradox here is that the more we live as "free individuals with no Master," the more we are in fact non-free, caught within the existing frame of possibilities—we have to be pushed/disturbed into freedom by a Master.[21]

Lenin was fully aware of this urgent need for a new Master. In his extraordinary analysis of Lenin's much-maligned *What Is to Be Done?* (1902), Lars T. Lih convincingly refuted the usual reading of this book as an argument for a centralized elitist professional revolutionary organization. According to this reading, Lenin's main thesis is that the working class cannot achieve its adequate class consciousness "spontaneously," through its own "organic" development; this truth has to be introduced into it from outside (by the Party intellectuals who provide "objective" scientific knowledge).[22] There are in fact elements in Lenin's writings which support this interpretation— just recall his letters to Gorky from fall 1913[23] in which, deeply disturbed by Gorky's support for the humanist ideology of the "construction of God," Lenin implies that Gorky succumbed to this deviation because of his bad nerves, and advises him to go to Switzerland and get the best medical treatment. In one of the letters, after making it clear how shocked he is by Gorky's ideas—"Dear Alexei Maximovitch, what are you doing, then? Really, it is terrible, simply terrible! / Why are you doing this? It is terribly painful. Yours, V.I."—Lenin adds a strange postscript: "P.S. *Take care of yourself more seriously, really, so that you will be able to travel in winter without catching cold* (in winter, it is dangerous)." Obviously, Lenin is worried that, apart from catching cold, Gorky will catch a much more serious ideological disease, as is clear from the subsequent letter (posted together with the previous one):

"Perhaps I don't understand you *well?* Perhaps *you were joking* when you wrote 'for the moment'? Concerning the 'construction of God,' perhaps you didn't write that seriously? Good heavens, take care of yourself a little bit better. Yours, *Lenin.*" What should surprise us here is the way the root of ideological deviation is located in a physical condition (overexcited nerves) that needs medical treatment. Is it not a supreme irony that, in Trotsky's dream from 1935 in which the dead Lenin appears to him, he gives him exactly the same advice?

> He was questioning me anxiously about my illness. "You seem to have accumulated nervous fatigue, you must rest ..." I answered that I had always recovered from fatigue quickly, thanks to my native *Schwungkraft*, but that this time the trouble seemed to lie in some deeper processes ... "Then you should seriously (he emphasized the word) consult the doctors (several names)."[24]

So, to bring this logic to its conclusion, I am tempted to imagine a scene between Lenin and Stalin in the last year of Lenin's life, after his stroke and collapse, when, with his remaining energy, he ferociously attacks Stalin, and Stalin answers him patronizingly: "Good heavens, comrade Lenin, you seem to have accumulated nervous fatigue, you must rest! You should more seriously consult the doctors!" ... Here, Lenin would have gotten his own message back in its inverted-true form—an appropriate punishment for his mistake. There is nonetheless a crucial cut here between Lenin and Stalin: while Lenin remained at this level, claiming access to the "objective meaning" of events, Stalin took a fateful step further and *resubjectivized* this objective meaning. In the Stalinist universe, there are, paradoxically, ultimately no dupes, everyone knows the "objective meaning" of his/her acts, so that, instead of illusory consciousness, we get direct hypocrisy and deceit: the "objective meaning" of your acts is what you *really wanted*, and your good intentions are merely a hypocritical mask. Furthermore, all of Lenin cannot be reduced to this subjective position of the privileged access to "objective meaning": there is another, much more "open," subjective position at work in Lenin's writings: the position of total exposure to historical contingency. From this position, there is no "true" Party line waiting to be discovered, no "objective" criteria to determine it: the Party "makes all possible mistakes," and the "true" Party line emerges from the zigzag of oscillations, i.e., "necessity" is constituted in praxis, it emerges through the mutual interaction of subjective decisions.

Along these lines, Lih changes the focus to the relationship between worker-followers and worker-leaders, and asks: "What happens when these two meet, when they interact? What happens can be summed up in one word: a miracle. This is Lenin's word, *chudo* in Russian, and, when you start looking, words like 'miracle,' 'miraculous,' are fairly common in Lenin's vocabulary."[25] To illustrate this "miracle," Lenin looks back to the Russian populist revolutionaries from the 1870s and, according to Lih, asks:

> Why are these people heroes? Why do we look up to them as model? Because they had a centralised, conspirational underground organisation? No, they are heroes because they were inspiring leaders. Here's what Lenin says about these earlier revolutionaries: "their inspirational preaching met with an answering call from the masses awakening in elemental [stikhiinyi] fashion, and the leaders' seething energy is taken up and supported by the energy of the revolutionary class."[26]

What Lenin expects from the Bolsheviks is something similar: not cold, "objective" (nonpartisan) knowledge, but a fully engaged subjective stance which can mobilize their followers—it is in this sense that even a lone individual can trigger an avalanche: "You brag about your practicability and you don't see (a fact known to any Russian praktik) what miracles for the revolutionary cause can be brought about not only by a circle but by a lone individual."[27] Lih reads along the same lines the famous claim from What Is to Be Done?: "Give me an organization of revolutionaries and I will turn Russia around!" Again, rejecting the interpretation that "a band of intelligentsia conspirators can somehow wave their hands and destroy tsarism," Lih provides his own paraphrase of Lenin:

> Comrades, look around you! Can't you see that the Russian workers are champing at the bit to receive the message of revolution and to act on it? Can't you see the potential for leadership that already exists among the activists, the praktiki? Can't you see how many more leaders would arise out of the workers if we set our minds to encouraging their rise? Given all this potential, what is holding things up? Why is the tsar still here? We, comrades—we're the bottleneck! If we could hone our underground skills and bring together what the tsarist regime wants so desperately to keep apart—worker leaders and worker followers, the message and the audience—then, by God, we could blow this joint apart![28]

What Lenin calls "miracle" is thus not some higher "objective knowledge" delivered to the ordinary proletarians by the intellectual leader, but the explosive encounter of a leader with his followers which makes all of them what they are. Such a Master is needed especially in situations of deep crisis. The function of a Master here is to enact an authentic division—a division between those who want to drag on within the old parameters and those who are aware of the necessary change. Such a division, not opportunistic compromises, is the only path to true unity. Let us take an example which surely is not problematic: France in 1940. Even Jacques Duclos, a key official in the

French Communist Party, admitted in a private conversation that if, at that point in time, free elections had been held in France, Marshal Pétain would have won with ninety percent of the votes. When de Gaulle, in his historic act, refused to acknowledge the capitulation to the Germans and continued to resist, claiming that it was only he, not the Vichy regime, who spoke on behalf of the real France (on behalf of the real France as such, not only on behalf of the "majority of the French"!), what he was saying was deeply true even if it was "democratically" not only without legitimization, but clearly opposed to the opinion of the majority of the French people.

Following the spirit of today's ideology, which demands a shift from traditional hierarchy, a pyramid-like subordination to a Master, to pluralizing rhizomatic networks, political analysts like to point out that the new antiglobalist protests all around Europe and the United States, from Occupy Wall Street to Greece and Spain, have no central agency, no Central Committee, coordinating their activity—there are just multiple groups interacting, mostly through social media like Facebook or Twitter, and coordinating their activity spontaneously. But is this "molecular" spontaneous self-organization really the most efficient new form of "resistance"? Is it not that the opposite side, especially capital, already acts more and more as what Deleuzian theory calls the post-Oedipal multitude? Power itself has to enter a dialogue at this level, answering Twitter with Twitter—the Pope and President Trump are now both on Twitter.

Tweet culture offers itself as a privileged space of this underground kingdom of obscenities: short snaps, retorts, sarcastic or outraged remarks, with no space for the multiple steps of a line of argumentation. One passage (a sentence, even part of it) is cut out and reacted to. For example, many critics reacted to my analysis of the anti-Semitic figure of the Jew as a foreign intruder that disturbs social harmony by accusing me of anti-Semitism, totally ignoring the fact that the claim about "Jews as the foreign intruder" is for me the very claim I reject as the exemplary ideological operation of obfuscating social antagonisms—they simply cut those words out of the line of argumentation and used them to attack me. ... The stance that sustains these tweet rejoinders is a mixture of self-righteousness, Political Correctness, and brutal sarcasm: the moment anything that sounds problematic is perceived, a reply is automatically triggered, usually a PC cliché. As such, tweet culture is deeply impregnated by the stance of *postfactuality*, which does not mean simply lying but an active ignorance of truth, a practice of indifference toward truth: statements continue to circulate even after they are proven factually wrong. Furthermore, as for the molecular self-organizing multitude against the hierarchical order sustained by the reference to a charismatic Leader, note the irony of the fact that Venezuela, a country praised by many for its attempts to develop modes of direct democracy (local councils, cooperatives, workers running factories), is also a country whose president was Hugo Chávez, a strong charismatic Leader if ever there was one. It is as if the Freudian rule of transference is at work here also: in order for individuals to "reach beyond themselves," to break out of the passivity of representative politics and engage as direct political agents, the reference to a Leader is necessary, a Leader who allows them to pull themselves out of the swamp like Baron Munchausen, a Leader who is "supposed to know" what they want. The only path to liberation leads through transference: in order to effectively rouse individuals from their dogmatic "democratic slumber," from their blind reliance on institutionalized forms of representative democracy, appeals to direct self-organization are not enough; a new figure of the Master is needed. Recall the famous lines from Arthur Rimbaud's "À une raison" ("To a Reason"):

A tap of your finger on the drum releases all sounds and initiates the new harmony.
A step of yours is the conscription of the new men and their marching orders.
You look away: the new love!
You look back,—the new love!

There is absolutely nothing inherently "Fascist" in these lines—the supreme paradox of the political dynamic is that a Master is needed to pull individuals out of the quagmire of their inertia and motivate them toward the self-transcending emancipatory struggle for freedom. Novalis, usually perceived as a representative of the conservative turn of Romanticism, was well aware of this paradox, and he proposed an extreme version of the infinite judgment: monarchy is the highest form of republic; "no king can exist without republic and no republic without a king":

the true measure of a Republic consists in the lived relation of the citizens to the idea of the whole in which they live. The unity that a law creates is merely coercive. ... The unifying factor must be a sensual one, a comprehensive human embodiment of the morals that make a common identity possible. For Novalis, the best such mediating factor for the idea of the republic is a monarch. ... While the institution might satisfy our intellect, it leaves our imagination cold. A living, breathing human being ... provides us with a symbol that we can more intuitively embrace as standing in relation to our own existence. ... The concepts of the Republic and monarch are not only reconcilable, but presuppose one another.[29]

Is not Badiou making a similar claim when he underscores the necessity of a Leader? Novalis's point is not just the banality that identification should not be merely intellectual (the point made also by Freud in *Group Psychology and the Analysis of the Ego*); the core of his argument concerns the "performative" dimension of political representation: in an authentic act of representation, people do not simply represent (assert through a representative) what they want, they become aware of what they want only through the act of representation: "Novalis argues that the role of the king should not be to give people what they think they want, but to elevate and give measure to their desires. ... The political, or the force that binds people together, should be a force that gives measure to desires rather than merely appealing to desires."[30]

However, no matter how emancipatory this new Master is, he has to be supplemented by another discursive form. As Moshe Lewin has noted, at the end of his life, even Lenin intuited this necessity when he proposed a new ruling body, the Central Control Commission. While fully admitting the dictatorial nature of the Soviet regime, he tried

> to establish at the summit of the dictatorship a balance between different elements, a system of reciprocal control that could serve the same function—the comparison is no more than approximate—as the separation of powers in a democratic regime. An important Central Committee, raised to the rank of Party Conference, would lay down the broad lines of policy and supervise the whole Party apparatus, while itself participating in the execution of more important tasks. ... Part of this Central Committee, the Central Control Commission, would, in addition to its work within the Central Committee, act as a control of the Central Committee and of its various offshoots—the Political Bureau, the Secretariat, the Orgburo. The Central Control Commission ... would occupy a special position with relation to the other institutions; its independence would be assured by its direct link to the Party Congress, without the mediation of the Politburo and its administrative organs or of the Central Committee.[31]

Checks and balances, division of powers, mutual control—this was Lenin's desperate answer to the question: Who controls the controllers? There is something dreamlike, properly fantasmatic, in this idea of a CCC: an independent, educational and controlling body with an "apolitical" edge, consisting of the best teachers and technocratic specialists keeping in check the "politicized" CC and its organs—in short, the neutral expert knowledge keeping the Party executives in check. ... However, everything hinges here on the true independence of the Party Congress, de facto already undermined by the prohibition of factions which allowed the top Party apparatus to control the Congress, dismissing its critics as "factionalists." The naivety of Lenin's trust in technocratic experts is all the more striking if we bear in mind that it comes from a politician who was otherwise fully aware of the all-pervasiveness of political struggle which allows for no neutral position.

However, Lenin's proposal cannot be reduced to this dimension; in "dreaming" (his expression) about the mode of work of the CCC, he describes how this body should resort

> to some semi-humorous trick, cunning device, piece of trickery or something of that sort. I know that in the staid and earnest states of Western Europe such an idea would horrify people and that not a single decent official would even entertain it. I hope, however, that we have not yet become as bureaucratic as all that and that in our midst the discussion of this idea will give rise to nothing more than amusement.
>
> Indeed, why not combine pleasure with utility? Why not resort to some humorous or semi-humorous trick to expose something ridiculous, something harmful, something semi-ridiculous, semi-harmful, etc.?[32]

Is this not an almost obscene double of the "serious" executive power concentrated in the CC and the Politburo, a kind of nonorganic intellectual of the movement—an agent resorting to humor, tricks, and the cunning of reason, keeping itself at a distance ... a kind of analyst? To properly locate this reading of Lenin, we should take note of the historicity inscribed into Lacan's matrix of four discourses, the historicity of modern European development.[33] The Master's discourse stands—not for the premodern master, but—for absolute monarchy, this first figure of modernity that effectively undermined the articulate network of feudal relations and interdependences, transforming fidelity to flattery, etc.: it is the "Sun King" Louis XIV, with his l'état, c'est moi, who is the Master par excellence. Hysterical discourse and the discourse of the University then deploy two outcomes of the vacillation of the direct reign of the Master: the expert rule of bureaucracy that culminates in contemporary biopolitics, which ends up reducing the population to a collection of Homo sacer (what Heidegger called "enframing," Adorno "the administered world," Foucault the society of "discipline and punish"); and the explosion of the hysterical capitalist subjectivity that reproduces itself through permanent self-revolutionizing, through the integration of the excess into the "normal" functioning of the social link (the true "permanent revolution" is already capitalism itself). Lacan's formula of four discourses thus enables us to deploy the two faces of modernity (total administration; capitalist-individualist dynamics) as the two ways to undermine the Master's discourse: doubt about the efficiency of the Master-figure (what Eric Santner called the "crisis of investiture")[34] can be supplemented by the direct rule of experts legitimized by their knowledge; or the excess of doubt, of permanent questioning, can be directly integrated into social reproduction as its essential driving force. And, finally, the Analyst's discourse stands for the emergence of a revolutionary-emancipatory subjectivity that resolves the split into University and Hysteria: in it, the revolutionary agent (a) addresses the subject from the position of knowledge which occupies the place of truth (i.e., which intervenes at the "symptomal torsion" of the subject's constellation), and the goal is to isolate, get rid of, the Master-Signifier which structured the subject's (ideologico-political) unconscious.

Or does it? As I have already mentioned, Miller[35] has recently proposed that, today, the discourse of the Master is no longer the "obverse" of the discourse of the Analyst; today, on the contrary, our "civilization" itself (its hegemonic symbolic matrix, as it were) fits the formula of the discourse of the Analyst: the "agent" of the social link today is a, surplus-enjoyment, the superego injunction to enjoy; this injunction addresses $\$$ (the divided subject) who is put to work in order to live up to this injunction. If there ever was a superego injunction, it is the famous Oriental wisdom: "Don't think, just *do* it!" The "truth" of this social link is S_2, scientific-expert knowledge in its different guises, and the goal is to generate S_1, the self-mastery of the subject, i.e., to enable the subject to "cope with" the stress of the call to enjoyment (through self-help manuals, etc.). Provocative as this notion is, it raises a series of questions. If it is true, where, then, is the difference between the discursive functioning of "civilization" as such and of the psychoanalytic social link? Here Miller resorts to a suspicious solution: in our "civilization," the four terms are kept apart, isolated, each operates on its own, while only in psychoanalysis are they brought together into a coherent link: "in the civilization, each of the four terms remains disjoined. … It is only in psychoanalysis, in pure psychoanalysis, that these elements are arranged into a discourse."[36]

However, is it not that the fundamental operation of psychoanalytic treatment is not synthesis, bringing elements into a link, but, precisely, analysis, separating what in a social link appears to belong together? This path, opposed to that of Miller, is indicated by Giorgio Agamben who, in the last pages of *The State of Exception*,[37] imagines two utopian options for breaking out of the vicious cycle of law and violence, of the rule of law sustained by violence. One is the Benjaminian vision of "pure" revolutionary violence with no relationship to the law; the other is the relationship to the law without regard to its (violent) enforcement—what Jewish scholars are doing in their endless (re)interpretation of the Law. Agamben starts from the correct insight that the task today is not synthesis but separation, distinction: not bringing law and violence together (so that right will have might and the exercise of might will be fully legitimized), but completely separating them, untying their knot. Although Agamben confers on this formulation an anti-Hegelian twist, a more proper reading of Hegel makes it clear that such a gesture of separation is what the Hegelian "synthesis" is actually about: in it, the opposites are not reconciled in a "higher synthesis"—it is rather that their difference is posited "as such." The example of Saint Paul may help us to clarify this logic of

Hegelian "reconciliation": the radical gap that he posits between "life" and "death," between life in Christ and life in sin, is in no need of further "synthesis"; it is itself the resolution of the "absolute contradiction" of Law and sin, of the vicious cycle of their mutual implication. In other words, once the distinction is drawn, once the subject becomes aware of the very existence of this other dimension beyond the vicious cycle of law and its transgression, the battle is formally already won.

However, is this vision not another case of our late-capitalist reality going further than our dreams? Are we not already encountering in our social reality what Agamben envisages as a utopian vision? Is the Hegelian lesson of the global reflexivization-mediatization of our lives not that it generates its own brutal immediacy which was best captured by Étienne Balibar's notion of excessive, nonfunctional cruelty as a feature of contemporary life, a cruelty whose figures range from "fundamentalist" racist and/or religious slaughter to the "senseless" outbursts of violence by adolescents and the homeless in our megalopolises, a violence one is tempted to call Id-Evil, a violence grounded in no utilitarian or ideological reasons? All the talk about foreigners stealing work from us, or the threat they represent to our Western values, should not deceive us: under closer examination, it soon becomes clear that this talk provides a rather superficial secondary rationalization. The answer we ultimately obtain from a skinhead is that it makes him feel good to beat up foreigners, that their presence disturbs him. What we encounter here is indeed Id-Evil, i.e., Evil structured and motivated by the most elementary imbalance in the relationship between the Ego and *jouissance*, by the tension between pleasure and the foreign body of *jouissance* at the very heart of it. Id-Evil thus stages the most elementary "short circuit" in the subject's relationship to the primordially missing object-cause of his desire: what "bothers" us in the "other" (Jew, Japanese, African, Turk) is that he appears to entertain a privileged relationship to the object—the Other either possesses the object-treasure, having snatched it away from us (which is why we don't have it), or he poses a threat to our possession of the object. What one should suggest here is a Hegelian "infinite judgment" asserting the speculative identity of these "useless" and "excessive" outbursts of violent immediacy, which display nothing but a pure and naked ("nonsublimated") hatred of Otherness, with the global reflexivization of society; perhaps the ultimate example of this coincidence is the fate of psychoanalytic interpretation. Today, the formations of the Unconscious (from dreams to hysterical symptoms) have definitely lost their innocence and are thoroughly reflexivized: the "free associations" of a typical educated analysand consist for the most part of attempts to provide a psychoanalytic explanation for their disturbances, so that one is quite justified in saying that we have not only Jungian, Kleinian, Lacanian, etc., interpretations of symptoms, but symptoms themselves which are Jungian,

Kleinian, Lacanian: i.e., whose reality involves implicit reference to some psychoanalytic theory. The unfortunate result of this global reflexivization of interpretation (everything becomes interpretation, the Unconscious interprets itself) is that the analyst's interpretation itself loses its performative "symbolic efficiency" and leaves the symptom intact in the immediacy of its idiotic *jouissance*.

Perhaps this is how the capitalist discourse functions: a subject enthralled by the superego call to excessive enjoyment, and in search of a Master-Signifier that would constrain his/her enjoyment, provide a proper measure of it, prevent its explosion into a deadly excess (of a drug addict, chain-smoker, alcoholic, and other -holics or addicts). How, then, does this version of the Analyst's discourse relate to the Analyst's discourse proper? Perhaps one reaches here the limit of Lacan's formalization of discourses, so that one should introduce another set of distinctions specifying how the same discourse can function in different modalities. What one should do here is distinguish between the two aspects of *objet a* clearly discernible in Lacan's theory: *objet a* as the void around which desires and/or drives circulate, and *objet a* as the fascinating element that fills in this void (since, as Lacan repeatedly emphasizes, *objet a* has no substantial consistency, it is just the positivization of a void). So in order to enact the shift from capitalist to analyst's discourse, one has merely to break the spell of *objet a*, to recognize beneath the fascinating agalma, the Grail of desire, the void that it covers. (This shift is homologous to the feminine subject's shift from Φ to the signifier of the barred Other in Lacan's graph of sexuation.)

7.4 CAPITALIST DISCOURSES

What, then, is our result? Perhaps it is wrong to search for a capitalist discourse, to limit it to one formula. What if we conceive capitalist discourse as a specific combination of all four discourses? First, capitalism remains Master's discourse. Capital, the Master, appropriates knowledge, the servant's *savoir-faire* extended by science, keeping under the bar the proletarian $ which produces *a*, surplus-enjoyment in the guise of surplus-value. However, owing to the displacement of the standard of domination in capitalism (individuals are formally free and equal), this starting point splits into two, Hysteria and University, so that the final result is the capitalist version of the Analyst's discourse, with surplus-enjoyment/value in in command.

To conclude with a short conceptual clarification: this complexity which culminates in the surprising fact that the same formula of a discourse can function as the formula of the capitalist discourse as well as the formula of the Analyst's discourse is grounded in the distinction between an element and the place this element occupies. Jean-Claude Milner[38] has shown how, with his theory of four discourses developed as a reaction to the turmoil of the events of May 1968, Lacan moved away from the strict structuralist paradigm in which elements are deprived of any substantial identity, since their identity is purely differential (a signifier "is" only its difference from other signifiers, or, as Saussure stated, in language there are no positive terms, only differences). The matrix of the four discourses is, on the contrary, based on the difference between a place and the element which occupies it: there are four places (agent, other, truth, product) and four elements (S_1, S_2, $\$$, a), each of which consecutively occupies each of the places, which means that each element must possess a distinctive identity independently of the place it occupies. However, upon closer inspection things immediately get complicated.

First, the paradox is that the four elements (S_1, S_2, $\$$, a), far from possessing a substantial identity, deploy the elementary structure of the differential signifying order: any differential network of signifiers has to be supplemented by an "empty" signifier which gives body to the difference as such; this signifier represents the void (subject) in the signifying network; however, this representation inevitably fails, and the product of this failure is a remainder (a), the subject's objectal counterpart. So while the elements are differential, the places occupied by these elements (agent, other, truth, product) are not; each of them has some kind of substantial weight.

Second, upon closer inspection, it is immediately obvious that all four discourses are not equal: the Master's discourse has clear priority, it is in a way "the discourse as such," and the other three discourses are ultimately the outcome of its failure, its variations or inversions. The Master-Signifier is the agent of the discourse, it stands for the initial gesture or intervention that establishes a discursive link; the Other is ultimately the signifying chain ("knowledge") into which the agent intervenes; the "truth" of the agent hidden beneath the agent's symbolic identity (provided by the Master-Signifier) is the abyss of the subject that eludes signifying representation; and, finally, the product of this failure of representation is *objet a*, a quasi-object in the guise of which the lack assumes positive existence (appears as an object).

Third and crucial point: how does it become possible for the gap between place and element to appear? (It is only this gap that enables different elements to occupy the same place one after another.) Lacan's answer is: through what Freud called "primordial repression," which is equivalent to the rise of the symbolic order as such. More precisely, this means that there is a self-redoubling that is immanent to the symbolic order—Saussure himself used a wonderful, simple example of a train which, according to the timetable, is supposed to depart from Paris to Lyon at, say, 4:10 p.m. In the symbolic order, this train remains "the 4:10 to Lyon" even if there is a delay, so that it is quite acceptable to say "the 4:10 to Lyon will depart at 4:25." In this way, the designation "the 4:10 to Lyon" becomes an "empty" signifier, a signifier emptied of its factual content: whenever it actually departs, or even if, by mistake or owing to an accident, it ends up in Bordeaux and not in Lyon, in all possible worlds it will remain "the 4:10 to Lyon." (Saul Kripke called such a signifier a "rigid designator.") Lacan calls this gap that separates the pure signifying determination "4:10 to Lyon" from the factual accidents of time and place "symbolic castration." (Another example would be the way one addressed kings in traditional societies: a king is called "his glorious, wise, beautiful, and courageous majesty" even if he is a stupid and ugly coward.)

The classic case of the fetishist disavowal of (symbolic) castration is, of course, that of a king who thinks he is in himself a king: what he is as the result of his location in the network of social-symbolic relations is misperceived as his immediate property. However, one should always bear in mind that we rarely encounter such a pure case; the predominant mode of disavowal is, rather, characterized by statements like "Don't be afraid, beneath my official insignia I am just an ordinary person with the dreams and fears we all share." True disavowal is at work here, in the illusion that beneath our official persona we are all the same "real people"—the point is that we are precisely *not* the same real people beneath the symbolic mask: that this mask affects our "real persona."[39]

But, still, how does this gap emerge? By what is a network of places occupied by arbitrary elements sustained? By a surplus moment described by Deleuze who, in *Logic of Sense*, demonstrated how the two series (of the signifier and the signified) always contain a paradoxical entity that is "doubly inscribed" (that is simultaneously surplus and lack): a surplus of the signifier over the signified (the empty signifier without a signified) and the lack of the signified (the point of nonsense within the field of Sense). In other words, as soon as the symbolic order emerges, a minimal difference is introduced between a structural place and the element that occupies or fills out this place: an element is always logically preceded by the place in the structure it fills out. The two series, therefore, can also be described as the "empty" formal structure (signifier) and the series of elements filling out the empty places in the structure (signified). From this perspective, the paradox consists in the fact that the two series never overlap: we always encounter an entity that is simultaneously (with regard to the structure) an empty, unoccupied place and (with regard to the elements) a rapidly moving, elusive object, an occupant without a place. We have thereby produced Lacan's formula of fantasy $\$–a$, since the matheme for the subject is $\$$, an empty place in the structure, an elided signifier, while *objet a* is, by definition, an excessive object, an object that lacks a place in the structure. Consequently, the point is not simply that there is a surplus of an element over the places available in the structure, or the surplus of a place that has no element to fill it out. An empty place in the structure would still sustain the fantasy of an element that will emerge to fill the place; an excessive element lacking its place would still sustain the fantasy of some as yet unknown place waiting to be filled. The point is, rather, that the empty place in the structure is strictly correlative to the errant element lacking its place: they are not two different entities, but two sides of one and the same entity, that is, one and the same entity inscribed onto the two surfaces of a Möbius strip. In other words, the gap that separates places from elements is sustained by an empty place (with no element to fill it in) which is the same as an excessive element for which there is no place: the moment all places in a structure were filled by elements (and all elements were to find their proper place), the structure would collapse into the Real.

CHAPTER 8

THE POLITICS OF ALIENATION AND SEPARATION

8.1 ALIENATION, CONSTITUTIVE AND CONSTITUTED

The topic of alienation plays a central role in so-called "warm" humanist Marxism. To put it briefly, humanist Marxism remains stuck within the confines of the abstract opposition of mechanism and organism, i.e., its vision of overcoming alienation remains that of the early, Romantic Hegel. As such, it does not provide a sufficient reply to "cold" Stalinist orthodoxy—it is not a solution, but part of the problem. It is here that Lacan's intervention is crucial: it enables us to break out of the alternative between "warm" humanist Marxism, which sees the main task of the revolutionary process in the overcoming of alienation and the establishment of a transparent society of free individuals, and the "cold" universe of dialectical and historical materialism with its "objective laws of history," a world in which there is no room for concepts like alienation. Lacan also asserts a fundamental alienation of the human subject, an alienation which is constitutive of being-human, alienation in the symbolic order: a human subject is not only a speaking being but, more radically, a being spoken, traversed by language; its truth lies outside itself, in the decentered symbolic order which forever eludes human control; every dream—of "appropriating" this alienated symbolic substance, of subordinating it to human subjectivity—is a humanist illusion. But does this mean that alienation (in the symbolic order) is simply an inevitable condition of human subjectivity, a kind of transcendental a priori of being-human?

Furthermore, when Marx writes about alienation, it is clear that he perceives the goal of revolutionary emancipation as the overcoming of alienation; even in his "mature" work, where the notion is rarely used, the vision of Communism is clearly that of a society organized in a transparent way and regulated by free collective subjectivity. "The flip side of commodity fetishism is the appearance that there is a more fundamental and unalienated position in the background, a position from which it would be possible to cognize the mistake that determines commodity fetishism"[1]—true, but is precisely this "appearance" not the basic premise not only of the early Marx but also of the "mature" Marx of the critique of political economy? So it is Marx himself who does not rigorously follow the basic axiom of his critique of political economy: the notion of alienation as a structural a priori which implies a gap between knowledge and truth, between a subject fully (self-)conscious of his social position and the properly politicized subject, a subject caught in an antagonistic process which precludes any self-transparency. If, however, we accept that the alienation of the labor force cannot be abolished, what are the precise political implications of this thesis? For Marx, alienation of the labor force is directly identified with its self-commodification; should we then distinguish some more "basic" ontological alienation, a kind of transcendental a priori of human history, from the specific case of self-commodification? To resolve this deadlock, Tomšič introduces "the distinction between constitutive alienation—alienation that is equivalent to structure—and constituted alienation—for instance, commodity fetishism, which follows from the misperception of the relation between the appearance of value and the structure that causes this appearance."[2] Conceived in this way, Communism stands not for the end of alienation but merely for the end of the commodity form as the form of social relations, i.e., not for the end of "constitutive" alienation but merely for the end of a historically specific form of "constituted" alienation. However, the question to be raised here is: but is not the greatest illusion the illusion that we can have "pure" constitutive alienation without its fetishistic mystification? How, then, can we bring together Marx and Lacan? Tomšič formulates the alternative between humanist-subjectivist Marxism and his version of reading Marx through Lacan in the following terms: "Does a radical political program of liberation necessitate the dissolution of the link between subjectivity and negativity? Should one not, rather, determine the subject of politics by following Marx's example when he recognized in the proletariat the symptomatic and negative point, from which the capitalist mode of production can be undermined?"[3]

But a Lukácsian Hegelo-Marxist approach has no difficulty in fully asserting the link between subjectivity and negativity—within this approach, the proletariat is precisely the "negative point, from which the capitalist mode of production can be undermined." In combining the assertion of proletarian subjectivity (as that of radical negativity) with the project of liberation as the overcoming of alienation, the young Lukács remains within the basic coordinates of Marx's thought—for Marx, the "critique of political economy" (with its notions of alienation, labor force as self-commodified subjectivity, etc.) is meaningful only against the background of the vision of a nonalienated, self-transparent society. In other words, Marx's theory simply does not provide the apparatus to conceive of some more primordial and constitutive alienation that precedes the alienation imposed by capitalism. In order to conceive of this Marxian notion of the proletariat, of the proletarian subjective position, correctly, one has to distinguish this subjective position from the "orthodox" Stalinist notion of the Communist Party as the bearer of "objective knowledge" about the historical process. Lacan himself is guilty of confusing the two:

> The proletariat means what? It means that labour is radicalized on the level
> of pure and simple commodity, which also reduces the labourer to the
> same price. As soon as the labourer learns to know himself as such through
> theory, we can say that this step shows him the way to the status of—call it
> what you want—a scientist [*savant*]. He is no longer a proletarian *an sich*, if I
> may say so, he is no longer pure and simple truth, but he is *für sich*, what we
> call class-consciousness. He can even become the Party's class-consciousness
> where one no longer speaks the truth.[4]

Here Lacan clearly conflates two distinct positions, two distinct notions of class consciousness. First, the Stalinist notion of consciousness as "objective knowledge," a cognition of objective social reality with no immanent practical dimension—praxis enters afterward, i.e., after I get to know how things objectively stand, I decide to act accordingly. This is how Stalinist Marxism distinguishes between scientific theory and proletarian ideology: first, objective theory provides a true insight into reality; then, on the basis of this insight, the revolutionary party develops a revolutionary ideology in order to mobilize the working class and their allies. It is in this sense that, in *On Dialectical and Historical Materialism*, Stalin wrote:

> we must not base our orientation on the strata of society which are no longer
> developing, even though they at present constitute the predominant force,
> but on those strata which are developing and have a future before them, even
> though they at present do not constitute the predominant force.
> In the eighties of the past century, in the period of the struggle between
> the Marxists and the Narodniks, the proletariat in Russia constituted an
> insignificant minority of the population, whereas the individual peasants
> constituted the vast majority of the population. But the proletariat was
> developing as a class, whereas the peasantry as a class was disintegrating. And
> just because the proletariat was developing as a class the Marxists based their
> orientation on the proletariat. And they were not mistaken; for, as we know,
> the proletariat subsequently grew from an insignificant force into a first-rate
> historical and political force.
> Hence, in order not to err in policy, one must look forward, not
> backward.[5]

In short, first I establish through cold, objective analysis which is the winning horse, and only then do I place my bet ... a stance totally opposed to that of Lukács who, in *History and Class Consciousness*, uses "(self-)consciousness" not as a term for passive reception/representation or awareness, but as the unity of intellect and will: "(self-)consciousness" is inherently practical, it changes its subject-object—once the working class arrives at its adequate class consciousness, it changes into an actual revolutionary subject in its very social reality. The idea that knowing changes reality is something quantum physics shares with psychoanalysis (for which interpretation has effects in the Real) as well as with historical materialism, for which the proletariat's act of acquiring self-consciousness (of becoming aware of its historical mission) changes its object—through this awareness, the proletariat in its very social reality turns into a revolutionary subject. Adorno observed somewhere that every great philosophy is a variation on the ontological proof of God's existence: an attempt to pass directly from thought to being, first formulated by Parmenides in his assertion of the sameness of thinking and being. Even Marx follows this line: is not his idea of "class consciousness" precisely that of a thought which directly intervenes in social being? The ontological paradox of this Lukácsian position is that it combines universal truth with radical "partiality," with taking sides (for the oppressed in the class struggle): a universal truth can be accessed only from an engaged "partial" position; every stance of neutrality ("to see the truth, one should elevate oneself above the mêlée of particular struggles") is false, it masks its own hidden partiality.

Lacan thus blurs the distinction between the dialectical-materialist notion of Consciousness as the cognitive reflection of objective reality, as a medium passively mirroring it, and György Lukács's notion (explained in *History and Class Consciousness*) of the act of Self-Consciousness as the constitution of a historical agent, an act of cognition which changes the object of cognition—this "performative" dimension is what is missing in the dialectical-materialist notion of cognition. What disappears thereby is the surprising proximity of Lukács and Lacan, who is interested precisely in how gestures of symbolization are entwined with and embedded in the process of collective practice. What Lacan elaborates as the "twofold moment" of the symbolic function reaches far beyond the standard theory of the performative dimension of speech as it was developed in the tradition from J. L. Austin to John Searle: "The symbolic function presents itself as a twofold movement in the subject: man makes his own action into an object, but only to return its foundational place to it in due time. In this equivocation, operating at every instant, lies the whole progress of a function in which action and knowledge alternate."[6] The historical example evoked by Lacan to clarify this "twofold movement" is significant in its hidden references: "in phase one, a man who works at the level of production in our society considers himself to belong to the ranks of the proletariat; in phase two, in the name of belonging to it, he joins in a general strike."[7] One can venture that Lacan's (implicit) reference here is to Lukács's *History and Class Consciousness*, whose widely acclaimed French translation was published in the mid-1950s. For Lukács, consciousness is opposed to the mere knowledge of an object: knowledge is external to the known object, while consciousness is in itself "practical," an act which changes its very object. (Once a worker "considers himself to belong to the ranks of the proletariat," this changes his very reality: he acts differently.) One does something, one counts oneself as (declares oneself) the one who did it, and, on the basis of this declaration, one does something new—the proper moment of subjective transformation occurs at the moment of declaration, not at the moment of the act. Marx's name for such engaged universality is "proletariat," which is why the following observation misses the point: "One can sometimes hear astonishment over the fact that Marx does not use the term 'proletariat' or 'proletarian' in *Capital*. He does not need to because 'labour power,' 'surplus population' and 'industrial reserve army' designate the very same subjective position."[8] "Surplus population" and "industrial reserve army" precisely do not designate a subjective position—they are empirical social categories. In a subtle, implicit way (not unlike Freud's implicit distinction, unearthed by Lacan, between Ego-Ideal and superego), Marx does distinguish between proletariat (a subjective position) and working class (an objective social category).

8.2 MARX AND LACAN

This compels us to ask:

> what does the combination "Marx and Lacan" stand for? Lacan next
> to Marx questions the optimistic and humanist readings, according to
> which Marx's critique aims to break out of symbolic determinations,
> negativity and alienation. Marx next to Lacan questions the pessimistic
> and apolitical readings, according to which Lacan's reformulation of the
> structuralist project supposedly amounts to the recognition of the "universal
> madness" and autism of *jouissance* which dissolve the social links, and to
> the affirmation of the discursive a priori which determines human actions
> and presumably reveals the illusionary features of every attempt in radical
> politics.[9]

What does this "third way" (neither a naive Marxist idea of sexual and economic liberation which allows us to break out of alienation, nor a psychoanalytic dismissal of every revolutionary project as imaginary illusion) in fact amount to? It is all too easy to resolve the problem by introducing a distinction between general alienation constitutive of humankind and commodity alienation as one of its species (or historical forms): capitalism gives birth to a desubstantialized subject and, in this way, functions as a unique symptomal point for the whole of history. We should mobilize here the dialectic of universal and particular: just as Marx simultaneously claimed that all history hitherto is the history of class struggle, *and* that the bourgeoisie is the only true class in the history of humanity, we should say that all history is the history of alienation, *and* that the only true alienation is the capitalist one.

It seems that Hegel himself misses this dialectical coincidence of opposites when, in his political thought, he criticizes universal democracy as abstract-formal: individuals partake directly in the universal by casting their vote as abstract individuals, independently of their concrete position in the social edifice. Against this immediacy, which precludes any actual representation, Hegel advocates corporate representation mediated by my particular belonging to an estate: I participate in the universal through my engagement in some specific field which constitutes my concrete identity (an artisan, a farmer, a professor, etc.). What Hegel ignores here is the fact that in our societies, as a rule, the particular place I occupy in the social edifice is deeply antagonistic; it is experienced as thwarting the full deployment of my potential. What he ignores is a class antagonism that cuts across the entire social edifice—it is being caught in this antagonism that makes a subject universal, it is an antagonism that cannot be reduced to particularity. More precisely: when and how do I experience myself as universal (subject), i.e., when does my universality become "for myself," a feature of how I relate to myself, not just "in itself," not just my objective property? When I am brutally dislocated from my particular identity. For instance, how does my desire become universal? Through its hystericization, when no particular object can satisfy it, when, apropos of every particular object, I experience how *ce n'est pas ça!* (That's not it!). This is why, for Marx, the proletariat is the universal class: because it is a class which is a non-class, which cannot identify itself as a class.

We thus have to reverse the standard Platonic notion of particularity as a failed universality, as a fall from the purity of the universal Idea: the Universal emerges only at the site of a failed particularity. Jean-Claude Milner wrote: "Value represents what of labour-power is contained in each object that carries value, but it can only represent it in commodity exchange, that is, for another value. But labour-power is simply the subject. It is Marx's name for the subject."[10] It is true that, for Marx, the labor force is subject in the precise Hegelian sense of *substanzlose Subjektivität*, the zero-point of pure potentiality deprived of any substantial content.[11] Frantz Fanon wrote in *Black Skin, White Masks*: "There is a zone of nonbeing, an extraordinarily sterile and arid region, an incline stripped bare of every essential from which a genuine new departure can emerge. In most cases, the black man cannot take advantage of this descent into a veritable hell."[12] Not all Black men lack this advantage: Malcolm X was certainly aware that, in order to attain freedom, one has to descend into the European Hell. ... While in prison, the young Malcolm joined the Nation of Islam, and, after his parole in 1952, he engaged in its struggle, advocating Black supremacy and the separation of White and Black Americans—for him, "integration" was a fake attempt by the Black to become like the White. In 1964, however, he rejected the Nation of Islam and, while continuing to emphasize Black self-determination and self-defense, he distanced himself from every form of racism, advocating emancipatory universality; as a consequence of this "betrayal," he was killed by three Nation of Islam members in February 1965. When Malcolm adopted "X" as his family name, thereby signaling that the slave traders who brought the enslaved Africans from their homeland brutally deprived them of their family and ethnic roots, of their entire cultural lifeworld, the point of this gesture was not to mobilize the Blacks to fight for the return to some primordial African roots, but precisely to seize the opening provided by X, an unknown new (lack of) identity engendered by the very process of slavery which rendered those African roots forever lost. The idea is that this X which deprives the Blacks of their particular tradition offers them a unique chance to redefine (reinvent) themselves, to freely form a new identity much more universal than white people's professed universality. Although Malcolm X found this new identity in the universalism of Islam, he was killed by Muslim fundamentalists. That is the hard choice to be made: yes, Blacks are marginalized, exploited, humiliated, mocked, also feared, at the level of everyday practice; yes, they experience daily the hypocrisy of liberal freedoms and human rights; but in the same movement they experience the promise of true freedom compared to which the existing freedom is false—it is this freedom that fundamentalists escape.

What this means is that, in the struggle for Black emancipation, one should leave behind the lament for the loss of authentic African roots—let us leave this lament to TV series like the one based on Alex Haley's *Roots*. Consequently, instead of desperately searching for our authentic roots, the task is to lose our roots in an authentic way—this loss is the birth of emancipatory subjectivity. To put it in speculative Hegelian terms, the true loss is the loss of the loss itself: when a Black African is enslaved and torn up from his roots, he in a way not only loses these roots—retroactively, he has to realize that he never really fully had these roots. What he, after this loss, experiences as his roots is a retroactive fantasy, a projection filling in the void.

8.3   THE POLITICS OF SEPARATION

But is this contraction of subjectivity to a substanceless evanescent point the ultimate fact? In other words, is alienation the unsurpassable horizon of our existence? Although Tomšič seems to endorse this notion, he points the way beyond it when he claims that constitutive alienation does not address solely the alienation of the subject but above all the alienation of the Other: it makes the Other appear in its split, incompleteness, contradiction and therefore inexistence. The correlate of this inexistence is the existence of the subject, the actual agency of the revolutionary process, which, however, does not assume the position of knowledge but the place of truth, as Lacan persistently repeated. Because the subject is produced, brought into existence in and through the gap in the Other, in other words, because there is a social entity, the proletariat, which articulates a universal demand for change in the name of all (being the social embodiment of a universal subjective position), this very enunciation grounds politics on the link between inexistence, alienation and universality. [13]

We should be careful when we talk about "constitutive alienation." There are two (main) ways to think the topic of alienation. From the humanist perspective, alienation is conceived as a temporal inversion, a state of things which should be set straight when humanity succeeds in reappropriating the alienated substance of its existence. From the tragic perspective, alienation is irreducible, since it is constitutive of being-human, grounded in the finitude of human existence. Lacan's theory is unique in proposing a third position: alienation is not our ultimate destiny, it can be overcome, but not in the triumphalist humanist sense. For Lacan, alienation is by definition the *subject's* alienation, and he has a specific concept for the "alienation of the Other"— *separation*. The core of Lacan's atheism is best discerned in the conceptual couple of "alienation" and "separation" which he develops in his *Four Fundamental Concepts of Psychoanalysis*. [14] In a first approach, the big Other stands for the subject's alienation in the symbolic order: the big Other pulls the strings, the subject doesn't speak, he is "spoken" by the symbolic structure. In short, this "big Other" is the name for the social substance, for all that on account of which the subject never fully dominates the effects of his acts, i.e., on account of which the final outcome of his activity is always something other than what he aimed at or anticipated. Separation takes place when the subject takes note of how the big Other is in itself inconsistent, lacking ("barred," as Lacan liked to put it): the big Other does not possess what the subject is lacking. In separation, the subject experiences how his own lack with regard to the big Other is already the lack that affects the big Other itself. To recall Hegel's immortal dictum apropos of the Sphinx: "The mysteries of the Ancient Egyptians were mysteries also for the Egyptians themselves." Along the same lines, the elusive, impenetrable *Dieu obscur* has to be impenetrable also to Himself; He has to have a dark side, something that is in Him more than Himself. [15]

The same goes for Christianity: we are not first separated from God and then miraculously united with Him; the point of Christianity is that this very separation unites us—it is in this separation that we are "like God," like Christ on the Cross, i.e., our separation from God is transposed into God Himself. So when Meister Eckhart speaks about how, in order to open oneself to the grace of God, to allow Christ to be born in one's soul, one has to "empty" oneself of everything "creaturely," how is this kenosis related to the properly divine kenosis (or, for that matter, even to the kenosis of alienation, of the subject being deprived of its substantial content)? Chesterton is fully aware that it is not enough for God to separate man from Himself so that mankind will love Him—this separation has to be reflected back into God Himself, so that God is abandoned by Himself:

> When the world shook and the sun was wiped out of heaven, it was not at the crucifixion, but at the cry from the cross: the cry which confessed that God was forsaken of God. And now let the revolutionists choose a creed from all the creeds and a god from all the gods of the world, carefully weighing all the gods of inevitable recurrence and of unalterable power. They will not find another god who has himself been in revolt. Nay (the matter grows too difficult for human speech), but let the atheists themselves choose a god. They will find only one divinity who ever uttered their isolation; only one religion in which God seemed for an instant to be an atheist.[16]

Because of this overlapping between man's isolation from God and God's isolation from himself, Christianity is "terribly revolutionary." We are one with God only when God is no longer one with Himself, but abandons Himself, "internalizes" the radical distance which separates us from Him. Our radical experience of separation from God is the very feature which unites us with Him—not in the usual mystical sense that only through such an experience do we open ourselves to the radical Otherness of the God, but in the sense similar to the one in which Kant claims that humiliation and pain are the only transcendental feelings: it is preposterous to think that I can identify myself with the divine bliss—only when I experience the infinite pain of separation from God do I share an experience with God Himself (Christ on the Cross). This moment of "Father, why have you abandoned me?," of the separation of God from Himself, causes great difficulty for commentators—here is a typical discussion by Mark D. Roberts:

> This side of heaven, we will never fully know what Jesus was experiencing in this moment. Was he asking this question because, in the mystery of his incarnational suffering, he didn't know why God had abandoned him? Or was his cry not so much a question as an expression of profound agony? Or was it both? What we do know is that Jesus entered into the Hell of separation from God. The Father abandoned him because Jesus took

upon himself the penalty for our sins. In that excruciating moment, he experienced something far more horrible than physical pain. The beloved Son of God knew what it was like to be rejected by the Father. As we read in 2 Corinthians 5:21, "God made him who had no sin to be sin for us, so that in him we might become the righteousness of God." I can write these words. I can say, truly, that the Father abandoned the Son for our sake, for the salvation of the world. But can I really grasp the mystery and the majesty of this truth? Hardly. As Martin Luther once said, "God forsaking God. Who can understand it?"[17]

Separation is thus not simply a redoubled alienation but a specific case of the "negation of negation." When the subject's alienation (in the Other) is redoubled by the (self-)alienation of the Other itself, this redoubling radically changes the status of the alienated subject: the alienation of the Other itself (the lack/antagonism that undermines the consistency of the Other from within) opens up a unique space of freedom, of active intervention by the subject into the Other. Fully assuming the Other's lack and inconsistency means that the Other is no longer a complete mechanism that controls me: I can exploit its inconsistencies, play the Other against itself. So instead of getting caught in desperate attempts to distinguish between constitutive and constituted alienation, one should focus on *how to determine separation in political terms*. According to Tomšič, in traditional Marxism, the standard social-democratic scenario proposes

> including the workers in a more just distribution of profit, collective ownership of the means of production, regulating financial speculation and bringing the economy down to the solid ground of the real sector. More radical political experiments were equally unsuccessful in abolishing alienation: "It's not because one nationalizes the means of production at the level of socialism in one country that one has thereby done away with surplus-value, if one doesn't know what it is." Nationalization does not produce the necessary global structural change, which would abolish the market of labour and thereby the structural contradiction that transforms the subject into a commodity-producing commodity. The non-relation between labour-power and surplus-value remains operative, and nationalization in the last instance evolves into a form of state capitalism. Marx, however, did not claim that the appropriation of surplus-value would abolish the capitalist forms of alienation and fetishization. This would suggest that the abolition of capitalists, these social fanatics of the valorization of value and personifications of capital, would already solve the problem. Marx's point is rather that capitalism can exist without capitalists because the capitalist drive to self-valorization is structural, systemic and autonomous—but there cannot be any capitalism without the proletariat.[18]

OK, nationalization doesn't work—but what, then, *does* work? In what, then, does consist "the necessary global structural change, which would abolish the market of labour and thereby the structural contradiction that transforms the subject into a commodity-producing commodity"? Again, if signifying alienation is constitutive of subjectivity, and if the homology between surplus-enjoyment and surplus-value is complete, is economic alienation, then, also inevitable? If yes, in what precise sense? What, then, can the overcoming of capitalism achieve, what is its goal or horizon? What is the third way between resigning oneself to capitalist alienation and the humanist fantasy of a reconciled, transparent society? My wager is that, even if we take away the teleological notion of Communism (the society of fully unbridled productivity) as the implicit standard by which Marx, as it were, measures the alienation of the existing society, the bulk of his "critique of political economy," his insight into the self-propelling vicious cycle of capitalist (re)production, survives.

The task of today's thought is thus double: on the one hand, to repeat the Marxist "critique of political economy" without the utopian-ideological notion of Communism as its inherent standard; on the other, to imagine effectively breaking out of the capitalist horizon without falling into the trap of returning to the eminently premodern notion of a balanced, (self-) restrained society (the "pre-Cartesian" temptation to which most of today's ecology succumbs). A return to Hegel is crucial in order to perform this task, a return which gets rid of all the classic anti-Hegelian topics, especially that of Hegel's voracious narcissism, of a Hegelian Idea which endeavors to swallow/ internalize the whole of reality. Instead of trying to undermine or overcome this "narcissism" from the outside, emphasizing the "preponderance of the objective" (or the fact that "the Whole is the non-true" and all other similar themes of Adorno's rejection of "identitarian" idealism), we should, rather, problematize the figure of Hegel criticized here by asking a simple question: but which Hegel is our point of reference here? Do not both Lukács and Adorno refer to the "idealist-subjectivist" (mis)reading of Hegel, to the classic image of Hegel as the "absolute idealist" who asserted Spirit as the true agent of history, its Subject-Substance? Within this framework, Capital can in effect look like a new embodiment of the Hegelian Spirit, an abstract monster which moves and mediates itself, parasitizing upon the activity of actual really existing individuals. This is why Lukács also remains all too idealist when he proposes to simply replace the Hegelian Spirit with the proletariat as the Subject-Object of History: here Lukács is not really a Hegelian, but a pre-Hegelian idealist.[19]

If, however, one problematizes this shared presupposition of Lukács and Adorno, another Hegel appears: a more "materialist" Hegel for whom reconciliation between subject and substance does not mean that the subject "swallows" its substance, internalizing it into its own subordinate moment. Reconciliation, rather, amounts to a much more modest overlapping or redoubling of the two separations: the subject has to recognize, in its alienation from the Substance, the separation of the Substance from itself. This overlapping is what is missed in the Feuerbachian-Marxian logic of disalienation, in which the subject overcomes its alienation by recognizing itself as the active agent which itself posited what appears to it as its substantial presupposition. In the Hegelian "reconciliation" between Subject and Substance, there is no absolute Subject which, in total self-transparency, appropriates/internalizes all objective substantial content. But neither does "reconciliation" mean (as it does in the line of German Idealism from Hölderlin to Schelling) that the subject should renounce its *hubris* of perceiving itself as the axis of the world, and accept its constitutive "decentering," its dependence on some primordial abyssal Absolute which is beyond/beneath the subject/object divide, and, as such, also beyond subjective conceptual grasp. The subject is not its own origin: Hegel firmly rejects Fichte's notion of the absolute I which posits itself and is nothing but the pure activity of this self-positing. But neither is the subject just a secondary, accidental appendix/outgrowth of some presubjective substantial reality: there is no substantial Being to which the subject can return, no encompassing organic Order of Being in which the subject has to find its proper place. "Reconciliation" between subject and substance means the acceptance of this radical lack of any firm foundational point: the subject is not its own origin, it comes second, it is dependent upon its substantial presuppositions; but these presuppositions also do not have a substantial consistency of their own, but are always retroactively posited.

This also means that Communism should no longer be conceived as the subjective (re)appropriation of the alienated substantial content—all versions of reconciliation as "the subject swallows the substance" should be rejected. So, again, "reconciliation" is the full acceptance of the abyss of the desubstantialized process as the only actuality there is: the subject has no substantial actuality, it comes second, it emerges only through the process of separation, of overcoming its presuppositions, and these presuppositions are also just a retroactive effect of the same process of their overcoming. The result is thus that there is, at both extremes of the process, a failure-negativity inscribed in the very heart of the entity we are dealing with. If the status of the subject is thoroughly "processual," that means it emerges through the very failure to fully actualize itself. This brings us again to one of the possible formal definitions of the subject: a subject tries to articulate ("express") itself in a signifying chain, this articulation fails, and by means of and through this failure the subject emerges: the subject is the failure of its signifying representation—this is why Lacan writes the subject of the signifier as $, as "barred." In a love letter, the writer's very failure to formulate his declaration in a clear and efficient way, his oscillations, the letter's fragmentation, etc., can in themselves be the proof (perhaps the necessary and the only reliable proof) that the professed love is authentic—here, the very failure to deliver the message properly is the sign of its authenticity. If the message is delivered in a smooth way, it arouses suspicions that it is part of a well-planned approach, or that the writer loves himself, the beauty of his writing, more than his love object, i.e., that the object is in effect reduced to a pretext for engaging in the narcissistically satisfying activity of writing.

And the same goes for substance: substance is not only always-already lost, it comes to be only through its loss, as a secondary return-to-itself—which means that substance is always-already subjectivized. In the "reconciliation" between subject and substance, both poles thus lose their firm identity. Let us take the case of ecology: radical emancipatory politics should aim neither at complete mastery over nature nor at humanity's humble acceptance of the predominance of Mother Earth. Rather, nature should be exposed in all its catastrophic contingency and indeterminacy, and human agency should assume the whole unpredictability of the consequences of its activity—viewed from this perspective of the "other Hegel," the revolutionary act no longer involves as its agent the Lukácsian substance-subject, the agent who knows what it is doing while doing it.

8.4 FROM KANT TO HEGEL, POLITICALLY

The inner logic of the passage from Kant to Hegel, the key reversal that defines the very core of German Idealism, is much more convoluted than it may appear. One totally misses this logic when one simply reproduces Hegel's critique of Kant—if one does only this, it is easy for Kantians to demonstrate that Hegel is criticizing a straw man, that he in effect reduced Kantian thought to its primitive caricature. What we should do is to begin with the simplified version of Hegel's critique of Kant, and then listen to the Kantian reply to it—and when we do it thoroughly, things start to get interesting: we soon discover that, in their defense of Kant, the Kantians have to bring in the gap between what Kant literally says (more precisely: what he seems to be saying in a first, immediate, reading) and what he is actually saying without being fully aware of it (a dimension revealed only through their detailed interpretation of Kant) … in short, they defend Kant by showing how Kant is really more refined, not what Hegel's critique targets, even if Kant simplifies himself and sometimes writes as if he does not know it. And then comes the crucial Hegelian countermove: to show that this self-corrected Kant asserted against Hegel's critique is Hegel. "Hegel" is not a simple overcoming of Kant, Hegel is the Kant who emerges as a reaction to the standard

Hegelian critique of Kant, the Kant (self-)corrected through this reaction, the Kant whose unsaid is brought to awareness through it.

Let us take just one simplified example. According to the standard Hegelian critique, the limitation of the Kantian universalistic ethic of the "categorical imperative" (the unconditional injunction to do one's duty) lies in its formal indeterminacy: the moral Law does not tell me *what* my duty is, it merely tells me *that* I should accomplish my duty, and so leaves room for an empty voluntarism (whatever I decide will be my duty *is* my duty). It is easy for a true Kantian to reply that, far from being a limitation, this very feature brings us to the core of ethical autonomy: it is not possible to derive the concrete obligations pertaining to one's specific situation from the moral Law itself—which means that the subject himself must assume the responsibility of translating the abstract injunction into a series of concrete obligations. The full acceptance of this paradox compels us to reject any reference to duty as an excuse: "I know this is difficult and can be painful, but what can I do, this is my duty. ..." Kant's ethics is often taken as justifying such an attitude—no wonder Adolf Eichmann himself referred to Kant when trying to justify his role in planning and executing the Holocaust: he was simply doing his duty and obeying the Führer's orders. However, the aim of Kant's emphasis on the subject's full moral autonomy and responsibility was precisely to prevent any such maneuver of putting the blame on some figure of the big Other. But are we here still fully in Kant? Are Kant's statements often not ambiguous when it comes to the full meaning of moral autonomy? My point is, of course, that by defending Kant in this way, *we are already in Hegel.*

While the Kantian approach relies on the insurmountable gap that forever separates the universal transcendental form from its contingent empirical content, Hegel overcomes this gap with his notion of "concrete universality" which mediates form and content. The Kantian subject can be said to be "castrated" in the sense that it is constitutively separated from the real Thing (the supreme Good which remains forever out of reach), and the universal form (of the ethical injunction) is a stand-in for the absent content (the real Thing). Here we find a specifically Laclauian dialectic of universal and particular: since universality is empty, since all content is by definition particular, the only way for a universality to get filled in with content is to elevate/transubstantiate some particular content into its placeholder, and the struggle for which element this will be is the struggle for hegemony.

An exemplary case of Laclau's theory of hegemony is his detailed analysis of populism.[20] For Laclau, populism is inherently neutral: a kind of transcendental-formal political structure that can be incorporated into different political engagements. Populism is not a specific political movement, but the political at its purest: the "inflection" of the social space that can affect any political content. Its elements are purely formal, "transcendental," not ontic: populism occurs when a series of particular "democratic" demands (for better social security, better health services, lower taxes, an end to war, etc.) is enchained in a series of equivalences, and this enchainment produces "people" as the universal political subject. What characterizes populism is not the ontic content of these demands, but the mere formal fact that, through their enchainment, the "people" emerges as a political subject, and all the various particular struggles and antagonisms appear as parts of a global antagonistic struggle between "us" (the people) and "them." Again, the content of "us" and "them" is not prescribed in advance but, precisely, the stake of the struggle for hegemony: even ideological elements like brutal racism and anti-Semitism can be enchained in a populist series of equivalences, in the way "them" is constructed.

It is clear now why Laclau prefers populism to class struggle: populism provides a neutral "transcendental" matrix of an open struggle whose content and stakes are themselves defined by the contingent struggle for hegemony, while "class struggle" presupposes a particular social group (the working class) as a privileged political agent; this privilege is not itself the outcome of hegemonic struggle, but grounded in the "objective social position" of this group—the ideologico-political struggle is thus ultimately reduced to an epiphenomenon of "objective" social processes and their conflicts. For Laclau, on the contrary, the fact that some particular struggle is elevated to the "universal equivalent" of all struggles is not a predetermined fact, but itself the result of the contingent political struggle for hegemony—in one constellation, this struggle can be the workers' struggle; in another constellation, the patriotic anticolonialist struggle; in yet another constellation, the antiracist struggle for cultural tolerance; *there is nothing in the inherent positive qualities of some particular struggle that predestines it for such a hegemonic role* of the "general equivalent" of all struggles. The struggle for hegemony thus presupposes not only an irreducible gap between the universal form and the multiplicity of particular contents, but also the contingent process by means of which one among these contents is "transubstantiated" into the immediate embodiment of the universal dimension—for instance (Laclau's own example), in 1980s Poland, the particular demands of Solidarność were elevated into the embodiment of the people's global rejection of the Communist regime, so that all the different versions of the anti-Communist opposition (from the conservative-nationalist opposition through the liberal-democratic opposition and cultural dissidence to Leftist workers' opposition) recognized themselves in the empty signifier "Solidarność." Does not Laclau come uncannily close what Hegel calls concrete universality? In the struggle for hegemony, universality is never neutral, it is always colored by some particular element that hegemonizes it. Laclau's difference from Hegel resides merely in the fact that, for Laclau, the mediation between universality and particularity ultimately always fails, since the gap between empty universal form and the element filling it in persists, and the struggle for hegemony goes on forever. Laclau's basic argument is summarized succinctly by Oliver Marchart:

> on a formal level, *every* politics is based on the articulatory logics of "a combination and condensation of inconsistent attitudes," not only the politics of fascism. As a result, the fundamental social antagonism will always be displaced to some degree since, as we have noted earlier, the ontological level—in this case, antagonism—can never be approached directly and without political mediation. It follows that distortion is constitutive for every politics: politics as such, not only fascist politics, proceeds through "distortion."[21]

This criticism remains caught in the "binary" tension between essence and appearance: the fundamental antagonism never appears as such, directly, in a directly transparent way (in Marxist terms: the "pure" revolutionary situation in which all social tensions would be simplified/reduced to the class struggle never takes place, it is always mediated by other—ethnic, religious, etc.—antagonisms)—the "essence" never appears directly, but always in a displaced/distorted way. So while it is true that "human relations exist in the way in which they are distorted. There are no human relations without distortion,"[22] this reference to distortion allows for different readings. It can be read in the conventional way, as a reminder of the complexity of historical situations—recall how, in 1916, Lenin replied to those who dismissed the Irish uprising as a mere "putsch" of no interest for the proletarian struggle:

> To imagine that social revolution is *conceivable* without revolts by small nations in the colonies and in Europe, without revolutionary outbursts by a section of the petty bourgeoisie *with all its prejudices*, without a movement of the politically non-conscious proletarian and semi-proletarian masses against oppression by the landowners, the church, and the monarchy, against national oppression, etc.—to imagine all this is to *repudiate social revolution*. So one army lines up in one place and says, "We are for socialism," and another, somewhere else and says, "We are for imperialism," and that will be a social revolution! Only those who hold such a ridiculously pedantic view could vilify the Irish rebellion by calling it a "putsch."
> Whoever expects a "pure" social revolution will *never* live to see it. Such a person pays lip-service to revolution without understanding what revolution is.
> The Russian Revolution of 1905 was a bourgeois-democratic revolution. It consisted of a series of battles in which *all* the discontented classes, groups and elements of the population participated. Among these there were masses imbued with the crudest *prejudices*, with the vaguest and most fantastic aims

of struggle; there were small groups which accepted Japanese money, there were speculators and adventurers, etc. But *objectively*, the mass movement was breaking the back of tsarism and paving the way for democracy; for this reason the class-conscious workers led it.

The socialist revolution in Europe *cannot* be anything other than an outburst of mass struggle on the part of all and sundry oppressed and discontented elements. Inevitably, sections of the petty bourgeoisie and of the backward workers will participate in it—without such participation, *mass struggle is impossible*, without it no revolution is possible—and just as inevitably will they bring into the movement their prejudices, their reactionary fantasies, their weaknesses and errors. But *objectively* they will attack *capital*, and the class-conscious vanguard of the revolution, the advanced proletariat, expressing this objective truth of a variegated and discordant, motley and outwardly fragmented, mass struggle, will be able to unite and direct it, capture power, seize the banks, expropriate the trusts which all hate (though for different reasons!), and introduce other dictatorial measures which in their totality will amount to the overthrow of the bourgeoisie and the victory of socialism, which, however, will by no means immediately "purge" itself of petty-bourgeois slag.[23]

A biographical detail should be kept in mind when we read these lines: they were written immediately after the period at the beginning of World War I when, out of despair at the nationalist breakdown of almost all social democracies, Lenin withdrew into "pure" theory and engaged in a detailed reading of Hegel's logic. One usually associates Hegel with linear teleology and progressive "historical necessity"—but the basic lesson Lenin drew from Hegel was exactly the opposite one: the complex contingency of the historical process, overdetermination of every "basic" tendency by an intricate network of specific historical conditions where "the exception is the rule." Lenin goes so far as to say that, in a concrete situation, the fate of the entire revolutionary process can hinge on seizing (or not) a particular historical opening. (Later, in 1917, he wrote that if the Bolsheviks did not seize the unique revolutionary chance, it might be decades before the next chance would arrive.) This is Lenin's own "materialist reversal of Marx" (of Marx's historicist evolutionism whose manifesto is the [in]famous "Preface" to the *Critique of Political Economy*) into Hegel. One should thus note that the reference to Hegel enabled Lenin to get rid of the very feature of orthodox Marxism that Althusser attributed to Hegel's influence on Marx (linear historical determinism, etc.).

For Laclau, these ruminations of Lenin's remain all too "essentialist": despite all his flexibility, Lenin clearly privileges the "class-conscious vanguard of the revolution, the advanced proletariat," able to express the "objective truth of a variegated and discordant, motley and outwardly fragmented, mass struggle." So although a revolution can "by no means immediately 'purge' itself of petty-bourgeois slag," in its further development it will none-theless be obliged to enforce "dictatorial measures" which will amount to the purge of petit-bourgeois slag. The problem is, of course, where to set the limit, i.e., whom can the "class-conscious vanguard" accept as partners in their struggle? Today, it is obvious that (at least some version of) feminism, ecology, struggle for religious freedoms, etc., fits the bill—but what about, say, Boko Haram? For its members, the liberation of women looks like the most visible feature of the destructive cultural impact of capitalist modern-ization, so that Boko Haram (whose name can be roughly and descriptively translated as "Western education is forbidden," specifically the education of women) can perceive and portray itself as an agent fighting the destruc-tive impact of modernization, by imposing a hierarchical regulation of the relationship between the sexes. The enigma is: why do Muslims, who have undoubtedly been exposed to exploitation, domination, and other destruc-tive and humiliating aspects of colonialism, target in their response what is (for us, at least) the best part of the Western legacy: our egalitarianism and personal freedoms, inclusive of a healthy dose of irony and a mocking of all authorities? The obvious answer is that their target is well chosen: what for them makes the liberal West so unbearable is not only that it practices exploitation and violent domination but that, to add insult to injury, it pre-sents this brutal reality in the guise of its opposite: freedom, equality, and democracy.

So, again, how to enact Lenin's insight here? Laclau's solution is obvi-ous: why even continue to talk about the "fundamental social antagonism"? All we have is a series of antagonisms which (can) build a chain of equiva-lences, metaphorically "contaminating" each other, and which antagonism emerges as "central" is the contingent result of the struggle for hegemony. However, is the rejection of the very notion of "fundamental antagonism" the only alternative to "class essentialism"? My Hegelian answer is a resounding *no*. Laclau's position here is Kantian: struggle for hegemony is his transcen-dental a priori, a form filled in with different contingent contents, or, to put it another way, Laclau's Kantian position is the one of symbolic castration as the ultimate horizon of our experience. "Castration" refers here to the irre-ducible gap between the transcendental form and its contingent content, and, for Laclau, Hegel disavows castration by enacting the move from the Kantian split ("castrated") subject, a subject divided between its form and its contin-gent content, to the Hegelian allegedly self-reconciled subject in which all antagonisms are sublated (*aufgehoben*) through dialectical mediation. However, the move from Kant to Hegel in no way abolishes "negativity, in the guise of castration" and enacts a return to "essentialism"; on the contrary, it radical-izes negativity (or the Kantian gap) in a very precise way. In Kant, negativity is located in the gap that forever separates us, finite humans, from the Thing, so that we have access only to its placeholder, the empty form of the Law. What Hegel does is to transpose the gap between appearance and the inaccessible Thing into the Thing itself, thoroughly redefining it as the coincidence of opposites at its most radical—the Real as that which is always distorted in its symbolic representations and the Real as the very force (thrust) of this distortion.

This means that "castration" is not just the gap between the empty form and its content but a torsion in content itself which gives rise to form, or more precisely, to the gap between content and form. We attain the level of proper dialectical analysis of a form only when we conceive a certain formal procedure not as expressing a certain aspect of the (narrative) content, but as marking/signaling the part of content that is excluded from the explicit narrative line, so that—and this is the properly theoretical point—if we want to reconstruct "all" of the narrative content, we must reach beyond the explicit narrative content as such, and include some formal features which act as the stand-in for the "repressed" aspect of that content.[24] To take the well-known elementary example from the analysis of melodrama: the emotional excess that cannot express itself directly in the narrative line finds its outlet in the ridiculously sentimental musical accompaniment, or in other formal features. One very good example is the way Claude Berri's Jean de Florette and Manon des Sources displace Marcel Pagnol's original film (and his own later novelization of it) on which they are based. That is to say: Pagnol's original retains traces of the "authentic" French provincial community life in which people's acts follow old, quasi-pagan religious patterns, while Berri's films fail in their effort to recapture the spirit of the closed premodern community. However, unexpectedly, the inherent obverse of Pagnol's universe is the theatricality of the action and the element of ironic distance and comicality, while Berri's films, while shot more "realistically," emphasize destiny (their musical leitmotiv is based on Verdi's La forza del destino), and the melodramatic excess which often borders on the ridiculous (like the scene in which, after the rain passes over his parched field, the desperate Jean cries and shouts at heaven). So, paradoxically, the closed ritualized premodern community implies theatrical comicality and irony, while the modern "realistic" rendering involves Fate and melodramatic excess. In this respect, Berri's two films are to be opposed to Lars von Trier's Breaking the Waves: in both cases, we are dealing with the tension between form and content; however, in Breaking the Waves, the excess is located in the content (the subdued pseudo-documentary form underlines the excessive content), while in Berri, the excess in the form obfuscates and thus exposes the flaw in content, the impossibility today of realizing the pure classical tragedy of Destiny.

That is the key consequence of the move from Kant to Hegel: the very gap between content and form is to be reflected back into content itself, as an indication that this content is not-all, that something has been repressed/ excluded from it. This exclusion which establishes the form itself is the "primordial repression" (Ur-Verdrängung), and no matter how much we bring out all the repressed content, this gap of primordial repression persists; again, why? The immediate answer is the identity of the repression with the return of the repressed, which means that the repressed content does not preexist repression, but is retroactively constituted by the very process of repression. Through different forms of negation/obfuscation (condensation, displacement, denegation, disavowal, etc.), the repressed is allowed to penetrate public conscious speech, to find an echo in it (the most direct example from Freud: when one of his patients said "I do not know who this woman in my dream is, but I am sure she is not my mother!" the mother entered the speech)—we get here a kind of "negation of negation," i.e., the content is negated/repressed, but this repression is in the same gesture itself negated in the guise of the return of the repressed (which is why we are definitely not dealing here with the proper Hegelian negation of negation). The logic here seems similar to that of the relationship between sin and Law in Saint Paul, where there is no sin without Law, i.e., where the Law/prohibition itself creates the transgression it tries to subdue, so that, if we take away the Law, we also lose what the Law tried to "repress," or, in more Freudian terms, if we take away the "repression," we also lose the repressed content.

But still, what do all these obscure distinctions amount to politically? How do they open up the space for a political practice that reaches beyond the alternative of Leninist "class essentialism" and Laclauian "chain of equivalences" with no element destined in advance to play the hegemonic role? We should make a detour here and bring into the debate another paradoxical figure of universality which we can provisionally call "supernumerary universality," the universality embodied in the element which sticks out of the existing Order, i.e., the element which, while internal to it, has no proper place within it—what Jacques Rancière calls the "part of no-part" and what Hegel called *Poebel* (the rabble). In its very status of the destructive excess of social totality, the rabble is the "reflexive determination" of the totality as such, the immediate embodiment of its universality, the particular element in the guise of which the social totality encounters itself among its elements, and, as such, the key constituent of its identity. Although the two universalities seem to share a minimal common feature (a particular element stands for universality), what separates them is the aspect of negativity that pertains to the second one: in hegemonic universality, all elements emphatically identify with the particular feature that hegemonizes universality ("Solidarity is all of us!" in the case of Poland), while the supernumerary universality is experienced as the excremental element of nonidentification, as a negation of all particular qualities. The struggle is ultimately not just about which particular content will hegemonize the empty form of universality but *the struggle between these two universalities*, the hegemonic one and the supernumerary one. More precisely, the two universalities are not completely incompatible; rather, they operate at different levels, so the task is to combine them. How? Hegemonic universality designates an empty place, while the supernumerary element is the element in the social space which lacks a proper place and is as such a stand-in for universality among the elements. The minimal definition of radical politics is thus that the "part of no-part," the excremental element, occupies the hegemonic place—or, to quote the line from "the Internationale," that those who are nothing (excrement) become all (hegemonize the entire field).

We are dealing with three main positions here. According to the first, orthodox Marxist, one, class opposition provides a hermeneutic key to decoding other struggles (feminist, ecological, national liberation) which are all forms of appearance of the "true" class struggle, and can be resolved only through the victorious proletarian revolution. The second position, the conservative-populist one, turns this relationship around: Leftist multiculturalism, ecology, etc., are a matter of upper-class elitism which despises the "narrowness" of the hard-working lower classes. The third, Laclauian, position asserts open struggle for hegemony: there is no ontological guarantee that feminist struggle, ecological struggle, etc., will become part of the same "chain of equivalences" with economic class struggle; their enchainment is the stake of the open struggle for hegemony. There is, however, a fourth position: class antagonism is not the ultimate signified of other struggles but the "bone in the throat" of all other struggles, the cause of the failure of Meaning of other struggles. The relation of each of these struggles toward class antagonism is an index of its inherent limitation/inadequacy—mainstream American liberal feminism, for example, at some point obfuscates the basic dimension of women's exploitation; or, today's humanitarian compassion for refugees obfuscates the true causes of their predicament. Class struggle/antagonism is thus not the ultimate referent-signified, the hidden meaning, of all other struggles but a measure of the "(non-)authenticity" of all other struggles—and the paradox is that the same holds for class struggle itself: in Hegelese, class struggle necessarily encounters itself in its oppositional determination (*gegensätzliche Bestimmung*)—for instance, when, in the United States, Tea Party members "encode" their opposition to multiculturalism, feminism, their racism, etc., in class terms, as a working-class opposition to the preoccupations of the rich educated classes, this direct class reference functions as a false screen dissimulating the true link between class antagonism and the issue at stake (feminism, racism, etc.); again, class difference can serve as its own best mask.[25]

With regard to the ongoing tension on the Left between identity politics focused on antiracist and antisexist struggle and the new forms of class struggle for economic justice, the standard *doxa* is that we should avoid both extremes, especially "class essentialism," and bring all these struggles together into one big all-encompassing coalition. However, such a "balanced" position advocating a "synthesis" or a "right measure" between the two extremes is a totally empty lifeless abstraction: there is no "synthesis of opposites" here, class struggle should be given a full and clear priority, but class struggle as a *concrete universality*. *Every* serious mention of economic struggle is denounced as "class essentialism" by the partisans of identity politics, i.e., the mantra gender–race–class secretly occludes class: although it mentions class as one element in the series, it effectively keeps its place empty. The focus on economic struggle is also wrong—not because it puts too much weight on the economy and neglects other struggles, but because it precisely occludes class struggle itself. As Saroj Giri pointedly noted, it is possible that

> the immigrants who secure rights thanks to the anti-racist anti-colonial struggle might be securing the right to free capitalist enterprise, refusing to see, refusing to "open your eyes", as the angry black yelled at the postcolonial immigrant. This right to free enterprise is another way to capital accumulation powered by the postcolonial entrepreneur: it produces "unfree labor" and racialized class relations in the name of challenging the colonial rule of difference.
>
> There is a closet Ayn Randian class position underpinning the anti-racism of hyperbolic anti-colonialists—it is then not difficult to see that the non-modern, radical alterity upon which the anti-colonial is premised now stands for the capitalist universal.[26]

Giri's last sentence should be taken in all its Hegelian stringency: the "concrete universal" of today's global capitalism, the particular form which over-determines and colors its totality, is that of the "anti-colonial" non-European capitalist. Giri's point is not simply to assert the primacy of economic "class struggle" over other struggles (against racism, for sexual liberation, etc.)— if we simply decode racial tension as a passive reflection of class difference, such a direct displacement of race onto class effectively is class reduction whose function is to obfuscate the very dynamic of class relations. Giri refers here to Jared Sexton's writings in the aftermath of the 1992 Los Angeles uprising, where he "critiques scholars like Sumi Cho who argue that 'the ability (of Korean Americans) to open stores (in black neighbourhoods) largely depends upon a class variable.' Hence, 'many of the tensions (between these groups) may be class-, rather than racially based, actually reflecting differences between the store-owning Korean immigrants and the African-American customers.'"[27] As Sexton shows, this class analysis does not have anything to do with class struggle, as class is abstracted from any real unequal social relations. Secondly, "the mention of class-based relation is done in order to mitigate the resentment and hostility supposedly born of 'cultural differences and racial animosities'."[28] Thus for Cho, "the ability to open stores (Korean businesses) largely depends upon a class variable, *as opposed to* a racial one."[29] A watered-down, politically sterile notion of class is invoked even as the question of anti-Black racism is diluted. Sexton calls this approach "subordinating the significance of race while pacifying the notion of class."[30] ... "This is where we encounter the familiar story of the postcolonial immigrant making great entrepreneurs and keeping the American Dream alive even as other 'illegal' and undocumented migrants are pushed to the bottom and even as a vast majority of blacks are reduced to not just marginalization and deprivation but 'social death'. ... this backhanded emphasis on class is a way to reduce the overdetermined status of the black poor to what looks like the natural outcome of (free) market relations."[31]

Do we not encounter here an exemplary case of the very reference to class as a means of obfuscating the concrete functioning of class struggle (which can be grasped only through the way class struggle overdetermines racial tensions)? Class difference itself can be the fetish which obfuscates class struggle. This is how one should approach what is arguably Mao's central contribution to Marxist philosophy, his elaborations on the notion of contradiction: one should not dismiss them as a worthless philosophical regression (which, as one can easily demonstrate, relies on a vague notion of "contradiction" which simply means "struggle of opposite tendencies"). The main thesis of his great text *On Contradiction*, on the two facets of contradictions, "the principal and the non-principal contradictions in a process, and the principal and the non-principal aspects of a contradiction," deserves a close reading. Mao's criticism of "dogmatic Marxists" is that they "do not understand that it is precisely in the particularity of contradiction that the universality of contradiction resides":

> For instance, in capitalist society the two forces in contradiction, the proletariat and the bourgeoisie, form the principal contradiction. The other contradictions, such as those between the remnant feudal class and the bourgeoisie, between the peasant petty bourgeoisie and the bourgeoisie, between the proletariat and the peasant petty bourgeoisie, between the non-monopoly capitalists and the monopoly capitalists, between bourgeois democracy and bourgeois fascism, among the capitalist countries and between imperialism and the colonies, are all determined or influenced by this principal contradiction.
>
> When imperialism launches a war of aggression against such a country, all its various classes, except for some traitors, can temporarily unite in a national war against imperialism. At such a time, the contradiction between imperialism and the country concerned becomes the principal contradiction, while all the contradictions among the various classes within the country

(including what was the principal contradiction, between the feudal system and the great masses of the people) are temporarily relegated to a secondary and subordinate position.[32]

This is Mao's key point: the principal (universal) contradiction does not overlap with the contradiction which should be treated as dominant in a particular situation—the universal dimension literally *resides* in this particular contradiction. In each concrete situation, a different "particular" contradiction is the predominant one, in the precise sense that, in order to win the fight for the resolution of the principal contradiction, one should treat a particular contradiction as the predominant one to which all other struggles should be subordinated. In China under the Japanese Occupation, patriotic unity against the Japanese was the most important thing if the Communists wanted to win the class struggle—*in these conditions, any direct focusing on class struggle went against class struggle itself*. (That, perhaps, is the main feature of "dogmatic opportunism": to insist on the centrality of the principal contradiction at the wrong moment.) So yes, we should without shame assert class essentialism, on condition that we grasp "essence" in a properly Hegelian way—not as the substantial base of a series of phenomena, but as the principle of their complex overdetermination.

8.5 BRINGING IN THE CHORUS

This brings us to the key feature of what one could call the politics of separation: the ultimate separation to be fully assumed and endorsed is the separation of the very goal of the emancipatory process, the separation of this goal from itself. What I have in mind here is neither accepting different ways of reaching this goal (the old mantra "each country will build socialism in its own way") nor the historical relativization of the goal itself ("each country will build its own socialism"), but the full acceptance of the fact that, in the process of its actualization, the goal itself changes. Étienne Balibar opposes Hegel (teleological movement toward a final resolution) and Spinoza (antagonism, being on the way toward ..., without a final guarantee of the outcome, since the same logic that causes and multiplies the Good—that of *imitatio affecti*—also causes and multiplies the Evil). (It is easy to note how this opposition is analogous to the one between the Jewish notion of wandering on a divine mission without the ultimate teleological closure and the Christian eschatology.) But is the opposition of Hegel and Spinoza really the one described by Balibar? Hegel's position is subtly different: yes, at the end we reach the goal *because the goal is the state of things we reach*, i.e., whatever (contingently) happens, whichever turn things take, a teleological order is established retroactively which changes contingency into necessity. Recall how the Hegelian dialectical *process* begins with some affirmative idea toward which it strives, but in the course of its actualization *this idea itself undergoes a profound transformation* (not just a tactical accommodation, but an essential redefinition), because the idea itself is caught into the process, (over)determined by its actualization.[33] Say we have a revolt motivated by a request for justice: once people get really engaged in it, they become aware that much more is needed to bring true justice than just the limited requests with which they started (to repeal some laws, etc.). A revolutionary process is not a well-planned strategic activity, with no place in it for a full immersion into the Now, without regard to long-term consequences. Quite the contrary: the suspension of all strategic considerations based upon hope for a better future, the stance of *on attaque, et puis, on le verra* (Lenin often referred to this slogan of Napoleon), is a key part of any revolutionary process.

Lukács himself later changed his position on this key point: the unexplored obverse of his accommodation to Marxist orthodoxy (he no longer conceives the social practice of collective historical subjectivity as the ultimate horizon of thinking, but endorses a general ontology with humanity as a special region of being) is his acceptance of the tragic dimension of the revolutionary subject. This unexplored aspect of Lukács's thought is brought out in Jeremy Glick's *The Black Radical Tragic*,[34] a book we were all waiting for *without knowing it*. Glick goes much further than the usual notion of the revolutionary tragic deployed by Marx and Engels, who locate the tragedy of a revolution in the figure of a hero who comes too early, ahead of his time, and is therefore destined to fail although, in the long view, he stands for historical progress (their exemplary figure is Thomas Müntzer). For Glick, tragedy is immanent to a revolutionary process, it is inscribed into its very core, defined by a series of oppositions: leader(ship) versus masses, radicality versus compromise, etc. For example: with regard to the first opposition, there is no easy way out; the gap between leader(ship) and masses, their miscommunication, emerges ineluctably—Glick quotes a touching passage from Édouard Glissant's play *Monsieur Toussaint* (Act IV, Scene 5), where Toussaint, laughing in delirium, sadly reflects how he "can barely write": "I write the word 'Toussaint,' Macaia spells out 'traitor.' I write the word 'discipline' and Moyse without even a glance at the page shouts 'tyranny.' I write 'prosperity'; Dessalines backs away, he thinks in his heart 'weakness.' No, I do not know how to write, Manuel."[35] (Note the irony of the way this passage refers to the racist cliché about the Black who cannot write.) The background of this passage is the tension in the revolutionary process as reflected in personal relations: Toussaint's nephew Moyse advocated uncompromising fidelity to the Black masses, and wanted to break up large estates, while Toussaint himself was possessed by a fear of the masses, and saw as his task maintaining discipline and the smooth running of the production process, so he ordered Moyse to be executed for sedition. Dessalines later triumphed and, after the establishment of a Black state, proclaimed himself emperor of Haiti, introducing a new form of domination (as well as ordering the massacre of all remaining white inhabitants of Haiti) in the very triumph of the revolution. In order to grasp these tragic twists, it is crucial to count the crowd (which, in the dramatic structure, appears as the Chorus) as one of the active agents, not just as the passive commentator on the events—the title of chapter 2 of Glick's book is, quite appropriately, "Bringing in the Chorus" (and I realized with pleasure that I did the same in my version of *Antigone* where, at the end, the Chorus intervenes, arresting and executing both Antigone and Creon).

The principal antagonism which underlies this tension is the one between fidelity to the universal Cause and the necessity of compromise—and, at least from my standpoint, Glick's deployment of this antagonism is the theoretical and political climax of his book. Glick's starting point is the reference to C. L. R. James, who clearly saw that the early Christian revolutionaries "were not struggling to establish the medieval papacy. The medieval papacy was a mediation to which the ruling forces of society rallied in order to strangle the quest for universality of the Christian masses."[36] Revolutions explode with radical millenarian demands of actualizing a new universality, and mediations are symptoms of its failure, of thwarting people's expectations. The quest for universality of the masses "forbids any mediation."[37] (Was not the tragic turn-around of the Syriza government the last major case of such a "mediation"? The principled no to European blackmail was immediately followed by a yes to the "mediation." ...) Glick mentions György Lukács, the great advocate of "mediation" who, in 1935, wrote "Hölderlin's *Hyperion*," a weird, but crucial, short essay in which he praises Hegel's endorsement of the Napoleonic Thermidor against Hölderlin's intransigent fidelity to the heroic revolutionary utopia:

> Hegel comes to terms with the post-Thermidorian epoch and the close of the revolutionary period of bourgeois development, and he builds up his philosophy precisely on an understanding of this new turning-point in world history. Hölderlin makes no compromise with the post-Thermidorian reality; he remains faithful to the old revolutionary ideal of renovating "polis" democracy and is broken by a reality which has no place for his ideals, not even on the level of poetry and thought.[38]

Here Lukács is referring to Marx's notion that the heroic period of the French Revolution was the necessary enthusiastic breakthrough followed by the unheroic phase of market relations: the true social function of the Revolution was to establish the conditions for the prosaic reign of bourgeois economy, and true heroism resides not in blindly clinging to the early revolutionary enthusiasm but in recognizing "the rose in the cross of the present," as Hegel liked to paraphrase Luther: i.e., in abandoning the position of the

Beautiful Soul and fully accepting the present as the only possible domain of actual freedom. It is thus this "compromise" with social reality which enabled Hegel's crucial philosophical step forward, that of overcoming the proto-Fascist notion of "organic" community in his *System der Sittlichkeit* manuscript, and engaging in dialectical analysis of the antagonisms of bourgeois civil society. It is obvious that this analysis of Lukács is deeply allegorical: it was written a couple of months after Trotsky—another figure who appears in Glick's book—launched his thesis of Stalinism as the Thermidor of the October Revolution. Lukács's text has thus to be read as an answer to Trotsky: he accepts Trotsky's characterization of Stalin's regime as "Thermidorian," giving it a positive twist—instead of bemoaning the loss of utopian energy, one should, in a heroically resigned way, accept its consequences as the only actual space of social progress. For Marx, of course, the sobering "day after" which follows the revolutionary intoxication represents the original limitation of the "bourgeois" revolutionary project, the falsity of its promise of universal freedom: the "truth" of universal human rights is the rights of commerce and private property. If we read Lukács's endorsement of the Stalinist Thermidor, it implies (arguably against his conscious intention) an utterly anti-Marxist pessimistic perspective: the proletarian revolution itself is also characterized by the gap between its illusory universal assertion of freedom and the ensuing awakening in the new relations of domination and exploitation, which means that the Communist project of realizing "actual freedom" necessarily failed—or does it?

There is a third way beyond the alternative of principled self-destruction and compromise: not some kind of "proper measure" between the two extremes, but focusing on what one might call the "point of the impossible" of a certain field. The word "synthesis" is totally misleading here: the concluding moment of a dialectic is not some kind of middle term between the two extremes, maintaining what is good in both of them and combining them into a balanced unity, but a total change of terrain. My friends from Israel reported to me enthusiastically how, in a Palestinian village near Jerusalem, there were joint demonstrations in which veiled Palestinian women marched together with provocatively dressed Jewish lesbians; my reaction was that yes, such events are miracles, but, like all miracles, they are rare, they will forever remain marginal: it is illusory to see in them a germ of future solidarity, of a common front that will be built through patient work and will gradually encompass a majority. This, of course, does not mean that the battle is lost in advance—it means that a much more radical change is needed where the basic identity of each of the two groups will be completely transformed: Palestinian women will have to drop their identity as part of the traditional Palestinian community, and Israeli women will have to drop their middle-class multicultural stance. The third term of the Hegelian "synthesis" is something genuinely new: an invention which breaks the deadlock of the existing situation.

The great art of politics is to detect it locally, in a series of modest demands which are not simply impossible but appear possible although they are de facto impossible. The situation is like the one in science-fiction stories where the hero opens the wrong door (or presses the wrong button, etc.) and all of a sudden the whole of the reality around him disintegrates. In the United States, universal healthcare is obviously such a point of the impossible; in Europe, it seems to be the cancellation of the Greek debt, and so on. It is something you can (in principle) do, but de facto you cannot or should not do it—you are free to choose it *on condition you do not actually choose it*.

Today's political predicament provides a clear example of how *la vérité surgit de la méprise*, of how the wrong choice has to precede the right choice. The general epistemological premise that underlies this necessary role of misrecognition can be neatly summarized by the reversal of the well-known phrase "You have to be stupid not to see that!"—*la vérité surgit de la méprise* means precisely that you *have* to be stupid to see that: i.e., as Lacan put it, *les non-dupes errent*, those who are not duped are in the wrong (this is the best critical description of cynics). In order to arrive at the truth, one has to be taken in by an illusion—just recall how emancipatory politics can be sustained only by a belief in the (in some sense obviously "illusory") axiom of universal justice.

In principle, the choice of Leftist politics is one between social-democratic reformism and radical revolution, but the radical choice, although correct and true in the abstract, is self-defeating and gets stuck in Beautiful Soul immobility: in Western developed societies, calls for a radical revolution have no mobilizing power. Only a modest "wrong" choice can create subjective conditions for an actual Communist prospect: whether it fails or succeeds, it sets in motion a series of further demands ("in order really to have universal healthcare, we also need ...") which will lead to the right choice. There is no short cut here; the need for a radical universal change has to emerge through such mediation with particular demands. To begin straight off with the right choice is therefore even worse than making the wrong choice: it is a version of the Beautiful Soul, it amounts to a position of "I am right and the misery of the world which got it wrong just confirms how right I am." Such a stance relies on a wrong ("contemplative") notion of truth; it totally neglects the practical dimension of truth. In his (unpublished) *Seminar XVIII* on a "discourse which would not be that of a semblance," Lacan provided a succinct definition of the truth of interpretation in psychoanalysis: "Interpretation is not tested by a truth that would decide by yes or no, it unleashes truth as such. It is only true inasmuch as it is truly followed." There is nothing "theological" in this precise formulation, only an insight into the properly dialectical unity of theory and practice in (and not only in) psychoanalytic interpretation: the "test" of the analyst's interpretation is in the truth-effect it unleashes in the patient. This is how we should also (re)read Marx's Thesis XI: the "test" of Marxist theory is the truth-effect it unleashes in its addressee (the proletarians), in transforming them into emancipatory revolutionary subjects. The true art of politics is thus not to avoid mistakes and to make the right choice, but to make the right mistake, to select the right (appropriate) wrong choice. In this sense, Glick writes of "the revolutionary leadership as vanishing mediator—the only responsible vanguard model. Political work in order to qualify as radical work should strive toward its redundancy."[39] Here he combines a sober and ruthless insight into the necessary tragic twists of the revolutionary process with an unconditional fidelity to this process; he stands as far away as possible from the standard "antitotalitarian" claim that since every revolutionary process is destined to degenerate, it is better to abstain from it. This readiness to take the risk and engage in the battle, although we know that we will probably be sacrificed in the course of the struggle, is the most precious insight for us who live in new dark times. The moment when particular political acts explode into a universal emancipatory break is not the big event of liberation, the triumphant eschatological moment, but rather the beginning of a mess, of a long and arduous confused process full of new dangers.

We should thus fully accept the fact that, since revolutionary activity is also not a self-transparent act but an act caught in conditions of alienation, it inevitably includes tragic reversals, acts whose final outcome is the opposite of what was intended. Here one should follow Badiou, who elaborated three distinct ways for a revolutionary movement to fail. First there is, of course, a direct defeat: one is simply crushed by the enemy forces. Then there is a defeat in the victory itself: one defeats the enemy (temporarily, at least) by taking over the enemy's main power agenda (the goal is to take state power, either in a parliamentary-democratic—social-democratic—way, or in a direct identification of Party with State, as in Stalinism). As well as these two versions, there is perhaps the most authentic, but also the most terrifying, way: guided by the correct instinct telling it that every consolidation of the revolution into a new state power equals its betrayal, but unable to invent and impose on social reality a truly alternative social order, the revolutionary movement engages in a desperate strategy of protecting its purity by the "ultra-Leftist" resort to all-destroying terror. Badiou aptly calls this last version the "sacrificial temptation of the void":

One of the great Maoist slogans from the red years was "Dare to fight, dare to win." But we know that, if it is not easy to follow this slogan, if subjectivity is afraid not so much to fight but to win, it is because struggle exposes it to a simple failure (the attack didn't succeed), while victory exposes it to the most fearsome form of failure: the awareness that one won in vain, that victory prepares repetition, restoration. That a revolution is never more than a between-two-States. It is from here that the sacrificial temptation of the void comes. The most fearsome enemy of the politics of emancipation is not the repression by the established order. It is the interiority of nihilism, and the cruelty without limits which can accompany its void.[40]

What Badiou is saying here is in fact the exact opposite of Mao's "Dare to win!"—one should be afraid to win (to take power, to establish a new socio-political reality), because the lesson of the twentieth century is that victory either ends in restoration (return to the State-power logic) or gets caught in the infernal cycle of self-destructive purification. This is why Badiou proposes replacing purification with subtraction: instead of "winning" (taking over power) one maintains a distance toward state power, one creates spaces subtracted from the State. ... But is this solution adequate? What about heroically accepting the risk of self-obliteration? In other words, isn't there a fourth mode of defeat (in addition to the three enumerated by Badiou), another mode of defeat in victory where defeat does not mean simply that the revolution is appropriated by what it wanted to overcome but, more radically, that in winning, in realizing its goals, the revolutionary process produces something unexpected, so that, in the course of the process, we have to redefine the goal itself? This is why Lukács (surprisingly for a Marxist) fully endorses Hegel's refusal to engage in any project for a better future society: "That Hegel stops at the present is related ... to the most profound motives of his thinking—to be precise, of his historico-dialectical thinking."[41] In other words, it is precisely Hegel's silence about the future which opens up the space for it: namely, for a future that is not just an extrapolation of the predominant tendencies of the present, but the unforeseeable result of risky decisions.

We thus need to subtly change the formula of the big revolutionary Event as the moment of final Judgment when, as Benjamin put it, even the past of the failed revolutionary attempts will be redeemed, the moment first clearly formulated in Joel 3:14: "Multitudes, multitudes, in the valley of decision! For the day of the Lord is near in the valley of decision."[42] But the decision is always risky, with no ontological guarantee, destined to fail and to be repeated. It can happen that the Lord (or whatever agent stands for Him) makes the wrong judgment, that the wrong multitude is finished off in the valley of decision. The true emancipatory work of love enters at this tragic moment.

CHAPTER 9

APPENDIX: DEATH, LIFE, AND JEALOUSY
IN COMMUNISM

9.1 THE CHANGING ETERNITY

The Moranbong Band, which made its debut in 2012, is an immensely popular all-female music group in North Korea whose members were selected by Kim Jong-un himself. Immaculately clad in dazzling dresses with short skirts, they perform in the styles of pop, soft rock, and fusion, with an overall mood of pleasing symphonic harmony (what we in the West would immediately identify as the pre-rock kitschy pop music from the late 1950s). Their repertoire combines Western popular culture (music from Disney cartoons like *Snow White*, the theme from *Rocky*, Sinatra's "My Way"), older Western operetta music (waltzes by Strauss, "Czardas"), some international revolutionary and popular songs (like "Guantanamera"), and songs that directly praise Kim Jong-un ("We Can't Live without Your Help," "We Will Go to Baekdusan"), so that it effortlessly moves between the extremes of nightclub experience and Communist Party gathering. And, in fact, the truly surprising thing in the performance of the Moranbong Band is how all these completely different pieces of music *sound the same*: they perform an official party song like a pop kitsch with sweet violins, and a Strauss operetta aria like a Communist marching chant. Recall Jacques Rancière's reading of Dziga Vertov's *Man with a Movie Camera* (mentioned in chapter 1 above), where Communism is presented not so much as the hard struggle for a goal (the new society to come), but as a fact, a present collective experience, a symphonic texture of life in all its positive diversity where the most disparate phenomena operate at the same level, as in an ironic cinematic version of Stalin's first law of dialectics, "everything is connected with everything else." Although, of course, we should never forget that the predominant tone of the Moranbong "synthesis" is neo-Romantic popular kitsch, nor that Moranbong music is clearly addressed to the new North Korean middle classes, destined to create the illusion of an easy life, should we nonetheless discern in it the last trace of a properly Communist utopia?

In my youth, when Communism was still widely considered a realistic political option, there were many speculations about how the so-called ultimate questions of everyday life would appear there—love, death, jealousy, happiness. ... Maybe we should engage again in such speculations, just in a slightly darker mode.

Modest socio-psychological experiments definitely have their uses when they indicate the historical specificity or even outright falsity of many claims about "natural" human dispositions, so let us begin with a nice case. David Brooks[1] explains how we inherently desire to do good, but society's assumptions of selfishness affect our behavior; he thereby almost reverses the conventional wisdom according to which the invisible hand of the market makes our natural selfishness work for the common good. Two examples from his short essay make his point clear. Six daycare centers in Haifa imposed a fine on parents who were late picking up their kids, but, surprisingly, the proportion of parents who arrived late doubled—how could this have happened? Before the fine was imposed, the key factor for the parents when they had to decide when to pick up their kids was simple consideration for the staff— they were well aware that being late could ruin their free evening. The introduction of the fine for being late changed the entire situation and made the parents perceive it as concerning a financial transaction: how much were they ready to pay for the privilege of arriving late for the pickup? From this new standpoint, many of them decided that paying a little bit of money is worth it to gain an hour or two of additional free time—moral consideration was out; it became irrelevant, since the price for being late was paid in money. The other example: in 2001, the Boston fire commissioner canceled the policy of unlimited sick days and imposed a limit of fifteen days per year—for those who exceeded this limit, a fine was deducted from their salary. The unexpected result of this measure was that absence from work in the Christmas and New Year period increased tenfold: again, the ethical stance of serving the city was replaced by a utilitarian paid agreement, and the firefighters simply decided that the price for extra holidays was worth paying. In both cases, a financial incentive "prompts people to see their situation through an economic lens." We have here a clear case of how the utilitarian selfish subject is not a fact of nature but is engendered by the socioeconomic frame.

The overall picture is nonetheless not so bright: what Brooks leaves out of consideration is a behavior which, while it is not motivated by egotism, works against the welfare of others, even if their welfare is profitable also for me, and satisfies my egotistic interests. I am talking, of course, about the tremendous power of envy, which makes me desire my neighbor's misfortune even if I have to pay a price for it—better for me to lose a cow than not, if I know that my neighbor will lose three cows.[2] A decade or so ago, there was a rebellion of Cuban refugees detained at the Guantanamo base: its direct cause was that one group of refugees received lower-quality orange juice than another. The very trifling character of what triggered the violent uprising is indicative: not a big injustice or large-scale suffering, but a minimal, ridiculous difference, especially for people who had just come from Cuba, a country with severe food shortages. Does this not make it clear that the cause immediately triggering a rebellion is, by definition, trifling, a pseudo-cause indicating that what is at stake is the relationship to the Other? However, we should not dismiss such squabbles as ridiculous. In Poland during the German Occupation, all Polish sport clubs were officially disbanded, but football (soccer) matches were tolerated by the occupying authority. Especially in the Kraków governorship, dozens of clubs formed and competed, and every summer a big Kraków championship was organized. In 1943, weird things happened (remember, we are in a country united against the German occupiers, whose treatment of the local population was extremely brutal, where starvation was a permanent threat, etc.). During and after the games, players, officials, and supporters would fight each other—on August 1, 1943, during a game between Łagiewianka and Wisła, a group of Łagiewianka officials and fans invaded the pitch to beat up the referee and Wisła players. The game was ended eight minutes before time. A week later, there were disturbances during the Groble–Nadwiślan (in Borek Fałęcki) and Dąbski–Czarni (in Rakowice) games, and the police had to intervene. Due to those disturbances, on August 10, 1943, all games were canceled. The decision was changed after the August 15 meeting, but it did not help, as soon afterward, during the Rakowiczanka–Cracovia game, further riots took place.

On Sunday, October 17, 1943, at 3 p.m., the final game of the 1943 Kraków Championship took place at Garbarnia Stadium, with some 10,000 spectators. The game between Wisła and Cracovia ended with a gigantic fight between supporters of both teams when referee Tadeusz Milusiński awarded a penalty kick to Cracovia, after a Wisła player touched the ball with his hand in the box. In response, Wisła's Mieczysław Gracz kicked the referee, and the Wisła players left the pitch, urged on by their officials. Fights between angry fans moved onto the streets of Kraków's Podgórze district.[3]

Is there not a touch of Bataillean sovereignty in such a stance of momentarily forgetting the big struggle for survival against the brutal foreign enemy, and focusing on a trifling competition? Can we imagine Polish soccer fans fighting each other in front of the true enemy (German soldiers) in public? Was this not a demonstration of inner strength and freedom? However, despite this continuity of envy, there is something unique in contemporary capitalism: it can no longer be thought of as a totalizing system threatened by erratic "sites of resistance," since it is already in itself structured as a multiplicity of erratic excesses:

the more varied, and even erratic, the better. Normalcy starts to lose its hold. The regularities start to loosen. This loosening of normalcy is part of capitalism's dynamic. It's not a simple liberation. It's capitalism's own form of power. It's no longer disciplinary institutional power that defines everything, it's capitalism's power to produce variety—because markets get saturated. Produce variety and you produce a niche market. The oddest of affective tendencies are okay—as long as they pay. Capitalism starts intensifying or diversifying affect, but only in order to extract surplus-value. It hijacks affect in order to intensify profit potential. It literally valorizes affect. The capitalist logic of surplus-value production starts to take over the relational field that is also the domain of political ecology, the ethical field of resistance to identity and predictable paths. It's very troubling and confusing, because it seems to me that there's been a certain kind of convergence between the dynamic of capitalist power and the dynamic of resistance.[4]

We can supplement this analysis in many directions—the very process of escaping to "liberated territories" outside the domain of the State was reappropriated by capitalism. Exemplary instances of the logic of global capitalism are so-called "Special Economic Zones," geographical regions within a (usually Third World) state with economic laws more liberal than the state's normal economic laws (fewer or no import and export taxes, free flow of capital, limitation or direct prohibition of trade unions, no minimum working hours, etc.) in order to increase foreign investment; the name covers a whole range of more specific zone types (Free Trade Zones, Export Processing Zones, Free Zones, Industrial Estates, Free Ports, Urban Enterprise Zones, etc.). So when Naomi Klein writes that "neoliberal economics is biased at every level toward centralization, consolidation, homogenization. It is a war waged on diversity,"[5] is she not focusing on a figure of capitalism whose days are numbered? Would she not be applauded by contemporary capitalist modernizers? Is not the latest trend in corporate management itself "diversify, devolve power, try to mobilize local creativity and self-organization?" Is not anti-centralization the topic of the "new" digitized capitalism? The problem here is even more "troubling and confusing" than it may appear. As Lacan pointed out apropos of his discussion of the structural homology between surplus-value and surplus-enjoyment, what if surplus-value does not simply "hijack" a preexisting relational field of affects—what if what appears to be an obstacle is in fact a positive condition of possibility, the element which triggers and propels the explosion of affective productivity? What if, consequently, one should precisely "throw the baby out with the bathwater" and renounce the very notion of erratic affective productivity, etc., as the libidinal support of revolutionary activity?

Badiou also recognizes the exceptional *ontological* status of capitalism whose dynamic undermines every stable frame of re-presentation: what is usually the task of critico-political activity (namely, the task of undermining the re-presentational frame of the State) is already performed by capitalism itself. In precapitalist formations, every State, every re-presentational totalization, implied a founding exclusion, a point of "symptomal torsion," a "part of no-part," an element which, although part of the system, did not have a proper place within it—and emancipatory politics had to intervene on behalf of this excessive ("supernumerary") element which, although part of the situation, cannot be accounted for in its terms. However, what happens when the system no longer excludes the excess, but directly posits it as its driving force—as is the case in capitalism, which can reproduce itself only through its con-stant self-revolutionizing, through the constant overcoming of its own limit? To put it in a simplified way: if a political event, a revolutionary emancipa-tory intervention into a determinate historical world, is always linked to the excessive point of its "symptomal torsion," if it by definition undermines the contours of this world, how, then, are we to define the emancipatory politi-cal intervention into a universe which is already in itself worldless, which, for its reproduction, no longer needs to be contained by the constraints of a "world"? (This impasse is the same as the one that occurs at the end of True Life where, as we have already seen,[6] Badiou—in a strict homology with the prospect of the rise of a new World—advocates a new symbolization of the two sexes.)

An excellent example of this deadlock is Hardt's and Negri's[7] continu-ous oscillation between their fascination for global capitalism's "deterritori-alizing" power, and the rhetoric of the struggle of the multitude against the One of capitalist power. Financial capital, with its wild speculations detached from the reality of material labor, this standard bête noire of the traditional Left, is celebrated as the germ of the future, as capitalism's most dynamic and nomadic aspect. The organizational forms of today's capitalism—decentralization of decision-making, radical mobility and flexibility, inter-action of multiple agents—are perceived as pointing toward the oncoming reign of the multitude. It is as if everything is already here, in "postmodern" capitalism, or, in Hegelese, the passage from In-itself to For-itself—all that is needed is an act of purely formal conversion, like the one developed by Hegel apropos of the struggle between Enlightenment and Faith, where he describes the "silent, ceaseless weaving of the Spirit."

Even the fashionable parallel with the new cognitivist notion of human psyche is here: just as brain sciences teach us how there is no central Self in the brain, how our decisions emerge from the interaction between a pan-demonium of local agents, how our psychic life is an "autopoietic" process which, without any imposed centralizing agency (a model which, inciden-tally, is explicitly based on the parallel with today's "decentralized" capi-talism), so the new society of the multitude which rules itself will be like today's cognitivist notion of the ego as a pandemonium of interacting agents with no central deciding Self running the show. ... However, although Hardt and Negri see today's capitalism as the main site of the proliferating multitudes, they continue to rely on the rhetoric of the One, the sovereign Power, against the multitude; how they bring these two aspects together is clear: while capitalism generates multitudes, it contains them in the capitalist form, thereby unleashing a demon it is unable to control. The question to be asked here is nonetheless if Hardt and Negri do not commit a mistake analogous to that of Marx: is not their notion of the pure multitude ruling itself the ultimate *capitalist* fantasy, the fantasy of capitalism's self-revolutionizing perpetual movement freely exploding when relieved of its inherent obstacle? In other words, is not the capitalist *form* (the form of the appropriation of surplus-value) the necessary form, the formal frame/condition, of the self-propelling productive movement?

This immanent tension between the capitalist erratic dynamic and its reterritorialization through the form of profit extraction is redoubled by an even more radical tension, the one between the two aspects of modernity: the dynamic interaction of desiring and producing individuals self-regulating itself through the market, and different forms of social control and regulation whose emblematic figure is Bentham's Panopticon and whose contemporary versions are not only organizations like the National Security Agency but, perhaps even more, corporations like Google, which unite the two aspects. Google is a medium of "free" social interaction and, simultaneously, a very efficient medium of control which regulates and registers these interactions—no free interplay of multitudes without the NSA overlooking it.

What underlies this deadlock is the deeply ambiguous status of capitalism's exceptional nature, mentioned above: capitalism is unique, but it is precisely because of this exceptional status that it seems to directly echo what one might hypostasize as universal "human nature."[8] At the level of libidinal economy, capitalism is also an exception which reveals the underlying universal rule. Human desire is constitutively metonymic— the object we get is never "that," the real Thing; the object-cause of desire is always in excess of every obtainable object, and lacking in it. In the libidinal economy of traditional societies, this constitutive instability is contained or masked by some form of the supreme Good which serves as the ultimate object of desire. In capitalism, however, the instability of desire (which compels it forever to the reproduction of the paradox of lack which appears as a surplus) is directly inscribed into its functioning, not only in late-capitalist consumerism but already in the circular movement of capital, which can reproduce itself only through permanent self-expansion. Here we have yet another case of the dialectical paradox of an exception (an "unnatural," unstable, "decadent" social form corrosive of all traditional forms) as the point at which the universal rule obfuscated by all other (traditional) social forms becomes visible. So there is a grain of truth in the apologetic saying that capitalism corresponds to human nature, and this, perhaps, is the reason why capitalism so easily expands into a global machine that can accommodate itself to all particular cultural forms.[9]

The first reaction of a Marxist historicist to this hypothesis is, of course, derisive laughter: is not the claim that capitalism somehow corresponds to human nature (with the implication that other modes of production are "artificial") ideology at its worst, the naturalization of a historically specific form of production? And is not this very talk about "human nature" the worst case of philosophy as ideology? However, a much more refined case for this claim can be made, based on the key dialectical insight that a universal feature valid for all times and places appears "as such," in its pure state, only as an exception, since the very function of every "normal" state (or species of a genus) is to repress or obfuscate or cope with the antagonism that pertains to this universality. Marx himself illustrates this dialectic of universality and its exception with the category of labor:

> Labor seems a quite simple category. The conception of labor in this general form—as labor as such—is also immeasurably old. Nevertheless, when it is economically conceived in this simplicity, "labor" is as modern a category as are the relations which create this simple abstraction.
> … Indifference toward any specific kind of labor presupposes a very developed totality of real kinds of labor, of which no single one is any longer predominant. … Indifference toward specific labors corresponds to a form of society in which individuals can with ease transfer from one labor to another, and where the specific kind is a matter of chance for them, hence of indifference. … Here, then, for the first time, the point of departure of modern economics, namely the abstraction of the category "labor," "labor as such," labor pure and simple, becomes true in practice. The simplest abstraction, then, which modern economics places at the head of its discussions, and which expresses an immeasurably ancient relation valid in all forms of society, nevertheless achieves practical truth as an abstraction only as a category of the most modern society. … This example of labor shows strikingly how even the most abstract categories, despite their validity—precisely because of their abstractness—for all epochs, are nevertheless, in the specific character of this abstraction, themselves likewise a product of historic relations, and possess their full validity only for and within these relations.[10]

If, then, capitalism somehow corresponds to universal "human nature," what is this "nature"? Here, of course, irony comes in: the universal "nature" of human beings is precisely their counter-nature, the fact that a human being is "by nature" deprived of a stable natural (instinctual) foundation. I am referring here to the central topic of philosophical anthropology from the late eighteenth century: a human being is a deformed, crippled animal, an animal which is constitutively out of joint, destabilized, an animal whose existence precedes its essence (as Sartre would have put it), and, for this reason, an animal which has to be made into what it is, through self-creativity or through tough discipline and education (a human being as an animal which needs a Master, as Kant put it). This "unfinished" character of a human being which pushes humanity to continuous creativity, to the development of all kinds of external supplements and supports, from tools to language, can be given a Leftist-libertarian or a Rightist-authoritarian spin—Sartre or Gehlen, we might say. Either we celebrate human creativity, the permanent push toward self-transcendence (a human being "is what it is not," as Sartre put it): a human being is never satisfied with a given state, it always strives for more, it experiences every limitation as a constraint on its freedom which is grounded in its basic ontological structure. Or we insist that, precisely because of its ontologically uncertain, open status, a human being needs tough external authority to discipline it, to keep its self-destructive potential in check. (Or—the third, and darkest, option—we focus on how the libertarian aspect necessarily turns into its opposite: did not Stalinist authoritarianism, one of the worst nightmares of the twentieth century, arise out of the very attempt to realize human freedom and creativity?)

And this brings us to Aaron Schuster's provocative thesis: this "counternatural" status of a human being, this ontological incompleteness, the precarious status of every stable form of communal being, which was obfuscated in the whole of human thought in the past, and became visible only in modern anthropology, seems to find its echo in the form of subjectivity that characterizes not so much capitalism as such as its latest phase, in our "age of austerity" and universalized indebtedness. Here I am tempted to posit a kind of short circuit between precariousness as a universal feature of "human nature" and today's precariat (the more and more hegemonic role of precarious work). Precarious workers experience the ambiguity of precariousness in an extreme form: they are "condemned to be free," free to reinvent themselves all the time, to search for new form of expressing their creativity, but the price they pay for it is that their daily existence is marked by eternal insecurity, helplessness, and anxiety. Schuster conceives this "precarious" form of subjectivity as the last stage in the succession of the modes of capitalist subjectivity: the Protestant autonomous agent, the corporate "organization man," the consumerist hedonist of Fukuyama's happy 1990s, and, today, after the end of the end of history signaled by events like September 11 and the 2007–2008 financial crisis, the precarious subjectivity that fits our age of austerity. It is only in this last stage that capitalism directly echoes the precariousness, instability, etc., of the "eternal" human nature. This short circuit gives a new, dark and unexpected, spin to Fukuyama's thesis on the end of history: history will end when the existing mode of production finally fits human nature.

At this point, of course, we immediately encounter the big question: is this short circuit between "eternal" human nature and capitalism final, i.e., is the only way out a new ideological mystification that again obfuscates precarious "human nature," or should we continue to hope (as Deleuze and Negri do) that today's capitalism is merely a perverted "reterritorialized" version of erratic excess, and that a new, fully "deterritorialized" social order is possible, an order in which negativity will no longer be constrained by the form of capital?

Maybe what we should put into question is this very anthropological premise of a disoriented/perverted "human nature," all the poetry of the human being as a sick animal, all the ontology of lack, out-of-jointness, etc. The first thing to do is to supplement it with its opposite: an irreducible excess—what if what constitutes being-human is a traumatic encounter with a surplus for which there is (or, rather, should be) no place in our reality, with a too-muchness, as Eric Santner would have put it? Negativity and surplus are two sides of the same coin. The second thing to do is to historicize this very "eternal human nature": yes, the parallax duality of lack/surplus is "eternal," constitutive of being-human, but its very universality acquires different shades in particular epochs, and the "pessimistic" anthropology of dislocation is just one among its figurations. There is a subtle difference between this view and direct historicism: transhistorical "eternity" is not directly denied-historicized but caught in history as "eternity"—eternity itself has a history; this is arguably the deepest insight of German Idealism.

9.2 JEALOUSY BEYOND ENVY

Capitalist consumerism is a civilization of envy, its moving force is mimetic desire: I want not what I need but what others (desire to) have, and it is this mimetic game of overcoming the other (of "keeping up with the Joneses") which fuels the permanent hystericization, the permanent desire for more. Communism breaks this spell of competitive mimetic desire neither through egalitarianism (Marx made this very clear when he insisted that equality is a bourgeois principle) nor with distributive justice (again and again rejected by Lacan). Here we also encounter the fateful limit of the famous formula "from each according to his/her ability, to each according to his/her needs"— who determines what my needs are? Can we talk, especially in a developed society, of needs independently of how these needs are determined through sociosymbolic networks and interaction with others? Does this mean, then, that Communism remains caught in the spell of envy? But what if, even if we break this spell of envy, jealousy remains, preventing harmonious social collaboration?

The basic idea is that, at the level of libidinal economy, the passage from capitalism to Communism functions as the passage from (the predominant role of) envy to jealousy. Jean-Pierre Dupuy[11] systematically deployed the difference between envy and jealousy, a difference often neglected by René Girard, Fredric Jameson, but not by Lacan (the famous lines from Saint Augustine that he often quotes refer to envy, not jealousy—what causes envy in the small boy is the vision of his brother's exclusive access to the mother's breast). Envy implies a triangle: the subject, his rival, and the object possessed by the rival (and desired because the rival desires it). In jealousy, on the contrary, "rival" and object coalesce into One, a self-enclosed circle of full satisfaction, as in Munch's (deservedly) famous painting *Jealousy*. The jealous subject is excluded from this circle, entry into it is prohibited to him, and it is this exclusion which triggers his desire—jealousy is not caused by desire (I am jealous of my object of desire possessed by someone else), it is desire itself which is caused by jealousy. The closed circle of a fully satisfied couple happy in their seclusion is mostly fantasized, of course; it does not exist in itself.

Jealousy is thus the exemplary case of supposed enjoyment, of a fantasized enjoyment projected onto an Other who is the "subject-supposed-to-enjoy." This category also provides a key to what one should perhaps risk calling "religious-terrorist enjoyment." A terrorist is not a sadist who pretends to do the work of God while secretly enjoying the suffering he causes; the enjoyment that motivates him is the divine Other's presupposed enjoyment. Perhaps the libidinal economy of terrorist attacks was best encapsulated by Nietzsche when he wrote: "'All evil is justified if a god takes pleasure in it': so ran the primitive logic of feeling—and was this logic really restricted to primitive times? The gods viewed as the friends of *cruel* spectacles—how deeply this primeval concept still penetrates our European civilization!"[12] One should be very careful in quoting Nietzsche, especially his pseudo-radical "amoral" axioms, since, as Sloterdijk noted perspicaciously, "as soon as one quotes Nietzsche, one shoots way above the target."[13] Here, however, Nietzsche hit the target full on: instead of speculating on the perverse pleasures of the terrorists themselves, we must focus on the figure of the big Other for the imagined pleasure of whom/which the terrorists did what they did.

A different version of this type of enjoyment is clearly discernible in the way Greece (among many other nations) was humiliated for its inability to repay its debts. One cannot fail to recall Nietzsche's famous reflections on the repayment of a debt by the pleasure of torturing the powerless other in his *Genealogy of Morals*:

The equivalency is provided by the fact that instead of an advantage directly making up for the wrong (so, instead of compensation in money, land or possessions of any kind), a sort of *pleasure* is given to the creditor as repayment and compensation,—the pleasure of having the right to exercise power over the powerless without a thought, the pleasure *"de faire le mal pour le plaisir de le faire"* [doing wrong for the pleasure of doing it], the enjoyment of violating. ... To what extent can suffering be a compensation for "debts"? To the degree that *to make* someone suffer is pleasure in its highest form, and to the degree that the injured party received an extraordinary counter-pleasure in exchange for the injury and distress caused by the injury: to *make* someone suffer,—a true *feast*.[14]

Back to jealousy: in Mozart's *Don Giovanni*, Zerlina and Masetto form a very happy couple, and the hero cannot stand such a couple, which seems so satisfied in itself—he seduces Zerlina only to ruin the couple, and if his seduction had not been interrupted by Elvira, he would have dropped Zerlina immediately after the amorous act, since his only goal was to ruin the happy couple; love played no role in it. Another distinction is that envy (what Rousseau called l'*amour-propre*) calculates; it matters who got more of it, me or my rival, while jealousy does not calculate, it is simply transfixed by the fantasized perfection of the One couple from which the subject is excluded—Lacan calls this fascination with the imagined perfect unity *jalouissance* (a condensation of jealousy and *jouissance*).[15] Consequently, hatred in jealousy is not hatred of the obstacle (my competitor) but hatred of the entire circle of the perfect couple, a hatred which easily reverts to self-hatred on account of my exclusion from the circle. In envy, the "mediator" (my competitor who possesses what I desire) is simultaneously my model (I want to be like him, possessing the object) and my obstacle (I want him destroyed so that I can have free access to the object), but the paradox is that the moment I get rid of him, my desire for the object also disappears. In jealousy, however, there is no mediator and no imitation of the mediator—I don't want to be like him, I want to destroy the Whole of him and his love object. This Whole can also be located in the past: I can be jealous when I learn that my present partner enjoyed a deep love relationship before I met him/her—just imagining what they were doing can drive me crazy.

In a famous TV advertisement for Nespresso coffee, George Clooney acts as if he enjoys the coffee—but we all know he is probably indifferent toward it, i.e., he is pretending to enjoy it because he is being well paid for doing so. How, then, does this advertisement work? We don't desire coffee because Clooney desires it, since we know very well that he probably isn't enjoying it, so Clooney is a kind of "mediator without desire," he mediates our desire for coffee without desiring it himself. There is a further twist at work here: while Clooney is drinking his coffee, a young woman approaches him, and he smiles with narcissistic satisfaction, thinking the woman wants him—but we soon learn she is attracted by the smell of the coffee, not by him. ... It is as if the woman (who stands for us, consumers) is not attracted by the mediator who also desires the object. The enigma is thus, again: how does the advertisement work, when we all know that Clooney probably doesn't really desire the advertised product, so it cannot be that we will desire it in imitation of him; moreover, we know that the woman ignoring him but actually enjoying the coffee is a double cheat (we assume that she is really attracted by Clooney, and that her ignoring him is a complex act designed to arouse his curiosity and—maybe—desire for her)? What we get here is a redoubled fetishist disavowal: we (the spectators) know very well that Clooney probably doesn't enjoy Nespresso, but we nonetheless believe he does; we know very well that the woman is focused on Clooney and not on the stupid coffee, but we nonetheless believe she really cares for the smell of the coffee ... a lesson in the autonomous efficiency of the symbolic order.

To recapitulate: insofar as desire is in itself "impossible," self-sabotaging, i.e., insofar as the fundamental function of prohibition is not to serve as an obstacle to desire but to sustain desire (to sustain the illusion that, if we overcome the prohibition, we will attain full satisfaction), the moment when the prohibition disintegrates is the most dangerous one, since it compels the subject to confront the immanent impossibility of desire (to put it in popular terms: the fact that the most horrible thing is to get what one wants). As Lacan pointed out, social prohibitions never simply serve the aim of those in power by legitimizing deprivation: they certainly serve those in power, but they are obeyed, they "function," because the ruling ideology deftly manipulates the immanent impossibility (self-sabotaging) of desire. By obeying the prohibition (which serves and sustains the power structure), the subject profits in that this obedience enables it to avoid the deadlock of desire: it appears that desire is in itself consistent, striving toward satisfaction in an unproblematic way, and that impediments to this satisfaction are purely external. We can now see the libidinal problem of Communism: insofar as Communism is supposed to abolish "oppressive" prohibitions that serve relations of domination, the subject has to confront the debilitating deadlock of desire. This means is that, instead of introducing a new era of relations of solidarity and solidary satisfaction, Communism threatens to unleash explosive imbalances and self-destructive cycles of resentment.

What, then, happens with jealousy in Communism? Are we simply condemned to it as the ultimate a priori of human experience? The duo "Oh! Rimembranza!" from Act I of Bellini's *Norma* (between Norma, the Druid high priestess in Gaul under Roman occupation, and Adalgisa, her subordinate priestess) is one of the most sublime examples of the triangle of mimetic desire. They are both in love with Pollione, the Roman governor of the province with whom Norma had two children a couple of years ago. Adalgisa approaches Norma and confesses she has fallen in love with a Roman whom she does not name. As she describes how she fell in love while waiting at the temple and seeing "his handsome face" appear, Norma recalls (as an aside) her own feelings for Pollione ("my passions too burned like this"), and more and more, their experiences of falling in love run parallel. Adalgisa pleads for help and forgiveness, and Norma pledges that she will accede and will also free her from her vows as a priestess: "Yes, take heart, embrace me. I forgive you, and sympathize with you." Then things take a wrong turn: Norma asks Adalgisa to describe the man whom she loves, and Adalgisa replies that he is a Roman and, at that moment, turns to indicate that it is Pollione, who is just then entering the room. While Pollione shows fear that Norma will hurt Adalgisa, Norma furiously confronts him: "O faithless man, do not tremble for her. She is not guilty, you are the wicked one."[16]

The sublime echoing of emotions reverts to explosive hatred the moment the object of love is identified as the same—in a strange twist to the basic logic of jealousy, it seems as if the One that emerges is the One of the duo itself, the couple of Norma and Adalgisa whose vein of emotions forms a closed loop, the two reinforcing each other. (Although one should also note that their respective positions are not completely symmetrical: Adalgisa reports on her feelings now, about her present love, while Norma remembers, i.e., she sings in a nostalgic mode about moments of the happy past.) Harmony works as the harmony of two separate Ones (love couples) echoing each other; the unity is violently broken when the two women discover they are talking about the same man—however, interestingly, Norma's hatred turns not toward her competitor for stealing the love object, but toward the object itself: the object is perceived as the active agent who has chosen another union. In short, Norma does not envy Adalgisa for having Pollione, she is jealous of the love union between Adalgisa and Pollione.

Religion seems to be able to avoid this explosive turn: a religious community is a community of those who share their love for the same (divine) object. This works insofar as the object remains unknown, so that each of us loves "his/her own God." Only God can work in this way: He can remain the same while being an exclusive love object for each of us. There is, however, another way beyond jealousy within its very coordinates. Recall the fate of Stella Dallas in the final scene of the Hollywood melodrama of the same name: from outside the grand house where the ceremony is in progress, Stella watches through the big window the marriage of her daughter to her rich suitor—the harmonious paradise of a happy, rich family from which she is excluded. This, precisely, is the illusion of a fantasy par excellence: by erasing oneself (the disturbing excess) from the picture—and this erasure can go right up to actual suicide—the picture will be that of a harmonious Whole.

What we get here is what Dupuy calls the geometry of jealousy—the subject excluded from the One of full enjoyment—but *without jealousy*, with jealousy replaced by a kind of ecstatic happiness generated by the view of the happy One (couple) from which the subject is excluded. The scene enacted in *Stella Dallas* exemplifies a sacrificial logic ignored by René Girard: the scapegoat is the subject him-/herself, ready to sacrifice him-/herself in order to bring about the fantasized One. (In the film, the heroine starts to behave in a vulgar and promiscuous way not because she really is such a person but because she is pretending to be to make it easier for her daughter to cut her links with her without regret, and marry her rich boyfriend from a grand family.) Is this constellation not a kind of fulfillment-through-negation of the normal logic of jealousy (the subject endeavoring to destroy the One of the perfect couple which gives rise to his/her jealousy)? Instead of brutally destroying the stain which disturbs the harmony of the One, the subject grasps that it is he/she who is the stain. So why does the subject destroy itself as the stain even though, as a jealous subject, it wants to destroy the One? We could even argue that the implicit insight on which this gesture is based is that the ultimate stain is the One itself, the fantasy of a harmonious couple which has no place in reality, and which is, as such, immanent to the subject itself.

And there is a more radical cure for jealousy: to perceive a crack in the closed circle of the (two united in) One. In his "Postface" to Dupuy's book, Olivier Rey moves a step further from Girard, for whom only the imitation of Christ can save us from the infernal cycle of mimetic desire—and of envy, since he is a model which is not an obstacle but remains at a distance, uniting all of us who imitate him.[17] Rey points out that jealousy is not resolved in this way: after we accept the crack in the (two united in) One, our loss is irreparable, the encircled closure of the One is forever lost. But we might add that the gesture of Christianity is even more unique here: in the highest moment of the mystery of crucifixion ("Father, why have you abandoned me"?), it displaces the loss into God Himself, i.e., Father and Son no longer form a harmonious One, so that what we imitate in *imitatio Christi* is this gesture of assuming-the-loss itself—I become one with Christ when I recognize, in my experience of being abandoned by God, the self-abandonment of God on the Cross.

9.3 LOVE BEYOND DEATH

Is this self-abandonment, then, the ultimate horizon of our experience? To put it in the most naive way, can love overcome death? If yes, in what precise way, insofar as we want to remain materialists? In chapter II C ("You Shall Love Your Neighbour") of his *Works of Love*, Kierkegaard develops the thesis that the ideal neighbor whom we should love "as ourselves" is a dead one—the only good neighbor is a dead neighbor. His line of reasoning is surprisingly simple and cogent: in contrast to poets and lovers, whose object of love is distinguished by its particular outstanding qualities, "to love one's neighbor means equality": "Forsake all distinctions so that you can love your neighbour."[18] However, it is only in death that all distinctions disappear: "Death erases all distinctions, but preference is always related to distinctions."[19] A further consequence of this reasoning is the crucial distinction between two perfections: the perfection of the object of love and the perfection of love itself. The lover's, poet's, or friend's love contains a perfection belonging to its object, and is, for this very reason, imperfect as love; in contrast to this love,

> precisely because one's neighbour has none of the excellences which
> the beloved, a friend, a cultured person, an admired one, and a rare and
> extraordinary one have in high degree—for that very reason love to one's
> neighbour has all the perfections. ... Erotic love is determined by the object;
> friendship is determined by the object; only love to one's neighbour is
> determined by love. Since one's neighbour is every man, unconditionally
> every man, all distinctions are indeed removed from the object. Therefore
> genuine love is recognisable by this, that its object is without any of the
> more definite qualifications of difference, which means that this love is
> recognisable only by love. Is not this the highest perfection?[20]

To put it in Kant's terms: what Kierkegaard is trying to articulate here are the contours of a non-pathological love, of a love which would be independent of its (contingent) object, a love which (again, to paraphrase Kant's definition of moral duty) is motivated not by its determinate object, but by the mere form of love—I love for the sake of love itself, not for the sake of what distinguishes its object. The implication of this stance is thus weird, if not outright morbid: perfect love is utterly indifferent toward the beloved. No wonder Kierkegaard was so obsessed with the figure of Don Juan: do not Kierkegaard's Christian love for the neighbor and Don Juan's serial seductions share this crucial indifference toward the object? For Don Juan also, the quality of the seduced object did not matter: the ultimate point of Leporello's long list of conquests, which categorizes them according to their characteristics (age, nationality, physical features), is that these characteristic are indifferent—the only thing that matters is the pure numerical fact of adding a new name to the list. Is Don Juan not, in this precise sense, a properly Christian seducer, since his conquests were "pure," non-pathological in the Kantian sense, made for the sake of it, not because of any particular and contingent properties of their objects? The poet's preferred love object is also a dead person (paradigmatically the beloved woman): he needs her dead in order to articulate his mourning in his poetry (or, as in courtly love poetry, a living woman herself is elevated to the status of a monstrous Thing). However, in contrast to the poet's fixation on the singular dead love object, the Christian, as it were, treats the still living neighbor as already dead, erasing his or her distinctive qualities. The dead neighbor means: the neighbor deprived of the annoying excess of *jouissance* which makes him/her unbearable. It is thus clear where Kierkegaard cheats: in trying to sell us as the authentic difficult act of love what is in effect an escape from the effort of authentic love. Love for the dead neighbor is an easy feat: it basks in its own perfection, indifferent toward its object—what about not only "tolerating," but loving the other *on account of its very imperfection?*

Lacan's name for this "imperfection," for the obstacle which *makes me* love someone, is *objet petit a*, the "pathological" tic which makes him/her unique. In authentic love, I love the other not simply as alive, but on account of the very troubling excess of life in him/her. Even the common wisdom is somehow aware of this: as they say, there is something cold in perfect beauty; one admires it, but one falls in love with an imperfect beauty, on account of this very imperfection. An opinion poll conducted two decades ago made it clear that, for Americans at least, there was something all too cold in Claudia Schiffer's perfection: it was somehow easier to fall in love with Cindy Crawford on account of her very small imperfection (the famous tiny pimple close to her lip—her *objet petit a*).[21] This failure by Kierkegaard also accounts for the problems which emerge when we apply the Kierkegaardian triad of the Aesthetic, the Ethical, and the Religious to the domain of sexual relations: what is the religious mode of the erotic, if its aesthetic mode is seduction and its ethical mode is marriage? Is it at all meaningful to speak of a religious mode of the erotic in the precise Kierkegaardian sense of the term? Lacan's point is that this, precisely, is the role of *courtly love*: the Lady in courtly love suspends the ethical level of universal symbolic obligations and bombards us with totally arbitrary ordeals in a way which is analogous to the religious suspension of the Ethical; her ordeals are on a par with God's ordering Abraham to slaughter his son Isaac. And, contrary to our first impression that sacrifice reaches its apogee here, it is only here that, finally, we confront the Other *qua* Thing that gives body to the excess of enjoyment over mere pleasure.

In exactly the same way as Kierkegaard's love for the dead neighbor, this tragic vision of courtly love is not only false, but ultimately even unchristian. In Hitchcock's *Vertigo*, the low-class Judy who, under the pressure exerted from and out of her love for Scottie, endeavors to look and act like the high-class fatal and ethereal Madeleine, turns out to *be* Madeleine: they are the same person, since the "true" Madeleine Scottie encountered was already a fake. However, this identity of Judy and Judy-Madeleine reveals all the more clearly the absolute otherness of Madeleine with regard to Judy—the Madeleine who is nowhere, who is present merely in the guise of the ethereal "aura" that envelops Judy-Madeleine. In a strictly analogous gesture, Christianity asserts that there is nothing beyond appearance—nothing but the imperceptible X that changes Christ, this ordinary man, into God. In the absolute identity of man and God, the divine is the pure *Schein* of another dimension that shines through Christ, this miserable creature. It is only here that the iconoclasm is truly brought to its conclusion: what is in fact "beyond the image" is that X that makes the man Christ God. In this precise sense, Christianity inverts the Jewish sublimation into a radical desublimation: not desublimation in the sense of the simple reduction of God to man, but desublimation in the sense of the descent of the sublime Beyond to the everyday level. Christ is a "ready-made God" (as Boris Groys put it); he is fully human, inherently indistinguishable from other humans in exactly the way Judy is indistinguishable from Madeleine in *Vertigo*—it is only the imperceptible "something," a pure appearance which can never be grounded in a substantial property, that makes him divine. This is why Scottie's obsessive love for Madeleine in *Vertigo* is a fake: if his love were true, he should have accepted the full identity of (the common, vulgar) Judy and (the sublime) Madeleine.

There is, nonetheless, an indifference which pertains to true love: not the indifference toward its object, but the indifference toward the positive properties of the beloved object. This indifference of love is closely linked to that of the Lacanian "empty signifier": of course, this signifier is never actually "empty"—a king, for example, is always identified with a series of personal idiosyncratic features which characterize him; however, we, his subjects, are at all times aware that these features are completely indifferent and replaceable; that it is not these features which make him a king. The difference between the "empty" and "full" signifier lies not in the absence or presence of positive features of the object designated by it, but in the different *symbolic status* of these features: in the first case, these features are a positive magnitude (the subject's properties), while in the second case, they function as a negative magnitude, i.e., their very "full presence" is a stand-in for— holds the place of—the "emptiness" of the signifier (of the symbolic mandate) "King." "Fullness" and "emptiness" are thus not directly opposed: the very "emptiness" of the empty signifier is sustained by a specific "negative" fullness. And the same goes for love: to say "I love you because … (you have a nice nose, attractive legs)" is a priori false. With love, it is the same as with religious belief: I do not love you because I find your positive features attractive, but, on the contrary, I find your positive features attractive because I love you and therefore observe you with a loving gaze. Consequently, all the "fullness" of the positive features which I adore in the beloved are a stand-in for the "emptiness" which I really love—even if each of them were to be obliterated, I would still love you.

How does all this relate to sex? In Catherine Breillat's *Romance*, there is a fantasmatic scene which perfectly stages this radical split between love and sexuality: the heroine imagines herself lying naked on her belly on a low, small table divided in the middle by a partition with a hole just large enough for her body. With the upper side of her body, she faces a nice tender guy with whom she exchanges gentle loving words and kisses, while her lower part is exposed to one or more sex-machine studs who penetrate her wildly and repeatedly. However, the true miracle occurs when these two series momentarily coincide, when sex is "transubstantiated" into an act of love. There are four ways to disavow this impossible/real conjunction of love and sexual enjoyment: (1) the celebration of asexual "pure" love, as if the sexual desire for the beloved demonstrates love's inauthenticity; (2) the opposite assertion of intense sex as "the only real thing," which reduces love to a mere imaginary lure; (3) the division of these two aspects, their allocation to two different people: one loves one's gentle wife (or the idealized inaccessible Lady), while one has sex with a "vulgar" mistress; (4) their false immediate merger, in which intense sex is supposed to demonstrate that one "truly loves" one's partner, as if, in order to prove that our love is a true one, every sexual act has to be the proverbial "fuck of the century." All these four stances are wrong, an escape from accepting the impossible/real conjunction of love and sex; a true love is enough in itself, it makes sex irrelevant—but precisely because "fundamentally, it doesn't matter," we can fully enjoy it without any superego pressure. . . .

And, unexpectedly, this brings us to Lenin: when, in 1916, Lenin's (at that point former) mistress Inessa Armand wrote him that even a fleeting passion was more poetic and cleaner than kisses without love between man and woman, he replied: "Kisses without love between vulgar spouses are filthy. I agree. These need to be contrasted . . . with what? . . . It would seem: kisses with love. But you contrast 'a fleeting (why a fleeting) passion (why not love?)'—and it comes out logically as if kisses without love (fleeting) are contrasted to marital kisses without love. . . . This is odd."[22] Lenin's reply is usually dismissed as proof of his petit-bourgeois sexual constraint, sustained by his bitter memory of the past affair; however, there is more to it: the insight that marital "kisses without love" and the extramarital "fleeting affair" are two sides of the same coin—they both shrink from combining the Real of an unconditional passionate attachment with the form of symbolic proclamation. Lenin is profoundly right here, although not in the standard prudish sense of preferring "normal" marriage out of love to illicit promiscuity.[23] The underlying insight is that, contrary to all appearances, love and sex are not only distinct, but ultimately incompatible: that they operate at completely different levels, like agape and eros: love is charitable, self-effacing, ashamed of itself; while sex is intense, self-assertive, possessive, inherently violent (or the opposite: possessive love versus generous indulging in sexual pleasures). However, the true miracle occurs when (exceptionally, not "as a rule") these two series momentarily *coincide*, when sex is "transubstantiated" into an act of love—an achievement which is real/impossible in the precise Lacanian sense, and as such marked by an inherent *rarity*. The state of love is characterized by a permanent surprise at this coincidence—when I am in love, I look at the beloved and am again and again surprised by the shocking realization: "My God, this really is *him/her!*" In short, I am surprised by the fact that "my lover keeps reminding me of him-/herself." This surprise makes it clear that the beloved is not fully identical with him-/herself, that he/she is characterized by an extreme tension, and the repeated surprise expresses my wonder that the disparate elements nonetheless hold together. Authentic love disappears when this surprise fades away, when I simply accept the beloved as what he/she is even if he/she remains a wonderful and attractive person. Or, as Lacan put it, love disappears when the amorous encounter no longer "stops not being written" but, instead, "doesn't stop being written"—when it loses the character of a shocking contingent encounter and turns into an ordinary permanent feature of my life.

Can we also imagine a similar shift in politics? An authentic political sequence persists as long as its agents are surprised by the fact that "this" (a series of often pragmatic and modest measures) is "that" (advancing the universal Cause)— that, for instance, bringing water and electricity to a poor village is part of a Communist project. Is this not what Eisenstein had in mind in the famous cream separator scene from his *Old and New* (*General Line*) (1928), where the demonstration to a group of backward peasants of how a cream separator works is staged as the ecstatic experience of a disclosure of the Grail? And could we also not read in the same way Lenin's famous formula "Communism = power of soviets + electrification"? We regress from authentic politics to ordinary administration when universal emancipation no longer finds its echo in a particular measure.

A pragmatic realist's instant retort would be that the surplus of the Cause over particular measures is precisely ideology, i.e., what we should get rid of: we should focus on particular measures which solve concrete problems. However, the universal dimension that echoes in particular measures is not some vague ideological universality but the universality of antagonism, the Real of a stumbling block, of the impossibility around which a society is structured. Abstract universality is the mute medium of all particular content, concrete universality *unsettles the identity of the particular from within*; it is a line of division which is itself universal, running across the entire sphere of the particular, dividing it from itself. Abstract universality is uniting; concrete universality is dividing. Abstract universality is the peaceful foundation of particulars; concrete universality is the site of struggle—it brings the sword, not love. ...

With regard to emancipatory struggle, a particular culture which tries desperately to defend its identity has to repress the universal dimension which is active at its very heart—that is, the gap between the particular (its identity) and the universal which destabilizes it from within. This is why the "allow us our culture" argument fails. Within every particular culture, individuals do suffer; for example, women do protest when they are forced to undergo clitoridectomy, and *these protests against the parochial constraints of one's culture are formulated from the standpoint of universality.* Actual universality is not the "deep" feeling that, above all differences, different civilizations share the same basic values, etc.; *actual universality "appears" (actualizes itself) as the experience of negativity, of the inadequacy-to-itself, of a particular identity.* "Concrete universality" does not concern the relationship of a particular entity with its wider encompassing Whole, the way this entity relates to others, to its context, but *the way this entity relates to* <u>itself</u>, the way its very particular identity is split in itself, from within. The standard problem of universality (how can I be sure that what I perceive as universality is not colored by my particular identity?) thereby disappears: "concrete universality" means that, precisely, my particular identity is corroded from within, that the tension between particularity and universality is inherent to my particular identity—or, to put it in more formal terms, in concrete universality, specific difference overlaps with generic difference.

9.4 *MENTEM MORTALIA TANGUNT*

How, then, can we come to terms with the ultimate loss, death itself, which is, as Gadamer put it, "one of the most unpleasant things that are part of life"?[24] In line 462 of Book I of the *Aeneid*, we get Aeneas's reaction to a mural found in a Carthaginian temple which depicts battles of the Trojan War where most of his friends and countrymen died—Aeneas is moved to tears and says: *sunt lacrimae rerum et mentem mortalia tangunt.* The line can be translated as "There are tears of things and mortal things touch the mind" or "There are tears for things and mortal things touch the mind," since the genitive *rerum* can be read as objective or subjective. Although this indeterminacy is poetically productive, in English we have to make a choice: if we take the genitive as *subjective* then the phrase means that things feel sorrow for the sufferings of humanity—the universe feels our pain; if we take it as *objective* then it means that we, humans, shed our tears for the horrible things that have happened (and that these horrors that happened to mortal things deeply affect our minds).[25] However, if the genitive is subjective, the second part of the line means something much more refined: things are crying for us and this crying of things, tears shed by things, is what affects our mind deeply, much more deeply than our own crying.

This, exactly, is how Dmitri Shostakovich's mind is touched in his Fourteenth Symphony. Although the symphony sets to music a series of great poems dedicated to death, it makes no great pathetic declaration about mortality which could be shared by the listener. When we, listeners, establish a link with the symphony, we relate to death not as if it is the deepest metaphysical enigma of our lives but as if it is a dirty and awkward personal secret, as in those well-known embarrassing moments when a fantasmatic intimacy is unexpectedly shared, often through a stupid misunderstanding. When I was talking with a friend about soprano operatic arias and tried to describe an aria the name of which I couldn't remember, he interrupted me with weird intensity: "You mean 'La mamma morta'?" (He was referring to the aria from Umberto Giordano's *Andrea Chénier* whose Callas version is known to the wider public from an unbearably pathetic scene from the movie *Philadelphia*.) In a split second he recognized that his choice was wrong, and that he had made it for an obvious personal reason—he was a bachelor who lived alone with his mother, with whom he was engaged in a strange pathological link, so that one line of his desire was obviously for his mother to die so that he could finally breathe freely; he blushed and quickly changed the subject. ... Another friend told me of a similar case: a colleague was describing to him the location of the Judd bookstore in London and, after failed attempts to make his description work, added: "It's close to a gay bookstore on the same street." My friend reacted all too quickly and intensely: "Yes, yes, now I know where it is!" but then he immediately realized that his answer revealed his intimate acquaintance with the gay bookstore, and thus his sexual orientation (this happened decades ago, when even in academic circles homosexuality was still frowned upon).

The Fourteenth Symphony is composed of eleven movements, each a setting of a poem (by Lorca, Apollinaire, Küchelbecker, and Rilke).[26] The work shows Shostakovich's willingness to adopt new techniques. Much of the setting is in a quasi-*parlando* style. In most of the movements we find themes using tone rows (getting close to Schoenberg's twelve-tone technique)—not to make death more palpable but, on the contrary, to convey a sense of the abstract. He also makes dramatic use of dissonant tone clusters, such as the fortissimo chord illustrating the lily growing from the suicide's mouth in the fourth movement. Shostakovich attached great importance to this work, commenting in a letter to Glikman: "Everything that I have written until now over these long years has been a preparation for this work."[27] Why?

The first movement begins with the violins playing a theme which echoes "*Dies irae*," which returns later. "Day of Judgment," but, precisely, no judgment at death, no full meaning of life. ... The Fourteenth Symphony was a creative response (not to official critique, like the Fifth, but) to Mussorgsky's *Songs and Dances of Death*, which Shostakovich had orchestrated in 1962. He added that he intended the symphony to prove a counterweight to the positive presentation of death in music:

I am trying to polemicize with the great classics who touched upon the theme of death in their work. ... Remember the death of Boris Godunov. When he dies, then a kind of brightening sets in. Remember Verdi's *Otello*. When the whole tragedy ends, and Desdemona and Othello die, we also experience a beautiful tranquility. Remember *Aida*. When the tragic demise of the hero and heroine occurs, it is softened with radiant music.[28]

(And we may add all great *Liebestode* from *Norma* to Wagner's *Tristan und Isolde*.) In Mussorgsky's song cycle Shostakovich found a model that spoke out against death; in his symphony, he attempted to expand this protest still further. The composer wrote in his preface to the score:

I want listeners to reflect upon my new symphony ... to realize that they must lead pure and fruitful lives for the glory of their Motherland, their people and the most progressive ideas motivating our socialist society. That is what I was thinking about as I wrote my new work. I want my listeners, as they leave the hall after hearing my symphony, to think that life is truly beautiful.[29]

While Shostakovich's intent may have been to emphasize that life is truly beautiful, he did so by starkly underlining the opposite—that the end of life is ugly and irredeemably negative. The work, written in the spring of 1969, received its official premiere in Leningrad on September 29, 1969. The pre-premiere performance was notable for the commotion caused in the audience by Pavel Apostolov, one of the composer's most vicious critics (in the 1948 anti-"formalist" campaign), who suffered a heart attack and died soon afterward (in a divine coincidence, death was triggered by a work on death). The negative reaction to the symphony ran across ideological divides: Solzhenitsyn criticized it as too hopeless—in yet another coincidence with official critics who "wanted the finale to be comforting, to say that death is only the beginning. But it's not a beginning, it's the real end, there will be nothing afterwards, nothing. I feel you must look truth right in the eyes."[30] The absence from the symphony of redemption or transcendence drew protests not only in the Soviet Union but also in the West, where the work was considered both obsessive and limited spiritually. Shostakovich was determined to avoid false consolation—embracing mortality without constraint, with no fingers crossed, is what motivated him. Does this mean that his Fourteenth Symphony belongs to the thought of finitude so forcefully criticized by Badiou, who asserted that

death is something that *happens to you*; it is not the immanent unfolding of some linear program. Even if we say that human life cannot go beyond a hundred and twenty years, for biological, genetic etc. reasons, death as death is always something that *happens to you*. ... And I would maintain that death always comes from the outside. Spinoza said something excellent on that score: "Nothing can be destroyed except by an external cause." ... This means that death is in a position of radical exteriority: we would not even say that a human reality, a *Dasein*, is mortal. Because "mortal" means to say that it contains the virtuality of death in an immanent fashion. In truth, all that is is generically immortal, and then death intervenes.[31]

The mention of Spinoza is crucial, and here one should oppose Spinoza to Hegel: while for Spinoza, every destruction comes from outside, thwarting every organism's immanent tendency to reproduce and expand its life power, for Hegel, negation is immanent, inscribed within the innermost identity of every living being, so that every destruction is ultimately self-destruction. To avoid misunderstanding: Hegel would have agreed that there is no deeper meaning in death, that death comes as a radically external meaningless contingency—but it is precisely as such that it corrodes from within the very core of human identity and its universe of meaning. Furthermore, like Badiou, Hegel asserts infinity/immortality, but for him immortality emerges precisely through "tarrying with the negative," through its immanent overcoming: only a being which is not constrained by its mortality can relate to its death "as such." This overcoming is, paradoxically, a form of "death in life": a human being overcomes its mortality through gaining a distance toward its life-substance (for example, through its readiness to risk its life for some spiritual cause). Death is not external, but neither is it the point toward which life moves, concluding the story of life, providing meaning, Judgment; it is external meaninglessness in life, detotalizing it from within.

In a strict parallel with his notion of death as a contingent cut totally external to the potential infinity of life, for Badiou, the end of an evental series is external to it; it should not be reduced to the immanent limitations of the Event in question. Let us take the case of the Chinese Cultural Revolution, which can be read on two different levels. If we read it as a part of historical reality (being), we can easily subject it to a "dialectical" analysis which perceives the final outcome of a historical process as its "truth": the ultimate failure of the Cultural Revolution bears witness to the inherent inconsistency of the very project ("notion") of Cultural Revolution, it is the explication-deployment-actualization of this inconsistency (just as, for Marx, the vulgar, nonheroic, capitalist daily life of profit-seeking is the "truth" of Jacobin noble revolutionary heroism). If, however, we analyze it as an Event, as an enactment of the eternal Idea of egalitarian Justice, then the ultimate factual result of the Cultural Revolution, its catastrophic failure and reversal into the recent capitalist explosion, does not exhaust its Real: the eternal Idea of the Cultural Revolution survives its defeat in sociohistorical reality, it continues to lead the underground spectral life of the ghosts of failed utopias which haunt future generations, patiently awaiting its next resurrection.

It is easy to discern in these two opposed readings the echo of the philosophical contrast between Kant and Hegel: Kant sees the Idea as an ideal exempt from the dialectics of history (which can only endlessly approach it, its actualization), while for Hegel an Idea is fully caught up in the historical process. Back to the Cultural Revolution: the supreme Hegelian irony of history is thus that it was Mao himself who created the ideological conditions for rapid capitalist development by tearing apart the fabric of traditional society. What was his call to the people, especially the young ones, in the Cultural Revolution? Don't wait for someone else to tell you what to do, you have the right to rebel! So think and act for yourselves, destroy cultural relics, denounce and attack not only your elders, but also government and Party officials! Sweep away the repressive state mechanisms and organize yourself in communes! And Mao's call was heard: what followed was an explosion of the unrestrained passion to delegitimize all forms of authority, so that, in the end, Mao had to call the army in to restore order. This does not mean that Hegel is a historicist for whom an Idea is simply part of a historical process: a true Idea persists, gets purified, transformed, through its process; the point is just that the fate of an Idea in its actualization is its inherent moment.

Shostakovich's ruminations about his mortality do not concern his intimate or private side in tension with official Communist optimism—it is here that Shostakovich is truly a Communist, much more than in the noisy "great" finales of some of his symphonies (like the Fifth or the Seventh). We should reject the nonsense that death is traumatic in capitalism because people are lonely individuals under that system, while in Communism it will be easier because our dying will be done in solidarity with others (or that dying for a noble Cause makes it easier)—if anything, it will be much harsher to die in Communism. To get an idea of this, we should return to the passage from Samuel Beckett with which this book begins, and from which it also took its title; it comes from one of Beckett's late absolute masterpieces, *Ill Seen Ill Said* (1981),[32] in which "language is pitilessly starved of prolixity and adornment but obstinately refuses to die."[33] It consists of the confused mumblings of an old woman living out her last days alone in an isolated cottage, and although it deals with the "universal" theme of the debilitating process of dying, it does not "sublate" this process into any higher meaning (like dying for a noble Cause) but just reduces it to its minimal form of the antagonism between refusal to die and longing for the peace of death. This minimum will survive in Communism.

9.5   A MATERIALIST CONSPIRACY OF FAITH

Does this mean that bitter despair is the ultimate horizon of our lives? We must add another turn of the screw here. Toward the end of *A Conspiracy of*

Faith (original title Flaskepost [Message in a bottle], a 2016 Danish noir directed by Hans Petter Moland), there is a remarkable dialogue between Carl Mørck, a burnt-out, terminally depressed detective, and Johannes, a handsome blond serial killer of children who is as interested in destroying their parents' faith as in snatching their offspring. (This dialogue occurs only in the film, not in Jussi Adler-Olsen's novel on which the film is based, so I am referring to Nikolaj Arcel's scenario.) Their final confrontation occurs in an isolated wooden seaside cottage where Johannes holds tied up as prisoners Mørck and the kidnapped children, a boy and a girl. After presenting himself as one of the Devil's sons whose task is to destroy faith, Johannes tells Mørck: "And now ... I'll take away your faith." Mørck promptly replies: "You're wasting time. I don't believe in God. I don't believe in anything." When Johannes then throws the young boy into the sea and keeps his head under water, Mørck desperately shouts: "Listen to me. Take me instead." Johannes: "You're rescuing people you've never met. Of course you have faith. I've never met anyone who's had as much faith as you." Mørck: "Take me!" Johannes: "Do you wish God would make you powerful enough to stop me?" When the boy seems to be dead, Johannes concludes: "I think you will remember this day. You were here and it changed nothing. And God ... never showed." He then turns to the boy's elder sister, cuts her bonds with scissors, pushes the scissors into her hand, and tells her: "Now you get this ... And then you get your revenge. Then you will be his, then you will be free. Stab me. Stab me and you'll be free." The girl refuses, and Johannes snaps at her: "You disappoint me." Then he tells Mørck: "Now you've seen. Now you must live." At this moment the sound of a police helicopter above the cottage is heard, as a kind of pseudo-divine last-minute intervention. ...

The film's concluding moments are ambiguous: in a church Mørck half-heartedly joins the prayer for the victims which celebrates the power of life over death, and when, in the very last shot of the film, he observes children playing in a green sunlit meadow, he says: "I thought what idiots they were. But maybe it's right ..."—again, an ambiguity: what is right? For the innocent children to remain in their illusion? Those final minutes are obviously a retreat from the thorny ethical dilemma that occurs in the confrontation between Mørck and Johannes. We should, of course, dismiss as ridiculous Johannes's idea of acting as the Devil's son, an idea which is meaningful only within the theological universe where there is a conflict between God and the Devil. If we follow T. S. Eliot's insight that the Devil's ultimate temptation is the reference to Good itself—"the highest form of treason: to do the right deed for the wrong reason," as he put it in Murder in the Cathedral—then it is Mørck himself who is the true Devil's son. The Devil's ultimate trump card is not "give way to your lust for power, enjoy life, abandon the chimera of higher ethical values!" but "do all the noble deeds your heart tells you to do, live the highest ethical life, and be aware that there is no need for a reference to God in all this, it is your own inner nature which is your guide here, you are following the law of your heart!"—is this stance not personified in Mørck's atheistic readiness to sacrifice himself for others?

The crux of the matter is thus the enigma of atheism and ethics: can one be fully ethical, up to being ready to sacrifice oneself for others, without believing in God? And, if we risk taking even a step further, what if only an atheist can be truly and unconditionally ethical? The point is not to ascribe to atheists some deeper belief too pure to be articulated in explicit dogmas— if there is anything good about religions, it is their dogmatic aspect. The title of the English translation of the novel and film—"a conspiracy of faith"— is brilliant, and immediately reminds us of G. K. Chesterton's famous essay "A Defense of Detective Stories," where he remarks how the detective story

> keeps in some sense before the mind the fact that civilization itself is the most sensational of departures and the most romantic of rebellions. When the detective in a police romance stands alone, and somewhat fatuously fearless amid the knives and fists of a thief's kitchen, it does certainly serve to make us remember that it is the agent of social justice who is the original and poetic figure, while the burglars and footpads are merely placid old cosmic conservatives, happy in the immemorial respectability of apes and wolves. [The police romance] is based on the fact that morality is the most dark and daring of conspiracies.[34]

Chesterton, of course, extends this logic to religion itself: orthodoxy, orthodox faith, is the most dark and daring of all conspiracies, while atheists are "merely placid old cosmic conservatives, happy in the immemorial respectability of apes and wolves." ... However, he is well aware that, in Christianity, things get more complicated: the "conspiracy" of Christianity is that "Christianity alone has felt that God, to be wholly God, must have been a rebel as well as a king"[35] —even more, that God Himself, the origin of all things, for a moment becomes an atheist and does not believe in Himself. That is the lesson of Christianity: it is not only that we do not believe in God, but that God Himself does not believe in Himself, so that He also cannot survive as the non-substantial symbolic order, the virtual big Other who continues to believe in our place, for us. Moreover, only a belief which survives such a disappearance of the big Other is belief at its most radical, a wager more crazy than Pascal's: Pascal's wager remains epistemological, concerning only our attitude toward God, i.e., we have to assume that God exists, our wager does not concern God Himself; while for radical atheism, the wager is ontological—the atheist subject engages itself (in a political, artistic, etc., project), "believes" in it, without relying on any guarantee.

My thesis is thus double: not only that *Christianity* (in its core disavowed by its institutional practice) *is the only authentic atheism*, but also that *atheists are the only true believers*.

Perhaps the only way out of these impasses is what, in his unpublished "secret" writings, Denis Diderot described under the title of the "materialist's credo." In "Entretien d'un philosophe avec la maréchale de ***," he concluded: "Après tout, le plus court est de se conduire comme si le vieillard existait ... même quand on n'y croit pas" (After all, the most straightforward way is to behave as if the old guy exists ... even if one doesn't believe it). This may appear to amount to the same as Pascal's wager apropos of custom: even if you don't believe in it, act as if you believe. ... However, Diderot's point is exactly the opposite: the only way to be truly moral is to act morally without regard to God's existence. In other words, Diderot directly reverses Pascal's wager (the advice to place your bet on the existence of God): "En un mot que la plupart ont tout à perdre et rien à gagner à nier un Dieu rémunérateur et vengeur" (In a word, it is that the majority of those who deny a remunerating and vengeful God have everything to lose and nothing to gain).[36] In his denial of the remunerating and vengeful God, the atheist either loses everything (if he is wrong, he will be damned forever) or gains nothing (if he is right, there is no God, so nothing happens). It is this attitude which expresses true confidence in one's belief, and makes one do good deeds without regard to divine reward or punishment. "As if the old guy exists"—this old guy is, of course, God-the-Father, which recalls Lacan's formula *le père ou pire*—father or worse. It is on this level that one should oppose Pascal and Diderot: while Pascal bets on God-the-Father, Diderot enjoins us to *parier sur le pire*, to put our money on the worst. In true ethics, one acts from a position of the inexistence of the big Other, assuming the abyss of the act deprived of any guarantee or support from the big Other.

When something crucial happens, even if it happens unexpectedly, we often get the impression that it *had* to happen, that it would violate some higher order if it were not to happen. More precisely, once it *does* happen, we see that it had to happen—but it may *not* have happened. Let us take a case of desperate love: I am deeply convinced that my love is not reciprocated, and I silently resign myself to a gloomy future of despair; but if all of a sudden I discover that my love is reciprocated, I feel that this had to happen, and I cannot even image the despair of my life without it. Or let us take a difficult and risky political decision: although we sympathize with it, we are skeptical, we don't trust the scared majority; but when, as if by a miracle, this decision is taken and enacted, we feel it was destined to happen. Authentic political acts take place like this: in them, (what was considered) the "impossible" happens and, by happening, it rewrites its own past, emerging as necessary, predestined even.

Here we should bring in the fact that *A Conspiracy of Faith* is a Danish movie based on a Danish novel: is not Mørck's "terminal depression" a form of what Kierkegaard called "infinite resignation," the crucial step toward the authentic religious experience? Kierkegaard's "God" is the name for the Absolute Other against which we can measure the utter contingency of reality—as such, it cannot be conceived as any kind of Substance, as the Supreme Thing (that would again make Him part of Reality, its true Ground). This is why Kierkegaard has to insist on God's complete "desubstantialization"—God is "beyond the order of Being," He is nothing but the mode of how we relate to Him, i.e., we do not relate to Him, He is this relating: "God himself is this: *how* one involves himself with Him. As far as physical and external objects are concerned, the object is something else than the mode: there are many modes. In respect to God, the *how* is the what. He who does not involve himself with God in the mode of absolute devotion does not become involved with God."[37] The Christian passage to the Holy Spirit as Love (Christ's "whenever there will be love between the two of you, I will be there") is to be taken literally: God as the divine *individual* (Christ) passes into the purely *non-substantial* link between individuals. This absolute devotion is enacted in the gesture of total self-renunciation: "in self-renunciation one understands one is capable of nothing."[38] This renunciation bears witness to the unbridgeable gap that separates man from God: the only way to assert one's commitment to the unconditional Meaning of Life is to relate *all* of our life, our entire existence, to the absolute transcendence of the divine, and since there is no common measure between our life and the divine, this sacrificial renunciation cannot be part of an exchange with God—we sacrifice all (the totality of our life) *for nothing*: "The contradiction which arrests [the understanding] is that a man is required to make the greatest possible sacrifice, to dedicate his whole life as a sacrifice—and wherefore? There is indeed no wherefore."[39]

This is why the entire theme of a sacrifice that grounds subjectivity is superfluous and misses the point: for a subject to emerge, there is no need for any sacrifice, since the subject itself (as a "barred" subject, as the void of negativity) already *is* the most radical sacrifice, the sacrifice of all substantial content, what Sade called the "second death," although he misses the true dimension of his own discovery. What, then, on a strict theoretical level, is wrong with this dream of the "second death" as a radical pure negation which puts a stop to the life-cycle itself?[40] In a superb display of his genius, Lacan provides a simple answer: "It is just that, being a psychoanalyst, I can see that the second death is prior to the first, and not after, as de Sade dreams it."[41] In what precise sense are we to understand this priority of the second death—the radical annihilation of the entire life-cycle of generation and corruption—over the first death, which remains a moment of this cycle? The total negation imagined by Sade does not come at the end, as a threat or prospect of radical destruction, it comes at the beginning, it always-already happened, it stands for the zero-level starting point from which fragile/inconsistent reality emerges. In other words, what is missing in the notion of Nature as a body regulated by fixed laws is simply *the subject itself*: in Hegelese, the Sadeian Nature remains a Substance, Sade continues to grasp reality only as Substance and not also as Subject, where "subject" stands not for another ontological level different from Substance but for the immanent incompleteness-inconsistency-antagonism of Substance itself. And, insofar as the Freudian name for this radical negativity is the death drive, paradoxically, what Sade misses in his celebration of the ultimate Crime of radical destruction of all life is precisely the death drive.

It was Kant who characterized a free autonomous act as an act which cannot be accounted for in the terms of natural causality, the texture of causes and effects: a free act occurs as its own cause, it opens up a new causal chain from its zero-point. So insofar as "second death" is the interruption of the natural life-cycle of generation and corruption, no radical annihilation of the entire natural order is needed for this—an autonomous free act already suspends natural causality, and subject as $ is already this cut in the natural circuit, the self-sabotage of natural goals. The mystical name for this end of the world is "night of the world"; the philosophical name is radical negativity as the core of subjectivity. And, to quote Mallarmé, a throw of the dice will never abolish the risk, i.e., the abyss of negativity remains forever the unsublatable background of subjective creativity. We may even risk here an ironic version of Gandhi's famous motto "You must be the change you wish to see in the world": the subject is itself the catastrophe it fears and tries to avoid. And is not the lesson of Hegel's analysis of the French revolutionary Terror exactly the same (which is why the parallel between Sade's absolute crime and revolutionary Terror is well grounded)? Individuals threatened by the Terror have to grasp that this external threat of annihilation is nothing but the externalized/fetishized image of the radical negativity of self-consciousness—once they grasp this, they pass from revolutionary Terror to the inner force of the moral Law.

This means that there is no guarantee that our sacrifice will be rewarded, that it will restore Meaning to our life – the only reward of radical sacrifice is sacrifice itself, i.e., sacrifice is its own reward. One has to make a leap of faith which, to an external observer, cannot but look like an act of madness (like Abraham's readiness to kill Isaac): "At first glance the understanding ascertains that this is madness. The understanding asks: what's in it for me? The answer is: nothing."[42] Or, to quote Michael Weston's concise formulation:

It is true that in terms of the measure an end remains, that "eternal happiness" of which Kierkegaard speaks, for which everything must be ventured, but it is an end which can be related to only as essentially absent. As soon as one thinks about it as something that could be present, and so as a reward, one ceases to venture everything and so ceases to have a relation to it. Such an end is not the satisfaction of human capacities, since if it is to be granted all such satisfaction must be given up as a goal.[43]

The Good is thus (not unlike the Kantian Thing-in-itself) a *negatively determined concept*: when, in the movement of "infinite resignation," I turn away from all temporal goods, goals, and ideals, then—to quote Simone Weil— "my reason for turning away from them is that I judge them to be false by comparison with the idea of the good. ... And what is this good? I have no idea. ... It is that whose name alone, if I attach my thought to it, gives me the certainty that the things of this world are not goods."[44] In short, Kierkegaardian "infinite resignation" displays the structure of what, following Freud, Lacan calls *Versagung*: the radical (self-relating) loss/renunciation of the very fantasmatic core of our being: first, I sacrifice all I have for the Cause-Thing which is for me more than my life; what I then get in exchange for this sacrifice is *the loss of this Cause-Thing itself*.[45]

However, does Mørck's "terminal depression" really reach this radical level of redoubled renunciation? There is a further step to be made. If we remain in Denmark, the finale of the last (third) season of the Danish noir series *The Killing (Forbrydelsen*, 2012) ends with an ethical act so shocking that it perplexed many of the series' most avid followers. The detective Sarah Lund (superbly played by Sofie Gråbøl) finally confronts the serial killer Rheinhardt, a corporate manager with high political connections. When the two of them are alone in a car, he coldly confesses to her his brutal murders but mockingly claims that she will never succeed in prosecuting him; desperate at her impotence, she executes him with a gun. Following the advice of her colleague and lover who has just confessed his love to her, she then illegally flies to Reykjavik to disappear forever. ... Her act of killing is *the* killing in the series dedicated to resolving criminal killing, and it seems weirdly appropriate that the series of crime killings concludes with the killing performed by the agent of law. Is her illegal act a crime or an ethical act ... or both? It has all the features of a supreme ethical act: Sarah's predicament when she commits the act is terrifying. She has just reconciled with her lover with the prospect of a shared life, plus she has made peace with her estranged son and happily accepted his girlfriend and their newborn child—and at this very moment when her happiness is so near, she faces the terrible choice—as Gråbøl, the actress, put it: "It would have been so easy to kill her but Søren Sveistrup [the writer] wanted her to pay the highest price. For Lund, death isn't the highest price. Everything she wanted for happiness is within her reach and she has to give it all up in order to do the right thing."[46]

But was this the right thing to do? It certainly meets the Kantian formal criteria of an ethical act: by doing it she loses everything, personal erotic fulfilment and family happiness, plus her career is ruined and, in the eyes of the law, she becomes a criminal; plus there is no narcissistic self-satisfaction or any other "pathological" gain in doing it. She finds herself in an absolute existential void, "between the two deaths," biologically alive but in a way worse than dead, excluded from her community, like Antigone after she is punished by Creon. Her act is nonetheless so problematic that even those spectators who view it with some sympathy perceive it as a crazy gesture done out of despair, as an impotent outburst of revenge—here is a *Guardian* comment which encapsulates this common reaction:

> What we got for the woman whose moral sense of right and wrong is as solid as a continent was an ending that found her committing herself to a man who can best be described as a volatile adulterer, carrying out a cold-blooded execution, and then, to add insult to fatal injury, doing precisely what the craggy-faced fella told her to do without a jot of complaint: skipping off for a life on the run. ... As I watched Lund taking the battery out of her phone and flying off like a common criminal I wished they had killed her, because death would have been preferable to this ignoble end.[47]

We should nonetheless insist on the thoroughly ethical nature of her act—although this is, if we may refer again to Kierkegaard, an ethics elevated to the level of the Religious, not unlike Abraham's readiness to kill his son, an ethics in conflict not only with the public law but with morality itself—to quote Kierkegaard, in her terrible predicament, *morality itself is the temptation*, the obstacle that threatens to divert her from accomplishing the proper act. Her act is criminal in the eyes of the moral big Other, but Kierkegaard's wager is that this big Other is not the ultimate point of reference of ethics. One cannot but note here the contrast with *A Conspiracy of Faith*, the contrast which overlaps with sexual difference: while Mørck is a man ready to sacrifice himself, to lose his life, Sarah is a woman who is ready to sacrifice herself much more radically, ready to enter the "ignoble" space of absolute loneliness, the space between the two deaths.

At this razor's edge where atheism and theology overlap, we get a unique form of negative theology indicated by Rowan Williams, who wrote about the work of four British Catholic novelists—O'Connor, Percy, Spark, and Ellis:

> All four create a world in which the secular majority account of what is going on is severely relativized, but there is no simple alternative that anyone can step into by a single decision or even a series of decisions.

> The "religious" dimension of these fictions lies in the insistent sense of incongruity, unmistakable even if no one within the fiction can say what we should be congruent with.[48]

The term "negative theology" is usually applied to the idea that God cannot be described by any positive determination, so we can circumscribe His place only in a negative way—God is neither infinite nor finite, neither ideal nor real, neither being nor nonbeing, and so on. But what if, in contrast to this notion of God as a pure In-itself beyond all categorial determinations, we locate negativity in God Himself, positing that the experience of the divine is, at its most elementary, a negative experience in the sense described by Williams, the experience of the out-of-jointness of our lives? At its most radical, religion is thus not the opium of the people (today, the opium of and for the people is, as they say, more and more opium itself, drugs), but an awareness of the incongruity and/or inconsistency of existing positive reality, the incongruity which we have pursued throughout this book whose basic premise is that the order of being is haunted by—and originating from—its own impossibility. This ontological paradox throws a new light on the problem of deontology, of how to derive Ought from Is: some kind of deontological tension is always-already at work at the level of being itself, making it incomplete/antagonistic—the order of being is always haunted by its own impossibility, it is never what it "ought to be."

Only a passage through this zero-point of "infinite resignation," of utter hopelessness, can ground a materialist ethics.

NOTES

INTRODUCTION

1. See S. J. Gould and R. C. Lewontin, "The Spandrels of San Marco and the Panglossian Paradigm," *Proceedings of the Royal Society of London*, ser. B, 205, no. 1161 (1979): 581–598.

2. Chapter 3 is in its entirety a slightly rewritten version of a text that first appeared in Slavoj Žižek, ed., *Cogito and the Unconscious* (Durham: Duke University Press, 1998).

I SOS: SEXUALITY, ONTOLOGY, SUBJECTIVITY

1. There are, of course, many other versions of UPS. Our global society clearly implies the triad of the Universal (global capitalism), Particular (cultures, "ways of life"), and Singular (political acts as a way to return to universality). On a more abstract, anthropological level, we could distinguish between the Universal (humanity), the Particular (specific properties that characterize groups of humans), and the Singular (the punctuality of a *cogito*, a singular individual who, abstracting from his/her particular properties, rejoins the universal); here, P is the vanishing mediator between abstract universality and singular universality (the singular point which is the void of *cogito*).

2. *SCTIW Review*, August 23, 2016, 5 (in-text page references and footnotes omitted).

3. See <https://www.theguardian.com/us-news/2016/may/07/professor-flight-delay-terrorism-equation-american-airlines>.

4. Alberto Toscano, "The Detour of Abstraction," in "Other Althussers," ed. Jason Barker and G. M. Goshgarian, special issue, *Diacritics* 43, no. 2 (2015): 78.

5. Quoted from ibid., 85.

6. Quoted from Jason Barker, "Are We (Still) Living in a Computer Simulation? Althusser and Turing," in "Other Althussers," 93.

7. Ibid., 94. In his text, Barker elaborates in detail how digital space is potentially much more "aleatory" than Althusser's "aleatory materialism" dares to dream.

1 THE BARRED ONE

1. Liu Cixin, *The Three-Body Problem*, trans. Ken Liu (New York: Tor Books, 2014).

2. Jacques-Alain Miller, "Un réel pour le XXIᵉ siècle," in *Un réel pour le XXIᵉ siècle* (Paris: Scilicet, 2013). English translation available at <http://www.congresamp2014.com/en/template.php?file=Textos/Presentation-du-theme_Jacques-Alain-Miller.html>.

3. Ibid.

4. Ibid.

5. See Peter Sloterdijk, *Was geschah im 20. Jahrhundert?* (Frankfurt: Suhrkamp, 2016), 93–136.

6. Jacques-Alain Miller, "A Reading of the Seminar *From an Other to the other*," *lacanian ink*, no. 29 (2007): 13.

7. Gilles Deleuze, *Difference and Repetition*, trans. Paul Patton (New York: Columbia University Press, 1994), 104–105 (original emphasis).

8. *The Seminar of Jacques Lacan, Book XVII: The Other Side of Psychoanalysis*, trans. Russell Grigg (New York: Norton, 2007), 107.

9. Alenka Zupančič, *What Is Sex?* (Cambridge, MA: MIT Press, 2017), 133–134; hereafter cited parenthetically as "AZ."

10. See Alain Badiou, *Being and Event*, trans. Oliver Feltham (New York: Continuum, 2006).

11. Immanuel Kant, *Critique of Pure Reason* (London: Everyman's Library, 1988), 264.

12. Ibid., 264–265.

13. I develop this line of thought in greater detail in chapter 11 of Slavoj Žižek, *Less than Nothing* (London: Verso, 2013).

14. Peter van Inwagen, *Material Beings* (Ithaca: Cornell University Press, 1990).

15. Nathan Ross, *On Mechanism in Hegel's Social and Political Philosophy* (New York: Routledge, 2008).

16. And are not the last traces of this keeping apart of the two dimensions discernible even in the two main problems with Hegel's *Phenomenology*? First, is not the break in the structure of the work, the one between the first three chapters and the rest (with an ambiguous position of the chapter on Reason), vaguely between epistemology and history, a reappearance of the old break between logic and metaphysics? Second, is not the position of *Phenomenology* itself as a book—is it part of the system, or a critical introduction into the system proper?—also not that of logic which is not yet metaphysics proper, of critical analysis which is not yet the positive speculative system?

17. The contrast between Hegel and communitarian Romantics is clear here: for Romantics, society is a living organism grounded in shared traditions, and the State is an artificial mechanism trying to regulate social life from above; while for Hegel, it is modern civil society which functions as a social mechanism (market interaction of individuals each of whom pursues his/her egotistic interests), and a degree of organic totality can be achieved only through state regulation.

18. What is abstraction? There is a well-known story about a screenwriter who awoke in the middle of the night, with a vivid dream of a perfect story for a movie; half-asleep, he wrote a couple of words on a notepad near his bed to remind him of it and fell asleep again immediately; in the morning, he took a look at his notepad and read: "A boy meets a girl." ... From a Hegelian standpoint, this was clearly a "bad" abstraction, a reduction of the dream to a general feature which totally obliterated its specific color. A "good" abstraction would have condensed the dream into a specific detail—something like "embarrassed encounter at a toilet" or "a hand dripping sperm"—that would immediately bring out the memory of the story.

19. G. W. F. Hegel, *Phenomenology of Spirit* (Oxford: Oxford University Press, 1977), 18–19.

20. Liu, *The Three-Body Problem*, 411–414.

21. Ross, *On Mechanism*, 35.

22. Ibid., 84.

23. G. W. F. Hegel, *Science of Logic* (Atlantic Highlands, NJ: Humanities Press International, 1989), 402.

24. For a more detailed exploration of this notion, see Slavoj Žižek, *Absolute Recoil* (London: Verso, 2015).

25. See Eric Hobsbawm and Terence Ranger, *The Invention of Tradition* (Cambridge: Cambridge University Press, 2012).

26. Hegel, *Science of Logic*, 50.

27. Ibid., 58.

28. *Hegel's Philosophy of Nature*, para. 220, quoted from <https://www.marxists.org/reference/archive/hegel/works/na/nature2.htm>.

29. Hegel, *Science of Logic*, 824.

30. For the latest formulation, see Manuel DeLanda, *Assemblage Theory* (Edinburgh: Edinburgh University Press, 2016).

31. Jane Bennett, *Vibrant Matter* (Durham: Duke University Press, 2010), 4–6.

32. Levi R. Bryant, *The Democracy of Objects* (Ann Arbor, MI: Open Humanities, 2011), 24.

33. I owe this reference to Vertov to Jacques Rancière, "Cinematographic Vertigo" (unpublished paper).

34. Manuel DeLanda, *A New Philosophy of Society* (London: Bloomsbury, 2006), 12.

35. Quoted from <https://larvalsubjects.wordpress.com/2010/09/08/drg-assemblages-against-totalities/>.

36. DeLanda, *A New Philosophy of Society*, 10.

37. So when Bryant claims that "in addition to something like Lacan's unconscious structured like a language, there's a material unconscious that's scarcely registered in political theory outside of media studies and ecotheory" (Bryant, *The Democracy of*

Objects), we should raise the question: in what precise sense is this "material unconscious" unconscious? Does it have anything to do with the Freudian unconscious, or does it simply designate the objective neuronal-biological processes that go on in our bodies?

38. Quoted from <https://larvalsubjects.wordpress.com/2016/11/21/zizek-on-the-democracy-of-objects-2/>.

39. More on this in chapter 5 below.

40. Quoted from <https://larvalsubjects.wordpress.com/2016/11/21/zizek-on-the-democracy-of-objects-2/>.

41. Quoted from Bryant, *The Democracy of Objects*.

42. The topic of "castration" has many other faces: for example, is the price a commodity pays for becoming a general equivalent of commodities (money) also not a kind of "castration," namely, being deprived of its use value? Or, in an analogous way, is the price a signifier pays for becoming the signifier of meaning as such not that of being deprived of any determinate meaning?

43. I rely here on a line of thought by Aaron Schuster.

44. Positivist social scientists often emphasize that they are simply cold observers of social reality, observing (and maybe manipulating) phenomena from a safe distance, outside any partial engagement. The proper way to reply to this stance is not direct moralism ("How can you adopt such a cold impartial stance toward reality full of suffering and injustices?"); one should rather explore how such a cold manipulative stance fits into observed reality itself, i.e., what social position is inscribed into it.

45. Quoted from <http://www.informationphilosopher.com/solutions/experiments/wave-function_collapse/>.

46. Quoted from <https://www.marxists.org/reference/archive/hegel/works/ph/phc1ac.htm>. For a more detailed elaboration of this point, see chapter II.2 of Žižek, *Absolute Recoil*.

2 ANTINOMIES OF PURE SEXUATION

1. Joan Copjec, *Read My Desire* (Cambridge, MA: MIT Press, 1994).

2. Quoted from <http://scienceblogs.com/goodmath/2006/08/04/irrational-and-transcendental/>.

3. In a first approach, it may appear that here we are as far as possible from Hegel: does not Cantor's concept of the transfinite as that which persists outside the finite, which stands side by side with it, which is exempted from it as its external frame, provide an exemplary case of what Hegel calls the "abstract infinite" which, insofar as it is externally opposed to the finite and excludes it, is in itself again finite? And, in contrast to this transfinite, the Hegelian "true infinite" immanent to the finite, is it not the very organic totality of the finite in its movement of self-sublation? It is, however, precisely such an "organic" notion of the infinite as the living totality of the finite that remains at the level of Substance since, in it, the infinite is not yet for

itself: it is crucial for Hegel that the infinite must appear, that it be "posited as such," in its difference to the finite—only thus do we pass from Substance to Subject. For Hegel, "subject" qua the power of absolute negativity designates the point at which the infinite is posited as such, in its negative relationship to everything finite.

4. Strictly speaking, the same goes for the transcendental dimension as such. The field of our experience is in principle "open," infinite, there is always something to be added to it; we attain the transcendental dimension when we decide to treat this "open" field of experience as a closed, framed totality, and to render thematic the frame which, although not part of our experience, a priori delineates its contours.

5. F. W. J. von Schelling, *Ages of the World* (Ann Arbor: University of Michigan Press, 1997), 181–182. For a more detailed reading of this notion, see chapter 1 of Slavoj Žižek, *The Indivisible Remainder* (London: Verso, 1997).

6. Jacques Derrida, *Adieu à Emmanuel Levinas* (Paris: Galilée, 1997), 87.

7. Incidentally, is it not weird to hear gay theorists rejecting the "gender binary" when gay sexuality is totally inscribed into this "gender binary": the choice of a male sexual partner (and not a female one) presupposes the established difference, and in no way undermines it?

8. Tim Dean, *Beyond Sexuality* (Chicago: University of Chicago Press, 2000), 23.

9. Ibid., 26.

10. Ibid., 19.

11. Quoted from <https://differentcolouredhats.wordpress.com/2016/08/03/slavoj-zizek-is-wrong-about-stuff/>.

12. Jacques Lacan, *Le séminaire, livre XX: Encore* (Paris: Éditions du Seuil, 1975), 37. Quoted from <http://www.lacaninireland.com/web/wp-content/uploads/2010/06/THE-SEMINAR-OF-JACQUES-LACAN-XX.pdf>.

13. Quoted from <http://www.pomoculture.org/2015/07/07/queering-zizek/>.

14. Sigmund Freud, *Dora: An Analysis of a Case of Hysteria* (New York: Macmillan, 1963), 101.

15. See the Introduction to Part II of this book.

16. Alenka Zupančič, *What Is Sex?* (unpublished manuscript), hereafter AZ.

17. Sigmund Freud, *The Interpretation of Dreams* (Harmondsworth: Penguin , 1988), 671.

18. A witty Catholic argument for the Pope's infallibility—to consider one person infallible is much less naive than to consider millions infallible (the implicit premise of democracy)—nonetheless misses the mark. The Pope's infallibility is the exception which grounds the universal fallibility of ordinary humans, while the premise of democracy follows the logic of non-All: although there is no human being who is not fallible, not all are fallible, i.e., they cannot be totalized in a universal set of fallible individuals.

19. See note 12 above.

20. *The Seminar of Jacques Lacan, Book XI: The Four Fundamental Concepts of Psycho-Analysis,* trans. Alan Sheridan (New York: Norton, 1978), 218–219.

21. Alain Badiou, "The Scene of Two," *lacanian ink,* no. 21 (2003): 55.

22. For a closer elaboration of this reflexive structure, see chapter 3 of Slavoj Žižek, *The Puppet and the Dwarf* (Cambridge, MA: MIT Press, 2003).

23. *The Seminar of Jacques Lacan, Book XI,* 268.

24. When, in this scene, the music "takes off," it is not melody which is added but a deep emotional background (violins, etc.); the libidinal effect is the same as when melody is added to the background accompaniment.

25. This subjectivity is clearly evident in Wilhelm Furtwängler's conducting, whose two main features are a permanent tension that is never resolved and an uninterrupted "organic" flow that blurs clear distinctions. The two are intimately connected: the flow goes on because the continuing tension does not allow for any stop. This is why Furtwängler is the ideal conductor for Beethoven and the composers who come after him (Wagner, Brahms, Bruckner), while his attempts to conduct Mozart failed miserably. (It is sufficient to recall his Salzburg *Don Giovanni* from 1950, which sounds ridiculously "heavy," like a Mozart approached through Beethoven's lenses, a Mozart deprived of the characteristic "lightness" of his music—in short, what Furtwängler does here is almost the exact opposite of Karl Böhm's Bayreuth live recording of Wagner's *Ring,* where his aim was to conduct the *Ring* as if it was written by Mozart.)

26. Unfortunately, Furtwängler also follows this cliché when he opposes Stravinsky's mechanical brilliance to German living spirituality.

27. Among other simplifications, one should bear in mind that I am referring to a break which can occur at different levels: between the background and the melody proper, within the melodic line itself between its preparatory part and its climax, etc.

28. Maybe this accounts for the unique position of Schubert, who, although already a Romantic if ever there was one, was the last composer who was able to write authentic beautiful melodies (with Schumann, such melodies are already marked by impossibility).

29. Another nice case of the surplus exploding at the end of a piece is found in the Jefferson Airplane version of "Wooden Ships" (from their *Volunteers* album). Similarly, in "Cosmic Dancer" (T. Rex), the main melody fails to reach its implied conclusion (it remains within the ascending tension), and it is as if this failure is supplemented by the elevation of the background rhythmic pattern into a main motif toward the end of the piece.

3 TOWARD A UNIFIED THEORY OF FOUR DISCOURSES AND SEXUAL DIFFERENCE

1. Lacan developed his matrix of four discourses in his *Seminar XVII: The Other Side of Psychoanalysis,* delivered in 1969–1970 (English translation: New York: Norton, 2007). We should note that this seminar was Lacan's reaction to the events of May 1968.

2. See James Naremore, *The Magic World of Orson Welles* (New York: Oxford University Press, 1978), 61–63.

3. Ibid., 48, 50.

4. Quoted from Joseph McBride, *Orson Welles* (New York: Da Capo, 1996), 36.

5. Ibid., 157.

6. Ibid., 47. The paradigmatic example of Kane's gesture of excessive generosity which characterizes the attitude of the Master is the famous scene in which, after firing Leland, his long-time friend, for writing a detrimental critique of his wife's opera debut, Kane sits down at Leland's desk, finishes Leland's critique in the same injurious spirit, and has it printed.

7. The point not to be missed here is that Prince Hal's father (King Henry IV) is, no less than Falstaff, an impostor whose throne is contested: Falstaff's mocking of royal rituals is so striking because it reminds us of the imposture which already character-izes the "true" bearer of the title. The two paternal figures of Prince Hal, his father the king and Falstaff, are thus opposed as the desiccated, dying man clinging to the symbolic title, and the generous ebullience which mocks all symbolic titles. However, it would be wrong to say that we should strive for the ideal father uniting the two sides: the message of Welles is precisely that this split of the paternal figure into the desiccated bearer of the symbolic title and the ebullient *jouisseur* is insurmountable— there must be two fathers.

8. The weakness of *The Fountainhead* with regard to Welles and Lynch is that it is unable to assume this radical ambiguity of the larger-than-life hero: for Rand, Roark simply is the ideal hero, and traces of madness can be discerned only in the formal excesses of the cinematic texture.

9. Ayn Rand, *The Fountainhead* (New York: Signet, 1992), 143–144.

10. Ibid., 217.

11. Ibid., 272–273.

12. Elisabeth Bronfen, "Kundry's Laughter," *New German Critique* 69 (Fall 1996): 147–162.

13. The subject of the University discourse is able to make the best choice (ratio-nal strategic decision) only within the conditions of the given situation—what he is not able to do is to perform an excessive gesture which, as it were, retroactively redefines/restructures these very conditions; i.e., in popular terms, a gesture which "changes the entire picture," so that, after it, "things are no longer the same."

14. It is well known that a thwarted (disavowed) homosexual libidinal economy forms the basis of a military community—it is for that very reason that armies as a rule adamantly oppose the admission of gays into their ranks. *Mutatis mutandis*, Rand's ridiculously exaggerated adoration of strong male figures betrays the underlying dis-avowed lesbian economy, i.e., the fact that Dominique and Roark, or Dagny and Galt, are in effect lesbian couples.

4 TRANSREAL, TRANSHUMAN, TRANSGENDER

1. Mao Tse-Tung, *On Practice and Contradiction* (London: Verso, 2007), 87.

2. Claude Lévi-Strauss, "Do Dual Organizations Exist?," in *Structural Anthropology*, trans. Claire Jacobson and Brooke Grunfest Schoepf (New York: Basic Books, 1963), 131–163; the drawings are at 133–134.

3. This short description shamelessly relies on the Wikipedia entry on Pokémon.

4. Apart from numerous reports in the media, see the concise description under "SixthSense" on Wikipedia.

5. Quoted from *Dnevnik* (Ljubljana), August 24, 2016, p. 28.

6. This description of VR, AR, and MR is condensed from <http://www.recode.net/2015/07/27/whats-the-difference-between-virtual-augmented-and-mixed-reality/>.

7. See Daniel C. Dennett, *Consciousness Explained* (Boston: Little, Brown, 1991).

8. Ibid., 132.

9. Ibid., 315.

10. See <https://en.wikipedia.org/wiki/Dual_consciousness_neuroscience>, and the original report in Michael S. Gazzaniga, "The Split Brain Revisited," *Scientific American*, July 1998.

11. Charles Foster, *Wired to God?* (London: Hodder, 2011), 21.

12. See David Chalmers, *The Conscious Mind* (Oxford: Oxford University Press, 1997).

13. I owe this idea to Todd McGowan.

14. I owe this reading of the novel to a conversation with Julian Assange, a well-known media theorist, currently staying at the Ecuadorian embassy in London.

15. See chapter 1 above.

16. See Jerry Aline Flieger, "Is Oedipus On-line?," *Pretexts* 6, no. 1 (July 1997): 81–94.

17. I rely here on Yuval Noah Harari, *Homo Deus: A Brief History of Tomorrow* (London: Harvill Secker, 2016).

18. Ibid., 338.

19. Ibid., 396.

20. Ibid., 305.

21. Ibid., 306.

22. Thomas Metzinger, *Being No One: The Self-Model Theory of Subjectivity* (Cambridge, MA: MIT Press, 2003), 620.

23. Ibid., 621.

24. Harari, *Homo Deus*, 311.

25. Ibid., 397.

26. Ibid., 273.

27. Ibid., 346.

28. Especially suspicious here is the category of Allies: why should heterosexuals who have sympathy for transgender people count as a special category of sexual identities? Is their sympathy not a fact of their morality, which has nothing to do with their sexuality? The hidden normativity of transgenderism is clearly perceptible here: "allies" are "honest enemies" in almost the same sense in which historians of Nazism like to discover an "honest Nazi," a Nazi who admits the criminal nature of Nazism. ...

29. See <http://heatst.com/culture-wars/here-are-the-31-gender-identities-new-york-city-recognizes/>.

30. Alain Badiou, *La vraie vie* (Paris: Fayard, 2016).

31. Ibid., 82.

32. I disagree here with Badiou's description of the nihilist dimension of contemporary consumerist hedonism: he claims that in it, "the life-drive is secretly inhabited by the death-drive" (ibid., 16)—a clear case of misunderstanding this notion of Freud's.

33. See Lee Edelman, *No Future: Queer Theory and the Death Drive* (Durham: Duke University Press, 2005).

34. In his *Dark Deleuze* (Minneapolis: University of Minnesota Press, 2016), Andrew Culp systematically opposes to the popular figure of Deleuze as the thinker of creativity, joyous affirmation, and rhizomatic assemblages—the Deleuze easily appropriated by postmodern capitalism—another Deleuze, the Deleuze of the hatred of this world, advancing toward Nothing, of "breakdown, destruction, ruin." But, again, is this other, Dark Deleuze more than the dark obverse of the joyous one?

35. Badiou, *La vraie vie*, 106.

36. Ibid., 105.

37. Ibid., 107.

38. Ibid., 109.

39. Along these lines, some Italian feminists have proposed the notion of the "Name-of-the-Mother," with the idea that in today's Western world, where men are more and more deprived of their symbolic authority and prone to narcissistic hedonism, it is the mother who takes care of the offspring and keeps together (whatever remains of) family life. For theoretical reasons, one should reject the "Name-of-the-Mother" as an illusory notion.

40. Peter Sloterdijk, *Das Schelling-Projekt* (Frankfurt: Suhrkamp, 2016), 144.

41. Ibid.

42. Jacques Lacan, *The Other Side of Psychoanalysis* (New York: Norton, 2007), 162.

43. See Hans Blumenberg, *The Laughter of the Thracian Woman* (London: Bloomsbury, 2015). For a more general analysis, see Mladen Dolar, "Philosophy and Sexual Difference—from Thales to Heidegger" (unpublished manuscript).

44. Quoted from <http://www.graziano-raulin.com/supplements/History/2-01 .htm>.

45. This description shamelessly relies on <https://en.wikipedia.org/wiki/The _School_of_Athens>.

46. Quoted from <http://www.naturalthinker.net/trl/texts/Hegel,G.W.F/Hegel ,_G.W.F._-_The_Phenomenology_Of_Mind.pdf>.

II THE BELATED ACTUALITY OF MARX'S CRITIQUE OF POLITICAL ECONOMY

1. François Truffaut, *Hitchcock* (New York: Simon and Schuster, 1985), 257.

5 THE VARIETIES OF SURPLUS

1. Jacques Lacan, *Les non-dupes errent*, lesson 11 (April 9, 1974), quoted from <http:// www.valas.fr/IMG/pdf/S21_NON-DUPES---.pdf>.

2. Samo Tomšič, *The Capitalist Unconscious: Marx and Lacan* (London: Verso, 2015), 63.

3. Ibid., 122.

4. Thomas Aquinas, *Summa Theologica*, Supplementum Tertia Partis, Question 94, Article 1.

5. Ibid.

6. Ibid., Question 94, Article 2.

7. Ibid., Question 92, Article 3.

8. Peter Sloterdijk, *Das Schelling-Projekt*, Frankfurt: Suhrkamp 2016, pp. 234–5. Here Sloterdijk misreads the deepest core of the Freudian death drive, which is not the drive toward a nirvana-like self-obliteration but an obscene immortality, a drive that persists beyond life and death.

9. Quoted from <http://research.calvin.edu/german-propaganda-archive/goeb36 .htm>.

10. I owe this term and point to Jela Krečič, Ljubljana.

11. See <http://www.robert-pfaller.com/20-years-of-interpassivity>.

12. Quoted from <https://www.marxists.org/reference/archive/hegel/works/pr/ prcivils.htm#PR245>.

13. Guy Le Gaufey, *Une archéologie de la toute-puissance* (Paris: EPEL, 2014), 111.

14. Frank Ruda, *Abolishing Freedom: A Plea for a Contemporary Use of Fatalism* (Lincoln: University of Nebraska Press, 2016).

15. Le Gaufey, *Une archéologie de la toute-puissance*, 20.

16. The gap that separates Hegel and modern science is obvious: according to Hegel, our knowledge progresses through self-relating critique, through the immanent analysis of our own inconsistencies, reflexively undermining every external measure of truth; while modern science is never a self-immanent movement, it needs some

external measure, even in quantum physics where the observer seems to constitute external reality.

17. Jacques Lacan, *Le séminaire, livre XII: Problèmes cruciaux pour la psychanalyse* (unpublished), lesson of June 9, 1965.

18. Jacques Lacan, *Seminar XVII: The Other Side of Psychoanalysis* (New York: Norton, 2007), 177.

19. Tomšič, *The Capitalist Unconscious*, 235.

20. Thomas Presskorn-Thygesen and Ole Bjerg, "The Falling Rate of Enjoyment: Consumer Capitalism and Compulsive Buying Disorder," *Ephemera* 14, no. 2 (2014): 197–220, <http://www.ephemerajournal.org/contribution/falling-rate-enjoyment-consumer-capitalism-and-compulsive-buying-disorder>.

21. Ibid., 197.

22. Ibid., 202.

23. Ibid., 205. We can, of course, easily imagine a consumer reasoning thus: "I hate stone-washed jeans, they are ridiculous, I'll just buy and wear them to project a certain image of myself!" However, in this case, the consumer's desire is neither for a commodity nor for his own identity, he is just playing a game of deceiving others as to what he is.

24. Ibid., 212.

25. Ibid.

26. Ibid., 206.

27. Ibid., 199.

28. In *Mother*, Brecht provides a nice formula against the subject-supposed-to-know: "What you do not know for yourself, you do not know. Check the bill. You will have to pay it."

29. Gilles Deleuze, *The Logic of Sense* (New York: Columbia University Press, 1990), 166.

30. Manuel DeLanda, *Intensive Science and Virtual Philosophy* (New York: Continuum, 2002), 115.

6 *IN DER TAT*: THE ACTUALITY OF FANTASY

1. Karl Marx, *Capital, Volume One*, available online at <https://www.marxists.org/archive/marx/works/1867-c1/ch01.htm>.

2. Ibid.

3. Ibid.

4. Ibid.

5. David Harvey, *A Companion to Marx's "Capital"* (London: Verso, 2010), 29.

6. Marx, *Capital, Volume One*.

7. Harvey, *A Companion to Marx's "Capital,"* 29.

8. Anson Rabinbach, "From Emancipation to the Science of Work: The Labor Power Dilemma" (unpublished manuscript).

9. Ibid.

10. See David Harvey, "Marx and the Labour Theory of Value" (unpublished manuscript).

11. Ibid.

12. *MEGA (Marx-Engels-Gesamtausgabe)*, Abteilung II (Berlin: Dietz, 1976), 6:41.

13. Harvey, "Marx and the Labour Theory of Value."

14. Quoted from <https://www.marxists.org/archive/marx/works/1867-c1/cho1.htm> (footnote omitted).

15. Ibid.

16. Ibid.

17. Ibid.

18. This term was elaborated by Samo Tomšič in *The Capitalist Unconscious: Marx and Lacan* (London: Verso, 2015).

19. Sigmund Freud, *Introductory Lectures on Psychoanalysis* (Harmondsworth: Penguin, 1973), 261–262.

20. Sigmund Freud, *The Interpretation of Dreams* (Harmondsworth: Penguin, 1976), 561.

21. Ibid., 446.

22. Karl Marx, *Capital, Volume One*, quoted from <https://www.marxists.org/archive/marx/works/1867-c1/cho4.htm>.

23. Ibid.

24. Ibid.

25. Ibid.

26. *MEGA*, 6:41.

27. Ibid. (Original emphasis.)

28. This line of argumentation is presented in a more detailed way in chapter 3 of Slavoj Žižek, *Living in the End Times* (London: Verso, 2011). (Original emphasis.)

29. Quoted from <https://www.marxists.org/archive/marx/works/1859/critique-pol-economy/preface.htm>.

30. Kojin Karatani, *The Structure of World History* (Durham: Duke University Press, 2014), 9. It was Adorno who, in his *Three Studies on Hegel*, critically characterized Hegel's system in the same "financial" terms as a system that lives off a credit it can never pay up. See Theodor W. Adorno, *Hegel: Three Studies*, trans. Shierry Weber Nicholsen (Cambridge, MA: MIT Press, 1994), 67.

31. G. W. F. Hegel, *Hegel's Science of Logic* (Atlantic Highlands, NJ: Humanities Press International, 1989), 824.

7 CAPITALIST DISCOURSES

1. Jacques Lacan, *Television*, ed. Joan Copjec (New York: Norton, 1990), 15.

2. Ibid., 16.

3. <https://www.yahoo.com/news/lawyer-asks-israel-destroy-homes-palestinians -killers-083739507.html>.

4. Samo Tomšič, *The Capitalist Unconscious: Marx and Lacan* (London: Verso, 2015), 151.

5. Jacques Lacan, *Je parle aux murs* (Paris: Éditions du Seuil, 2011), 74.

6. Tomšič, *The Capitalist Unconscious*, 151–152.

7. Ibid., 152.

8. <http://www.positionusfinance.com/investing/31980-how-sleeping-on-the-job -can-actually-improve-your-performance.html>.

9. See Jacques Lacan, *The Four Fundamental Concepts of Psychoanalysis* (New York: Norton, 1979).

10. See "La passe: Conférence de Jacques-Alain Miller," paper presented at the fourth Congrès de l'AMP, Comandatuba, Bahia, Brazil, August 2004.

11. This is also why, as Lacan made clear, the structure of courtly love is perverse: in it, the woman is placed in the same position as that of the master in ancient Greek homosexual love, and the subject posits himself as the object-instrument serving the Other (for Lacan, in the case of male homosexuality, the mother "sets down the law for the father"; see Jacques Lacan, *Le séminaire, livre V: Formations de l'inconscient* [Paris: Éditions du Seuil, 1998], 207–212).

12. For a more detailed reading of *The Matrix*, see chapter 6 of Slavoj Žižek, *Enjoy Your Symptom!*, new edition (New York: Routledge, 2007). However, just as films whose main topic is psychoanalysis are as a rule of little interest to those who want to know more about the real breakthrough of Freud, one cannot get rid of the impression that films which directly deal with cyberspace mostly remain stuck in traditional narrative procedures: they refer to cyberspace in an objective way, and ignore the key question of its effect on the basic coordinates of our subjectivity. What still lies ahead is the task of artistically appropriating cyberspace in the way early modern art appropriated feminine hysteria or Raymond Chandler appropriated the urban wasteland of Los Angeles. Perhaps we can learn more about cyberspace from films like Altman's *Short Cuts* or Lynch's *Mulholland Drive* than from paranoid cyberspace exercises like *The Matrix*.

13. Tomšič, *The Capitalist Unconscious*, 228.

14. Ibid.

15. Ibid., 227.

16. Ibid., 228.

17. Ibid., 229.

18. See Nestor Braunstein, "Le discours capitaliste: 'cinquième discours'?," *Savoirs et Clinique*, no. 14 (October 2011): 94–100.

19. Jacques Lacan, *The Seminar of Jacques Lacan, Book XVII: The Other Side of Psychoanalysis* (New York: Norton, 2007), 174.

20. Personal communication, April 2013.

21. It is not as easy as it may seem to be a true Master—the problem with being a Master is the one formulated succinctly by Deleuze: *si vous êtes pris dans le rêve de l'autre, vous êtes foutu* (If you're trapped in the dream of the other, you're fucked up!). And a Master definitely is caught in the dream of others, his subjects, which is why his alienation is much more radical than that of his subjects—he has to act in accordance with this dream image, i.e., he has to act as a person in another's dream. When Mikheil Chiaureli, the ultimate Stalinist director, held a screening of *The Vow* (*Klyatva*, 1946) for Stalin, the latter disapproved of the final scene, in which he is shown kissing Varvara's (the heroine's) hand. Stalin told Chiaureli that he had never kissed a woman's hand in his life, to which Chiaureli gave the perfect reply: "The people know better what Stalin does and doesn't do!" (Andrei Konchalovsky and Alexander Lipkov, *The Inner Circle: An Inside View of Soviet Life under Stalin* [New York: Newmarket, 1992], 29). Fortunately for him, this reply didn't cost him his head (probably because he was Stalin's drinking buddy).

22. For a more detailed reading of this topic, see Slavoj Žižek, *Revolution at the Gates* (London: Verso, 2011).

23. Available online at <https://www.marxists.org/archive/lenin/works/1913/>.

24. Leon Trotsky, *Diary in Exile*, 1935, trans. Elena Zarudnaya (Cambridge, MA: Harvard University Press, 1976), 145–146.

25. Lars T. Lih, "'We Must Dream!' Echoes of 'What Is to Be Done?' in Lenin's Later Career," available online at <http://links.org.au/node/1980>.

26. Ibid.

27. Lars T. Lih, *Lenin Rediscovered* (London: Historical Materialism Books, 2008), 770.

28. Lih, "'We Must Dream!'"

29. Novalis, *Glauben und Liebe*, quoted from Nathan Ross, *On Mechanism in Hegel's Social and Political Philosophy* (New York: Routledge, 2008), 27.

30. Ibid.

31. Moshe Lewin, *Lenin's Last Struggle*, trans. A. M. Sheridan Smith (Ann Arbor: University of Michigan Press, 2005; French original published in 1968), 132.

32. V. I. Lenin, "Better Few, but Better," available online at <https://www.marxists.org/archive/lenin/works/1923/mar/02.htm>.

33. Lacan deploys the matrix of four discourses in *Le séminaire, livre XVII: L'envers de la psychanalyse* (1969–1970) (Paris: Éditions du Seuil, 1996).

34. Eric Santner, *My Own Private Germany* (Princeton: Princeton University Press, 1996).

35. See Miller, "La passe."

36. Ibid.

37. Giorgio Agamben, *The State of Exception* (Stanford: Stanford University Press, 2004).

38. Jean-Claude Milner, "1938, 1953, 1968," conference in Ljubljana, March 1, 2016.

39. Today's aggressive Zionism provides another clear case of disavowing castration. That is to say: with regard to the Jews, "castration" refers to the price they paid for their exceptional position and extraordinary role in the intellectual and cultural life of humanity: their homelessness. Just as money can be a universal equivalent of all commodities only if it loses its use value, the Jews can function as the direct embodiment of universality only insofar as they are a people without a land. The ongoing endeavor of the State of Israel to grab land and assert itself as a normal nation-state clearly implies the loss of the universal dimension of being the Jews, their transformation into just another particular nation, but this is obviously a price Zionists are not prepared to pay: they "disavow castration" and want to remain the exception (a universal nation), while functioning as another nation-state with a land of their own.

8 THE POLITICS OF ALIENATION AND SEPARATION

1. Samo Tomšič, *The Capitalist Unconscious: Marx and Lacan* (London: Verso, 2015), 92.

2. Ibid.

3. Ibid., 234.

4. Jacques Lacan, *Le séminaire, livre XVI: D'un Autre à l'autre* (Paris: Éditions du Seuil, 2006), 173.

5. Quoted from <https://www.marxists.org/reference/archive/stalin/works/1938/09.htm>.

6. Jacques Lacan, *Écrits*, trans. Bruce Fink (New York: Norton, 2007), 72–73.

7. Ibid.

8. Tomšič, *The Capitalist Unconscious*, 89.

9. Ibid., 237.

10. Jean-Claude Milner, *Clartés de tout* (Paris: Verdier, 2011), 90.

11. What raises a question is Milner's implicit reference to Lacan's formula of the signifier (which represents the subject for another signifier): is not the appropriate homology that of exchange value and use value where, as Marx put it, the exchange value of a commodity can be represented only in the use value of another commodity?

12. Frantz Fanon, *Black Skin, White Masks*, trans. Richard Philcox (New York: Grove, 2008), xii.

13. Tomšič, *The Capitalist Unconscious*, 92–93. However, in Lacan's formula of the discourse of the Analyst, knowledge and truth are no longer opposed, they coincide as element and place: in this discourse, knowledge is not replaced by truth, it occupies the place of truth. It is in the Master's discourse that the subject occupies the place of truth.

14. See *The Seminar of Jacques Lacan, Book XI: The Four Fundamental Concepts of Psychoanalysis*, trans. Alan Sheridan (New York: Norton, 1977), chapter 11.

15. The same goes for woman in psychoanalysis: the masquerade of femininity means that there is no inaccessible feminine X beneath the multiple layers of masks, since these masks ultimately conceal the fact that there is nothing to conceal.

16. G. K. Chesterton, *Orthodoxy* (San Francisco: Ignatius, 1995), 145.

17. Quoted from <http://www.patheos.com/blogs/markdroberts/series/the-seven -last-words-of-christ-reflections-for-holy-week/>.

18. Tomšič, *The Capitalist Unconscious*, 65–66.

19. Although some themes seem to connect the Frankfurt School appropriation of psychoanalysis and Lacan's "return to Freud," actual contacts between the two are more or less nonexistent. As for the "Kant avec Sade" theme, there are no clear indi- cations that Lacan was directly influenced by Adorno and Horkheimer's *Dialectic of Enlightenment*: his approach is totally different, so we have nothing more than a con- tingent overlapping. There is only one proven direct contact: Juan Pablo Lucchelli (in his "Lacan et l'École de Francfort," <http://www.journaldumauss.net/?Lacan-et -l-Ecole-de-Francfort-1304>) discovered that Lacan, in his early *écrit* "Les complexes familiaux dans la formation de l'individu" (1938), referred to Max Horkheimer's essay "Authority and Family" (from 1936) to support his thesis on the decline of (what Lacan at that time called) "the paternal imago." (The reason this reference to the Frankfurt School went unnoticed was that the documentation for Lacan's text [which he submitted] was printed at the end of the collective volume in which this text appeared.) Although one should not make too much of this (the notion of the decline of paternal authority was widespread among conservative critics of culture at that time), it does provide a further link between Lacan's early work and his Hegelian and Marxist background.

20. See Ernesto Laclau, *On Populist Reason* (London: Verso, 2005).

21. Oliver Marchart, "Acting and the Act: On Slavoj Žižek's Political Ontology," in *The Truth of Žižek*, ed. Paul Bowman and Richard Stamp (London: Continuum, 2007), 111.

22. Tomšič, *The Capitalist Unconscious*, 172.

23. Quoted from <https://www.marxists.org/archive/lenin/works/1916/jul/x01 .htm>.

24. The thesis that form is part of content, the return of its repressed, should, of course, be supplemented by its reversal: content is ultimately also nothing but an effect and indication of the incompleteness of form, of its "abstract" character.

25. The link between antagonism, *objet a*, and failed interpellation resides in the fact that interpellation as such always displaces, "betrays," obfuscates antagonism. The antagonistic character of "class struggle" means precisely that members of the two classes are never interpellated as pure class subjects (Capitalists and Proletar- ians) directly, but always in a mystified-displaced way (as in the case of fashion: today's rich are interpellated—like to experience themselves—as populists, wearing

stone-washed jeans, etc.). In this precise way, *objet a* is the remainder which emerges as the index of the failed interpellation, of the fact that the interpellation of individuals in their symbolic identity always displaces the underlying antagonism.

26. See Saroj Giri, "Parasitic Anticolonialism" (unpublished manuscript).

27. Jared Sexton, "Proprieties of Coalition: Blacks, Asians and the Politics of Policing," *Critical Sociology* 36, no. 187–188 (January 2010): 92–93.

28. Ibid., 93.

29. Ibid.

30. Ibid.

31. Quoted from Giri, "Parasitic Anticolonialism."

32. Mao Tse-Tung, *On Practice and Contradiction* (London: Verso, 2007), 87.

33. In his famous Preface to the *Contribution to the Critique of Political Economy*, Marx wrote (in his worst evolutionary mode) that humanity sets itself only tasks which it is able to solve: "Mankind thus inevitably sets itself only such tasks as it is able to solve, since closer examination will always show that the problem itself arises only when the material conditions for its solution are already present or at least in the course of formation" (quoted from <https://www.marxists.org/archive/marx/works/1859/critique-pol-economy/preface.htm>). I am tempted to turn this statement around and claim that humanity as a rule sets itself only tasks which it cannot solve, and thereby triggers an unpredictable process in the course of which the task (goal) itself gets redefined.

34. Jeremy Matthew Glick, *The Black Radical Tragic: Performance, Aesthetics, and the Unfinished Haitian Revolution* (New York: New York University Press, 2016).

35. Ibid., 117.

36. Ibid., 138.

37. Ibid., 139.

38. György Lukács, "Hölderlin's Hyperion," trans. Robert Anchor, in *Goethe and His Age* (London: Allen and Unwin, 1968), 137.

39. Glick, *The Black Radical Tragic*, 12.

40. Alain Badiou, *L'hypothèse communiste* (Paris: Lignes, 2009), 28.

41. György Lukács, "Moses Hess and the Problems of Idealist Dialectics," quoted in Glick, *The Black Radical Tragic*, 136.

42. The "valley of decision" is the location of God's punishment of His enemies at the moment of Armageddon: the armies of the world will gather in this valley, where God will announce His final judgment and destroy His enemies.

9 APPENDIX: DEATH, LIFE, AND JEALOUSY IN COMMUNISM

1. David Brooks, "The Power of Altruism," *International New York Times*, July 9–10, 2016, p. 9.

2. There is another Slovene joke along these lines: a fairy promises a farmer to grant two wishes; the farmer says his first wish is that his neighbor's cow should drop dead, and his second wish that his own cow should drop dead. The surprised fairy asks why this weird second wish, and the farmer promptly replies: "So that when my neighbor comes to me and asks me for some milk, I will be able to say no!"

3. Quoted from <https://en.wikipedia.org/wiki/Football_in_occupied_Poland _(1939-45)>.

4. Brian Massumi, "Navigating Movements," in *Hope*, ed. Mary Zournazi (New York: Routledge, 2002), 224.

5. Naomi Klein, *Fences and Windows: Dispatches from the Frontlines of the Globalization Debate* (London: Flamingo, 2002), 245.

6. See the end of chapter 2 above.

7. See Michael Hardt and Antonio Negri, *Multitude* (New York: Penguin, 2004).

8. Aaron Schuster, "The Debt Drive: Political Economy and Philosophical Anthropology," a talk delivered on December 17, 2016 at *Fantasies of Capital*, a Jnanapravaha Mumbai conference.

9. For a detailed elaboration, see Todd McGowan, *Capitalism and Desire* (New York: Columbia University Press, 2016).

10. Quoted from <https://www.marxists.org/archive/marx/works/1857/grundrisse/cho1.htm>.

11. See Jean-Pierre Dupuy, *La jalousie: Une géometrie du désir* (Paris: Éditions du Seuil, 2016).

12. Friedrich Nietzsche, *On the Genealogy of Morality*, trans. Carol Diethe (Cambridge: Cambridge University Press, 2007), 44. Quoted from <http://www.inp.uw.edu.pl/mdsie/Political_Thought/GeneologyofMorals.pdf>.

13. Peter Sloterdijk, *Das Schelling-Projekt* (Frankfurt: Suhrkamp, 2016), 14.

14. Nietzsche, *On the Genealogy of Morality*, 41–42.

15. Quoted from <http://www.lacaninireland.com/web/wp-content/uploads/2010/06/THE-SEMINAR-OF-JACQUES-LACAN-XX.pdf>.

16. This summary is shamelessly paraphrased from the Wikipedia entry on *Norma*.

17. Olivier Rey, "Postface," in Dupuy, *La jalousie*, 176.

18. Søren Kierkegaard, *Works of Love*, trans. Howard and Edna Hong (New York: Harper and Row, 1964), 75.

19. Ibid., 74.

20. Ibid., 77–78.

21. Incidentally, the status of the mark of imperfection significantly called the "beauty spot" (the discreet mole off to one side of an otherwise flawless face which slightly perturbs the face's symmetry) as *objet petit a* is directly evoked by Lacan in his seminar on anxiety (the lecture of May 22, 1963).

22. Quoted from Robert Service, *Lenin* (London: Macmillan, 2000), 232.

23. This line of argumentation is presented at greater length in Slavoj Žižek, *Revolution at the Gates* (London: Verso, 2011).

24. Jean Grondin, *Hans-Georg Gadamer* (New Haven: Yale University Press, 2003), 336.

25. I rely here on <https://en.wikipedia.org/wiki/Lacrimae_rerum>.

26. See <https://en.wikipedia.org/wiki/Symphony_No._14_(Shostakovich)>. Shostakovich was initially unsure what to call this work, eventually designating it a symphony rather than a song cycle to emphasize its musical and thematic unity: most of the poems deal with the subject of mortality. There are a few breaks between movements that effectively divide the work into a four-movement structure.

27. Elizabeth Wilson, *Shostakovich: A Life Remembered* (Princeton: Princeton University Press, 2004), 412.

28. Quoted from Laurel Fay, *Shostakovich and His World* (Princeton: Princeton University Press, 2004), 22.

29. Quoted in David Fanning, Notes to Deutsche Grammophon 437785, *Mussorgsky: Songs and Dances of Death; Shostakovich: Symphony No. 14*, p. 5.

30. Quoted from Solomon Volkov, *Testimony: The Memoirs of Dmitri Shostakovich* (New York: Harper and Row, 1979), 139.

31. "Badiou: Down with Death!," Verso Books blog, August 18, 2015, <http://www.versobooks.com/blogs/2176-badiou-down-with-death>.

32. The passage is quoted from Samuel Beckett, *Company / Ill Seen Ill Said / Worstward Ho / Stirrings Still* (London: Faber and Faber, 2009), 72.

33. Tim Martin, quoted from <http://www.sjsu.edu/faculty/harris/GothicNovelS10/Handouts/beckettpresentation.pdf>.

34. Gilbert Keith Chesterton, "A Defense of Detective Stories," in *The Art of the Mystery Story*, ed. H. Haycraft (New York: Universal Library, 1946), 6.

35. G. K. Chesterton, *Orthodoxy* (San Francisco: Ignatius, 1995), 145.

36. Denis Diderot, "Observations sur Hemsterhuis," in *Œuvres*, vol. 1 (Paris: Robert Laffont, 1994), 759.

37. Søren Kierkegaard, *Journals and Papers*, trans. Howard V. Hong and Edna H. Hong (Bloomington: Indiana University Press, 1970), entry 1405.

38. Kierkegaard, *Works of Love*, 355.

39. Søren Kierkegaard, *Training in Christianity*, trans. Walter Lowrie (Princeton: Princeton University Press, 1972), 121.

40. For a more detailed deployment of this point, see chapter 9 of Slavoj Žižek, *Disparities* (London: Bloomsbury Press, 2016).

41. Jacques Lacan, *The Seminar, Book XVII: The Other Side of Psychoanalysis* (New York: Norton, 2007), 67.

42. Kierkegaard, *Journals and Papers*, entry 1608.

43. Michael Weston, *Kierkegaard and Modern Continental Philosophy* (London: Routledge, 1994), 85–86.

44. Quoted from ibid., 89. I examine this reading of Kierkegaard in greater detail in chapter 2 of Slavoj Žižek, *The Parallax View* (Cambridge, MA: MIT Press, 2009).

45. Lacan provided a detailed interpretation of Claudel's *L'Ôtage* in his Seminar VIII on transference (*Le séminaire, livre VIII: Le transfert* [Paris: Éditions du Seuil, 1982]); see also my reading of *Versagung* in chapter 2 of *The Indivisible Remainder* (London: Verso, 1996).

46. Sofie Gråbøl, quoted from <www.theguardian.com/tv-and-radio/tvandradioblog/2012/dec/17/killing-perfect-ending>.

47. Quoted from <https://www.theguardian.com/tv-and-radio/tvandradioblog/2012/dec/15/killing-iii-final-episodes>.

48. Rowan Williams, *Dostoyevsky: Language, Faith and Fiction* (London: Continuum, 2008), 6.

INDEX